T0137847

IFIP Advances in Information and Communication Technology   **658**

Editor-in-Chief

Kai Rannenberg, Goethe University Frankfurt, Germany

Editorial Board Members

TC 1 – Foundations of Computer Science
  Luís Soares Barbosa, *University of Minho, Braga, Portugal*

TC 2 – Software: Theory and Practice
  Michael Goedicke, University of Duisburg-Essen, Germany

TC 3 – Education
  Arthur Tatnall, *Victoria University, Melbourne, Australia*

TC 5 – Information Technology Applications
  Erich J. Neuhold, University of Vienna, Austria

TC 6 – Communication Systems
  Burkhard Stiller, University of Zurich, Zürich, Switzerland

TC 7 – System Modeling and Optimization
  Fredi Tröltzsch, TU Berlin, Germany

TC 8 – Information Systems
  Jan Pries-Heje, Roskilde University, Denmark

TC 9 – ICT and Society
  David Kreps, *National University of Ireland, Galway, Ireland*

TC 10 – Computer Systems Technology
  Ricardo Reis, *Federal University of Rio Grande do Sul, Porto Alegre, Brazil*

TC 11 – Security and Privacy Protection in Information Processing Systems
  Steven Furnell, *Plymouth University, UK*

TC 12 – Artificial Intelligence
  Eunika Mercier-Laurent, *University of Reims Champagne-Ardenne, Reims, France*

TC 13 – Human-Computer Interaction
  Marco Winckler, *University of Nice Sophia Antipolis, France*

TC 14 – Entertainment Computing
  Rainer Malaka, University of Bremen, Germany

IFIP – The International Federation for Information Processing

IFIP was founded in 1960 under the auspices of UNESCO, following the first World Computer Congress held in Paris the previous year. A federation for societies working in information processing, IFIP's aim is two-fold: to support information processing in the countries of its members and to encourage technology transfer to developing nations. As its mission statement clearly states:

> IFIP is the global non-profit federation of societies of ICT professionals that aims at achieving a worldwide professional and socially responsible development and application of information and communication technologies.

IFIP is a non-profit-making organization, run almost solely by 2500 volunteers. It operates through a number of technical committees and working groups, which organize events and publications. IFIP's events range from large international open conferences to working conferences and local seminars.

The flagship event is the IFIP World Computer Congress, at which both invited and contributed papers are presented. Contributed papers are rigorously refereed and the rejection rate is high.

As with the Congress, participation in the open conferences is open to all and papers may be invited or submitted. Again, submitted papers are stringently refereed.

The working conferences are structured differently. They are usually run by a working group and attendance is generally smaller and occasionally by invitation only. Their purpose is to create an atmosphere conducive to innovation and development. Refereeing is also rigorous and papers are subjected to extensive group discussion.

Publications arising from IFIP events vary. The papers presented at the IFIP World Computer Congress and at open conferences are published as conference proceedings, while the results of the working conferences are often published as collections of selected and edited papers.

IFIP distinguishes three types of institutional membership: Country Representative Members, Members at Large, and Associate Members. The type of organization that can apply for membership is a wide variety and includes national or international societies of individual computer scientists/ICT professionals, associations or federations of such societies, government institutions/government related organizations, national or international research institutes or consortia, universities, academies of sciences, companies, national or international associations or federations of companies.

More information about this series at https://link.springer.com/bookseries/6102

Nathan Clarke · Steven Furnell (Eds.)

Human Aspects of Information Security and Assurance

16th IFIP WG 11.12 International Symposium, HAISA 2022
Mytilene, Lesbos, Greece, July 6–8, 2022
Proceedings

 Springer

Editors
Nathan Clarke 🆔
University of Plymouth
Plymouth, UK

Steven Furnell 🆔
University of Nottingham
Nottingham, UK

ISSN 1868-4238   ISSN 1868-422X (electronic)
IFIP Advances in Information and Communication Technology
ISBN 978-3-031-12174-6   ISBN 978-3-031-12172-2 (eBook)
https://doi.org/10.1007/978-3-031-12172-2

This Springer imprint is published by the registered company Springer Nature Switzerland AG
The registered company address is: Gewerbestrasse 11, 6330 Cham, Switzerland

Preface

It is now widely recognized that technology alone cannot provide the answer to cyber security problems. A significant aspect of protection comes down to the attitudes, awareness, behavior, and capabilities of the people involved, and they often need support in order to get it right. Factors such as lack of awareness and understanding, combined with unreasonable demands from security technologies, can dramatically impede their ability to act securely and comply with policies. Ensuring appropriate attention to the needs of users is therefore a vital element of a successful security strategy, and they need to understand how the issues may apply to them and how to use the available technology to protect their systems.

With all of the above in mind, the Human Aspects of Information Security and Assurance (HAISA) symposium series specifically addresses information security issues that relate to people. It concerns the methods that inform and guide users' understanding of security, and the technologies that can benefit and support them in achieving protection.

This book presents the proceedings from the sixteenth event in the series, held virtually due to the COVID-19 pandemic, during July 2022. A total of 25 reviewed papers are included, spanning a range of topics including security management, cyber security education and training, culture, and privacy. All of the papers were subject to double-blind peer review, with each being reviewed by at least two members of the International Program Committee. We are grateful to all of the authors for submitting their work and sharing their findings. We are also grateful to Spyros Kokolakis, from the University of the Aegean, for being the keynote speaker for this year's event.

The HAISA symposium is the official event of IFIP Working Group 11.12 on Human Aspects of Information Security and Assurance, and we would like to thank Kerry-Lynn Thomson for supporting the event as the Working Group 11.12 chair. We would also like to acknowledge the significant work undertaken by our International Program Committee, and recognize their efforts in reviewing the submissions and ensuring the quality of the resulting event and proceedings. Finally, we would like to thank Christos Kalloniatis and the organizing team for making all the necessary arrangements to enable this symposium to take place.

July 2022

Nathan Clarke
Steven Furnell

Organization

General Chairs

Nathan Clarke   University of Plymouth, UK
Steven Furnell   University of Nottingham, UK

IFIP WG 11.12 Conference Chair

Kerry-Lynn Thomson   Nelson Mandela University, South Africa

Local Organizing Chair

Christos Kalloniatis   University of the Aegean, Greece

Publicity Chair

Fudong Li   University of Portsmouth, UK

International Program Committee

Sal Aurigemma   University of Tulsa, USA
Maria Bada   University of Cambridge, UK
Peter Bednar   University of Portsmouth, UK
Matt Bishop   University of California, Davis, USA
Patrick Bours   Norwegian University of Science and Technology,
                             Norway
William Buchanan   Edinburgh Napier University, UK
Mauro Cherubini   University of Lausanne, Switzerland
Emily Colins   Cardiff University, UK
Jeff Crume   IBM, USA
Adele Da Veiga   University of South Africa, South Africa
Dionysios Demetis   University of Hull, UK
Ronald Dodge   Palo Alto Networks, USA
Paul Dowland   Edith Cowan University, Australia
Jan Eloff   University of Pretoria, South Africa
Simone Fischer-Huebner   Karlstad University, Sweden
Stephen Flowerday   Rhodes University, South Africa
Lynn Futcher   Nelson Mandela University, South Africa
Stefanos Gritzalis   University of Piraeus, Greece
Julie Haney   NIST, USA
Karen Hedström   Örebro University, Sweden
Kiris Helkala   Norwegian Defence University College, Norway

Contents

Cyber Security Education and Training

Visual Programming in Cyber Range Training to Improve Skill Development

Magdalena Glas[(✉)] [iD], Manfred Vielberth [iD], Tobias Reittinger [iD],
Fabian Böhm [iD], and Günther Pernul [iD]

University of Regensburg, Universitätsstr. 31, 93053 Regensburg, Germany
{magdalena.glas,manfred.vielberth,tobias.reittinger,fabian.boehm,
guenther.pernul}@ur.de
https://go.ur.de/ifs

Abstract. Cyber range training is a promising approach to address
the shortage of skilled cybersecurity experts in organizations worldwide.
Seeking to make the training of those experts as efficacious and efficient
as possible, we investigate the potential of visual programming languages
(VPLs) for training in cyber ranges. For this matter, we integrate the
VPL Blockly into an existing cyber range concept. To evaluate its effect
on the learning process of the trainees we conducted a user study with an
experimental group using the VPL and a control group using textual programming. The evaluation results demonstrated a positive impact of the
VPL on the trainees' learning experience. The trainees in the VPL group
achieved equally good learning outcomes as those in the control group
but rated the subjective workload as lower and perceived the training as
more interesting.

Keywords: Visual programming language · Cyber range training ·
Security operations center · Experiential learning

1 Introduction

A strong organizational security workforce is a promising way to address emerging cybersecurity challenges and to protect an organization's assets. However,
according to a recent study by ISC^2 [5], organizations face problems in seizing
this potential. 60% of all participants report a shortage of skilled cybersecurity experts in their organizations and, consequently, believe their organizations'
security posture is at risk. Globally, the study estimates this skills gap at 3
Million unfilled positions. Investing in organizational training is one approach to
overcome this problem [3]. In recent years, cybersecurity training in cyber ranges
has gained popularity in this regard. Cyber ranges are virtual environments that
enable hands-on cybersecurity training in a highly realistic infrastructure [10].
While this approach holds great promise, cyber range exercises that are customized to the infrastructure of an organization are a costly and time-consuming
endeavor [19]. For this reason, it is crucial not only to define the learning content

N. Clarke and S. Furnell (Eds.): HAISA 2022, IFIP AICT 658, pp. 3–13, 2022.
https://doi.org/10.1007/978-3-031-12172-2_1

conveyed in the process but to examine how training can be designed to be as efficacious and efficient as possible.

With the help of visual programming languages (VPLs), users can program using reusable graphical elements instead of producing text-based code [16]. VPLs are largely used in computer science education because they help to reduce often-complex syntax and, thus, facilitate the learners to solve computational problems. In short, the aim is to help learners to focus on *what* they want to express, not *how* they do it. Related studies demonstrate that participants using a VPL achieved better results, showed more interest in the topic and found the process more engaging compared to those using a textual programming language [9,11]. In organizational cybersecurity, a number of tasks require programming or the use of code-based commands and configurations. For this reason, we investigate the integration of a VPL into cybersecurity learning by addressing the following research question:

RQ. *Can a VPL support trainees in learning code-based cybersecurity skills?*

In detail, we want to investigate if using a VPL can make cyber range training more efficacious and efficient. We define efficacy as the learning outcome and the learning experience in the learning process. The efficiency of the cyber range training is to be improved by shortening the duration of the training - while retaining its learning content.

We tackle the research question by examining the learning process of a particular security skill in a SOC, namely code-based rule creation for a Security Information and Event Management (SIEM) system. As a foundation, we utilize a cyber range training proposed by Vielberth et al. [18], which aims to educate security analysts to learn to create JSON-based SIEM rules. We implement an extension of this concept allowing trainees to create SIEM rules using the VPL Blockly[1]. To investigate whether learners benefit from this approach, we conduct a user study evaluating the following hypotheses:

H1. *Trainees achieve better learning outcomes when using a VPL.*
H2. *Trainees find training more engaging and less stressful when using a VPL.*
H3. *Trainees learn faster when using a VPL.*

The remainder of this work is structured as follows. Section 2 gives an overview of the theoretical background of this research, while Sect. 3 briefly discusses related work. In Sect. 4, we introduce our concept of integrating a VPL into cyber range training. Subsequently, Sect. 5 presents and discusses the evaluation results of the concept's prototypical implementation in the form of a user study. Finally, Sect. 6 concludes this work and gives an outlook on future research.

2   Background

Security Operations Center (SOC). SOCs play a central role in modern organization-wide cybersecurity. Their goal is to improve the security posture of

---

[1] https://developers.com/blockly.

the organization by identifying security threats and taking appropriate measures. In addition to suitable technologies and processes, people are of central importance for successful SOCs [17], making SOCs dependent on a sufficient number of well-trained security experts. Therefore, it is not surprising that SOCs also suffer from the aforementioned skills gap [12].

Security Information and Event Management (SIEM). A SIEM system is the key technology in a SOC correlating security-relevant events from various sources across an organization [2]. Incoming security events are correlated by rules created by security experts within the SOC to detect incidents or at least anomalies. These rules are usually created with domain-specific languages, depending on the SIEM system used. Thus, not only security-related expert knowledge is required to create the rules, but also skills regarding the syntax and semantics of the respective languages. This provides a promising opportunity for cyber range-based training, which can be tailored to the specific corporate infrastructure and the SIEM system in use.

Cyber Range. The National Institute of Standards and Technology (NIST) defines cyber ranges as "interactive, simulated platforms and representations of networks, systems, tools, and applications" [10] that provide a safe and legal environment for security training, testing, and research. From a training perspective, this allows trainees to learn and practice offensive and defensive security skills in a training environment that closely resembles an actual digital infrastructure, such as that of a specific organization. The infrastructures replicated in cyber ranges are not limited to information technology (IT) but can also include operational technology (OT), then referred to as cyber-physical range [6]. Cyber ranges with a training purpose usually include a Learning Management System (LMS) that guides the trainees through a training scenario [20]. Typically, a LMS comprises learning material in the form of videos and texts as well as tasks for the trainee to solve during the training, often enhanced with gamification aspects such as a scoring system.

3   Related Work

A common application of VPLs is to teach basic programming concepts to first-time coders. In a study by Tsai [16], for example, participants were taught programming concepts over several weeks. During this time, the experimental group attended a class in which VPL was used. The control group attended a conventional computer science class. This study shows that those participants learning with the VPL outperformed the control group.

Beyond that, VPLs can be utilized to facilitate learners to gain domain-specific knowledge that requires programming to some extent. However, the goal is not to teach programming skills but a simpler, better understandable representation of source code. Rao et al. [13] present a VPL-based learning environment for data science and machine learning. The platform is built for learners to understand and apply complex computer-assisted analyses, despite having little programming experience. Lédeczi et al. [8] use a VPL in a networked robotics environment to introduce learners to networking aspects of cybersecurity. The latter two studies, however, focus on the overall learning environment rather than the specific impact of the VPL on the learning process. This paper aims to apply a VPL to transfer skills and knowledge in cybersecurity and investigate the specific impact of using the VPL on the learning process. For this reason, we perform a comprehensive user study following a two-group experimental design, similar to that of the previously mentioned study by Tsai [16]. This has – to the best of our knowledge – not been attempted in the field of cybersecurity learning yet.

4   Integrating a VPL into Cyber Range Training

We integrate a VPL into an existing cyber range concept proposed by Vielberth et al. [18] to investigate the potential of VPLs in cybersecurity training. What follows is a short description of this underlying concept before we describe the integration of the VPL approach.

4.1   Cyber Range Concept

The cyber range concept by Vielberth et al. [18] aims to train future SOC analysts. The virtual environment of the training is a simulation of an industrial control system against which a simulated attacker performs various attacks. The simulation produces live log data that is transferred to a SIEM system. In the web-based front end of the cyber range, the trainees interact with the SIEM system and a LMS, which provides information about the scenario and includes the tasks the trainees need to solve. For each attack, the trainees first need to manually detect the attack by analyzing the log data in the SIEM system. Leveraging this knowledge, they learn how to create correlation rules with which the respective attacks can be detected automatically by the SIEM system. The syntax of the rules of the SIEM system in use is JSON-based. After a first task, that serves as an introduction to the topic (Task 0), the trainees create increasingly complex SIEM rules in two different task types. In Tasks 1, 2 and 3, large parts of the rule are given and the trainees only fill out missing gaps (*Cloze Task*). In Tasks 4 and 5, the trainees create entire rules themselves, only using a text editor to create the rules in actual JSON (*Editor Task*). One SIEM rule the trainees create is shown in Fig. 1b. This rule triggers an alarm for every incoming security event "Firewall Warning". For a deeper insight into the cyber range scenario and technical implementation of the prototype, please refer to the original paper [18]. Based on this concept, we want to investigate whether trainees can learn better to create code-based SIEM rules when using a VPL. The integration of this approach in the existing cyber range is described in the following subsection.

4.2   SIEM Rule Creation with Blockly

For our study, we seek to integrate a VPL in Tasks 1–5 of the original cyber range. The introduction task (Task 0) remains unchanged. As a VPL we use the open-source library Blockly which fulfills essential requirements to successfully integrate it into the cyber range proposed by Vielberth et al. [18]. First of all, it is web-based and, therefore, can be directly used within the existing front-end. Additionally, Blockly is highly dynamic and allows the creation of custom blocks, which is necessary to map the domain-specific SIEM language used within the cyber range.

Blockly leverages graphical blocks to display concepts of the underlying domain-specific language (e.g., a programming language or a language to describe SIEM rules) without knowing the syntax of this language. With the Blockfactory[2], Blockly offers a simple way to define custom blocks for a specific language. Figure 1a illustrates the two custom blocks we defined for the integration into the cyber range: the green *header* block and the blue *rule* block. Comparing this Blockly-based rule with the JSON-based description of the same rule (Fig. 1b) highlights that Blockly allows for a more compact representation and does not contain syntax-specific characteristics. The full integration is publicly available on GitHub[3].

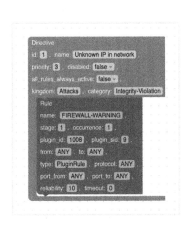

```
 1  {
 2      "directives": [
 3          {
 4              "id": 1,
 5              "name": "Unknown IP in network",
 6              "priority": 3,
 7              "disabled": false,
 8              "all_rules_always_active": false,
 9              "kingdom": "Attacks",
10              "category": "Integrity-Violation",
11              "rules": [
12                  {
13                      "name": "FIREWALL-WARNING",
14                      "stage": 1,
15                      "plugin_id": 1008,
16                      "plugin_sid": [
17                          9
18                      ],
19                      "occurrence": 1,
20                      "from": "ANY",
21                      "to": "ANY",
22                      "type": "PluginRule",
23                      "port_from": "ANY",
24                      "port_to": "ANY",
25                      "protocol": "ANY",
26                      "reliability": 10,
27                      "timeout": 0
28                  }
29              ]
30          }
31      ]
32  }
```

(a) Blockly-based SIEM rule.   (b) JSON-based SIEM rule.

Fig. 1. Comparison of the JSON-based and Blockly-based SIEM rules.

---

[2] https://blockly-demo.appspot.com/static/demos/blockfactory/index.html.
[3] https://github.com/BlocklyCyberRange.

5   Evaluation

To evaluate the impact of the VPL on the cyber range training, we formulate three hypotheses in the introduction to this paper, regarding the improvement of learning outcome (**H1**), learning experience (**H2**), and efficiency (**H3**) of the training. In the following, we illuminate the method and procedure of the evaluation before presenting the retrieved results.

5.1   Method and Procedure

To test our hypotheses, we conducted a Randomized Controlled Trial (RCT) [15] with $N = 30$ participants. While the experimental group ($n = 15$) used Blockly to create the SIEM rules, the control group ($n = 15$) created the rules in JSON. Each group had to solve both task types described in Sect. 4.1. As intended by the RCT experiment design, participants were randomly assigned to one of the two groups prior to training. Participants were students from undergraduate and graduate cybersecurity classes within business informatics curricula. Hereafter, we elaborate on the different aspects of the evaluation. The overall procedure of the user study in connection with the hypotheses is illustrated in Fig. 2.

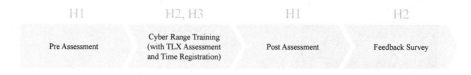

Fig. 2. Procedure of the evaluation.

H1 (Learning Outcome). The participants' skills and knowledge were assessed before and after the training to evaluate the learning outcome. In this way, each participant's learning outcome can be objectively determined to compare the average increase among the two groups subsequently. The assessment was conducted with a multiple-choice quiz consisting of twelve questions in four categories: *Non security-related knowledge, Attack-related knowledge, SIEM-related knowledge,* and *SIEM rule-related knowledge.*

H2 (Learning Experience). To evaluate the participants' perception of the learning process, the participants were assessed after each task during the training and in a post-training feedback survey. As outlined in Subsect. 4.1, the cyber range training entails tasks of increasing difficulty in two different task types. Evaluating H2 for each of these tasks makes it possible to distinguish precisely at which stages of the training the VPL subjectively improved the learning experience and where it did not. For this purpose, we utilize the NASA Task Load Index (TLX) [1] to assess the trainees' perceived workload.

The TLX was originally designed to measure subjective workload for operators interacting with a human-machine interface. The TLX consists of six subscales representing sources of workload: *Mental Demand (MD)*, *Physical Demand (PD)*, *Temporal Demand (TD)*, *Performance (PE)*, *Effort (EF)*, and *Frustration Level (FL)*. Participants are asked to rate each subscale for each task. These ratings are then combined to determine the TLX for the respective task. Today, the TLX is considered a common method for workload assessment in various application areas [4]. In this regard, the TLX is also used to capture purely cognitive workload, e.g., to evaluate the usability of web applications [14]. To fit our purpose, we exclude the subscales *Physical Demand* and *Effort*. The former because the training does not include any physical aspects, the latter because – in our case – this subscale is equivalent to *Mental Demand*. This results in a set of four TLX-specific questions, one for each remaining subscale.

- MD: How mentally demanding was the task?
- TD: How hurried or rushed was the pace of the task?
- PE: How successful were you in accomplishing what you were asked to do?
- FL: How insecure, discouraged, irritated, stressed, or annoyed were you?

To simplify the scoring for participants, we chose a Likert scale from 1 to 5 (*low* to *high* for MD, TD, and FL, respectively, *good* to *poor* for PE) instead of the original TLX scale from 1 to 100. We integrate a TLX-module in the LMS of the existing cyber range. The TLX-module is displayed each time a participant completes a task. To assess the participants' engagement in the training, we constructed a post-training feedback survey. The survey is based on the four conditions *Attention*, *Relevance*, *Confidence*, and *Satisfaction* as proposed within the ARCS model by Keller [7]. The model presumes that intrinsic motivation can be achieved when a learning process meets these conditions. We evaluate each condition with two statements, which the participants assess on a Likert scale from 1 (fully disagree) to 5 (fully agree).

H3 (Learning Efficiency). To measure the efficiency of the VPL used in the cyber range training (H3), we recorded the timestamp at the beginning of the training and whenever a participant started or completed a task during the training. This allows us to determine how long it takes a participant to complete each task.

5.2 Results and Discussion

In this section, we present the results of the RCT and discuss them with respect to our hypotheses. The data set and the SPSS outputs are published GitHub[4].

H1 (Learning Outcome). We performed a paired t-test across all knowledge categories to investigate learning efficacy, comparing the mean rate of correctly answered questions in pre and post assessment. For both groups, the average rate of correctly answered questions increased significantly from pre assessment

---

[4] https://github.com/BlocklyCyberRange/userStudy.

(Blockly: $M = .66, SD = .15$; JSON: $M = .52, SD = .13$) to post assessment (Blockly: $M = .87, SD = .10$; JSON: $M = .77, SD = .17$), $t(14) = -5.43$, $p < .001$ for Blockly and $t(14) = -4.61, p < .001$ for JSON. To compare the two groups, we examined the change in their performance, that is, the difference in the percentage of correctly answered questions between pre and post assessment. This variable was investigated with an unpaired t-test comparing the two groups for each knowledge category and across all categories, as shown in Table 1.

While this indicates equally good learning outcomes in both groups, the results could not prove that using Blockly led to a significantly different learning outcome. For this reason, H1 is rejected.

Table 1. Results of H1 (Learning Outcome).

Know. category	Blockly		JSON		t	df	Sig.
	M	SD	M	SD			
Non-sec.-related	.16	.33	.18	.28	−.20	27.21	.843
Attack-related	.13	.17	.16	.28	.27	23.11	.794
SIEM-related	.04	.17	.11	.30	−.75	22.32	.463
SIEM rule-related	.51	.49	.53	.33	−.15	24.59	.885
Overall	.21	.15	.24	.21	−.51	25.69	.616

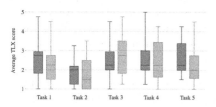

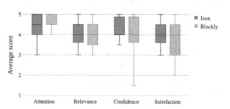

(a) Learning Experience based on TLX.   (b) Learning Experience based on ARCS.

Fig. 3. Graphical representation of H2 (Learning Experience) results.

H2 (Learning Experience). For H2, an unpaired t-test was performed to compare the TLX workload for the two groups (cf. Table 2 and Fig. 3a). The measured mean workload was lower for four of the five tasks in the Blockly group. This difference was particularly noticeable in Task 1 and Task 5, which could indicate that Blockly offers an advantage, especially in unfamiliar tasks (Task 1) and particularly complex tasks (Task 5).

Likewise, an unpaired t-test for the four conditions of the ARCS model was conducted (cf. Table 3 and Fig. 3b). While *Confidence* and *Satisfaction* were higher among the control group, *Attention* was higher in the Blockly group. The mean rating of *Relevance* was about the same in both groups. A possible explanation for this result is that the participants all had some prior experience in textual programming due to their study background. When solving the tasks with Blockly the participants had to engage with something new. Thus, the Blockly participants were less satisfied and confident than the JSON participants, yet found the learning process more interesting (*Attention*).

These results are consistent with the verbal feedback from participants, in which the Blockly approach was rated very positively overall. For this reason, we conclude that the use of Blockly has the potential to improve the learning experience to some extent. Although this cannot be shown to be significant in our user study, partly because of the relatively small number of participants, we consider the results to be a good indicator and therefore accept H2.

Table 2. Results of Learning Experience (H2): TLX assessment.

Task	Blockly		JSON		t	df	Sig.
	M	SD	M	SD			
Task 1	2.25	0.93	2.53	0.90	−0.85	27.97	.404
Task 2	1.78	0.83	1.88	0.68	−0.36	26.98	.721
Task 3	2.67	1.06	2.45	0.91	0.60	27.36	.552
Task 4	2.57	1.06	2.58	0.98	−0.04	27.80	.965
Task 5	2.35	1.01	2.62	0.85	−0.78	27.24	.442

Table 3. Results of Learning Experience (H2): ARCS assessment.

Condition	Blockly		JSON		t	df	Sig.
	M	SD	M	SD			
Attention	4.67	0.41	4.43	0.65	1.18	23.54	.251
Relevance	4.03	0.55	4.07	0.56	−0.16	27.99	.871
Confidence	4.00	0.98	4.30	0.53	−1.04	21.47	.309
Satisfaction	3.67	0.96	4.00	0.57	−1.16	22.74	.258

H3 (Learning Efficiency). For the third hypothesis, an unpaired t-test was performed to compare the average time it took the participants to solve each task for the two groups (H3). The total training duration (in minutes) ($M = 52:33$, $SD = 12:52$ for Blockly, $M = 52:16$, $SD = 11:23$ for JSON) was very close in the two groups, $t(27.59) = 0.06, p = .950$. Task 1 and Task 6 were completed faster by the Blockly group, Tasks 2, 3, and 4 were completed faster by the control group. For the full results, we refer to the aforementioned GitHub repository.

While conducting the evaluation, we realized that the duration for solving the tasks has more factors than the sheer modality of the task. Participants told us, e.g., that they interrupted the training for short breaks or were facing technical issues such as a weak internet connection. This is also shown by the high number of outliers and the associated poor significance. For this reason, we do not consider the results of the time recording to be meaningful and can therefore neither accept nor reject H3.

6   Conclusion

In this work, we integrated a VPL into an existing cyber range training and evaluated its effects on learning outcome, learning experience, and learning efficiency in a Randomized Controlled Trial. The study indicates an equally good learning outcome for the experimental group (using the VPL) and the control group (using text-based programming). While a successful learning outcome is considered the primary goal of cyber range training, it is also highly desirable to raise trainees' engagement. If trainees enjoy the training, it might raise their interest in the topic and thus be an incentive for further learning. Our experiments indicate that the use of VPL can improve the learning experience, as participants found the learning process more enjoyable. Due to the promising results of the conducted user study, the potential of VPL usage for other domains appears encouraging. However, further experiments are necessary to validate the statistical significance of our results and to determine the effectiveness of the training in terms of its long-term impact in the real world context of an organization. In addition, the aspects of ethicality and elegance of the VPL approach should also be investigated in an extended future evaluation.

Acknowledgment. This work is partly performed under the INSIST project, which is supported under contract by the Bavarian Ministry of Economic Affairs, Regional Development and Energy (DIK0338/01).

References

1. Development of NASA-TLX (Task Load Index): Results of Empirical and Theoretical Research. In: Hancock, P.A., Meshkati, N. (eds.) Human Mental Workload, Advances in Psychology, vol. 52, pp. 139–183. North-Holland (1988)
2. Bhatt, S., Manadhata, P.K., Zomlot, L.: The operational role of security information and event management systems. IEEE Secur. Priv. **12**(5), 35–41 (2014)
3. Furnell, S., Fischer, P., Finch, A.: Can't get the staff? The growing need for cybersecurity skills. Comput. Fraud Secur. **2017**(2), 5–10 (2017)
4. Hart, S.G.: NASA-task load index (NASA-TLX); 20 years later. In: Proceedings of the Human Factors and Ergonomics Society Annual Meeting, vol. 50, pp. 904–908 (2006)

5. ISC^2: A resilient cybersecurity profession charts the path forward - ISC^2 cyberse-curity workforce study 2021. Technical report, International Information System Security Certification Consortium (2021)
6. Kavallieratos, G., Katsikas, S.K., Gkioulos, V.: Towards a cyber-physical range. In: Proceedings of the 5th on Cyber-Physical System Security Workshop, pp. 25–34 (2019)
7. Keller, J.M.: Development and use of the ARCS model of instructional design. J. Instr. Dev. **10**(3), 2–10 (1987)
8. Lédeczi, Á., et al.: Teaching cybersecurity with networked robots. In: Proceedings of the 50th ACM Technical Symposium on Computer Science Education, pp. 885–891 (2019)
9. Lye, S.Y., Koh, J.H.L.: Review on teaching and learning of computational thinking through programming: what is next for K-12? Comput. Hum. Behav. **41**, 51–61 (2014)
10. National Initiative for Cybersecurity Education (NICE): The Cyber Range: A Guide. Technical report, National Initiative for Cybersecurity Education (NICE) (2020)
11. Ouahbi, I., Kaddari, F., Darhmaoui, H., Elachqar, A., Lahmine, S.: Learning basic programming concepts by creating games with scratch programming environment. Proc. Soc. Behav. Sci. **191**, 1479–1482 (2015)
12. Pescatore, J., Filkins, B.: Closing the critical skills gap for modern and effective security operations centers (SOCs). SANS Institute (2020)
13. Rao, A., Bihani, A., Nair, M.: Milo: a visual programming environment for data science education. In: 2018 IEEE Symposium on Visual Languages and Human-Centric Computing (VL/HCC), pp. 211–215 (2018)
14. Schmutz, P., Heinz, S., Métrailler, Y., Opwis, K.: Cognitive load in eCommerce applications-measurement and effects on user satisfaction. Adv. Hum.-Comput. Interact. **2009**, 1–9 (2009)
15. Torgerson, C.J., Torgerson, D.J.: The need for randomised controlled trials in educational research. Br. J. Educ. Stud. **49**, 316–328 (2001)
16. Tsai, C.Y.: Improving students' understanding of basic programming concepts through visual programming language: the role of self-efficacy. Comput. Hum. Behav. **95**, 224–232 (2019)
17. Vielberth, M., Bohm, F., Fichtinger, I., Pernul, G.: Security operations center: a systematic study and open challenges. IEEE Access **8**, 227756–227779 (2020)
18. Vielberth, M., Glas, M., Dietz, M., Karagiannis, S., Magkos, E., Pernul, G.: A digital twin-based cyber range for SOC analysts. In: Barker, K., Ghazinour, K. (eds.) DBSec 2021. LNCS, vol. 12840, pp. 293–311. Springer, Cham (2021). https://doi.org/10.1007/978-3-030-81242-3_17
19. Vykopal, J., Vizvary, M., Oslejsek, R., Celeda, P., Tovarnak, D.: Lessons learned from complex hands-on defence exercises in a cyber range. In: Proceedings - Frontiers in Education Conference, FIE, pp. 1–8 (2017)
20. Yamin, M.M., Katt, B., Gkioulos, V.: Cyber ranges and security testbeds: scenarios, functions, tools and architecture. Comput. Secur. **88**, 101636 (2020)

Survey of Users' Willingness to Adopt and Pay for Cybersecurity Training

Joakim Kävrestad[(✉)] [ID], Martin Gellerstedt [ID], Marcus Nohlberg [ID],
and Jana Rambusch

University of Skövde, Skövde, Sweden
{joakim.kavrestad,martin.gellerstedt,marcus.nohlberg,
jana.rambusch}@his.se

Abstract. The importance of user behaviour in the cybersecurity domain is widely acknowledged. Users face cyberthreats such as phishing and fraud daily, both at work and in their private use of technology. Using training interventions to improve users' knowledge, awareness, and behaviour is a widely accepted approach to improving the security posture of users. Research into cybersecurity training has traditionally assumed that users are provided such training as members of an organization. However, users in their private capacity are expected to cater for their own security. This research addresses this gap with a survey where 1437 Swedish adults participated. Willingness to adopt and pay for different cybersecurity training types was measured. The included types were; training delivered to users in a context where the training is of direct relevance, eLearning and game-based training. The participants were most willing to adopt and pay for contextual training, while eLearning was the second most favoured training type. We also measured if willingness to pay and adopt cybersecurity training was impacted by the participant's worry about various cyber threats. Surprisingly, no meaningful correlation was found, suggesting that something else than worry mediates willingness to adopt and pay for cybersecurity training.

Keywords: Cybersecurity · Training · User · Adoption · Willingness · Pay

1 Introduction

Cybersecurity training for end-users is an integral part of common frameworks and standards covering organizational cybersecurity operations [1, 2]. That is unsurprising given the many research publications which suggest cybersecurity training as a crucial part of promoting secure user behaviour [3–5]. Since user behaviour has long been acknowledged as one of, if not the, biggest cybersecurity risks, using training measures to support secure behaviour is reasonable [6, 7]. Indeed, several different options for cybersecurity training have been proposed. A broad classification of those is physical and digital efforts [8]. This research focuses on digital training efforts, which are argued to be more scalable and cost-efficient than lectures or other in-person training [9, 10]. While there are a plethora of different options for digital cybersecurity training methods, they can be grouped as follows [3, 8, 11]:

© IFIP International Federation for Information Processing 2022
Published by Springer Nature Switzerland AG 2022
N. Clarke and S. Furnell (Eds.): HAISA 2022, IFIP AICT 658, pp. 14–23, 2022.
https://doi.org/10.1007/978-3-031-12172-2_2

- E-learning platforms that users access on-demand or where the material is broadcasted to users at regular intervals.
- Game-based training where game mechanics are used for teaching. That includes competitive games, single-player story-based games, quizzes and more.
- Contextual training where users are provided with training when they encounter situations that pose an elevated cybersecurity risk or experience such situations as part of a simulation.

Previous research has shown that those approaches can have beneficial results in different circumstances [11]. As exemplified by [12, 13], those evaluations have assumed that cybersecurity training is to be implemented for users of an organization. To the best of our knowledge, no research evaluating cybersecurity training methods for users in their private capacity has been conducted. That is a gap that this research intends to fill, and the motivation is twofold. First, users in their private capacity are not safeguarded by other security mechanism provided to users in an organization. Consequently, the responsibility for ensuring private cybersecurity falls on the user alone. Second, without organizational support, a private user must seek out, and possibly pay for, cybersecurity measures of their own. As such, research into private users' willingness to adopt and pay for cybersecurity training is much needed. Three research questions have been developed for this research:

1. To what extent are private users willing to adopt the different types of cybersecurity training?
2. To what extent are private users willing to pay for the different types of cybersecurity training?
3. Does worrying about cyber threats impact private users' willingness to adopt or pay for cybersecurity training?

This research seeks to understand private users' willingness to adopt and pay for the different types of cybersecurity training. The rationale is that cybersecurity training can only be effective if users adopt it [14]. Further, willingness to pay becomes important when private users, in contrast to users in an organization, need to procure cybersecurity training for themselves. Finally, we assume that users who perceive cyberthreats as harmful are more willing to pay for protective measures than users who do not. The third research question tests that assumption. The research contributes to the scientific community by increasing the understanding of private users' willingness to use and pay for cybersecurity training. These insights can guide future research efforts. The research is also practically usable for organizations seeking to develop cybersecurity training products for the private market. They can also guide national and international efforts to raise national cybersecurity awareness, which is an emergent challenge [15, 16].

The remainder of this paper will, in turn, describe the method used before outlining the results and conclusions of this research.

2 Methodology

This research was conducted as a web-based survey using a web panel located in Sweden, which includes Swedish users. Following an informed consent and demographic questions, the survey included four sections. Sections one to three measured willingness to adopt (WTA) and willingness to pay (WTP) for the categories of cybersecurity training. WTA was measured using a Likert scale [17] with five statements that the participant responded to on a six-pointed scale ranging from "1-do not agree at all" to "6-fully agree". WTP was measured by asking the respondents if they would be willing to pay for cybersecurity training and, in that case, what amount. While WTP can be measured differently, directly asking the participants provides a simple and easily comparative metric [18]. The survey ended with a Likert scale developed to measure the participants' worry about cyberthreats. It contained six statements that the participant responded to on a six-pointed scale ranging from "1-do not agree at all" to "6-fully agree". The statements included in the scales are presented in the results section to preserve space.

As suggested by [19], the research group drafted the survey, which was then evaluated by an external survey professional before it was pilot tested by 34 participants who were asked to complete the survey and provide feedback on the questions. Following the pilot, 1437 participants were recruited using a web panel provided by Webropol[1]. That allowed for the use of a stratified sampling approach [20]. Strata were created based on gender, age and place of living to ensure a sample representative of the Swedish adult population.

For data analysis, an index value was created for each Likert scale. The index was calculated as the mean answer of all items on the scale. The indexes reflect the participants' overall WTA for each respective cybersecurity training type and the participants' overall worry about cybersecurity threats. Cronbach's Alpha was computed to measure the internal consistency of each scale, and 0.70 was accepted as the threshold for acceptance of a scale's internal consistency, as suggested by [21]. Repeated measures ANOVA was used to identify differences between the WTA indexes, as suggested by [22], and the Friedman test was used as a non-parametric alternative for ordinal data. Pearson's correlation coefficient [23] was calculated to identify correlations between WTA and WTP for the different training types and the worry index. The conventional significance level of 95% was adopted in this research.

The data set includes 1437 participants, and the demographic composition of the sample is shown in Table 1. As shown in Table 1, the gender and age distribution in the sample is roughly equal, but one age group, 28–37, is slightly overrepresented.

3 Results

Following the demographic questions, the participants were presented with a description of a cybersecurity training type and then asked to respond to the WTA and WTP questions. That was repeated for all three cybersecurity training types. Table 2 shows the statements used in the WTA scale, mean response values, mean index value and scale

---

[1] https://webropol.se/.

Table 1. Age and gender distribution in the data sample.

Variable	Answer	Proportion
Gender	Male	48.2%
	Female	51.3%
	Other/Prefer not to say	0.5%
Age	18–27	15.5%
	28–37	20.2%
	38–47	12.6%
	48–57	14.1%
	58–67	18.0%
	68 or above	19.0%
	Prefer not to say	0.6%

Alpha. Table 2 also reports the proportion of respondents who hand an index value of at least 4. At seen in Table 2, the answer values for the individual statements are systematically highest for contextual training, followed by eLearning and Game-based with the lowest score. The same tendency is seen for the index and reflected by the proportion of respondents with an index value of at least 4. Moreover, 71% of respondents had an index value over 4 for at least one of the included training types.

Table 2. Descriptive statistics for WTA scales. Note that the responses for statement 3 were inverted when computing the index and that the statements are translated from Swedish.

Statement	Contextual	eLearning	Game-based
I would use it if it was recommended by someone I trust	4.37	3.73	2.91
I would use it if a trusted organization recommended it	4.10	3.45	2.71
I would not use the product at all	2.37	2.92	3.50
I would actively search for it if I heard about it in news media, social media, etc	3.26	2.81	2.34
I would use the product if it came with a newly bought computer or cell phone	4.38	3.66	2.87
INDEX	4.15	3.55	2.87
Proportion of respondents with an index of at least 4	62%	39%	27%
Alpha (Acceptance threshold = 0.7)	0.76	0.86	0.93

A repeated-measures ANOVA with Greenhouse-Geisser correction was used to test if the tendency displayed in Table 2 was statistically significant. Greenhouse-Geisser correction was used since P = 0.000 for Mauchly's test of Sphericity. ANOVA tests for differences in mean values over two or more groups. The ANOVA showed a statistically significant difference (F = 668,945, P = 0.000). Post-hoc analysis with Bonferroni correction was used to test for pairwise differences and confirmed that WTA for contextual training was higher than the WTA for both eLearning and game-based training. The WTA for eLearning was higher than the WTA for game-based training. 95% Confidence intervals of the differences are reported in Table 3.

Table 3. Confidence intervals for the difference in WTA between cybersecurity training types.

Pairwise comparison	Confidence interval
Contextual – eLearning	0.535–0.672
Contextual – game-based	1.189–1.376
eLearning – game-based	0.590–0.767

WTP was measured by asking the participants if they would be willing to pay for the three types of cybersecurity training. The answer options and results are presented in Table 4. Note that only participants who reported being willing to pay were asked to submit their maximum price.

Table 4. Results for the WTP question. 10 SEK is ~1 EUR. * participants unwilling to pay were treated as 0.

Statement	Contextual	eLearning	Game-based
I would only use it if it was free	61.2%	67.8%	52.9%
I would not use it at all	8.9%	18.1%	38.0%
I would consider paying for it	29.9%	14.1%	9.1%
Mean maximum price (only participants willing to pay)	505 SEK	543 SEK	522 SEK
Mean maximum price (all participants) *	151 SEK	77 SEK	48 SEK

The general tendency shown in Table 4 is that WTP is highest for contextual training, followed by eLearning and Game-based last. The Friedman test confirmed that this tendency was statistically significant (P = 0.000).

The worry question asked the participant to reply to six statements about their worry about different cyberthreats by selecting how well they agreed with each statement on a scale from "1-do not agree at all" to "6-fully agree". An index was computed by calculating each participant's mean response value. The mean response values for the individual statements and the index are presented in Table 5. The Alpha for the scale was 0.89. It is also noticeable that the top concern was identify theft, while the least worrying statement was being conned for money.

Table 5. Data reflecting the participants' worry about cyberthreats

Statement	Mean
I worry about being conned for money on the Internet	3.05
I worry that my opinions can be registered without my knowledge	3.05
I worry that my behaviour is tracked without my knowledge and used to show ads	3.34
I worry about my phone or computer being hacked or getting malware	3.42
I worry about someone stealing my identity on the Internet	3.45
I worry about someone using my passwords	3.48
INDEX	3.30

The relationship between worry about cyberthreats, and WTA and WTP for the different types of cybersecurity training were analysed using Pearson's correlation coefficient. All coefficients are statistically significant and are presented in Table 6.

Table 6. Correlation coefficients

	Contextual WTA	Contextual WTP	eLearning WTA	eLearning WTP	Game-based WTA	Game-based WTP
Contextual WTA	–					
Contextual WTP	0.453	–				
eLearning WTA	0.533	0.267	–			
eLearning WTP	0.277	0.508	0.528	–		
Game-based WTA	0.282	0.108	0.450	0.228	–	
Game-based WTP	0.175	0.255	0.283	0.376	0.675	–
Worry	0.205	0.078	0.217	0.109	.150	0.101

A correlation coefficient is a number between 1 and −1. A positive number means a positive correlation, and a negative number means a negative correlation. A coefficient closer to zero signifies a weaker correlation. Correlations below 0.29 are considered very low, correlations between 0.30 and 0.49 are low and correlations between 0.50 and 0.69 are moderate [23]. Thus, while significant, the relationship between worry and WTA and WTP for the cybersecurity training types is weak. A moderate correlation between contextual training and eLearning is found, while the correlations between game-based and eLearning, and contextual and game-based are weak. It can also be seen that there is a moderate correlation between WTA and WTP within the cybersecurity training methods.

4   Discussion

This section ends the paper with a discussion on the results in relation to the research questions, the contributions made by this research and an outline of limitations and future work.

4.1   Answering the Research Questions

The first research question was *To what extent are private users willing to adopt different types of cybersecurity training?* A Likert scale was used to compute an index value that measured the participants' willingness to adopt (WTA) contextual, eLearning and game-based cybersecurity training. Repeated measure ANOVA showed a significant difference in WTA between the cybersecurity training types. Post-hoc tests showed that contextual training had the highest WTA, with eLearning in second place and game-based third. Those results were emphasized by showing that the proportion of participants who had a positive WTA for contextual training was 62%. In comparison, the corresponding eLearning and game-based numbers were 39% and 27%. In response to the research question, two conclusions can be made. First, 70% of the participants demonstrate a positive WTA towards at least one cybersecurity training method. Second, contextual training has the highest WTA scores. The first implication is that contextual training is more likely to be adopted by a large userbase than eLearning or game-based initiatives. Second, a large proportion of the respondents have a WTA lower than 4, suggesting a low interest in cybersecurity training. That would suggest that, even with freely available training, reaching the entire population is difficult, and other measures to support secure behaviour are needed.

The second research question, *To what extent are private users willing to pay for different types of cybersecurity training?*, was addressed by asking the participants if and what they could consider paying for the different types of training. At a glance, the results confirmed the results for the WTA questions by showing that more participants are willing to pay for contextual training compared to eLearning or game-based training. Likewise, the lowest proportion of participants who would not consider free training was found for contextual training, followed by eLearning and game-based training. However, the mean amount that users that were willing to pay would spend for cybersecurity training was relatively equal between the training types. To conclude, the maximum price for the three training types is similar, but the number of participants willing to pay for training differs significantly between the training types. Thus, the overall willingness to pay (WTP) is highest for contextual training, followed by eLearning and game-based training last.

The last research question was *Does worrying about cyber threats impact private users' willingness to adopt or pay for cybersecurity training?* It was motivated by the assumption that users worried about cyberthreats are more motivated to protect against those threats and, therefore, more willing to adopt cybersecurity training. To this end, an index reflecting the participants' cybersecurity worries was computed and correlated with the WTA and WTP for the cybersecurity training types. While significant, the correlation coefficients were low and suggest that worry about cybersecurity threats has a low impact on WTA and WTP for cybersecurity training. This surprising result calls for further investigation into the factors influencing willingness to adopt cybersecurity training. Further, the correlation analysis did reveal a moderate correlation between WTA and WTP within the different cybersecurity training types. As such, the data suggests that participants are willing to pay for cybersecurity training that they are positive about adopting.

4.2 Contributions

User perception of digital tools is a known factor that influences the adoption of such tools [24]. In the cybersecurity domain, user perception of cybersecurity training for organizations has been researched in several studies. This study, however, focuses on users' perception of cybersecurity training in the user's private capacity and is, to the best of our knowledge, the first of its kind. The first contribution of this research is that it shows what cybersecurity training types users are most willing to adopt and shows large differences between the included training types. About 40% of the respondents would not use game-based training even if it was free, while only 10% answered in that way for contextual training. As a result, this research suggests that user adoption is a concern that future research into game-based training needs to consider. A second and surprising contribution is that this research questions if worry about cybersecurity training types impacts users' willingness to adopt cybersecurity training. While we hypothesised that willingness to adopt cybersecurity training would be significantly influenced by the worry of cyberthreats, the gathered data did not support that hypothesis. A further contribution is the WTA scale, which future researchers can adopt as a comparative index of users' willingness to adopt cybersecurity training.

This research makes two contributions to the practice community. First, it demonstrates what types of training users are most likely to pay for, which could guide decisions to develop and sell cybersecurity training. Second, it demonstrates that most users are not ready to pay for cybersecurity training. This insight is important for national and international initiatives into cybersecurity. We argue that this suggests that national or international organizations must take the economic responsibility for supporting private users towards secure behaviour since the willingness to take that responsibility is low on the user side.

4.3 Limitations and Future Work

While this study aims to be reliable within its population, the extent to which the results are transferable to other populations remains unknown. Consequently, a given direction for future work is to replicate this research in other populations and compare the results.

A further limitation or question raised by this research is what factors influence WTA. This research shows little or no influence from worry about cybersecurity threats, which we found surprising. A suggested direction for future work would be continued data collection and analysis of this dataset to identify factors that greatly impact WTA for cybersecurity training. Understanding those factors is crucial for developing training that users will want to use. A suggested approach would be to quantify the impact of different variables, including worry, using regression analysis. That is beyond the scope of this paper but a viable option for continued work with this or other datasets. It could also be useful to employ a qualitative approach to better understand how users reason concerning WTP and WTA.

References

1. NIST: Framework for Improving Critical Infrastructure Cybersecurity. cited 20201230; Available from: https://nvlpubs.nist.gov/nistpubs/CSWP/NIST.CSWP.04162018.pdf (2018)
2. ISO/IEC: ISO/IEC 27001:2017 (2017)
3. Aldawood, H., Skinner, G.: Educating and raising awareness on cyber security social engineering: a literature review (2019)
4. Hu, S., Hsu, C., Zhou, Z.: Security education, training, and awareness programs: literature review. J. Comput. Inf. Syst. 1–13 (2021).
5. Chowdhury, N., Gkioulos, V.: Cyber security training for critical infrastructure protection: a literature review. Comput. Sci. Rev. **40**, 100361 (2021)
6. Klimburg-Witjes, N., Wentland, A.: Hacking humans? social engineering and the construction of the "deficient user" in cybersecurity discourses. Sci. Technol. Human Values **46**(6), 1316–1339 (2021)
7. Lain, D., Kostiainen, K., Capkun, S.: Phishing in organizations: findings from a large-scale and long-term study. arXiv preprint arXiv:2112.07498 (2021)
8. Al-Daeef, M.M., Basir, N., Saudi, M.M.: Security awareness training: a review. In: Proceedings of the World Congress on Engineering (2017)
9. Nagarajan, A., Allbeck, J.M., Sood, A., Janssen, T.L.: Exploring game design for cybersecurity training. In: 2012 IEEE International Conference on Cyber Technology in Automation, Control, and Intelligent Systems (CYBER). IEEE (2012)
10. Christopher, L., Choo, K.-K., Dehghantanha, A.: Honeypots for employee information security awareness and education training: a conceptual EASY training model. In: Contemporary Digital Forensic Investigations of Cloud and Mobile Applications, pp. 111–129. Elsevier (2017)
11. Kävrestad, J., Nohlberg, M.: Evaluation strategies for cybersecurity training methods: a literature review. In: Furnell, S., Clarke, N. (eds.) HAISA 2021. IAICT, vol. 613, pp. 102–112. Springer, Cham (2021). https://doi.org/10.1007/978-3-030-81111-2_9
12. Alshaikh, M., Maynard, S.B., Ahmad, A., Chang, S.: An exploratory study of current information security training and awareness practices in organizations (2018)
13. He, W., Zhang, Z.: Enterprise cybersecurity training and awareness programs: recommendations for success. J. Organ. Comput. Electron. Commer. **29**(4), 249–257 (2019)
14. Dahabiyeh, L.: Factors affecting organizational adoption and acceptance of computer-based security awareness training tools. Inf. Comput. Secur. (2021)
15. Amanowicz, M.: Towards building national cybersecurity awareness. Int. J. Electron. Telecommun. **66**(2), 321–326 (2020)
16. Van Steen, T., Norris, E., Atha, K., Joinson, A.: What (if any) behaviour change techniques do government-led cybersecurity awareness campaigns use? J. Cybersecur. **6**(1) (2020)
17. Joshi, A., Kale, S., Chandel, S., Pal, D.K.: Likert scale: explored and explained. Curr. J. Appl. Sci. Technol. 396–403 (2015)
18. Miller, R., Banerjee, N.K., Banerjee, S.: Within-system and cross-system behavior-based biometric authentication in virtual reality (2020)
19. Fowler Jr, F.J.: Survey research methods. Sage Publications (2013)

20. Henry, G.T.: Practical Sampling, vol. 21. Sage (1990)
21. Tavakol, M., Dennick, R.: Making sense of Cronbach's alpha. Int. J. Med. Educ. **2**, 53 (2011)
22. Park, E., Cho, M., Ki, C.-S.: Correct use of repeated measures analysis of variance. Korean J. Lab. Med. **29**(1), 1–9 (2009)
23. Asuero, A.G., Sayago, A., Gonzalez, A.: The correlation coefficient: an overview. Crit. Rev. Anal. Chem. **36**(1), 41–59 (2006)
24. Rahimi, B., Nadri, H., Afshar, H.L., Timpka, T.: A systematic review of the technology acceptance model in health informatics. Appl. Clin. Inform. **9**(3), 604 (2018)

A Thematic Content Analysis of the Cybersecurity Skills Demand in South Africa

Madri Kruger[(✉)] [ID], Lynn Futcher[ID], and Kerry-Lynn Thomson[ID]

Nelson Mandela University, Port Elizabeth, South Africa
{madri.kruger,lynn.futcher,kerry-lynn.thomson}@mandela.ac.za

Abstract. The cybersecurity skills demand is a growing concern both globally and in South Africa, creating what is known as the cybersecurity skills gap. This means that there is a shortage of Information Technology (IT) and cybersecurity professionals that have the required knowledge, skills and abilities, to effectively fill this gap. This study aims to provide a better understanding of the cybersecurity skills demand in South Africa having analysed job postings in South Africa over a 4-month period from 1st October 2020 to 31st January 2021. This was done by conducting a thematic content analysis of the 280 job postings identified during this period. Results indicate a condensed set of knowledge, skills and abilities (KSAs) categorised according to five main job categories, namely: Cybersecurity, Operations and Support, Data and Artificial Intelligence, Strategy and Governance, and Software and Application Development. These results can assist universities, training institutions and organisations to address the cybersecurity skills gap in South Africa.

Keywords: Cybersecurity · Skills demand · Thematic content analysis

1 Introduction

The global Cyber Exposure Index ranks South Africa sixth on the list of most-targeted countries for cyberattacks [1]. According to the Kaspersky laboratory, malware attacks in South Africa increased by 22% in the first quarter of 2019 compared to the same time in 2018. This equates to about 13842 attempted cyberattacks daily, or just over 9 attacks per second [2]. Due to this growth in cyberattacks in South Africa, cybersecurity needs to grow in response in order to mitigate such attacks.

Cybersecurity is seen as the practice of defending systems, networks and programs from cyberattacks [3]. There are many threats to cybersecurity, such as phishing, malware, trojans, ransomware, worms and Denial of Service attacks (DoS), among others [4]. In addition, the personal information stored on devices like computers and mobile phones can be used for identity theft, financial gain, blackmail and for gaining access to highly confidential information.

© IFIP International Federation for Information Processing 2022
Published by Springer Nature Switzerland AG 2022
N. Clarke and S. Furnell (Eds.): HAISA 2022, IFIP AICT 658, pp. 24–38, 2022.
https://doi.org/10.1007/978-3-031-12172-2_3

Human error is the main cause of 95% of cybersecurity breaches [5]. Through advances in the technological tools used in information and network security, a large majority of threat detection and monitoring has been automated, However, some tasks cannot be automated and require human intervention to successfully secure information and networks [6].

In a global survey by Oltsik, 82% of respondents reported a shortage of cybersecurity skills, and 61% of companies believed that cybersecurity-related job applicants are not qualified for the job [7]. In a follow-up survey in 2020, 45% of the respondents believed that the skills shortage, as well as its impact, has gotten worse over the last few years [8].

The aim of this paper is to provide a better understanding of the cybersecurity skills demand in South Africa, by analysing job postings in South Africa over a 4-month period from 1st October 2020 to 31st January 2021. This was done by conducting a thematic content analysis of 280 relevant job postings identified during this period.

This paper is structured as follows. Section 2 provides related literature regarding the cybersecurity skills gap both globally and in South Africa. In addition, it highlights several skills frameworks that provide insight into various cybersecurity work roles and their related knowledge, skills and abilities (KSAs). Section 3 discusses the thematic content analysis conducted as a key research method of this study, and Sect. 4 presents the results and findings from the thematic content analysis. Section 5 provides a discussion before concluding the paper in Sect. 6.

2   Related Literature

In 2019, ISACA conducted a survey to better understand the current state of cybersecurity globally. 58% of their respondents indicated that they have unfilled cybersecurity positions within their organisations. The study also indicated an annual 6% increase in the waiting time of positions being filled, sometimes taking as long as six months to fill such positions. Technically skilled cybersecurity professionals were considered the hardest to find, further contributing to the struggle of filling open cybersecurity positions [9].

According to Burning Glass Technologies, job postings for cybersecurity openings have grown three times as fast as openings for IT jobs overall [10]. Although some IT jobs can be filled easily without the need for extensive training, most cybersecurity jobs require specific KSAs, some of which can only be gained through specialised training.

There are many accredited certifications that a cybersecurity professional can attain, including: Certified Information Systems Security Professional (CISSP), CompTIA Security+ and Certified Ethical Hacker (CEH), to name just a few. Each certification targets a different need within industry and most of them are globally recognised. When taking into consideration that in order to apply for CISSP certification, applicants require at least 5 years of relevant experience, one can understand why there is such a huge need for skilled and trained cybersecurity employees [9]. Due to the high qualification and experience requirements for most cybersecurity-related jobs, the cybersecurity skills gap will not be easily addressed in the near future.

South Africa has also been affected by the worldwide shortage of cybersecurity skills. One of South Africa's largest banks, Absa, has collaborated with the Maharishi

Institute (MI) to set up the Absa Cybersecurity Academy in an attempt to address its skills shortage [11]. Despite these kinds of targeted efforts, there is a lack of cost-effective local cybersecurity training offered to South Africans. Most cybersecurity courses offered by international organisations are often unaffordable for most South Africans due to them being billed in US dollars [12]. This has resulted in several local universities, colleges and training institutions providing various forms of cybersecurity training and education. However, most of these would have been based on insight gained from international cybersecurity skills frameworks. For example, the National Initiative for Cybersecurity Education (NICE) framework developed by the National Institute of Standards and Technology (NIST), a United States based institute.

The NICE framework attempts to create a better understanding of what cybersecurity jobs entail and what knowledge, skills, and abilities (KSAs) are needed to complete certain tasks based on job roles. This is a useful tool for organisations seeking guidance on their cybersecurity workforce development. However, while the NICE framework is good at defining job descriptions, there are over 1600 KSA's and more than 50 job roles, making it rather unmanageable. In addition, some of their KSAs are vague and not well defined [13].

A further framework of particular interest to this study is the Skills Framework for Infocomm Technology (SFw for ICT). This framework aims to provide information on career paths, existing and emerging skills, as well as occupations and job roles and their respective knowledge, skills, abilities and tasks (KSATs). It is therefore useful for employers and educational facilities, as well as individuals who are job seeking or planning their careers. Although this framework does not focus specifically on cybersecurity, it does include cybersecurity as one of the seven career pathway tracks [14].

A study by Parker and Brown provides some insight into various cybersecurity jobs advertised in South Africa, together with the typical skills required by such cybersecurity professionals. However, Parker and Brown consider their work as an initial exploratory study providing a basis for future studies [6]. Further, it can be argued that cybersecurity skills are required by IT professionals at all levels of the profession since they are all personally responsible for the information they are entrusted with.

3   Thematic Content Analysis Using ATLAS.ti

Before starting the formal data collection process, it was decided to conduct a pilot study to gain a better understanding of the data to be collected for this study. In September 2020, the pilot study began. Data was collected weekly on three job posting websites, namely: LinkedIn, Careers24 and Career Junction. During the pilot study it was found that the adverts on LinkedIn provided greater depth of information compared to other job posting websites, and was therefore chosen for the rest of the study.

The official data collection for this study took place over a four-month period from 1st October 2020 to 31st January 2021. The search results were filtered by relevant IT and cybersecurity-related jobs each week and set to South African based job postings only. A total of 280 job postings were collected. These job postings were then analysed by conducting a thematic content analysis using ATLAS.ti, a popular software analysis tool for analysing qualitative data.

A three-phased approach was used for the thematic content analysis as proposed by [15]. Using ATLAS.ti in combination with this three-phased approach is considered a promising strategy for conducting a thematic content analysis [15]. Figure 1 presents the three phases of the thematic content analysis and the associated steps taken in ATLAS.ti.

Phases of thematic content analysis	Steps in ATLAS.ti
First phase: Pre-analysis.	Creating the project. Adding documents. Grouping documents into document groups. Writing first memos on the overall project aim including research questions.
Second phase: Material exploration.	Reading the data, selecting data segments and creating quotations. Creating and applying codes. Writing memos and comments. Grouping codes and memos
Third phase: Interpretation.	Exploring the coded data using various analysis tools. Linking quotations, codes, and memos on the conceptual level. Continuing memo writing. Generating network views. Extracting reports.

Fig. 1. Three-phased thematic content analysis [15]

These phases are discussed in more detail in the following sub-sections.

3.1 First Phase: Pre-analysis

Firstly, a new project was created in ATLAS.ti. All the data collected for the four months from 1st October 2020 to 31st January 2021 were added to this project by importing the MS Word documents containing the job postings for each month into the project. Once imported, these documents were grouped according to month, resulting in four groups named "OCT", "NOV", "DEC" and "JAN". Each monthly group contained four MS Word documents, one for each week of the month.

3.2 Second Phase: Material Exploration

To start the second phase of the thematic content analysis, a document group was opened, and a document was chosen. This started with the document group called "OCT", and the document for the first week of October was selected. This document was then read, and important data segments were selected, and quotations created for these segments. Each of the quotations were assigned a code. Thereafter the next document in the group was selected which in this case was called "Week 2 Oct" after it had been completed the same process was followed for the documents "Week 3 Oct" and "Week 4 Oct". Once document group "OCT" was completed, the next group was selected, that being document group "NOV", and the documents for each week in document group "NOV" completed. The same process was followed for document groups "DEC" and "JAN", as well as their respective documents. There was a total of 640 codes and 3580 quotations after completing the coding for each of the document groups. Each quotation was linked to only one data segment. Each quotation was assigned a single code, and a code belonged to only one code group. For example, the quotation "Ideal candidate must have a Security+ certification" would be assigned the code "Security+".

Once all job postings had been coded, these codes needed to be organised. To do this, a similar process to that used for the document groups was followed, called code groups. Each of the different types of codes were grouped according to their type. For example, all certifications were grouped into a group called Certifications. The same was done for all the other types of codes. A total of six code groups were identified, namely: Certifications, Industries, Job Levels, Job Roles, Job Types and Regions.

Once all codes had been grouped, each group was inspected individually to find possible duplications. For example, in the case of the Certifications group, it contained multiple occurrences of the same certifications due to them often being referred to in various ways by different employers. One such case was the certification Security+. It was referred to as S+ in some cases and as Security+ in others. In this case the two codes were merged into a single code, named Security+.

After the codes had been grouped and checked for duplicates, there was a total of 552 codes in the project, thus a reduction of 88 from the original 640 codes.

3.3 Third Phase: Interpretation

In the third phase, the primary focus was on the code group called "Job Roles" since these could be further analysed according to their related knowledge, skills and abilities (KSAs). A total of 223 job roles were identified in the "Job Roles" code group on starting this third phase of the thematic content analysis. However, on further analysis, some of these job roles were found to be similar, but were named differently due to employers using different naming conventions. For example, a job role named "Software Developer" and a job role named "Application Developer" were merged into a single job role named "Software Developer" since they were considered to be similar job roles.

Each job role was individually assessed according to their associated knowledge, skills and abilities (KSAs) and their required certifications were noted in a comment associated with the job role. To further determine whether job roles were the same, their KSAs were compared. If they had the same KSAs, the job roles were deemed similar and were merged into one. After the completion of this phase, the initial 223 job roles were substantially reduced to a total of 20 job roles, each having defined KSAs, as well as various certifications associated with them.

The completed thematic content analysis process resulted in 353 codes spread over five key job categories, down from the initial number of 640 codes at the beginning of the Material Exploration Phase.

4 General Results and Findings

Of the 280 postings analysed, approximately 90% were full-time positions. From the thematic content analysis conducted, the following key categories were deemed most relevant to this study, and were therefore defined and coded for further analysis. These key categories were derived from the code groups described in Sect. 3.2 and included:

- the industry (where five main industries were identified)
- the job location (this was indicated by province)
- the job level (ranging from entry-level to executive-level)
- the minimum qualifications and certifications.

These key categories are further analysed in their respective sub-sections below, while job roles and their related KSAs are discussed in Sect. 5.

4.1 Identified Industries

From the thematic content analysis conducted, it was found that most of the job postings indicated the specific industry of the job advertised. In total, there were 43 industries identified from the 280 job postings analysed. Of the identified industries Information Technology and Services was mentioned 140 times (25%), Financial Services was mentioned 122 times (21.7%) and Computer Software mentioned 84 times (15%).

4.2 Job Locations

South Africa has a total of nine provinces, eight of which had job listings during the four-month data collection period from 1st October 2020 to 31st January 2021. Gauteng accounted for most of the job postings (178 postings, 63.6%), followed by the Western Cape (67 postings, 23.9%). These two provinces, accounted for 87.5% of the total job postings.

4.3 Job Levels

Most job postings collected over the four-month period had a job level assigned to it. Each job posting was therefore classified according to whether it was entry-level, mid-level, senior level or executive-level. Those that did not specify the job level were classified under "Not Specified". Entry-level jobs made up the majority of the job postings (101 postings, 36.1%), followed by mid-level (87 postings, 31.1%) and senior level (65 postings, 23.2%). Executive-level only made up 3.5% of the total job postings, while 6.1% did not specify a job level.

4.4 Qualifications and Certifications

The minimum required qualifications and most common certifications listed in the job postings were analysed. Of the 280 job postings analysed, 231 job postings (82.5%) listed a specific requirement in terms of formal tertiary education. This implies a strong emphasis on meeting specific academic requirements to enter the IT industry. More than half of the job postings (65.8%, 152 job postings) specified that they require a degree in either Computer Science, Information Systems or Information Technology, as a minimum qualification. This indicates that there is a demand for academic qualifications needed for most of the job postings and that in most cases a diploma would not suffice. A diploma was specified as a requirement for 69 job postings (29.9%), with 10 job postings (4.3%) requiring either a master's degree or some form of relevant postgraduate qualification.

In terms of certifications, Certified Information Systems Security Professional (CISSP) was the most listed (55 times in the 280 job postings). This was followed by Information Technology Infrastructure Library (ITIL) with 46 listings, and two of the certifications provided by COMPTIA, namely, Network+ with 45 listings and A+ with 42 listings.

The following section discusses the identified job roles and their related KSAs.

5 Job Roles Results and Findings

The job roles and knowledge areas identified during the thematic content analysis were mapped against the following five job categories, namely:

- Cybersecurity [CS]
- Operations and Support [OS]
- Data and Artificial Intelligence [DA]
- Strategy and Governance [SG]
- Software and Application Development [SA].

Furthermore, the skills and abilities identified during the thematic content analysis were grouped according to whether they were technical or non-technical in nature.

5.1 Identified Job Roles, Knowledge, Skills and Abilities

Table 1 presents the 20 job roles categorised according to the five job categories listed above. Cybersecurity had seven related job roles (CSJ01 to CSJ07), followed by Strategy and Governance with six (SGJ01 to SGJ06) and Data and Artificial Intelligence with three (DAJ01 to DAJ03). Operations and Support (OSJ01 and OSJ02) and Software and Application Development (SAJ01 and SAJ02) each had two related job roles identified.

Table 1. Job roles identified per job category

Code	Description	Code	Description
Cybersecurity [CS]		**Strategy and Governance [SG]**	
CSJ01	Cybersecurity Specialist	SGJ01	Information Technology Manager
CSJ02	Digital Forensics Analyst	SGJ02	Information Technology Auditor
CSJ03	Security Engineer	SGJ03	Compliance Specialist

(continued)

Table 1. (*continued*)

Code	Description	Code	Description
CSJ04	Data Privacy and Protection Specialist	SGJ04	Project Manager
CSJ05	Cybersecurity Manager	SGJ05	Quality Assurance Analyst
CSJ06	Application Security Specialist	SGJ06	Chief Information Officer
CSJ07	Penetration Tester	**Data and Artificial Intelligence [DA]**	
Operations and Support [OS]		DAJ01	Systems Administrator
OSJ01	Desktop Technician	DAJ02	Data Warehousing Engineer
OSJ02	Network Engineer	DAJ03	Cloud Architect
Software and Application Development [SA]			
SAJ01	Software Developer		
SAJ02	DevOps Engineer		

Table 2 presents the 54 knowledge areas identified and categorised according to their relevant job category. The most knowledge areas fall within the Strategy and Governance job category (SGK01 to SGK15), followed by Operations and Support (OSK01 to OSK13).

Table 2. Knowledge areas identified per job category

Code	Description	Code	Description	Code	Description
Cybersecurity [CS]		**Strategy and Governance [SG]**		**Software and Application Development [SA]**	
CSK01	Security Proxies	SGK01	Project Management	SAK01	SDLC
CSK02	Security Frameworks	SGK02	IT Risk	SAK02	Secure Coding
CSK03	Anti-Virus Software	SGK03	NIST	SAK03	Application Security
CSK04	Security Best Practices	SGK04	ISO	SAK04	SQL
CSK05	Penetrating Testing	SGK05	COBIT	SAK05	Coding Languages
CSK06	Security Vulnerabilities and Exploits	SGK06	Business Operations	SAK06	Functions
CSK07	Firewalls	SGK07	King IV	SAK07	Databases

(*continued*)

Table 2. (*continued*)

Code	Description	Code	Description	Code	Description
CSK08	SSL	SGK08	Problem Management	SAK08	Stored Procedures
CSK09	IPS/IDS	SGK09	Incident Management	SAK09	Database Design
Operations and Support [OS]		SGK10	Access Management	SAK10	SAK10
		SGK11	Compliance	SAK11	Version Control
OSK01	Operating Systems	SGK12	Change Management		
OSK02	PC Hardware and Software	SGK13	IT Governance		
OSK03	Backups	SGK14	ITIL		
OSK04	VMWare	SGK15	IT Security Policies		
OSK05	Active Directory	**Data and Artificial Intelligence [DA]**			
OSK06	VPN				
OSK07	IIS	DAK01	Data Warehousing		
OSK08	OWASP	DAK02	Data Analysis		
OSK09	Routers	DAK03	Data Modelling		
OSK10	Switches	DAK04	Machine Learning		
OSK11	IP/VOIP/TCP	DAK05	Cloud Services		
OSK12	Network Security	DAK06	Automation		
OSK13	Network Monitoring Tools				

Table 3 presents the 23 skills identified and categorised according to their technical or non-technical nature. 17 skills were identified as non-technical (NTS01 to NTS17) and six were considered to be technical (TS01 to TS06).

Table 3. Non-technical and technical skills identified

Code	Description	Code	Description
Non-technical skills		**Technical skills**	
NTS01	Planning Skills	TS01	Troubleshooting Skills
NTS02	Leadership Skills	TS02	Technical writing Skills
NTS03	Presentation Skills	TS03	Diagnostic Skills
NTS04	Analytical thinking Skills	TS04	General programming Skills
NTS05	Communication Skills	TS05	Administration Skills
NTS06	Adaptability Skills	TS06	Problem solving Skills
NTS07	Fast learner Skills		
NTS08	Organisational Skills		
NTS09	Time management Skills		
NTS10	Attention to detail Skills		
NTS11	Conflict management Skills		
NTS12	Collaboration Skills		
NTS13	Customer service Skills		
NTS14	Strategic thinking Skills		
NTS15	Negotiation Skills		
NTS16	Decision making Skills		
NTS17	Logical thinking Skills		

Table 4 presents the 16 non-technical abilities (NTA01 to NTA16) and 11 technical abilities (TA01 to TA11) that were identified.

Table 4. Non-technical and technical abilities identified

Code	Description	Code	Description
Non-Technical Abilities		**Technical Abilities**	
NTA01	Ability to manage human resources	TA01	Ability to solve technical problems
NTA02	Ability to lead teams	TA02	Ability to write reports
NTA03	Ability to work with leadership	TA03	Ability to obtain forensic evidence
NTA04	Ability to work in teams	TA04	Ability to provide technical assistance

(continued)

Table 4. (*continued*)

Code	Description	Code	Description
NTA05	Ability to maintain confidentiality	TA05	Ability to troubleshoot
NTA06	Ability to research	TA06	Ability to maintain hardware and software
NTA07	Ability to manage many priorities concurrently	TA07	Ability to analyse data
NTA08	Ability to engage and contribute	TA08	Ability to investigate malware, intrusion attempts and vulnerabilities
NTA09	Ability to execute instructions	TA09	Ability to learn new technology independently
NTA10	Ability to be proactive and efficient	TA10	Ability to create network diagrams and related documentation
NTA11	Ability to work under pressure	TA11	Ability to write secure code
NTA12	Ability to adapt to changing environments		
NTA13	Ability to stay organised		
NTA14	Ability to communicate effectively and efficiently		
NTA15	Ability to prioritise		
NTA16	Ability to work independently		

The skills depicted in Table 3 and the abilities shown in Table 4 were further analysed and mapped against the five main job categories, as discussed in the next sub-section.

5.2   Mapping of Identified Skills and Abilities to Job Categories

Table 5 highlights the four most relevant non-technical skills, namely: NTS04 (Analytical thinking skills), NTS05 (Communication skills), NTS10 (Attention to detail skills), as well as NTS17 (Logical thinking skills). NTS04, NTS05, NTS10 and NTS17 are required by all job categories. Further, both Cybersecurity [CS] and Strategy and Governance [SG] require 15 of the 17 identified non-technical skills.

Notable technical skills shown in Table 6 are TS01 (Troubleshooting skills) and TS06 (Problem solving skills). TS01 is present in all job categories identified and TS06 had been identified in all but one category, Software and Application development [SA]. Cybersecurity [CS] has been shown to require all but one of the technical skills identified.

Table 5. Non-technical skills mapped according to job categories

Non- Technical Skills																	
Job Category	NTS 01	NTS 02	NTS 03	NTS 04	NTS 05	NTS 06	NTS 07	NTS 08	NTS 09	NTS 10	NTS 11	NTS 12	NTS 13	NTS 14	NTS 15	NTS 16	NTS 17	TOTAL
CS																		15
OS																		8
DA																		8
SG																		15
SA																		9
TOTAL	2	3	2	5	5	4	3	4	3	5	2	3	1	2	2	4	5	

Table 6. Technical skills mapped according to job categories

Technical Skills						
Job	TS01	TS02	TS03	TS04	TS05	TS06	TOTAL
CS							5
OS							4
DA							4
SG							3
SA							4
TOTAL	5	3	3	3	2	4	

It can be seen in Table 7 that TA01 (Ability to solve technical problems) and TA05 (Ability to troubleshoot) have been identified as required for all the identified job categories. Cybersecurity [CS], Operations and Support [OS] as well as Data and Artificial Intelligence [DA] mapped against 7 of the 11 technical abilities.

Table 7. Technical abilities mapped according to job categories

Technical Abilities											
Job	TA01	TA02	TA03	TA04	TA05	TA06	TA07	TA08	TA09	TA10	TA11	TOTAL
CS												7
OS												7
DA												7
SG												5
SA												5
TOTAL	5	2	1	4	5	2	4	1	3	2	2	

As seen in Table 8, both NTA04 (Ability to work in teams) and NTA09 (Ability to execute instructions) are required by all identified job categories. Further, Cybersecurity [CS] and Strategy and Governance [SG] both required 13 of the 17 non-technical abilities identified.

The mappings of the various skills and abilities to the five job categories identified by this study provides valuable detail for companies offering positions relating to these job categories and related job roles.

Table 8. Non-technical abilities mapped according to job categories

Job Category	Non-Technical Abilities																TOTAL
	NTA 01	NTA 02	NTA 03	NTA 04	NTA 05	NTA 06	NTA 07	NTA 08	NTA 09	NTA 10	NTA 11	NTA 12	NTA 13	NTA 14	NTA 15	NTA 16	
CS																	13
OS																	7
DA																	10
SG																	13
SA																	6
TOTAL	1	3	2	5	3	3	4	3	5	3	3	4	2	4	1	3	

6 Discussion and Implications

From this study it is evident that IT professionals with cybersecurity KSAs are required in various industries in South Africa. Many job postings specified the job as an entry-level position, despite there being a need for security knowledge, and in some cases, certifications related to cybersecurity for these entry-level positions. CISSP was the most mentioned certification, yet it requires a minimum of 5 years cybersecurity experience to qualify for the certification. In 65.8% of the job postings, the employers expect the ideal candidate to have a degree in either Computer Science, Information Systems or Information Technology. In addition, cybersecurity-related certifications were considered an advantage, if not a requirement, for many of the 280 job postings analysed. It was interesting to note that there were some cases where an entry-level job required a CISSP certification, as well as a relevant degree, further indicating the high level of experience and academic requirements for IT professionals with cybersecurity KSAs. Skills and abilities relating to the Cybersecurity [CS] job category is by far the most in demand based on the job postings analysed.

Several trends were identified from this study. Table 2 presents the knowledge areas found in the 280 job postings analysed. However, many of the knowledge areas could be considered as technical skills rather than knowledge areas. For example, Penetration Testing (CSK05) and Secure Coding (SAK02) are often considered to be technical skills. However, employers seem to focus more on knowledge requirements and non-technical skills, with the technical skills mentioned being less specific and more generalised, for example Problem-Solving skills (TS06). This is also evident in Table 3, when comparing the number of technical (6) and non-technical (17) skills. It is interesting to note the emphasis on non-technical skills and abilities especially in the Cybersecurity [CS] and Strategy and Governance [SG] job categories.

Based on this study one can more clearly determine what is required in terms of KSAs when employing IT professionals in the five identified job categories. This information could be used towards a cybersecurity skills framework for South Africa, which may contribute to improving the South African cybersecurity posture.

The KSAs identified in this study closely align with the Skills Framework for Infocomm Technology (SFw for ICT), sharing many knowledge areas, skills and abilities. Due to this study's alignment with (SFw for ICT), it could provide a good baseline for a cybersecurity skills framework for South Africa. This could be used to better inform employers and future employees, as well as to assist in the further development of cybersecurity curricula in the education sector.

7   Conclusion

Despite the limitation of only analysing job postings over a four-month period from 1st October 2020 to 31st January 2021, this study contributed further understanding of the cybersecurity skills demand in South Africa. In addition, it demonstrated that ATLAS.ti is a suitable tool to use for analysing such datasets using the three-phased approach as proposed by [15].

Most countries are developing their own workforce and skills frameworks for IT and cybersecurity professionals. Australia, Canada, the United Kingdom and Singapore are among those who have developed, or are in the process of developing, their own frameworks. South Africa has a need for a similar framework that identifies cybersecurity knowledge, skills and abilities for different IT and cybersecurity job roles in the South African context. Future work will therefore use the results of this study to propose a cybersecurity skills framework for the South African context.

References

1. CEI: Country statistics – cyber exposure index (2020). https://cyberexposureindex.com/country-statistics/
2. Smith, C.: Major spike in SA cyber attacks, over 10 000 attempts a day. News24 (2019). https://www.fin24.com/Companies/ICT/major-spike-in-sa-cyber-attacks-over-10-000-attempts-a-day-security-company-20190429
3. Cisco: What is cybersecurity? - Cisco (2017). https://www.cisco.com/c/en/us/products/security/what-is-cybersecurity.html
4. Tunggal, A.T.: What is a cyber threat? Upguard (2020). https://www.upguard.com/blog/cyber-threat
5. Ahola, M.: The role of human error in successful cyber security breaches. Usecure (2019). https://blog.getusecure.com/post/the-role-of-human-error-in-successful-cyber-security-breaches
6. Parker, A., Brown, I.: Skills requirements for cyber security professionals: a content analysis of job descriptions in South Africa. In: Venter, H., Loock, M., Coetzee, M., Eloff, M., Eloff, J. (eds.) ISSA 2018. CCIS, vol. 973, pp. 176–192. Springer, Cham (2019). https://doi.org/10.1007/978-3-030-11407-7_13
7. Oltsik, J.: 2017 ISSA ESG survey results - information systems security association (2017). https://www.members.issa.org/page/2017_issaesg_surv
8. Oltsik, J.: ESG Research report: the life and times of cybersecurity professionals 2020, July 2020. https://www.esg-global.com/research/esg-research-report-the-life-and-times-of-cybersecurity-professionals-2020
9. ISACA: ISACAs State of Cybersecurity 2019 Survey Retaining Qualified Cybersecurity Professionals (2019). https://www.isaca.org/why-isaca/about-us/newsroom/press-releases/2019/isacas-state-of-cybersecurity-2019-survey-retaining-qualified-cybersecurity-professionals
10. Burning Glass Technologies: The State of Cybersecurity Hiring, pp. 1–26, June 2019
11. Bucchianeri, S.: The cybersecurity skills gap offers SA an opportunity to lead in the 4IR (2019). https://www.iol.co.za/business-report/opinion/the-cybersecurity-skills-gap-offers-sa-an-opportunity-to-lead-in-the-4ir-31762949

12. Doyle, K.: Wanted: cyber security expertise | ITWeb. ITWeb's Corporate IT Training Guide, 4th Issue, p. 27 (2016). http://books.itweb.co.za/tg/
13. NIST: NICE Cybersecurity Workforce Framework Use Cases and Success Stories. Engl. J. 1–21 (2020). https://www.nist.gov/news-events/events/2020/03/nice-webinar-nice-cybersecurity-workforce-framework-use-cases-and-success
14. IMDA: Skills Framework For ICT (2017). https://www.imda.gov.sg/cwp/assets/imtalent/skills-framework-for-ict/index.html
15. Soratto, J., de Pires, D.E.P., Friese, S.: Thematic content analysis using ATLAS.ti software: potentialities for researchs in health. Rev. Bras. Enfermagem **73**(3), e20190250 (2020). https://doi.org/10.1590/0034-7167-2019-0250

Applying PDCA to Security, Education, Training and Awareness Programs

Olivier de Casanove$^{(\boxtimes)}$, Nicolas Leleu, and Florence Sèdes

Institut de Recherche en Informatique de Toulouse – IRIT, Université Toulouse
III – Paul-Sabatier, 118 route de Narbonne, 31062 CEDEX 9 Toulouse, France
{olivier.decasanove,florence.sedes}@irit.fr,
Nicolas.leleu@ut-capitole.fr

Abstract. Security standards help to create security policies, but they are often very descriptive, especially when it comes to security awareness. Information systems security awareness is vital to maintain a high level of security. SETA programs (Security Education, Training and Awareness) increase information systems security awareness and play an important role in finding the strategic balance between the prevention and response paradigms. By reviewing the literature, we identify guidelines for designing a SETA program following a PDCA (Plan Do Check Act) cycle.

Keywords: PDCA · Information systems security · Awareness · SETA · Guidelines

1 Introduction

Defining security awareness and more specifically its goals is a challenging task. This leads to a diversity of approaches and Tsohou et al. [1] conclude their paper saying that it creates frustration among security experts; this could be a reason why security awareness remains an issue. In this paper we will consider that the objective of security awareness is to reduce the share of security incidents caused by humans. To decrease the proportion of security incidents caused by well-meaning users, we need to educate them. As stated in [2] "Accountability must be derived from a fully informed, well-trained and aware workforce". To promote a security culture, we can use security, education, training and awareness programs (SETA programs). "SETA programs aim to provide employees with the knowledge and motivation necessary to comply with security policies when confronted with a security risk" [3]. Some information system security standards define objectives for promoting a security culture and for raising awareness. Two of the most famous standards addressing this concern are the ISO/IEC 27000 family [4] and the NIST Cybersecurity Framework [5]. Unfortunately, information system security standards are very descriptive [6]. They set goals to reach, but rarely provide process or methodology

© IFIP International Federation for Information Processing 2022
Published by Springer Nature Switzerland AG 2022
N. Clarke and S. Furnell (Eds.): HAISA 2022, IFIP AICT 658, pp. 39–48, 2022.
https://doi.org/10.1007/978-3-031-12172-2_4

on how to reach them; there is a need for guidelines. We propose to apply the Plan Do Check Act (PDCA) method to SETA programs to fulfil this need.

Plan Do Check Act

The Deming wheel (Fig. 1), also called continuous improvement wheel is a concept that illustrates the PDCA principle. It was made popular by William Edwards Deming. It aims to improve and optimise the gains and reduce the losses of products, processes or services. In the PDCA technique, the slope represents process improvement, the turning wheel continuously cycles Plan Do Check Act and thus climbs the hill, increasingly optimising the product, process or service with the aim of achieving the desired objective. Deming's representation also contains a wedge, it represents the quality system resulting from the previous improvement processes, the experience acquired which prevent the processes from going back. It must imperatively follow the upward movement of the wheel to avoid stagnating or even regressing. In other words, beyond the visual metaphor, it is necessary each time to improve the way of proceeding by avoiding repeating the errors of the past. We believe this tool can help design better SETA programs. With PDCA, we can limit the risk of failure, avoid repeating the same mistakes and provide guidelines.

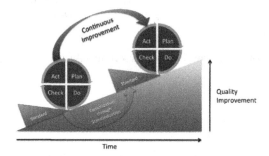

Fig. 1. Deming's wheel illustration

In this paper, we will extract guidelines from the literature to promote a security culture and raise awareness thanks to SETA programs. We do not seek to provide an exhaustive literature review but rather a useful compilation of SETA practices. These guidelines are presented in four sections, each section corresponds to a step in the PDCA cycle. Then, we discuss the future of SETA programs and security awareness. Finally, we conclude.

2 Plan the SETA Program

A SETA program is designed to make people adopt safe behaviours. People will still make mistakes even if they behave safely, but if we are successful, they will make fewer. The most effective way to change security behaviours is to make people adopt a security culture [7]. To adopt a new culture, it is advised to generate an intrinsic motivation [8]. In other words, SETA programs should increase empowerment, which is a strong lever to increase security awareness [9]. A SETA program designed to generate intrinsic motivation is more likely to be successful over a long period of time. To design such a program, we need to identify four elements: the source of the message, the type of message, the media of the message and the target of the message. Making the right choice decrease the risk of failing the SETA program.

2.1 The Source

First, we need to understand who is the source of the message [7]. Depending on its hierarchical level, the program will not have the same degree of complexity. For instance, if the message is from executives, the objective will be to teach non-technical ideas, for example *how to have good digital hygiene?* As executives have less understanding of the production environment than team leaders, their messages should not be about technical matters. It is the role of the team leaders to translate the non-technical messages into technical messages that are relevant to what their team is facing. For example, the team leader can turn the previous non-technical message into *how to use the shared mailbox safely?*

2.2 The Type of Message

There are two forms of communication that the SETA program should adopt [2, 8]:

- **Persuasive communication/education:** it answers the question "why" in the user's mind. It should increase people's insight and motivation.
- **Active participation/training** it answers the question "how" in the user's mind. It should develop skills and competences.

Both are equally important; people will not be satisfied if the only reason given for improving security is "just do it" and they cannot do anything if they do not know how. A good program is a combination of active training and persuasive communication [8].

There are five themes to conduct a security awareness campaign [10]: deterrence, morality, regret, incentive or feedback. They are defined as follows:

- **Deterrence messages** associate sanction to a bad action. This assumes that people are rational and will choose the best option for them, which will not be the one with the expected penalty. Empirical evidence that SETA programs are suitable for deterrence messages can be found in [11]. This finding is confirmed by the literature review [12]. Lowry et al. [13] advise staying careful when using this theme, as deterrence messages create reactance and can "result in unintended negative consequences" [13].
- **Morality messages** attempt to evoke our own moral principles to avoid bad decisions. Empirical evidence that moral reasoning has an impact on security behaviour can be found in [14]. The authors also argue that appropriate punishment activities are important for moral reasoning to be effective. Punishment activities obviously cannot be carried out during a SETA program.
- **Regret messages** assume that people can anticipate the emotional consequences of their choices before making a decision. This anticipation would encourage people to make the right choice. Empirical evidence of the positive effect of regret on security

behaviour is found in [15] but is not distinguished from deterrence or morality. No significant evidence is found in [16].

- **Incentive messages** assume that giving rewards for doing the right thing helps people improve their behaviour. This can be seen as the opposite of regret messages. Empirical studies show that rewards for compliance with security policies and procedures are not associated with the individual's perceived mandatoriness of the established set of policies and procedures [17] or with compliance [18]. A survey also concludes that rewards do not directly influence security behaviour [12]. However, [19] finds theoretical evidence of positive effects on security behaviour and [15] finds empirical evidence that the incentive has a positive effect. Financial rewards also have a positive effect on security behaviour according to [20].
- **Feedback messages** assume that people will change their behaviour if they receive feedback on their actions, this can be positive or negative reinforcement. In [21], West explains that classical feedback mechanisms do not work in information systems security; the consequence of a bad action is often delayed, and the consequence of a good one is not to be under attack. In other words, nothing happens. Reinforcement learning is therefore not effective in this context.

In [22], the authors compared the effectiveness of different themes for a password policies awareness campaign to a control group and they found no significant difference between the groups' willingness to comply. They suggest that, on a motivate public, theme does not matter.

2.3 The Media

There are different media for conveying a SETA program and choosing the right one is an important decision.

The choice of media depends on multiple factors, seven have been identified in [2]:

- **The population we are targeting:** we will not use the same media if the targeted audience is computer literate or if it is not, for example.
- **The why or the how:** some media are more suited for persuasive communication, and others for active participation. [2] lists the possible media according to the question they answer. [23] suggests that video-based communication is more effective than text-based communication to answer the question "why" (the objective of the study was motivating users to adopt password managers)
- **The price:** [2] details which media are cheap and which are expensive.
- **Ease of use:** How easy is it to access, deploy, update and maintain the SETA program?
- **Scalability:** Can the material be used for different sized audiences and in different locations?
- **Support:** Will support for the program be internal or external? Is it easy to find help to use the material?
- **Accountability:** Which statistics can be used to measure the effectiveness of the program? How comprehensive are these measures?

As mentioned in the previous Subsect. 2.2, we need to use media that allow us to answer the question of how (active training) and why (persuasive communication).

2.4 The Target

Finally, a SETA program should be audience-specific. Unfortunately, little work has been done to study the relationship between public types and other factors, such as the theme of a SETA program. However, one paper finds that there might be a correlation between personality traits and the effectiveness of a theme [10]. The most relevant advice found regarding the public is to divide the population by groups of interest. This recommendation is found several times in the literature, regardless of the study publication date [2, 24, 25].

Summary
To plan a SETA program we should assess available resources, understand who is the source of the message, what message we want to communicate, how we want to promote it and who is the target. If these attributes are identified, we decrease the risk of failing the campaign.

3 Do the SETA Program

During the Do step, we apply the choices made in the previous step and we conduct the SETA program. When we carry out the program, the most important thing is the public's willingness to participate [27]. Security gamification is a tool "to strengthen employees' motivations to encourage learning, efficacy, and increased employee compliance with organisational security initiatives" [3]; we can therefore use it to design a successful SETA program. Guidelines on how to properly implement gamification are provided [3]. Yet, as shown by [32] and [33], gamification in the context of security awareness does not always hit. Providing social interactions during a session increases the effectiveness of the SETA program and triggers positive changes in security behaviour [7, 12, 26–28]. This argument seems to demonstrate that e-learning is not appropriate since there are no interactions. On the other hand, Kävrestad et al. [29, 30] show that e-learning could be effective if "information [is] presented in short sequences to the learner. It should also include a practical element and be of direct relevance to the user's intention." [31] Organised SETA programs in short sessions is a good practice, even if we are not doing e-learning [25]. At the end of the program, giving gifts is a good way to spread our message and reinforce the commitment [25].

If the SETA program happens in a company or in an industrial context, the session needs to have as little impact as possible on production; therefore we should communicate the plan to all stakeholders [2, 12]. This means the people we are training, but also their immediate superiors and other people they work with who are not involved in the program. During the session, the trainees will not be able to maintain production; everyone working with them must be prepared for the consequences.

Summary
A program is more likely to succeed if it offers human interaction. If the program happens in a company, attendees' coworkers should be warned that attendees will not be available to maintain production.

4 Check the SETA Program

In the check step, we should verify whether we have processes to monitor the effectiveness and efficiency of the SETA program. To evaluate our program, we need to collect data. They can be feedback, questionnaires or notes taken during the session. We identified three types of evaluation in the literature: measure of behavioural intention, knowledge oriented and ulterior incident rate. A non-exhaustive list of papers related to each category can be found in Table 1.

- **Measure of behavioural intention:** The assumption behind this type of evaluation is that system, method or tool use can be estimated using many other measures, and that the behavioural intention to use is a good estimator of actual usage. For example, if we run a campaign to promote password managers, the higher the user's intention to use them, the more successful the campaign is.
- **Knowledge oriented:** This evaluation method posits that people who have less understanding of security concepts are more likely to be victims of an attack. Therefore, assessing the knowledge gained after the SETA program can be an indicator of the effectiveness of the program.
- **Ulterior incident rate:** This method consists of measuring the incident rate ulterior to the campaign. For example, if we run a campaign against bad password management and the rate of incidents related to bad password management decreases after the campaign, we can consider the campaign successful.

Table 1. Evaluation methods (* is a review)

Evaluation methods	References
Measure of behavioural intention	[34–36]* [37]
Knowledge test	[22, 38–41]
Ulterior incident rate	[2]

Regardless of the solution we choose for evaluating our program, we need to think about automating the evaluation [2, 39]. Some SETA programs can be huge; the process of collecting the data and then interpreting it can be time consuming. Obviously, some types of data are better suited for automation than others. Hand notes of the session, open-ended questions and oral feedback need a human to interpret them; therefore this is difficult to process automatically. On the other hand, online questionnaires or at least multiple-choice questionnaires are easier to process automatically.

Summary
We establish a process to evaluate our program. As the SETA program will grow, it will be harder to evaluate it without automation. Some evaluation methods are most suited for automation than others; this should be taken into consideration when choosing the method to evaluate our program.

5   Adjust the SETA Program

During the Act phase (also known as Adjust phase), we establish a process to ensure we perform a review on a periodic basis to confirm the continuing applicability, adequacy, effectiveness and efficiency of the SETA programs. In the first place, we take in consideration the data collected in the previous section to improve our program. Then, we verify if the campaign is consistent with the new policies and environment. The IT environment is an ever-evolving place, it is important to check if the messages provided are not obsolete. If so, we need to update them or add new ones. Once we have our new program, we should consider launching a new campaign. This cycle is the single-loop learning of the prevention paradigm described in [42]. Since we are considering SETA program as a continuous process, a new campaign should be launched on a regular basis. Exactly as it seems obvious to everyone to update their antivirus software, security culture must also be updated.

Summary
The improvement process is in two parts: first improve the program based on the feedback, second verify if the messages are still up to date. A new campaign must be planned at the end of the previous one.

6   Discussion and Perspectives

SETA programs are an important aspect of security. It differs from other aspects of security by putting the user back at the centre of the information system. This is associated with the field of "Human-Centred Security and Privacy" (HCSP), see [43] for a brief overview of this field.

While many tools in information system security are automated, non-technical security measures are exceptions to this rule. The PDCA cycle permits at least to create a clear process which will facilitate the creation of a SETA program. We used the PDCA cycle because it is a widely used tool in the industry, but other continuous improvement tools should be studied, or created if needed, to better suit the needs of information system security. We seek, in future works, to develop a PDCA-based method for the implementation of organisational SETA work.

SETA programs have been researched extensively, but some aspects have been neglected. For example, how themes interact with other variables, like the target of a campaign, is not well studied in the literature. We want to extract other weaknesses in future works, thanks to techniques such as content analysis.

Khan et al. [27] identify that information systems security awareness lags behind other domains such as ecological or public health awareness. They propose to imitate techniques from other fields to improve information systems security awareness. For example, in public health, a reference model is the EPPM (Extended Parallel Process Model) [44]. This model works well with messages fear-based (they are similar to deterrence-based messages), which are effective for SETA programs according to what we found in the literature (see Subsect. 2.2).

At the check step, we listed models allowing measuring the SETA campaign effectiveness (see Table 1). The lack of common datasets makes it difficult to compare them together and to conclude if one is better than another. In addition, there is a need for reproducibility since the datasets are not public.

7 Conclusion

Security awareness is a major concern in information system security. To promote awareness, we use SETA program. However, there is a lack of methodology on how to implement them in the state of the art. This is the problem we try to address in this paper. By reviewing the literature, we identify guidelines for designing SETA programs following a PDCA cycle. The PDCA cycle allows us to be prescriptive and not just descriptive as many current standards do. In addition, PDCA facilitates the continuous improvement of awareness campaigns which, as every security tool, should stay updated.

We believe this work can help information system security actors to design better prevention programs but not only. This work can also be used by researchers who want to study the various topics related to prevention. They can find in this paper guidelines to create effective programs to convey messages, leading to more efficient prevention campaign and more significant results.

References

1. Tsohou, A., Kokolakis, S., Karyda, M., Kiountouzis, E.: Investigating information security awareness: research and practice gaps. Inf. Secur. J. Glob. Perspect. **17**, 207–227 (2008)
2. Wilson, M., Hash, J.: Building an information technology security awareness and training program (2003)
3. Silic, M., Lowry, P.B.: Using design-science based gamification to improve organizational security training and compliance. J. Manag. Inf. Syst. **37**, 129–161 (2020)
4. ISO, ISO 27000 framework (2018)
5. Stine, K.M., Quill, K., Witte, G.A.: Framework for improving critical infrastructure cybersecurity, February 2014
6. Barlette, Y., Fomin, V.V.: The adoption of information security management standards: a literature review, pp. 69–90. IGI Global (2010)
7. von Solms, R., von Solms, B.: From policies to culture. Comput. Secur. **23**, 275–279 (2004)
8. Siponen, M.T.: A conceptual foundation for organizational information security awareness. Inf. Manag. Comput. Secur. **8**, 31–41 (2000)
9. Dhillon, G., Backhouse, J.: Current directions in IS security research: towards socio-organizational perspectives. Inf. Syst. J. **11**, 127–153 (2001)
10. Kajzer, M., D'Arcy, J., Crowell, C.R., Striegel, A., Van Bruggen, D.: An exploratory investigation of message-person congruence in information security awareness campaigns. Comput. Secur. **43**, 64–76 (2014)
11. D'Arcy, J., Hovav, A., Galletta, D.: User awareness of security countermeasures and its impact on information systems misuse: a deterrence approach. Inf. Syst. Res. **20**, 79–98 (2009)
12. Abraham, S.: Information security behavior: factors and research directions. In: AMCIS - 2011 Proceedings - All Submissions (2011)
13. Lowry, P.B., Moody, G.D.: Proposing the control-reactance compliance model (CRCM) to explain opposing motivations to comply with organisational information security policies. Inf. Syst. J. **25**, 433–463 (2015)

14. Myyry, L., Siponen, M., Pahnila, S., Vartiainen, T., Vance, A.: What levels of moral reasoning and values explain adherence to information security rules? An empirical study. Eur. J. Inf. Syst. **18**, 126–139 (2009)
15. Bulgurcu, B., Cavusoglu, H., Benbasat, I.: Information security policy compliance: an empirical study of rationality-based beliefs and information security awareness. MIS Q. **34**, 523–548 (2010)
16. Wright, C., Ayton, P.: Focusing on what might happen and how it could feel: can the anticipation of regret change students' computing-related choices? Int. J. Hum.-Comput. Stud. **62**, 759–783 (2005)
17. Boss, S.R., Kirsch, L.J., Angermeier, I., Shingler, R.A., Boss, R.W.: If someone is watching, I'll do what I'm asked: mandatoriness, control, and information security. Eur. J. Inf. Syst. **18**, 151–164 (2009)
18. Pahnila, S., Siponen, M., Mahmood, A.: Employees' behavior towards IS security policy compliance (2007)
19. August, T., Tunca, T.I.: Network software security and user incentives. Manag. Sci. **52**, 1703–1720 (2006)
20. Goel, S., Williams, K.J., Huang, J., Warkentin, M.: Can financial incentives help with the struggle for security policy compliance? Inf. Manag. **58**, 103447 (2021)
21. West, R.: The psychology of security. Commun. ACM **51**, 34–40 (2008)
22. Mayer, P., Kunz, A., Volkamer, M.: Motivating users to consider recommendations on password management strategies. In: HAISA 2018 (2018)
23. Albayram, Y., Liu, J., Cangonj, S.: Comparing the effectiveness of text-based and video-based delivery in motivating users to adopt a password manager. In: European Symposium on Usable Security 2021, pp. 89–104. Association for Computing Machinery, New York (2021)
24. Bauer, S., Bernroider, E.W.N., Chudzikowski, K.: Prevention is better than cure! Designing information security awareness programs to overcome users' non-compliance with information security policies in banks. Comput. Secur. **68**, 145–159 (2017)
25. Thomson, M.E., von Solms, R.: Information security awareness: educating your users effectively. Inf. Manag. Comput. Secur. **6**, 167–173 (1998)
26. Das, S., Dabbish, L.A., Hong, J.I.: A typology of perceived triggers for end-user security and privacy behaviors (2019)
27. Khan, B., Alghathbar, K.S., Khan, M.K.: Information security awareness campaign: an alternate approach. In: Kim, T., Adeli, H., Robles, R.J., Balitanas, M. (eds.) ISA 2011. Communications in Computer and Information Science, vol. 200, pp. 1–10. Springer, Heidelberg (2011). https://doi.org/10.1007/978-3-642-23141-4_1
28. Das, S., Kim, T.H.-J., Dabbish, L.A., Hong, J.I.: The effect of social influence on security sensitivity. In: 10th Symposium On Usable Privacy and Security (SOUPS 2014), Menlo (2014)
29. Kävrestad, J., Skärgård, M., Nohlberg, M.: Users perception of using CBMT for information security training. In: Human Aspects of Information Security & Assurance (HAISA 2019) International Symposium on Human Aspects of Information Security & Assurance (HAISA 2019), Nicosia, Cyprus, 15–17 July 2019 (2019)
30. Kävrestad, J., Hagberg, A., Nohlberg, M., Rambusch, J., Roos, R., Furnell, S.: Evaluation of contextual and game-based training for phishing detection. Future Internet **14**, 104 (2022)
31. Kävrestad, J., Nohlberg, M.: ContextBased MicroTraining: a framework for information security training. In: Clarke, N., Furnell, S. (eds.) HAISA 2020. IFIP Advances in Information and Communication Technology, vol. 593, pp. 71–81. Springer, Cham (2020). https://doi.org/10.1007/978-3-030-57404-8_6
32. Ophoff, J., Dietz, F.: Using gamification to improve information security behavior: a password strength experiment. In: Drevin, L., Theocharidou, M. (eds.) WISE 2019. IFIP Advances in Information and Communication Technology, vol. 557, pp. 157–169. Springer, Cham (2019). https://doi.org/10.1007/978-3-030-23451-5_12

33. Baxter, R.J., Holderness, K., Wood, D.A.: Applying basic gamification techniques to IT compliance training: evidence from the lab and field. Rochester (2015)
34. Huang, D.-L., Patrick Rau, P.-L., Salvendy, G., Gao, F., Zhou, J.: Factors affecting perception of information security and their impacts on IT adoption and security practices. Int. J. Hum.-Comput. Stud. **69**, 870–883 (2011)
35. Johnston, A.C., Warkentin, M.: Fear appeals and information security behaviors: an empirical study. MIS Q. **34**, 549–566 (2010)
36. Lebek, B., Uffen, J., Neumann, M., Hohler, B., Breitner, M.H.: Information security awareness and behavior: a theory-based literature review. Manag. Res. Rev. **37**, 1049–1092 (2014)
37. Shropshire, J., Warkentin, M., Sharma, S.: Personality, attitudes, and intentions: predicting initial adoption of information security behavior. Comput. Secur. **49**, 177–191 (2015)
38. Drevin, L., Kruger, H., Bell, A.-M., Steyn, T.: A linguistic approach to information security awareness education in a healthcare environment. In: Bishop, M., Futcher, L., Miloslavskaya, N., Theocharidou, M. (eds.) Information Security Education for a Global Digital Society. FIP Advances in Information and Communication Technology, vol. 503, pp. 87–97. Springer, Cham (2017). https://doi.org/10.1007/978-3-319-58553-6_8
39. Kruger, H.A., Kearney, W.D.: A prototype for assessing information security awareness. Comput. Secur. **25**, 289–296 (2006)
40. Kruger, H., Drevin, L., Steyn, T.: A vocabulary test to assess information security awareness. Inf. Manag. Comput. Secur. **18**, 316–327 (2010)
41. Mayer, P., Schwartz, C., Volkamer, M.: On the systematic development and evaluation of password security awareness-raising materials. In: Proceedings of the 34th Annual Computer Security Applications Conference (2018)
42. Baskerville, R., Spagnoletti, P., Kim, J.: Incident-centered information security: managing a strategic balance between prevention and response. Inf. Manag. **51**, 138–151 (2014)
43. Renaud, K., Flowerday, S.: Contemplating human-centred security & privacy research: suggesting future directions. J. Inf. Secur. Appl. **34**, 76–81 (2017)
44. Witte, K.: Putting the fear back into fear appeals: the extended parallel process model. Commun. Monogr. **59**, 329–349 (1992)

Exploring CyBOK with Topic Modeling Techniques

Ana I. González-Tablas$^{(\boxtimes)}$ [ID] and Mohammed Rashed [ID]

Universidad Carlos III de Madrid, Leganés, Spain
{aigonzal,mrashed}@inf.uc3m.es

Abstract. Several frameworks that cover cyber security education and professional development have been introduced as a guidance for learners, educators and professionals to the different knowledge areas of the field. One of the most important frameworks is the Cyber Security Body of Knowledge (CyBOK). In this paper, we apply the BERTopic topic modeling technique to CyBOK. We aim, by using this technique, to identify the most relevant topics related to each CyBOK's knowledge area in an automated way. Our results indicate that it is possible to find a meaningful topic model describing CyBOK and, thus, suggests the possibility of applying related techniques to texts to identify their main themes.

Keywords: Natural language processing · NLP · Topic modeling · Cyber security framework · CyBOK · Cyber security body of knowledge

1 Introduction

As time passes, cyber security is more recognised as a field on its own. Hence, there is more focus on areas like creating specific standards, developing new educational programs and industrial certificates for cyber security among others. Yet, such recognition is just a step to fulfill the needs of the industry. As per Furnell et al. [11], the shortage in the number of qualified cyber security personnel has been alerted for several years now. One of the causes of such shortage is the ambiguity in the skills required for cyber security related job offers. Furnell [10] highlighted how such vacancies required security related certifications. However, in a single vacancy, recruiters may ask for certifications that cover distinct groups of skills and areas of knowledge.

This research was supported by the Ministerio de Ciencia, Innovación y Universidades (Grant No. PID2019-111429RB-C21), by the Region of Madrid grant CYNAMON-CM (P2018/TCS-4566), co-financed by European Structural Funds ESF and FEDER, and the Excellence Program EPUC3M17. The opinions, findings, conclusions, or recommendations expressed are those of the authors and do not necessarily reflect those of any of the funders.

© IFIP International Federation for Information Processing 2022
Published by Springer Nature Switzerland AG 2022
N. Clarke and S. Furnell (Eds.): HAISA 2022, IFIP AICT 658, pp. 49–65, 2022.
https://doi.org/10.1007/978-3-031-12172-2_5

To fill the gap between the knowledge required and the existing roles in cyber security in the job market, existing cyber security frameworks [1–3,7,23, 24] may be used as a reference. Even though the list of underlying topics in these frameworks is not definitive, they establish a basis that designers of both academic programmes and professional certificates can depend on for preparing their course materials. Yet, as discussed by Furnell and Collins in [12], it might be difficult to understand how the different frameworks cover the wide spectrum of topics addressed in the cyber security field or to identify what can be expected when some material is said to be 'about security'. Moreover, the analysis that can be undertaken to identify the specific topics needs to be done mainly by manual means nowadays [14].

Topic modeling techniques use Natural Language Processing (NLP) as a means to find hidden semantics in a collection of documents through clustering the themes as topics [17]. Within the NLP field, a topic is usually represented by a set of words. Hence, topic modeling helps identifying keywords that maybe used as a reference by educators as well as researchers and professionals to find out what the focus of any text is.

In this paper, we explore how topic modeling tecniques can help identify the most significant topics in cyber security documents. Particularly, as the main contribution of this work and a proof-of-concept of the previous idea, we apply the BERTopic algorithm to CyBOK [24]. On one hand, BERTopic [13] is a flexible and competitive topic modeling algorithm, that leverages modern pre-trained language models. On the other hand, CyBOK is already a clear reference in the field that counts with the CyBOK Mapping Framework[1]. This framework facilitates finding the CyBOK knowledge areas related to a document by making use of an extensive keyword list. By no way our method aims at replacing the method in the CyBOK Mapping Framework but paving the way to developing a complementary and automated method leveraging NLP techniques.

In summary, the main contributions of our work are:

– Exploring how topic modeling techniques can be used to identify the main topics in CyBOK; specifically through applying BERTopic [13].
– Paving the way to a complementary and automated method for determining the knowledge area of a text in addition to the CyBOK Mapping Framework.

The paper is organized as follows. In Sect. 2, we address related work. Next, in Sect. 3, we discuss the focus of this paper and explain the system design along with the experiments. Then, Sect. 4 addresses the results of the experiments. Afterwards, we extensively discuss the results in Sect. 5. Finally, we conclude our paper and address future work in Sect. 6.

2   Related Work

Because our work is related to several areas, we split this section into three parts covering the areas of *topic modeling, cyber security frameworks* and *text mining in cyber security.*

---

[1] https://www.cybok.org/resources/.

2.1   Topic Modeling

It is a class of unsupervised learning techniques that, given a collection of documents, analyses the latent topics that appear in the corpus and best identify each of the given documents; within this context, a topic is usually represented by a set of words carefully selected by leveraging statistics and word semantics. Some techniques return a weight that represents the relevance of each word in the topic. Good models have coherent and interpretable topics with a small number of overlapping words [8]. Topic modeling is mainly used to understand underlying themes in text collections within varied fields. However, it can be combined with another machine learning technique to make possible or enhance the results of other text mining tasks such as document classification.

Reference to topic modeling goes back to 1990 [9]. Deerwester et al. treated the unreliability emerging from term-document association data as a statistical problem. Such approach, in which they assumed that data had an underlying latent semantic structure, helped them to resolve term-matching retrieval deficiencies. To estimate the structure, which is hidden partially because of the random word choice with regards to retrieval, they used a statistical analysis known as Latent Semantic Indexing (LSI). In this analysis, which leverages singular-value decomposition, a large matrix is constructed and includes term-document association data for building 'semantic space'. The more the related the documents and terms, the closer they are to each other in the space. Afterwards, Hofmann introduced Probabilistic LSI (PLSI) [15], largely influenced by [9], which is considered to be the first genuine topic model [18].

Later, the Dirichlet Multinomial Mixture (DMM) and the Latent Dirichlet Allocation (LDA) [6] topic models were proposed to enhance the accuracy of LSI and PLSI [8]. Since then, many variants were introduced. These variants aim at improving the capabilities to model the evolution of topics and to process modern text formats, while others focus on dealing with noise. We refer interested readers to the in-depth analysis on topic modeling by Churchill and Singh in [8].

State-of-the-art models mix traditional topic models with NLP methods by leveraging prior knowledge on natural language. An NLP technique that stands out is word embeddings which represents words as real-value vectors; words that are semantically similar are close to each other in the vector space. This technique can be used also to represent phrases or documents in the same semantic space. State-of-the-art embeddings are even capable of word sense disambiguation and providing contextually-meaningful word embeddings, like BERT and GPT-2 [26]. Two recent topic modeling algorithms that incorporate contextual-word embeddings are Top2Vec[2] [5] and BERTopic[3] [13].

2.2   Cyber Security Frameworks

In the last decades several cyber security frameworks have been published by public and private organizations worldwide. One of the early frameworks

---

[2] https://github.com/ddangelov/Top2Vec.
[3] https://maartengr.github.io/BERTopic/index.html.

was 2017's *Cybersecurity Curricula-Curriculum Guidelines for Post-Secondary Degree Programs in Cybersecurity* [1] as an output of the Joint Task Force (JTF) formed collaboratively in 2015 by four major international computing societies. The publication aimed to support academic institutions with curricular guidance through a *"comprehensive view of the cybersecurity field, the specific demands of the base discipline, and the relationship between the curriculum and cyberse-curity workforce frameworks"*. Other frameworks include Skills Framework [7], Cyber security Body of Knowledge (CyBOK) [24], Common Body of Knowledge (CBK) [3], National Initiative for Cybersecurity Education (NICE) Cybersecurity Workforce Framework [23], among others. Frameworks' origins span industry and academic communities. Each framework has its own perspective of the break-down of cyber security topics as per Furnell [11] to which we refer readers to for more detailed discussion on the topic. Among those frameworks, we chose to explore CyBOK because of its availability and the extensiveness of its text.

2.3   Text Mining in Cyber Security

In their extensive literature review on text mining in cyber security, Ignaczak et al. [16] divided the type of content analyzed into 16 categories, with electronic documents being the top ranked one. The top 5 categories include social networks, online forums, web pages and security databases. Also, they divided the tasks into 5 different areas including text supervised-learning classification, text clustering, information extraction, topic modeling and finally sentiment analysis. With regards to topic modeling, they consider that it is beneficial for:

– Cyber Threat Intelligence (CTI) as it is capable of identifying the main topics from online communities, and
– Data Leak Prevention (DLP) because it is able to determine if a document's main topics are connected to confidential subjects.

   Sundarkumar et al. [25] used topic modeling for malware detection through leveraging the API call sequences' types, while Neuhaus et al. [22] used it on the vulnerability reports found in Common Vulnerability and Exposures (CVE) database to find the dominant vulnerabilities and the new vulnerability trends. We aim to extend the use of topic modeling to cyber security education by applying such technique to natural language based texts.

3   Materials and Methods

We reviewed the topic modeling literature and tools to find the algorithms that best suit our objective. We selected Top2Vec and BERTopic, as both use contextual-word embeddings and then apply dimensionality reduction and clustering techniques. After preliminary testing, we opted for BERTopic as we obtained better results with this algorithm. With the recommended configuration, BERTopic returned around 50 topics, most of them meaningful in our context, while Top2Vec only returned 2 or 3 topics.

3.1   BERTopic

BERTopic algorithm [13] considers three phases:

1. *Document embedding.* BERTopic uses a pre-trained BERT model by default although any other embedding model can be used as well.
2. *Document clusterization.* First, UMAP algorithm [20] is used to reduce the word embeddings' dimensionality. Then, HDBSCAN algorithm [19] is applied to cluster the reduced document embeddings in semantically similar document clusters.
3. *Topic extraction.* Each previously identified cluster is understood as a single topic. Topic representations are modeled from the reduced document embeddings in that cluster. To find the words that best represent each topic, TF-IDF is used within the cluster, referred to as c-TF-IDF by the author.

One limitation of BERTopic is that it only assigns one topic per document. However, we highlight that HDBSCAN is a soft clustering technique. Thus, although it assigns each document to a single topic, it also estimates the probability of a document being associated to all identified topics. Hence, the obtained probability matrix can be used to estimate the distribution of topics in a document.

3.2   Corpus Generation

Our corpus is composed of documents that contain the text paragraphs found in CyBOK v1.1.0. In order to build the corpus, we downloaded each of the 22 chapters of CyBOK v1.1.0 from its web page[4] in PDF format and extracted the text contained in each PDF file using text processing tools. Microsoft Word and Office 365 have been used to open PDF files and save them as UTF-8 text; the result is a text file without headers or footers.

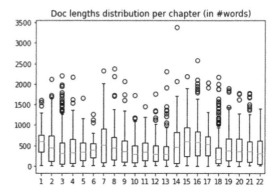

Fig. 1. Doc length distribution per chapter

---

[4] https://www.cybok.org/knowledgebase1_1/.

Table 1. Corpus. *KA* refers to Knowledge Area

Number	Title of KA	Version	Document count
1	Introduction to CyBOK	1.1.0	90
2	Risk Management & Governance	1.1.1	292
3	Law & Regulation	1.0.2	948
4	Human Factors	1.0.1	157
5	Privacy & Online Rights	1.0.2	161
6	Malware & Attack Technologies	1.0.1	124
7	Adversarial Behaviours	1.0.1	169
8	Security Operations & Incident Management	1.0.2	260
9	Forensics	1.0.1	237
10	Cryptography	1.0.1	350
11	Operating Systems & Virtualisation Security	1.0.1	164
12	Distributed Systems Security	1.0.1	223
13	Formal Methods for Security	1.0.0	243
14	Authentication, Authorisation & Accountability	1.0.2	253
15	Software Security	1.0.1	182
16	Web & Mobile Security	1.0.1	212
17	Secure Software Lifecycle	1.0.2	152
18	Applied Cryptography	1.0.0	341
19	Network Security	2.0.0	209
20	Hardware Security	1.0.1	170
21	Cyber Physical Systems	1.0.1	202
22	Physical Layer and Telecom Security	1.0.1	153

The text is then preprocessed so only the meaningful paragraphs remain. Preprocessing is mainly done manually using text processing tools combined with some Python scripts.

First, some sections are removed manually (cover, copyright, changelog, cross-reference of topics vs reference material, further reading, notes —except for the Law & Regulation chapter—, references, acronyms, glossary and index). Then, text retrieved from figures and tables is also manually identified and removed. Lines containing only a list of references[5] are removed as well.

After training the topic model with the cleaned corpus, we noticed that titles of sections *Introduction* and *Conclusions* introduced too much noise (a specific topic was identified for these documents). Hence, we removed them as well. For similar reasons, we removed the note numbers in the *Law & Regulation* chapter. The resulting corpus contains 5292 documents, each document being a paragraph

---

[5] E.g. line 3 in page 4 of *Cryptography* chapter is literally '[3, c8–c9, App B] [4, c1–c5]'.

from the original chapters. Table 1 specifies the contents of each chapter and the final number of documents in each of them, while Fig. 1 shows the document length distribution per chapter.

3.3   Topic Modeling with BERTopic

BERTopic is quite a flexible algorithm that embeds several algorithms. Each of these algorithms has a set of parameters, and selecting one or another value for them will influence the results. Next, we describe the values used for the main parameters. Any not mentioned parameter has been set with the default values.

We used the *all-MiniLM-L6-v2*[6] embedding model for english language included in the BERT Sentence Transformer framework. It is a general-purpose model trained on a large and diverse dataset which presents a faster performance than other models in the framework while still offering a good quality.

Regarding topic extraction, we set the number of words to extract per topic[7] to 10 and the minimum topic size[8] to 20. We used a customized vectorizer model so stop words are removed before finding topic representations with c-TF-IDF; we configured it to work with unigrams. Finally, we set the option that allows to calculate the probabilities of all topics per document to true.

All the experimentation has been done in Google Colaboratory, using the Python notebook provided by the author of BERTopic[9] as a template.

4   Results

4.1   Topic Model Analysis

We found 51 topics in the built corpus plus the additional topic identified as -1, which contains the documents that do not belong to any identified topic. The list of topics, the number of documents assigned to them and their 10-words representation are shown in Table 2.

We further leverage the BERTopic API as it offers a set of functions that helps us visualize the obtained topic model and better understand it. Figure 2a shows the intertopic distance map, in which all the 51 identified topics are represented by a circle considering their semantic distance in a 2D space. Figure 2b shows the dendrogram of the hierarchical clustering of the topics.

Besides, not only did we leverage BERTopic to train the model, but we also used it to compute the probabilities of finding each topic in all documents.

---

[6] https://huggingface.co/sentence-transformers/all-MiniLM-L6-v2.

[7] BERTopic recommends a value between 10 and 20, but as we obtained similar results with both values, we chose the smaller one to preserve the topic model quality.

[8] This parameter establishes the minimum number of documents that must be found in a cluster to be recognized as a topic. The lower this value is, the higher the number of topics are. Default value is 10 but it obtained 107 topics while a value of 20 obtained around 50 topics, which we found more compact and easier to analyze.

[9] https://github.com/MaartenGr/BERTopic/blob/master/notebooks/BERTopic.ipynb.

Table 2. List of topics found in CyBOK. First column contains the topic identification number. Second column contains the number of documents assigned to that topic. Third column contains the 10-word list representing the topic.

Topic	Count	Top 10 words
−1	1499	Security, systems, information, data, used, devices, attacks, cyber, control, network
0	268	Malware, criminals, malicious, victims, botnet, crime, online, criminal, money, operations
1	225	Forensic, evidence, data, file, digital, forensics, acquisition, artifacts, storage, files
2	168	Privacy, data, users, information, technologies, techniques, adversary, anonymous, tor, metadata
3	156	Distributed, coordination, consistency, resources, resource, services, service, cloud, consensus, systems
4	155	Properties, proofs, logic, verification, formal, model, methods, language, programs, trace
5	139	Encryption, key, adversary, scheme, block, cipher, algorithm, ae, rsa, pke
6	122	43, concepts, 41, methods, 42, 61, analysis, 31, 21, principles
7	114	Access, control, policies, policy, rights, user, users, capabilities, object, rbac
8	114	Cryptography, cryptographic, algorithms, libraries, developers, fhe, schemes, api, encryption, secure
9	113	Web, mobile, javascript, apps, browser, applications, html, application, security, browsers
10	111	Data, gdpr, personal, protection, law, processing, art, eu, subjects, european
11	111	State, international, law, jurisdiction, states, territory, persons, cyber, conflict, constitute
12	110	Key, keys, certificate, public, certificates, tls, protocol, parties, pki, exchange
13	109	Distance, signal, signals, receiver, attacker, wireless, spoofing, communication, prover, position
14	100	Detection, siem, alerts, anomaly, ids, alert, events, soim, sensors, network
15	99	Security, tasks, task, people, awareness, human, training, behaviour, organisation, employees
16	91	Risk, assessment, management, governance, impact, risks, cyber, outcomes, likely, likelihood
17	90	Copyright, patent, intellectual, trade, infringement, rights, trademark, patents, property, registered
18	85	Authentication, identity, user, authorisation, oauth, token, identities, saml, client, credentials
19	81	Network, networking, sdn, networks, lan, security, ntp, internet, layer, nfv
20	77	Mod, 01k1, k0, rm, keygenr, 01k0, k1, bits, true, pksk
21	75	Hardware, trusted, secure, attestation, abstraction, processor, software, design, level, trust
22	74	Cpss, control, cps, systems, attacks, physical, industrial, security, power, grid
23	62	Lifecycle, software, practices, development, secure, microsoft, organisation, security, processes, devops
24	57	Operating, systems, domains, security, ring, isolation, kernel, privileged, virtual, hypervisor
25	56	Passwords, password, unlock, authentication, users, biometric, people, device, patterns, features
26	56	Peers, p2p, routing, peer, attacks, overlay, sybil, discovery, eclipse, unstructured
27	50	Liability, tort, tortfeasor, victim, harm, tortious, duty, law, care, negligence
28	49	Signature, signatures, scheme, group, message, key, signing, ecdsa, signer, schnorr
29	47	Memory, address, page, kernel, code, pointer, program, operating, buffer, pages
30	46	Sidechannel, sidechannels, attacks, power, hardware, timing, information, leakage, channel, attacker
31	39	Hash, function, functions, sponge, output, length, construction, mac, oracle, sha3
32	38	Vulnerabilities, software, implementation, objective, categories, coding, vulnerability, programming, prevention, topic
33	38	Program, analysis, static, values, fuzzing, tools, vulnerabilities, execution, technique, taint
34	36	Law, legal, legislation, states, civil, laws, authority, secondary, study, legislative
35	35	Sql, output, injection, structured, input, query, database, statements, generation, command
36	34	Content, origins, qa, shell, cap, notes, pk, experience, authors, world
37	33	Verifier, prover, zeroknowledge, protocol, run, proof, public, apparently, noninteractive, simulator
38	33	Crimes, act, computer, crime, uk, criminal, 1990, 201340, directive, misuse
39	32	Incident, incidents, response, management, organisation, plan, procedures, plans, followup, handle
40	32	Ip, ddos, bgp, traffic, nat, syn, attacks, dos, address, icmp
41	29	Disclosure, vulnerability, disclosures, disclosing, vendor, responsible, finders, practitioners, upstream, benefits
42	25	Warranty, contract, contractual, goods, warranties, exclusions, contracts, liability, quality, vendor
43	25	Syslog, logs, log, format, events, generating, logging, 26, text, applications
44	23	Cybok, knowledge, area, kas, management, security, incident, cyber, human, areas
45	23	Interception, providers, communications, lawful, service, state, states, legal, intercepting, public
46	22	Network, netflow, packet, pcap, packets, monitoring, traffic, ip, interface, capture
47	22	Attack, mitigation, represents, attacker, considered, attacks, proactive, control, actuators, controller
48	22	Design, bullet, security, open, requirements, 211, obscurity, controls, usable, section
49	21	Entropy, random, puf, pufs, numbers, circuits, prng, generator, number, noise
50	21	Logging, log, accountability, logs, audit, policies, collected, evidence, entries, tamper

Recall that BERTopic uses HDBSCAN to compute the clusters (i.e. our topics). Although each document is assigned to a single topic, HDBSCAN can also estimate the probability of a document belonging to each cluster (i.e. the probability of finding a topic in a document). E.g, if we had a certain document with probability values of 0.7 and 0.6 for topics 5 and 20, and very low probability values for the rest of the topics, we could understand that topics 5 and 20 are found in the document, but not the rest of them.

Figure 2c shows the distribution of the probabilities per topic for all the documents in the corpus without outliers and Fig. 2d shows them with outliers. The connection between the topics and the chapter in which they show high probability is generally comprehensible from a cyber security professional's point of view. We elaborate on this part more in the next section.

To analyze how specific the identified topics are with respect to the documents in the corpus, we count how many topics are found with a probability greater than a certain threshold for each document. Figure 2e presents the results considering a probability $p > 0.05$. Finally, to better grasp the number of documents that are related to each topic, we count how many of them present a probability greater than a different larger threshold. Figure 2f presents the results considering a probability $p > 0.5$.

4.2 Topic Model vs CyBOK Chapters

After analysing the topic model, we wanted to get a deeper insight on how the topics were represented in each chapter. Therefore, we depicted the probabilities of finding a topic in a document per chapter. Results are presented in Figs. 3, 4 and 5; we split the chapters' probabilities into 3 figures for better readability.

5 Discussion

5.1 Topic Model Analysis

Reading through the terms representing each topic (Table 2), we found that most extracted topics seem coherent and make sense in the context of CyBOK. Topics 6 and 20 together with topic 36 are the exception; they are represented with text left from mathematical equations (topic 6), numbers (possibly originating from the section numbering) and terms that appear in a significant number of section titles or general terms (topics 20 and 36). We believe that a deeper preprocessing of the texts used to build the corpus would generate better results.

Focusing on the topic model structure (Figs. 2a and 2b), we find that some of the groupings (clades) make more sense than others from the point of view of a cybersecurity-knowledgeable person. Some groupings appear to be semantically correct, like {18, 25, 5, 8, 20, 12, 28} and {11, 34, 17, 42}. Others, like {9, 49, 29, 31, 35} and {30, 45, 37, 47, 13, 14}, appear to mix topics that are not understood as semantically close from a cyber security perspective (e.g. topic 35: {sql, output, injection, structured, input, query,

(a) Intertopic distance map

(b) Hierarchical clustering

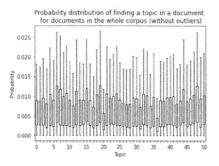

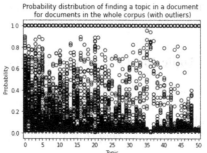

(c) Probability distribution of finding a topic in a document for the whole corpus (without outliers)

(d) Probability distribution of finding a topic in a document for the whole corpus (with outliers)

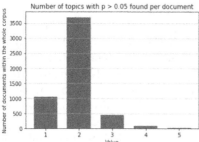

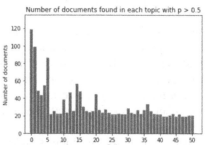

(e) Histogram of the number of topics with $p > 0.05$ found per document

(f) Number of documents with a probability p of finding a topic in them $p > 0.5$

Fig. 2. Topic model structure and topic probabilities

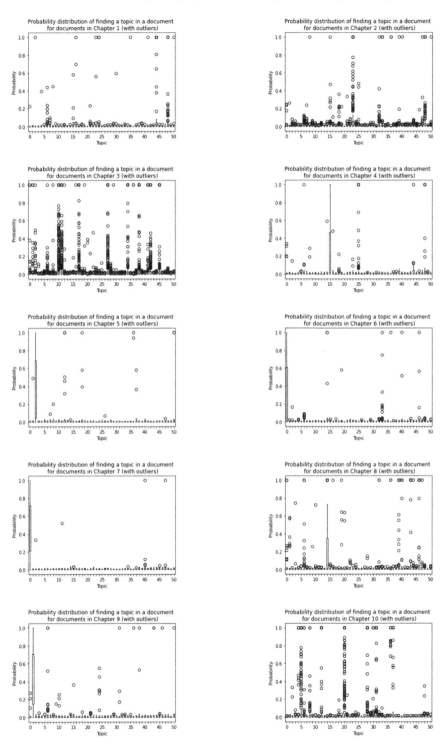

Fig. 3. Probability distribution of finding a topic in a document per chapter (I)

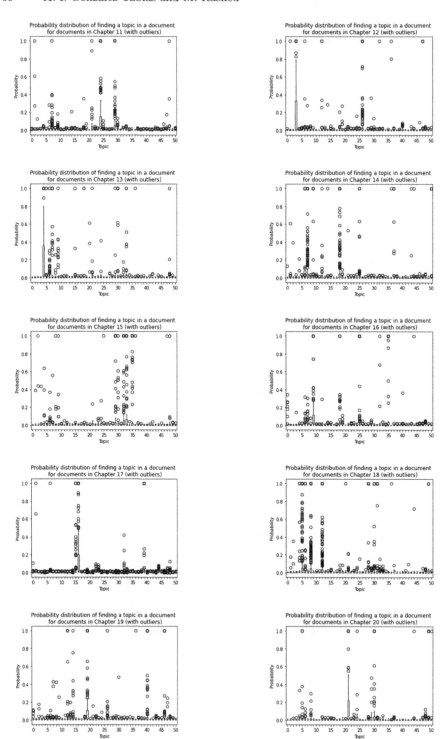

Fig. 4. Probability distribution of finding a topic in a document per chapter (II)

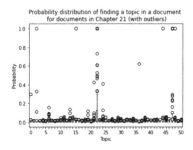 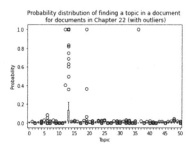

Fig. 5. Probability distribution of finding a topic in a document per chapter (III)

database, statements, generation, command} and topic 31: {hash, function, functions, sponge, output, length, construction, mac, oracle, sha3}). However, we point out the fact that the clustering has been computed according to the semantic representation of the topics, which has been derived with the support of a general-purpose pre-trained language model. Using a model specifically trained on a large and varied cyber security corpus would for sure output a different hierarchical clustering, probably more coherent from a cyber security point of view.

Regarding the distribution of the probabilities without outliers among the whole corpus (Fig. 2c), we observe that most probabilities are very low (with a mean value of around 0.006), presenting a very similar distribution for all chapters. With regards to the distribution of the outliers as shown in Fig. 2d, we notice that there is a significant number of them and that their values are present in the full range for the majority of the topics. Outliers can be viewed as documents sufficiently related to that topic.

In Fig. 2e, we find that most documents have one or two topics that we might consider as related (notice that we have selected $p > 0.05$, which is a very low value but that will include only probabilities considered as outliers). Hence, we infer that the identified topics are very specific compared to the documents in the corpus, being this result coherent with the documents' lengths. From Fig. 2f, we can observe that only a small fraction of the whole corpus is related to a certain topic with a (significant) probability $p > 0.5$. As expected, the topics more prevalent in the corpus present higher number of documents, although in general, the number is quite homogeneous (around 20 documents).

5.2   Topic Model vs CyBOK Chapters

Analysing results shown in Figs. 3, 4 and 5, we find several cases:

a) Chapters that present a single predominant topic, like Chapters 5, 7 or 17.
b) Chapters that seem to have several frequent topics among their documents, like Chapters 3, 10, 15 and 18.
c) The very special case of Chapter 1.

The fact that chapters are related to one or more topics depends in part on how many topics have been identified related to the subject treated in a given chapter. Some subjects are very specific and the terminology is used consistently throughout all the chapter (e.g. Chapter 6 *Malware Attack & Defences* and Chapter 7 *Adversarial Behaviours* are closely related to topic 0: {malware, criminals, malicious, victims, botnet, crime, online, criminal, money, operations}). On the other hand, some subjects have been the source of several topics and the probabilities of their documents reflect this situation (like Chapter 3 *Law & Regulation* and Chapter 10 *Cryptography*, that relate respectively to several topics closely connected to each of the subjects).

Chapter 1 is a very special case as it is the introduction to the whole Cyber Security Body of Knowledge, which makes it reasonable that it is not closely related to any specific topic.

In general, the analysis of the topics related to each chapter seems reasonable and the only unexpected result is that the model is not capable of identifying topic 16: {risk, assessment, management, governance, impact, risks, cyber, outcomes, likely, likelihood} as related to documents in Chapter 2 *Risk Mangement & Governance*.

5.3   Possible Expansions

We understand our work as a first step in a research line that would benefit users of cyber security frameworks. From our point of view, we identify two possible expansions whose results may interest to the cyber security community and that we believe feasible to achieve in the short-term.

In first place, although we have applied a topic modeling technique to CyBOK, we believe that these techniques could be also applied, at the same time, to several frameworks like the ones discussed in Sect. 2.2. Such a model would yield a list of topics covered by all the frameworks and an estimation of its distribution along the frameworks. Hence, results could be used to compare the different topics covered by each framework in an automated way and would serve as support to go further in the line of some recent works such as [11,14] and [12]. Such research would present additional challenges, as it is uncertain which topic modeling algorithms might provide good results when applied to several frameworks containing different text formats. To illustrate the differences, consider that CyBOK [24] is a book with proper paragraphs, while NICE [23] is mainly a list of really short descriptions of Knowledge, Skills and Abilities.

In second place, our results pave the way to develop a text classification model for cyber security materials with respect to CyBOK. Text classification is a supervised machine learning technique that yields a model that, once trained using a ground-truth labeled corpus, assigns labels to new documents. If there is no ground-truth labeled corpus (or it is not large enough), topic modeling techniques can be used to generate a labeled corpus, that can be used in turn as input in the training phase. Such a model would be really helpful in cases like the one described in [21], where the coverage of two cyber security programs respect to CyBOK knowledge areas is analysed using CyBOK's knowledge trees and mapping framework. Notice that we believe that text classification models should be seen as a supporting tool and not as a substitution of current approaches.

5.4 Limitations

There are several limitations to our work. First, we believe that our technique in cleaning the text from noise is not optimal, which results in the appearance of noisy topics and keywords that do not seem relevant (e.g. topic **6** included among its top 10 words `43, 41, 42, 61, 31, 21`). Also, the language model that we applied in the experiments causes some redundancy in the words that appear in the topics e.g. topic `47` has among its top 10 words: `attacker, attacks, attack`. Similarly, our topic model is not optimum as per [8] given that some topics have overlapping words, e.g. topics `5, 12, 28` include the word `key`. Finally, the language model is not a cyber security related one but rather a general-purpose pre-trained one.

6   Conclusion

In this paper, we applied topic modeling techniques using BERTopic's [13] Python library on CyBOK, one of the highly recognized cyber security frameworks. Our objective was to evaluate the possibility of identifying the most common topics for the CyBOK's knowledge areas in an automated way. Generally, the algorithm yielded acceptable results in which the most probable topics for each chapter made sense to a cybersecurity-knowledgeable person in terms of the words that define each topic. Our results pave the way to several interesting extensions, as discussed in Sect. 5.3.

6.1 Future Work

We plan to optimize the model by further cleaning the input texts and to formally evaluate the model quality. Additionally, we aim to carry out similar experiments on other frameworks (see Sects. 1 and 2.2) and to compare the results to the ones we obtained in this work. Besides, we would like to evaluate how different topic modeling algorithms perform on individual frameworks. For instance, although we have discarded Top2Vec for this exploratory work, we believe better results can be achieved after a thorough research on possible configurations.

In the medium term, we would like to address the extensions discussed in Sect. 5.3. Finally, we believe that building an enhanced cyber security language model that extends to all cyber security fields and not just vulnerabilities, as is the case of CyBERT [4], would be a great contribution to the scientific community.

References

1. Curriculum Guidelines for Post-Secondary Degree Programs in Cybersecurity. https://www.acm.org/binaries/content/assets/education/curricula-recommendations/csec2017.pdf. Accessed 03 Apr 2022
2. ISO/IEC 27002:2013 Information technology—Security techniques—Code of practice for information security controls. https://www.iso.org/standard/54533.html. Accessed 03 Apr 2022
3. The (ISC)² CBK. https://www.isc2.org/Certifications/CBK. Accessed 03 Apr 2022
4. Ameri, K., Hempel, M., Sharif, H., Lopez, J., Jr., Perumalla, K.: CyBERT: cybersecurity claim classification by fine-tuning the BERT language model. J. Cybersecur. Priv. **1**(4), 615–637 (2021)
5. Angelov, D.: Top2Vec: distributed representations of topics (2020)
6. Blei, D.M., Ng, A.Y., Jordan, M.I.: Latent Dirichlet allocation. J. Mach. Learn. Res. **3**(Jan), 993–1022 (2003)
7. Chartered Institute of Information Security: CIISec Skills Framework Version 2.4. https://www.ciisec.org/CIISEC/Resources/Capability_Methodology/Skills_Framework/CIISEC/Resources/Skills_Framework.aspx. Accessed 03 Apr 2022
8. Churchill, R., Singh, L.: The evolution of topic modeling. ACM Comput. Surv. (CSUR) (2022). https://doi.org/10.1145/3507900
9. Deerwester, S., Dumais, S.T., Furnas, G.W., Landauer, T.K., Harshman, R.: Indexing by latent semantic analysis. J. Am. Soc. Inf. Sci. **41**(6), 391–407 (1990)
10. Furnell, S.: The cybersecurity workforce and skills. Comput. Secur. **100**, 102080 (2021)
11. Furnell, S., Bishop, M.: Addressing cyber security skills: the spectrum, not the silo. Comput. Fraud Secur. **2020**(2), 6–11 (2020)
12. Furnell, S., Collins, E.: Cyber security: what are we talking about? Comput. Fraud Secur. **2021**(7), 6–11 (2021)
13. Grootendorst, M.: BERTopic: leveraging BERT and c-TF-IDF to create easily interpretable topics (2020). https://doi.org/10.5281/zenodo.4381785
14. Hallett, J., Larson, R., Rashid, A.: Mirror, mirror, on the wall: What are we teaching them all? Characterising the focus of cybersecurity curricular frameworks. In: 2018 USENIX Workshop on Advances in Security Education (ASE 2018) (2018)
15. Hofmann, T.: Unsupervised learning by probabilistic latent semantic analysis. Mach. Learn. **42**(1), 177–196 (2001)
16. Ignaczak, L., Goldschmidt, G., Costa, C.A.D., Righi, R.D.R.: Text mining in cybersecurity: a systematic literature review. ACM Comput. Surv. (CSUR) **54**(7), 1–36 (2021)
17. Kherwa, P., Bansal, P.: Topic modeling: a comprehensive review. EAI Endor. Trans. Scalable Inf. Syst. **7**(24), e2 (2020). https://doi.org/10.4108/eai.13-7-2018.159623
18. Liu, L., Tang, L., Dong, W., Yao, S., Zhou, W.: An overview of topic modeling and its current applications in bioinformatics. Springerplus **5**(1), 1–22 (2016). https://doi.org/10.1186/s40064-016-3252-8
19. McInnes, L., Healy, J.: Accelerated hierarchical density based clustering. In: 2017 IEEE International Conference on Data Mining Workshops (ICDMW), pp. 33–42. IEEE (2017)
20. McInnes, L., Healy, J., Melville, J.: UMAP: uniform manifold approximation and projection for dimension reduction. arXiv preprint arXiv:1802.03426 (2018)

21. Nautiyal, L., et al.: The United Kingdom's cyber security degree certification program: a cyber security body of knowledge case study. IEEE Secur. Priv. **20**(1), 87–95 (2022)
22. Neuhaus, S., Zimmermann, T.: Security trend analysis with CVE topic models. In: 2010 IEEE 21st International Symposium on Software Reliability Engineering, pp. 111–120. IEEE (2010)
23. Newhouse, W., Keith, S., Scribner, B., Witte, G.: National initiative for cybersecurity education (NICE) cybersecurity workforce framework. https://nvlpubs.nist.gov/nistpubs/specialpublications/nist.sp.800-181.pdf. Accessed 03 Apr 2022
24. Rashid, A., Chivers, H., Lupu, E., Martin, A., Schneder, S.: The cyber security body of knowledge version 1.1.0 (2021)
25. Sundarkumar, G.G., Ravi, V., Nwogu, I., Govindaraju, V.: Malware detection via API calls, topic models and machine learning. In: 2015 IEEE International Conference on Automation Science and Engineering (CASE), pp. 1212–1217. IEEE (2015)
26. Tripathy, J.K., Sethuraman, S.C., Cruz, M.V., Namburu, A., Mangalraj, P., Vijayakumar, V.: Comprehensive analysis of embeddings and pre-training in NLP. Comput. Sci. Rev. **42**, 100433 (2021)

COLTRANE – Towards a Methodology and Platform Supported Educational Basis for Cybersecurity Education

Jerry Andriessen[1], Steven Furnell[2], Gregor Langner[3],
Carmela Luciano[4,6], Gerald Quirchmayr[5], Vittorio Scarano[4(✉)],
and Teemu Johannes Tokola[6]

[1] Wise & Munro Learning Research, The Hague, The Netherlands
`jerry@wisemunro.eu`
[2] School of Computer Science, University of Nottingham, Nottingham, UK
`Steven.Furnell@nottingham.ac.uk`
[3] AIT Austrian Institute of Technology GmbH, Vienna, Austria
`gregor.langner@ait.ac.at`
[4] Dipartimento di Informatica, Università di Salerno, Fisciano, Salerno, Italy
`{cluciano,vitsca}@unisa.it`
[5] Fakultät für Informatik, Universität Wien, Vienna, Austria
`Gerald.Quirchmayr@univie.ac.at`
[6] Faculty of Information Technology and Electrical Engineering,
University of Oulu, Oulu, Finland
`teemu.tokola@oulu.fi`
`http://www.wisemunro.eu/`, `https://www.nottingham.ac.uk/`,
`https://www.ait.ac.at/`, `https://www.unisa.it/`,
`https://www.univie.ac.at/`, `https://www.oulu.fi/`

Abstract. Based on an analysis of current cybersecurity education in Europe and findings from a series of workshops conducted with selected groups of educators and learners in several European HEIs, this paper describes a methodology that is aimed at integrating the teaching of applied skills with the prevailing teaching, which is more focused on theoretical knowledge. The resulting COLTRANE Methodology aims at achieving this goal through providing a scenario-based and problem-oriented learning environment. A first case study is described and analyzed.

Keywords: Cybersecurity education · Learning · Awareness · Collaboration

1 Introduction

The field of cybersecurity education is highly dynamic considering the permanent change of knowledge and skills required to defend ICT systems. It is therefore

This project has been funded with support from the European Commission.

Published by Springer Nature Switzerland AG 2022
N. Clarke and S. Furnell (Eds.): HAISA 2022, IFIP AICT 658, pp. 66–76, 2022.
https://doi.org/10.1007/978-3-031-12172-2_6

very difficult for educators to keep their teaching materials current. At the same time the continuously growing market demand for cybersecurity experts cannot be met. Unmet student expectations are adding to the problem. The need to raise cybersecurity awareness not only in the field of computer science, but even more so in its application areas is highlighted by the introduction of significant European legislation, namely the GDPR and the NIS Directive. With privacy protection and the security of critical infrastructures having been the focus (also of teaching awareness and compliance [4]), the next logical step is to look at the protection of vital supply chains. Against this ever more demanding background, cybersecurity educators can no longer afford to teach alone (cf. [5,6]). That is why communities of educators are now starting to build around the sharing of teaching materials. As helpful as these activities are, a more structured approach is needed to effectively and efficiently tackle the wide range of problems the field of cybersecurity education is encountering. Giving community building efforts a realistic chance to deliver the educator networks needed, a common ground for the teaching of the subject must be established. Targeting these gaps, the COLTRANE project aims at providing a framework and toolbox for supporting educators, learners, and institutions through a teaching methodology that allows a practice-oriented and problem-driven approach to teaching, complemented with scenario-based teaching repositories and a technological platform for simulating realistic cases. This approach can integrate the teaching of soft skills which are so essential for successfully contributing to the workplace, especially raising, and gaining awareness, collaboration, teamwork, and communication.

The COLTRANE Project. COLTRANE is an Erasmus+ project [2] that aims to modernize and streamline cybersecurity education across Europe by introducing innovative education concepts in the context of collaborative awareness education. As most of the knowledge areas relating to cybersecurity are specific to certain areas and disciplines, cybersecurity awareness education creates an overarching theme to have the widest possible relevance, creating tangible impact on security, and creating a promise of not just academic discussion but real consequences in the security of European citizens.

Awareness of the critical nature of cybersecurity issues is the key ingredient for students to focus on, and lack of awareness is a source of tremendous issues. As such, success in improving awareness can deliver significant positive impacts. Few other fields require such a holistic and multidisciplinary view on things as cybersecurity does. In order to understand cybersecurity (and its problems), students have to be able to understand various related technological, legal, economic, social and psychological aspects that can influence it.

Traditional forms of education mainly focus on knowledge transmission, but in highly dynamic areas such as cybersecurity this does not lead to sufficient learning outcomes. We therefore need more innovative forms of education that aim at the development of joint action: being able to act in a variety of situations and knowing how to do this together.

The main innovations of COLTRANE are: (1) Establishing a holistic vision on cybersecurity, by not only focusing on resolving cyberthreats, but on the activities and implications in authentic organisational contexts; (2) Extending the view of awareness of cybersecurity, which expands the notion of 'being secure' to that of reflection and sharing of issues relevant to cybersecurity; (3) Promoting a view on cybersecurity as collaborative, implying that all stakeholders have a role in it, and that these roles need to be coordinated, during cyberthreats, but also after such events; (4) Enabling reflection on the relevance and coherence of cybersecurity education across domains, organisational and national borders.

2   COLTRANE Methodology

The Pressing Need for a Solution. Building a sustainable online community of cybersecurity educators obviously is a way to tackle the problem. This approach can however only be successful if it creates clearly identifiable benefits for educators and does in turn enable them to better meet student expectations and employer requirements. Starting with a collection of educator needs and expectations through questionnaires and online workshops, the current shortcomings and core requirements were identified. In parallel students were asked to provide their assessment of the current situation and express their expectations. While there were slight deviations in the perception of the importance of some issues, the identified issues as such showed a clear agreement between educators and learners on what the most pressing needs are. Meeting these needs is considered as being the central success factor for the COLTRANE project. In this section of the paper only a summary is presented. The actual questionnaire and workshop data is part of the project deliverables, which are available on the project website. Not surprising, the coverage of curricula and the adherence to established guides, such as CyBoK, or the ACM/IEEE/IFIP - driven recommendations and models, were a pointed out as a major concern, followed by the need to teach not only the knowledge, but also the skills necessary for applying it to problem solving in practice, and by the need to equip students with the associated soft skills, especially teamwork, collaboration, and communication (cf. [3]). The interdisciplinarity of cybersecurity was another prominently figuring aspect. These and other requirements indicate that the practical relevance of the content and how it is taught need to be changed to increase the job readiness of graduates and to better meet student expectations. It is obvious that given the resource limitations prevailing in most European HEIs, the efforts needed to deliver on these massive demands need to be shared. The modularity and reusability of learning materials are a prerequisite in this context. Ideally, the provided materials are customizable and can serve as templates for further development. A very promising way of enabling this sharing is through setting up online communities of educators pursuing the same goals. However, setting up the necessary environment is a major challenge, which has significant technical, organisational, and didactic components.

Background. The COLTRANE methodology, which is at the core of the project, follows a problem-oriented, scenario-based approach to teaching. It is also aimed at enabling a collaboration- and practice-oriented, case-based teaching style. The methodology rests on established and current scientific wisdom in cybersecurity education and in the learning sciences.

The domain aspect of the methodology has been inspired by the output of the SecTech project [4], in which seven higher education institutes collaborated on establishing a pan-European cybersecurity awareness curriculum, and the creation of related teaching materials. The strength of this curriculum is that it does not have a mere technical view, but a clear socio-technical approach, in which the role of human factors, organisational and legal context, as well as societal context are essential. In addition, the COLTRANE project elaborated the conceptual and practical approach to cybersecurity awareness as much as possible as situated in institutional contexts, which was studied in the CS-AWARE project [7]. There, we applied a holistic and collaborative approach to cybersecurity awareness, in which we recognise the responsibilities and involvement of all employees on a daily basis, as necessary for cybersecurity at the institutional level. In essence, this holistic view of cybersecurity necessitates an organisational context to be aware about the roles and responsibilities of all participants, in other words, implementing various forms of collaboration is essential [8].

This collaboration is in fact collaborative learning, as the cybersecurity landscape is changing all the time. The holistic view on an organisation asks for more collaboration, not only within the organisation, but also between organisations, that, for example are part of a supply chain of goods, or a critical sector such as electricity. Therefore, the collaborative learning of cybersecurity awareness in practice requires a collaborative learning approach for cybersecurity education. As a didactic approach we decided to look at approaches for problem-based or case-based learning [9]. For cybersecurity education, this approach is innovative.

Principles and Scenarios. The didactic approach of COLTRANE elaborates on this idea of cybersecurity awareness, by formulating a set of principles that can be used in constructing scenarios for lessons and exercises. We aim at developing and testing a number if innovative scenarios for cybersecurity awareness teaching. Our design approach is meant to be transparent and usable for teachers, for designing their own modules exploiting our principles. The principles have been designed by our project team, using theory, user needs, and reflecting on our own roles as teachers. Three groups of principles were constructed: (1) Principles for raising understanding about the need for cybersecurity awareness: e.g. linking to a knowledge domain, integration of knowledge and action in a realistic context, allow students time for reflection and discussion, support student agency; (2) Principles for designing collaboration in cybersecurity awareness education: e.g. make collaboration relevant and meaningful by explanation and design, allow collaboration to evolve over time, stress the importance of building trust and respect by building on the contributions of others; (3) Principles for course design and support for students: e.g. develop standards for awareness, try (within reason) to monitor collaboration, think about different degrees of (adaptive) support, consider including boundary objects for a collaborative assignment.

These principles are implemented in design scenarios, which can be understood as frameworks with a number of slots of course/lesson essential characteristics, whereby different principles can be applied to each of the slots. The first slot is called 'learning goals', an obvious choice, where we focus on what students are supposed to learn, for example what students have to master in terms of the domain knowledge. Even for a simple assignment, the topic can be related to a knowledge area, as well a task or role within an organisational context, such as cybersecurity risk management, or risk mitigation. Learning goals can also relate to collaborative learning or reflection. Other slots (there are ten slots) in the scenario are, for example, the contribution of the task to student awareness, or awareness of cybersecurity, the team and roles in the assignment, the prerequisite knowledge and skills, and the manner of evaluation of student activity and learning outcomes.

The final slot of a scenario involves reflection about the role of technology in the scenario. In COLTRANE, we make extensive use of two types of technology: a tool for collaborative sharing, analysing and mapping of data and data-sets, and a cyber range, allowing simulation of a cyber-incident in a realistic organisational setting.

Principles, scenarios and lesson examples will be part of a platform that can be used by teachers of cybersecurity. We make our approach usable for practice by presenting learning blocks and scenario building guidance.

Implementation. Modular design, flexible delivery, and an openness for contributions and adaptations to local circumstances are the main drivers for shaping the process models underlying the teaching material life cycle and the repository structure to be implemented.

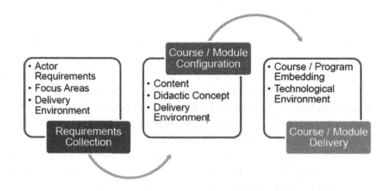

Fig. 1. Process architecture.

COLTRANE principles and scenario guidelines result in COLTRANE learning blocks that are part of a course and curriculum, that is set within cybersecurity domain content and cybersecurity organisational contexts. Implementation should be clear about the stakeholders involved, and what their interests are.

Furthermore, a course design should consider where in the teaching and delivery cycle a learning block is positioned: which requirements are set out by the organising department for participants, content and content delivery, which contents and content specifics are part of the configuration of a module of which the learning block is a part, and how will a learning block be structurally embedded within the learning program and the available technology.

The suggested process architecture (Fig. 1) needs to cover the whole teaching cycle, which in our approach will be structured in three major phases: (1) Requirements Collection; (2) Course/Module Configuration; (3) Course/Module Delivery.

These phases form a logical sequence with possible feedback loops from Course/Module Configuration and Course/Module Delivery to Requirements Collection and from and Course/Module Delivery to Course/Module Configuration. As this feedback can either concern the developed content or the process phase, we follow the proven double loop learning approach introduced by Argyris. This feedback mechanism is the central basis for maintain and adapting process and content materials, which is essential in a field that is changing as fat as cybersecurity.

Given the current situation in HEIs in Europe, temporary virtual ad-hoc communities of educators and learners working in small goal-oriented teams are expected to be the major user groups. The envisaged support of team teaching across disciplines, across cultures, across institutions, across national borders is a very demanding goal, but early experiments at the Universities of Salerno and Vienna are showing the feasibility and the benefits. In a first intensive course unit on cybersecurity for cloud computing, which was delivered in December 2021 in a mixed presence and online version, student feedback has confirmed the value of a tool-supported problem-oriented approach that incorporates real-world problems in the form of cases or scenarios. This course and the outcomes are described in more detail in the next section.

3 A Pilot Study

In COLTRANE we are going to apply and shape our methodology in several courses. In all the piloting, we will evaluate thoroughly the impact of methodology and technology on a particular course along a number of aspects: student achievement, impact on attitude towards cybersecurity, quality of the outcomes and of the collaboration.

The first of these case studies was carried out at the University of Salerno, in a class of the first year of Master degree in Computer Science, with specialization in Cloud Computing. The purpose of this study was to assess the impact of the COLTRANE methodology in a hybrid classroom setting (part of the students were in class and part were working from home, although great part of the work was conducted by remote), evaluating students' achievement, motivation and attitudes.

The primary collaboration platform used in this case was an on-line *Social Platform for Open Data*, named SPOD platform [1], where students can build, share, analyze and discuss data and related visualizations they build on it. SPOD is part of the project ROUTE-TO-PA (http://www.routetopa.eu), a three-years HORIZON 2020 European Funded project [9].

The main goal of the tool is to promote team-based, goal-oriented problem solving scenarios for students, which they can then use as vehicle for developing the skills necessary to apply their knowledge in practical settings. SPOD allows the co-creation of datasets and allows to easily build visualizations from Open Data (OD) using a user friendly wizard. Actually, SPOD supports several charts, geographical maps and other visualizations. SPOD is meant to enable collaboration among users to ensure creation of value for open data and provides the following tools that allow open discussion on data and *datalets* (i.e. real-time visualization of datasets) by an Open Agorá, but it also offers a group-based Data Co-Creation room, where each group can author a dataset, building datalets and discussing on the co-creation activities.

Each group of students created a private SPOD Data Co-creation room. They could then, meet and co-create the dataset either by importing existing files or by creating them from scratch, reusing other open data available. They were directed, first, to study the suggested sources or look for other sources, then structure the data. Finally, group discussion and collaboration led to shared visualizations of the dataset created.

Methodology. The participants in this study were 37 students (35 males (94.6%) and 2 females (5.4%) all for the Computer Science Master (curriculum Cloud Computing) all attending the "Cloud Computing" course of Department of Computer Science at the University of Salerno (Italy). The course was held in Fall 2021 and, being still valid the restrictions due to the COVID-19 pandemic, with 27 persons in presence and around 10 from remote (using Microsoft Teams). The experiment took place in one week in November 2021. In the first meeting, 2 h, we explained the purposes of the group work, the tools and gave some initial references to open datasets that were available. Each group was given one out of the three following tasks: (1) "Cybersecurity threats and their impact on industry/sectors", (2) "Data breach and their relevance in specific sectors", (3) "Data breach and their cost", with the instructions to collect data, possibly looking for other sources. In particular, each was asked to produce 3 datalets, on the theme assigned to each group, by comparing the data along different axes, (e.g., by time (semester, year, period), by geography (country, region, ..), by type (type of industry/sector, threats, ...), by type/diffusion of Internet access, etc.). Each datalet had to present a short description of 3–5 lines, to motivate the result of the assigned task. It was also asked to fill a Notes file (within the Co-creation room) to fully document the data sources used.

In the last day of the week, each group held a very short presentation (5 min) of the datalets they created and also a web-based survey was proposed to the students to gather their feedback, with several open ended questions. The questions were: (1) Having completed the group task, what are your considerations about the importance of cybersecurity for companies and society?; (2) How has the experience of this group work changed your perception of cybersecurity? (3)

What are the two most positive aspects of this experience? (4)What are the two most difficult/problematic aspects of this experience? (5) How much do you feel you have gained from this activity that you wouldn't have obtained by simply reading and studying the supplied material? (6) Other comments, suggestions, opinions?

Qualitative Data Analysis. Question 1 responses were overwhelming. All the students were absolutely convinced about the importance of cybersecurity, especially recognizing the costs associated and the risks that can be incurred if securities measures are not taken, risks that involve both companies and society at large.

For Questions 2 and 3, that contained richer and more different answers, the content analysis was carried out by using QDA Miner Lite v2.0.9 qualitative data analysis software. A step was to code the 33 questions manually and to process the identification of the codes gradually (refer to Figs. 2). The transcription of Question 2 for each student was analysed with open coding approach by using QDA Miner Lite. The distribution of codes referring to *Awareness focus* is graphically expressed on the left side Fig. 2. It shows distribution frequency of keywords in % regarding the Cybersecurity focus area for the Question 1): *awareness of cs relevance* (38.2%), *risks and consequences* (29.4%), *groupwork* (14.70%), *others items* (11.8%), *cybersecurity in real life* (8.8%), *costs* (5.9%), *multidisciplinary of the cs* (% 2.9). Students' opinions towards using Awareness of CS relevance with a level of appreciation (38.2%).

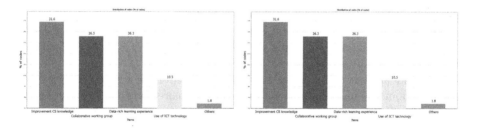

Fig. 2. On the left side, cybersecurity focus (Awareness of CS relevance 38.2%). On the right side, positive aspects (i.e. Improvement CS knowledge (31.6%))

The right side of Fig. 2 shows a frequency distribution of the codes generated in QDA Miner Lite for the Question 3) (i.e. "(Q3) *What are the two most positive aspects in this experience?*"). The analysis follows the basic routines of open coding where words or pieces of text are related to concepts. We prepared a set of codes that were significant for understanding the topic, which in this case are the positive aspects such as a) *Improvement CS knowledge*, b) *Collaborative working group*, c) *Data-rich learning experience* d) *Use of ICT technology*, and e) *Others*. The distribution of codes referring to *Positive aspects* is graphically expressed on the right side of the Fig. 2. It shows that the students are pleased to have deepened the topics on cybersecurity in the way the training was organized (*Improvement CS knowledge* (31.6%)), *Collaborative working group* (26.3%) that may predict student satisfaction for experiences addressing of workgroup; *Data-rich learning experience* (26.3%) is a data-driven approach.

Questions 4 only contained no answer (no negative aspects) or aspects related to the interaction mode. In fact, the tool was meant to stimulate collaboration via a chat and the students complained about the video call being more quick and efficient.

Question 5 also had an overwhelming majority of answers that outlined how the group work experience was able to generate a deeper knowledge of the issues related to cybersecurity and its impact. Many suggested that comparing their findings with others' in the group was really very helpful in comprehension of the topics.

Questions 6 contained only few answers with suggestions to repeat the experience in other courses, and (again) the suggestion to include a video chat into the collaboration tool.

Discussion of Results. Students' independence in the task was significant. Although there was a forum for support in the platform, only 2–3 groups used it and mostly only in order to be sure that their work was heading in the right direction (like ensuring that they were indeed allowed to use other sources). All the groups were able to provide significant output, and (with some variations) fully answered in a satisfactory way to the requests of the assignment.

The awareness of cybersecurity importance was really high. Some students were enthusiastic about the data supporting the position that cybersecurity is a serious issue for ours society.

The methodology proposed for group work, the analysis and co-creation of data, with the visualization to show some outcomes or results was also considered very interesting and effective.

The students liked the cooperation and the synchronous activity, widely complaining about the unavailability of a video chat (paired with our instruction to use the chat for communication). Almost all students were citing it as a weak point. It must be said that the tool was designed before the pandemic, and the actual widespread usage of videocommunication tools probably makes the student aware of the lower efficiency of the chat tool.

4   Outlook and Conclusion

COLTRANE project aims at addressing the challenges that are facing the providers of higher education for cybersecurity, by supporting the educators to fully address their need for community building, for sharing, for online delivery, for teaching collaboration in virtual teams, and for having to meet employer demand and learner expectations on employability.

As early project outcomes at the University of Salerno have shown, being able to offer students practice-oriented cases to work on and teach them in a problem-oriented and scenario-based way is highly motivating for them, especially when the teaching incorporates modern tools that allow a collaborative, team-oriented way of working and enable technology-based groupwork and communication. That is why the next series of case studies will continue to focus on collaborative aspects, this time to be led by the University of Vienna. The deployment of collaborative technologies will be in close cooperation with the University of Salerno and the AIT with the intention to bring an integrated technology platform into the classroom. This platform, consisting at its core of the SPOD tool and the AIT cyber range, is intended to serve as strategic basis for the further development of practice-oriented hands-on teaching materials. With the COLTRANE methodology building the didactic umbrella and the teaching content being developed in the form of modules that are compatible with CyBOK and NIST/CSF, educators will be put into a much better position as far as the teaching of applied knowledge is concerned. Delivering these more practical educational outcomes is expected to raise the employability of graduates and thereby help to better address the current cybersecurity skills shortage. In addition, the repository materials, such as templates derived from the COLTRANE method, associated guides and processes, and the scenarios and cases can also contribute to making continuous and distance education efforts more effective.

Acknowledgements. The authors gratefully thank EU ERASMUS+ project COLTRANE (grant number KA2-Projekt 2020-1-AT01-KA203-078070) for supporting our research.

References

1. Andriessen, J., et al.: Increasing public value through co-creation of open knowledge. In: 2017 Fourth International Conference on eDemocracy & eGovernment (ICEDEG), Quito, Ecuador, pp. 47–54. IEEE (2017). https://doi.org/10.1109/ICEDEG.2017.7962512
2. Langner, G., et al.: The need for a collaborative approach to cyber security education. In: 6th IEEE European Symposium on Security and Privacy, 6–10 September 2021, all-digital event (2021)
3. Tokola, T., et al.: A collaborative cybersecurity education program. In: Cybersecurity Education for Awareness and Compliance, Hershey, USA, pp. 181–200. IGI Global (2019). ISBN 1948-9730, 1948-9749/9781522578475, 9781522578482
4. Quirchmayr, G.: An international security education perspective. In: IFIP TC11 WG 11.8 - Information Security Education Workshop (2004)
5. Quirchmayr, G., Slay, J., Kurzel, F., Hagenus, K.: IFIP TC11 WG 11.8 - information security education workshop. In: Fifth Australasian Computing Education Conference (ACE 2003) (2003)
6. Schaberreiter, T., et al.: A cybersecurity situational awareness and information-sharing solution for local public administrations based on advanced big data analysis: the CS-AWARE project. In: Bernabe, J.B., Skarmeta, A. (eds.) Challenges in Cybersecurity and Privacy - The European Research Landscape, pp. 149–180. River Publishers, Gistrup (DK) (2019)

7. Andriessen, J., Pardijs, M.: Awareness of cybersecurity: implications for learning for future citizens. In: Kubincová, Z., Lancia, L., Popescu, E., Nakayama, M., Scarano, V., Gil, A.B. (eds.) MIS4TEL 2020. AISC, vol. 1236, pp. 241–248. Springer, Cham (2021). https://doi.org/10.1007/978-3-030-52287-2_24

8. Hmelo-Silver, C.E., DeSimone, C.: Problem-based learning. In: The International Handbook of Collaborative Learning. Routledge (2011). https://doi.org/10.4324/9780203837290.ch21

9. Cordasco, G., Malandrino, D., Pirozzi, D., Scarano, V., Spagnuolo, C.: A layered architecture for open data: design, implementation and experiences. In: Proceedings of the 11th International Conference on Theory and Practice of Electronic Governance, pp. 371–381, April 2018. https://doi.org/10.1145/3209415.3209466

An Investigation into Educational Process Models for Teaching Secure Programming

Vuyolwethu Mdunyelwa[1]([⊠]) [iD], Lynn Futcher[1] [iD], and Johan van Niekerk[1,2] [iD]

[1] Nelson Mandela University, Port Elizabeth, South Africa
{vuyolwethu.mdunyelwa,lynn.futcher}@mandela.ac.za
[2] Noroff University College, Kristiansand, Norway
johan.vanniekerk@noroff.no

Abstract. Despite the many advantages that software applications provide in our daily lives, there are also numerous threats that target vulnerabilities in these applications. There is therefore a demand for new technologies and approaches to secure software development. Educational institutions are responsible for equipping computing graduates with the requisite secure programming knowledge, skills and abilities. However, despite various curricula guidelines being provided by the ACM and other professional bodies, many educational institutions have not successfully implemented such changes within their curricula. One of the problems is that the available curricula guidelines focus more on *what* secure programming concepts should be taught, rather than *how*. This paper therefore investigates *how* educational process models could be used for teaching secure programming. It further identifies various themes and sub-themes from different educational process models and argues how these can be used to teach secure programming.

Keywords: Educational process model · Secure programming · Secure coding education

1 Introduction

The reliance on software applications for everyday operations has increased drastically in recent years. This is due to their central and underpinning role in enabling many functions in modern society [1]. However, the threats to software applications have also increased dramatically, often due to vulnerabilities existing within the application itself. A key challenge for software developers is therefore to ensure the security of these applications [2]. Educational institutions typically offer programming courses to learners enrolled in Computer Science, Information Technology, Information Systems, Software Engineering and other related qualifications [3]. In all these fields of study,

The financial assistance of the National Research Foundation (NRF) towards this research is hereby acknowledged. Opinions expressed and conclusions arrived at, are those of the author, and are not necessarily to be attributed to the NRF.

© IFIP International Federation for Information Processing 2022
Published by Springer Nature Switzerland AG 2022
N. Clarke and S. Furnell (Eds.): HAISA 2022, IFIP AICT 658, pp. 77–90, 2022.
https://doi.org/10.1007/978-3-031-12172-2_7

learners are required to acquire at least some programming skills either at introductory level or throughout the qualification.

Programming is a complex activity with many challenges in teaching it since it draws on different knowledge domains and a variety of cognitive processes. Teaching secure programming adds to this challenge. Existing curricula guidelines focus on *what* secure programming topics should be taught and only provide limited guidance in terms of *how* this should be done [4, 5]. This paper therefore investigates how educational process models could be used for teaching secure programming through a thematic content analysis of existing models, critical reasoning and a practical example.

This paper starts with a discussion of the Research Methodology in Sect. 2, followed by Related Literature regarding secure programming education and training in Sect. 3 and Educational Process Models in Sect. 4. Section 5 follows with the Thematic Analysis of the most common educational process models and Sect. 6 provides a discussion of the educational process model elements most suited to teaching secure programming. Section 7 concludes the paper.

2   Research Methodology

This study entailed a literature study to highlight current research relating to secure programming education and educational process models. Furthermore, it included a thematic content analysis to determine the key elements of existing educational process models, and critical reasoning to identify and argue those elements most relevant to teaching secure programming.

A thematic content analysis was deemed relevant for this study since it is a form of analysis for qualitative data [6]. In a thematic content analysis, the researcher is required to closely examine the data to identify common themes, topics, ideas, and patterns of meaning that come up repeatedly [7]. This method of analysis is a more flexible approach to data analysis and can be adapted to many different kinds of research [8]. Various approaches to conducting a thematic content analysis exist. However, the most common form follows a six-step process, which includes familiarization, coding, generating themes, reviewing themes, defining and naming themes, and writing up, as described below: [6, 9, 10].

– **Familiarization -** is the first step and refers to understanding all the data collected to provide an overview for the analysis of the individual items.
– **Coding -** refers to highlighting sections of text or phrases. This leads to coming up with labels to describe their codes.
– **Generating Themes -** is where themes are generated from patterns identified from the codes that have been created.
– **Reviewing Themes -** includes a comparison of the data set to the generated themes for accuracy of the representation of data.
– **Defining and Naming Themes -** here the defining of themes involves the exact formulation for determining what they mean, while the naming of themes involves coming up with brief and easily understandable names for each theme.
– **Writing Up -** includes writing the analysis of data. This includes how data was collected, and how the thematic content analysis was conducted.

This six-step process has been applied to the thematic content analysis as discussed in Sect. 5.

3   Secure Programming Education and Training

To mitigate cybersecurity incidents in software applications, many researchers have proposed a Secure Software Development Life Cycle approach which suggests that security should be considered in all the phases in the SDLC [11]. In adhering to this approach, many software development teams in industry are required to attend security training for their relevant tasks [12]. Software development is an intensive and demanding task, which means that finding time for such training might be challenging, especially for developers who may not have the underlying security knowledge or who lack a security mindset [13]. Various successful approaches have been used to equip software development teams with secure programming knowledge, skills through the use of gaming, challenges and continuous cybersecurity educational approaches [14]. Many researchers propose the integration of such approaches throughout the undergraduate curriculum [13, 15].

Even though industry provides secure programming training for their software development teams, it is reported that their first encounters with the training is normally challenging since they would be required to think of their jobs with a security mindset [16]. It has been argued that the development and application of secure programming knowledge, skills and abilities in industry would be less challenging if developers had some fundamental academic background related to secure programming to draw upon [17]. Many security researchers also agree that secure programming is best integrated from introductory courses in first year to progressively more advanced courses throughout the qualification [18]. While existing computing curricula guidelines suggest topics for inclusion, this is often not done in many computing disciplines due to various challenges, including:

- Finding space in the curriculum which is already full [19].
- Lack of sufficient security relevant knowledge amongst computing instructors
- [20].
- Existing computing curricula's lack of guidance on *how* security should be taught [16].

In terms of instructors' knowledge relating to secure programming, this relates to *what* should be taught and what secure programming knowledge, skills and abilities the instructor should be equipped with. Some researchers assert that secure programming refers to programming that adheres to specific security requirements [13, 21]. An example of these requirements can be more generic, such as avoiding user problems by validating input or not using concatenated SQL commands [22].

This form of programming is referred to as *robust programming*, or defensive programming [23]. This requires the programmer to think more about what the program *can be made to do*, rather than thinking more about *what it should do*. This requires an attacker mindset which would guide programmers when developing software applications. Not only the attacker mindset is required when developing such applications, but an implementation of security best practices which would address any unintended functions for the program. Such security best practices are secure coding practices which the programmer should know and implement when developing software applications [24–26].

Secure coding practices are not entirely new programming concepts that need to be adopted, these are existing security best practices which require certain implementations to make them effective in securing software applications [25, 27]. An example would be securing an application against SQL injection which is a manipulation of SQL statements to modify data in the database. This can occur if input in a software application is not properly validated, or when developing the application, the programmers made use of concatenated SQL strings. In this case, addressing SQL injection would require a programmer to validate all input fields and make use of store procedures or parameterised SQL commands. Newly developed curricula guidelines provide a first step towards answering the question as to *what* these computing disciplines' cybersecurity should encompass [3, 15, 28]. Many computing curricula guidelines suggest the integration of cybersecurity throughout the computing curriculum, instead of treating it as a separate entity from the computing content. The 2017 Cybersecurity Curricula Guidelines (CSEC2017) provides recommendations for these computing disciplines and outlines various cybersecurity knowledge areas, broken into knowledge units and topics [15].

While the issue on the space in the curriculum might seem like one of the gatekeepers for software security education, a more concerning issue is the assumption that separate or new secure coding concepts are required to ensure a software application's security requirements are met during software development, which is not the case [29]. The reality is that programming curricula already include secure programming concepts that the instructor may teach unknowingly to learners. This would lead to instructors not correcting any insecurely written code in learners' assessment due to the lack of knowledge relating to secure coding practices amongst instructors [30]. While this lack of knowledge amongst programming instructors is also a gatekeeper, various standards, security organizations and curricula guidelines provide educational materials and guidelines which learners and instructors can use as resources for teaching and learning [25, 31–33]. This material would be useful to teaching programming and addressing their lack of knowledge relating to secure coding practices.

In terms of addressing the *how* question in teaching secure programming, this seems to be an issue, since educational settings differ.

4   Educational Process Models

An educational process model is a system of educational components which may be derived from different process models or theoretical frameworks, which focuses on how the learning process takes places in different or specific educational settings [34]. While educational settings may differ according to whether teaching is done online, face-to-face or any combination of these educational settings, the underlying elements remain constant across these settings [35]. These underlying elements include learners, instructors, institutions, educational technology, and accrediting boards [36]. These diverse, yet necessary elements, can be integrated through a conceptual framework, provided by an educational process model [37]. The diverse nature of educational settings and disciplinary subject matter has resulted in the development of various such educational process models. These include:

- **Systems Model of the Educational Process** - this educational process model builds on a Rhetoric process model, and include inputs, integrative process, output and feedback [35]. This is used to integrate educational components in a distance learning environment, and also provides room for virtual learning environments.
- **The Teaching/Learning Process Model** - This process model has been developed to categorize the variables which address how learners learn, and why learners learn better than others in a classroom environment [38]. This is designed for classroom settings and includes components such as inputs, teaching processes and outputs.
- **A Generalized Educational Process Model** - this presents a generic educational process model. This process model is based on three models, which are, the Information Space to provide resources for information, Nonaka's Model for knowledge acquisition and Bloom's Taxonomy for evaluating the effectiveness of education [39].
- **e-Learning Educational Process Model** - this provides a model for identifying the correct educational technologies for use in a virtual learning environment [36]. This process model is specific for virtual learning environments.
- **Educational Process Model for Research** - this provides an analysis of the educational process, and considers a variety of input components, and how these interact to affect the educational experience of learners [37]. Outputs from this educational process model are measured in different domains of learning, which includes the cognitive, affective and psycho-motor.

An example of the differences in educational subject matter may be depicted in applied subjects, such as programming when compared to more theoretical subjects, such as philosophy. In theoretical subjects, learners are required to absorb knowledge transmitted by the instructor, or read from a book, whereas in programming modules, learners are required to construct code, building recursively on pre-existing knowledge [40]. This provides a different view of teaching, where the instructor helps the learner to learn with more practical work, requiring immediate feedback, rather than simply presenting information to the learners [39]. The educational process models highlighted above focus on the input and outputs of such models, as well as the integration of the diverse elements required for educational settings.

While similarities exist amongst these educational process models, their use and interpretation differ. Some focus specifically on online educational settings, while some provide a generic process model for both online, traditional classroom, or a blended learning approach [39–41]. Therefore, no single process model satisfies all needs for secure programming education since this can be taught in various educational settings. This study argues that specific elements across the different process models exist which can be used to teach secure programming. Generic process models consider a number of elements, such as educational environment, faculty, and target audience.

5   Thematic Content Analysis of Educational Process Models

As discussed in Sect. 2, a thematic content analysis was conducted to determine the themes and sub-themes relating to the five educational process models as discussed in Sect. 4. These educational process models were selected based on the researcher's interpretation of their applicability in teaching secure programming. The selected process models are specific for education and include elements which are relevant for teaching secure programming. Table 1 shows the data sets resulting from the thematic content analysis.

Table 1. Thematic content analysis data set.

Educational process model	Data set extracts
Systems model of the educational process	input, integration, output, internal and external feedback, outcomes, experience, instructional technology, method, purpose, pedagogy, educational philosophy, resources
The teaching/learning process model	input, teacher/learner characteristics, classroom process, teacher/student behaviour, output, student achievement, school characteristics, context, school process
A generalized educational process model	Information Space (knowledge, data, information), Nonaka's model (socialization, externalization, combination, instructional material, Bloom's taxonomy
e-learning educational process model	participants (teachers, web content developers, web content, learners), context, media, output, experience
Educational process model for research	input, student, media, environment, instruction, teacher, curriculum, output, combination, cognitive, psychomotor, affective

The first step in the thematic content analysis is the *familiarization* which was done by reviewing the different elements of the educational process models discussed in Sect. 4. Common educational process models include three major components, which may include sub-components depending on the specific process model. Such components include inputs, integration/combination, and outputs from the different process models [37, 38]. A few educational process models which are specific for distance or online learning include feedback or reflection since the learning occurs in a virtual environment [35, 36]. Step two, *coding*, included identifying texts and phrases in the data sets collected from the identified educational process models and their elements. These texts and phrases are clearly shown in Table 1.

The third step, *generating the themes*, was achieved by identifying patterns from the codes created from the elements existing in the selected educational process models. The patterns were identified from the elements which share the same meaning, or have the same function. It was found that various educational process models use different terms to refer to the educational experience provided by using the different input components in an educational setting. Educational process models also use different terms to refer to the process, such as combination, integration, or classroom process.

Step four, *reviewing of themes*, was achieved by comparing the themes to the exact codes of the educational process model elements for accuracy of their representation in the themes generated.

Step five, the *defining of themes* is provided in the discussion below where each generated theme (inputs, integration, output, and reflection) and their related sub-themes are discussed.

Figure 1 depicts the themes and sub-themes for this research which were generated from the data sets of the elements of the identified educational process models.

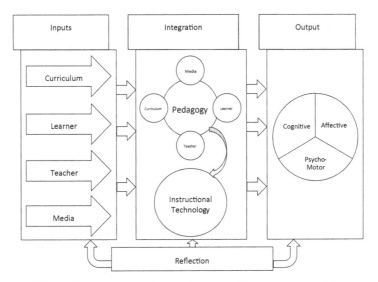

Fig. 1. Themes and sub-themes from educational process models.

The next section defines and reports on the identified themes and sub-themes identified.

5.1 Inputs

Inputs into the educational process model would need to be well thought through since they would determine the ultimate experience and whether the achievement of the desired goals will be successful. These inputs differ depending on the specific process model and its use. Inputs into educational process models refer to elements that enhance instructor and learners' teaching and learning experiences. The identified inputs include:

– **Curriculum** – this sub-theme refers to the content or the subject matter information, which is organised into a communicable form, to be conveyed to the learner [37]. This includes characteristics such as structure, organisation, and sequence which refers to how the flow of the information should be when teaching the learners [28].

- **Instructor** – the instructor sub-theme refers to the implementor of the curriculum [38]. This may take two forms, either an *instructor-implementor*, referring to a human being who is equipped with knowledge regarding the subject matter and is able to implement the curriculum, or the *implementor*, which refers to the technology used to implement and deliver the curriculum.
- **Learner** – the learner sub-theme includes the receptors in the educational process. This is important since it considers elements such as the learners' learning style, individual needs, and cultural differences [36, 42].
- **Media** – this sub-theme includes the different types of instructional material which is available for use inside and outside of the classroom [37]. Such instructional material includes internet, textbooks, slides, or videos and any medium learners use to received information.

Once the inputs have been identified, these need to be integrated in the educational process, creating an effective learning experience. The next section discusses the integration themes and its related sub-themes.

5.2   Integration (Combination)

This theme refers to the instructor and learner behaviour during the teaching and learning process as well as the learner and instructor relationships [35, 37, 38]. This takes into consideration the various input sub-themes and normalises them into a specific learning domain. The identified integration themes include various sub-themes, namely:

- **Purpose** – this sub-theme includes determining the essential learning objectives, and aligning such objectives to the specialised needs of the inputs to the model, specifically those of the learners [35, 37].
- **Pedagogy** - this sub-theme refers to the integration of the input sub-themes of the educational process model in order to produce an educational experience [35]. The instructor enhances the educational experience through modifying the original objectives to suite the learners' needs and the available educational resources both from learner and the instructor [36].
- **Instructional Technology** - this sub-theme covers the available technology for instruction, taking into account the learners' ability to interact with the technology [37]. This combines the learner and the instructors' ability to use the instructional material to provide an effective educational experience.

Once the integration of the input sub-themes has occurred, there are a number of measurable and immeasurable results that can either be the expected or unexpected outputs from the learning experience [39]. The next sub-section discusses the output theme and sub-themes generated from the educational process model data sets.

5.3 Output

This theme provides the outcomes of the learning experience [43]. Different learning outcomes and experiences may be produced depending on a number of factors, including learners, environment, and pedagogy [43].

The different learning outcomes also depend on the subject matter, since different learning outcomes are measured using different learning domains such as cognitive, psycho-motor, and affective as described below:

– **Cognitive** - this sub-theme refers to the *thinking* domain. This relates to how the learners acquire and process knowledge, and the different levels in which learners process the knowledge, as depicted in the Bloom's Taxonomy [37, 44].
– **Psycho-Motor** - once the learners have acquired the knowledge, they would be required to use the knowledge to produce some form of an artefact which would ensure that knowledge acquired is used [45].
– **Affective** - this sub-theme relates to how the learner feels after the learning experience. This depends on the learning experience and how the learner interacted with the content [45].

Some educational process models focus on all these learning domains, while some focus only on a single domain of learning.

The output theme provides the ability to address any unexpected results in the learning experience, since this provides feedback to an instructor. The next section discusses the final theme generated from the thematic content analysis data sets.

5.4 Reflection

The final theme identified from the educational process models is reflection/feedback, where the results from the output sub-theme could be used to suggest changes to the learning experience. Such changes may occur on the educational experience itself, or the technology, or any of the inputs.

6 Educational Process Model Elements for Teaching Secure Programming

This section discusses how the identified themes and sub-themes can be used to teach secure programming. An example of secure programming would include the use of stored procedures and validating input to address SQL injection, and this will be used to provide context in the following discussion.

6.1 Inputs for Teaching Secure Programming

This sub-section discusses the inputs relevant for teaching secure programming as generated from the data sets of the selected educational process models. The sub-themes for input in the model are listed below:

- **Curriculum -** this is necessary since it provides the topics and areas to focus on when teaching. This would require the instructor to acquire secure programming knowledge when preparing the content so that outputs can be measurable when the teaching and learning process is complete [38].
- **Instructor -** the instructor is required to have secure programming knowledge. For the above example, the instructor would have to be equipped with knowledge relating to SQL, input validation, stored procedures, and how these are implemented in order to deliver a software application which is not prone to SQL injection.
- **Learner -** in learning secure programming, the learner should have some prior programming knowledge to support what they are learning. When learning about SQL injection, they are required to have basic knowledge on input validation, SQL, and stored procedures providing an understanding of how SQL injection occurs when these are not implemented securely. They should also be provided with guidelines on how these should be implemented to provide a secure software application which will not be vulnerable to SQL injection.
- **Media -** this sub-theme is important for any teaching and learning environment, and in programming, this needs to address both the knowledge and behaviour of the learners and ensure effectiveness of both these aspects [2].

The inputs into the educational process model are important and differ on how they are used, providing a unique educational experience. Their use is further discussed in the integration theme, with the necessary sub-themes for teaching secure programming which are discussed in the next sub-section.

6.2   Integration for Teaching Secure Programming

This sub-section presents the integration of the inputs for teaching secure programming as generated from the different data sets of the selected educational process models:

- **Purpose -** the purpose provides the learning objective, and in referencing the SQL injection prevention example, this would include identifying concepts surrounding SQL injection which would be covered for teaching secure programming, such as SQL, input validation, and stored procedures.
- **Pedagogy -** in secure programming, an adopted pedagogy should be suitable for all the target audience needs. Also, this should address both the knowledge and behaviour aspects of learners by ensuring that learners acquire secure programming knowledge and are able to write secure code [46].
- **Instructional Technology -** this includes the technology required for teaching secure programming and what technology learners would be required to learn secure programming. For example, when teaching SQL injection, learners would be required to have database management software, an integrated development environment, and a computer which is able to run the software.

Once the integration of the sub-themes has occurred, outputs resulting from the integration would be evident. The next sub-section discusses the outputs which would be required for measuring the effectiveness of the secure programming educational process.

6.3 Outputs for Teaching Secure Programming

In programming, measuring effectiveness of education requires both the knowledge and behaviour aspects [47]. This sub-section discusses and aligns the output theme and its sub-themes.

– **Cognitive** - this is the primary requirement in any measurement of knowledge acquisition. However, in secure programming, this is not sufficient since learners need to demonstrate this through writing secure code.
– **Psycho-Motor** - in programming, a learner would be required to produce some form of an artefact which would be used to measure their behaviour relating to programming, and also to determine whether secure programming practices are adhered to when developing the artefact.
– **Affective** - this relates to the experience of the learner during the learning process. This can be enhanced by the instructor expanding on the planning of their course, including the teaching, activities and the teaching of secure programming.

The above output sub-themes are relevant for secure programming, however, an instructor may not be able to measure the affective domain in some environments such as the virtual environment. The final theme identified is reflection, as discussed in the next sub-section.

6.4 Reflection

Reflection provides feedback on the learning experience and allows for the improvement in the learning process to enhance the educational experience. In a secure programming environment, this is required since programming in general changes, and the vulnerabilities targeting software applications also change. New approaches to teaching which address such vulnerabilities should be provided as well as updates and changes to the curriculum [35].

7 Conclusion

This paper investigated the use of educational process models for teaching secure programming. Five educational process models were reviewed for common educational elements resulting in themes and sub-themes generated from the data sets extracted from the thematic content analysis conducted. This study argues that the identified themes and sub-themes are required for teaching secure programming and can be used in different educational settings. It also motivates the importance of the reflection theme which allows the educational experience to the improved, through changing the various themes and sub-themes. This study only focused on five educational process models due to the researchers interpretation of their applicability in teaching secure programming. Future research will include case study of the selected themes and sub-themes used in different educational settings putting into context the selected themes and sub-themes to teach secure programming.

References

1. Auch, M., Weber, M., Mandl, P., Wolff, C.: Similarity-based analyses on software applications: a systematic literature review. J. Syst. Softw. **168**, 110669 (2020). https://doi.org/10.1016/j.jss.2020.110669
2. Gasiba, T., Lechner, U., Cuellar, J., Zouitni, A.: Ranking secure coding guidelines for software developer awareness training in the industry. OpenAccess Ser. Inform. **81**(11), 1–11 (2020)
3. Sabin, M., Alrumaih, H., Impagliazzo, J., Lunt, B., Zhang, M.: ACM/IEEE. 2017 information technology curricula 2017: curriculum guidelines for baccalaureate degree programs in information technology. Technical report (2017)
4. I.E. Commission and S. S. Division, SANS 27034-1: 2013 South African National Standard Information technology—Security techniques—Application security Part 1: Overview and concepts (2013)
5. Lunt, B., Sabin, M., Hala, A., Impagliazzo, J., Zhang, M.: Information technology curricula 2017. Association for Computing Machinery (ACM) IEEE Computer Society, Technical report (2017)
6. Anderson, R.: Thematic content analysis (TCA). Descriptive Present. Qual. Data **15**, 1–4 (2007)
7. Xiao, Y., Watson, M.: Guidance on conducting a systematic literature review. J. Plan. Educ. Res. **39**(1), 93–112 (2019)
8. Cairns, A.H., et al.: Using semantic lifting for improving educational process models discovery and analysis. In: CEUR Workshop Proceedings, vol. 1293, pp. 150–161 (2014)
9. Caulfield, J.: How to do thematic analysis—a step-bystep guide & examples. Scribbr, pp. 1–9 (2020). https://www.scribbr.com/methodology/thematic-analysis/
10. Nowell, L.S., Norris, J.M., White, D.E., Moules, N.J.: Thematic analysis: striving to meet the trustworthiness criteria. Int J Qual Methods **16**(1), 1–13 (2017)
11. Nehouse, W., Keith, S., Scribner, B., Witte, G.: NIST 2017 national initiative for cybersecurity education (NICE) cybersecurity workforce framework. Technicl report, November 2017. https://nvlpubs.nist.gov/nistpubs/SpecialPublications/NIST.SP.800-181.pdf
12. Gasiba, T., Lechner, U., Rezabek, F., Pinto-Albuquerque, M.: Cybersecurity games for secure programming education in the industry: gameplay analysis. In: Queirós, R., Portela, F., Pinto, M. (eds.) First International Computer Programming Education Conference (2020)
13. Nance, K., Hay, B., Fairbanks, A., Bishop, M.: Secure coding education: are we making progress?, pp. 83–88 (2012)
14. Gasiba, T., Lechner, U., Pinto-Albuquerque, M., Zouitni, A.: Design of secure coding challenges for cybersecurity education in the industry. In: Shepperd, M., Brito e Abreu, F., Rodrigues da Silva, A., Pérez-Castillo, R. (eds.) QUATIC 2020. CCIS, vol. 1266, pp. 223–237. Springer, Cham (2020). https://doi.org/10.1007/978-3-030-58793-2_18
15. Burley, D., Bishop, M., Buck, S., Ekstrom, J., Futcher, L.: Cybersecurity Curricula 2017, no. December (2018)
16. Carneiro, D., Silva, R.: Game elements, motivation and programming learning: a case study. In: First International Computer Programming Education Conference (2020)
17. Zuzana, K., Iveta, D.: Using code review at school and at the programming club. In: First International Computer Programming Education Conference (2020)

18. Espinha Gasiba, T., Lechner, U., Pinto-Albuquerque, M., Mendez, D.: Is secure coding education in the industry needed? An investigation through a large scale survey, no. February, pp. 241–252 (2021)
19. Bishop, M., et al.: Cybersecurity curricular guidelines. In: Bishop, M., Futcher, L., Miloslavskaya, N., Theocharidou, M. (eds.) WISE 2017. IAICT, vol. 503, pp. 3–13. Springer, Cham (2017). https://doi.org/10.1007/978-3-319-58553-6_1
20. Dark, M.J., Lauren, S., Ngambeki, I., Bishop, M.: Effect of the secure programming clinic on learners' secure programming practices (2016)
21. Taylor, B., Bishop, M., Hawthorne, E., Nance, K.: Teaching secure coding- the myths and the realities. In: Proceeding of the 44th ACM Technical Symposium on Computer Science Education (SIGCSE 2013), no. March 2013, pp. 281–282 (2013)
22. Conde, V., Queirós, R.: First International Computer Programming Education Conference Ricardo Queirós Filipe Portela Mário Pinto (2020)
23. Bishop, M., Dai, J., Dark, M., Ngambeki, I., Nico, P., Zhu, M.: Evaluating secure programming knowledge. In: Bishop, M., Futcher, L., Miloslavskaya, N., Theocharidou, M. (eds.) WISE 2017. IAICT, vol. 503, pp. 51–62. Springer, Cham (2017). https://doi.org/10.1007/978-3-319-58553-6_5
24. Mdunyelwa, V., Futcher, L., Van Niekerk, J.: A framework for teaching secure coding practices through a blended learning approach (2020)
25. OWASP: OWASP Top 10 Web Application Security Risks. Technical report (2020). https://owasp.org/www-project-top-ten/
26. SANS Institute: 2011 CWE/SANS Top 25 Most Dangerous Software Errors. SANS Institute, pp. 1–25 (2011). http://cwe.mitre.org/top25/#CWE-78
27. Rindell, K., Ruohonen, J., Holvitie, J., Hyrynsalmi, S., Leppänen, V.: Security in agile software development: a practitioner survey. Inf. Softw. Technol. **131**(November 2020), 106488 (2021)
28. Ardis, M., Budgen, D., Hislop, G.W., Offutt, J., Sebern, M., Visser, W.: SE 2014: curriculum guidelines for undergraduate degree programs in software engineering. Computer **48**(11), 106–109 (2015)
29. Scholte, T., Balzarotti, D., Kirda, E.: Have things changed now? An empirical study on input validation vulnerabilities in web applications. Comput. Secur. **31**(3), 344–356 (2012)
30. Espinha Gasiba, T., Lechner, U., Pinto-Albuquerque, M.: Sifu - a cybersecurity awareness platform with challenge assessment and intelligent coach. Cybersecurity **3**(1), 1–23 (2020)
31. SANS/CWE: CWE - 2019 CWE Top 25 Most Dangerous Software Errors. Technical report (2019). https://cwe.mitre.org/top25/
32. The Acunetix Team: Acunetix Web Application Vulnerability Report 2019. Technical report (2020)
33. IBM: Security Cost of Data Breach (2019). https://www.ibm.com/downloads/cas/
34. Ruan, Y.: Educational process modelling with workflow and time petri nets. Ph.D. dissertation (2005)
35. Beck, C.E., Schornack, G.R.: Systems Model of Educational Processes. Encyclopedia of Distance Learning, 2nd edn., pp. 2008–2016 (2011)
36. Rashty, D.: eLearning processes models, pp. 1–7 (1998)
37. Armstrong, J.R.: An educational process model for use in research. J. Exp. Educ. **39**(1), 2–7 (1970)
38. Huitt, W.: A transactional framework of the teaching/learning process: a summary (2003). http://www.edpsycinteractive.org/materials/mdltlp.html
39. Tujarov, H., Avramova, S., Kalchev, S., Stefanova, M.: Educational process model. In: Proceedings of the 9th International Conference on Computer Systems and Technologies and Workshop for PhD Students in Computing, CompSysTech 2008, no. January 2008 (2008)
40. Adkins, M., Nitsch, W.: Student retention in online education. In: Encyclopedia of distance learning (1944)

41. Dees, D.M., Ingram, A., Kovalik, C., Allen, M., Mcclelland, A., Justice, L.: A transactional model of college teaching. Int. J. Teach. Learn. High. Educ. **19**(2), 130–139 (2007)
42. Kwek, C.L., Lau, T.C., Tan, H.P.: Education quality process model and its influence on students' perceived service quality. Int. J. Bus. Manag. **5**(8), 154 (2010)
43. Münch, J., Armbrust, O., Kowalczyk, M., Soto, M.: Descriptive process models, no. March (2012)
44. Bloom, B.S., Engelhart, M.D., Furst, E.J., Hill, W.H., Krathwohl, D.R.: The Classification of Educational Goals (1956)
45. Fawcett, G., Juliana, M.: Teaching in the digital age. In: Designing Instruction for Technology-Enhanced Learning, pp. 71–82 (2015). http://opentextbc.ca/teachinginadigi talage/%5Cn, http://services.igiglobal.com/resolvedoi/resolve.aspx?doi=10.4018/978-1-930 708-28-0.ch004
46. Mdunyelwa, V.S., Van Niekerk, J.F., Futcher, L.A.: Secure coding practices in the software development capstone project. In: Proceedings of the Eleventh International Symposium on Human Aspects of Information Security & Assurance (HAISA 2017) Secure, no. HAISA, pp. 282–291 (2017)
47. Mdunyelwa, V., Futcher, L., van Niekerk, J.: An educational intervention for teaching secure coding practices. In: Drevin, L., Theocharidou, M. (eds.) WISE 2019. IAICT, vol. 557, pp. 3–15. Springer, Cham (2019). https://doi.org/10.1007/978-3-030-23451-5_1

Cybersecurity Knowledge Requirements for a Water Sector Employee

R. Thomani[1], A. Marnewick[1], S. von Solms[2(✉)], and M. Malatji[1]

[1] School of Engineering Management, University of Johannesburg, Gauteng 2094, South Africa
{amarewick,masikem}@uj.ac.za
[2] Department of Electrical and Electronic Engineering, University of Johannesburg, Gauteng 2094, South Africa
svonsolms@uj.ac.za

Abstract. Critical infrastructure in South Africa remains highly vulnerable to cybercrime threats due to a poor cyber-crime fighting capacity and a lack of a strong cybersecurity policy. South Africa appears to have fallen behind in securing and protecting cyberspace, considering the country's dependability as well as the interconnectedness to the internet. Globally, the water and wastewater sector were ranked number four in the global security incidents. This study presents the findings of a systematic literature review conducted to assess the cybersecurity knowledge necessary for a general employee in the water sector. The study proposes a framework for determining the minimum knowledge that a general employee in the water sector should have. The frameworks start by defining the eight different types of cybersecurity challenges, then move on to mitigation strategies for dealing with such attacks. Several approaches and strategies were provided for mitigating various cybersecurity challenges. To deal with such risks, mitigations such as cybersecurity knowledge and skills, cybersecurity awareness, and cybersecurity training were proposed. The strategies for developing knowledge to deal with various sorts of dangers were provided at both the individual and organizational levels.

Keywords: Awareness · Critical infrastructure · Cybersecurity knowledge · Water sector employee

1 Introduction

Globally, the water and wastewater sector was ranked number 4 in the global security incidents based on the Repository of Industrial Security Incidents [1]. South Africa, in particular, has fallen behind in securing and protecting cyberspace, especially in state organisations which are facing an increasing amount of cybersecurity attacks and cybercrime [1, 2]. The critical infrastructure in South Africa remains highly vulnerable to cybercrime threats due to lack of a strong cybersecurity policy and poor cybercrime-fighting capacity [1].

© IFIP International Federation for Information Processing 2022
Published by Springer Nature Switzerland AG 2022
N. Clarke and S. Furnell (Eds.): HAISA 2022, IFIP AICT 658, pp. 91–105, 2022.
https://doi.org/10.1007/978-3-031-12172-2_8

Water management is South Africa is the responsibility of a range of organisations, from national departments to local municipalities. A wide range of corporate information technologies (IT) and operational technologies (OT) are deployed in the water and sanitation sector as utilities are increasingly using smart or connected industrial control systems. These connected technologies are vulnerable to cybersecurity threats, which includes sabotage or even damage by means of contamination injection, cyberattacks or physical destruction. South African organisations continuously invest in technological resources to reinforce their connectivity, automation and security dispositions, but regularly fall victim to unwanted intrusions to their information systems due to vulnerabilities caused by human activity on these systems. A shortage in cybersecurity professionals and general organisational cybersecurity awareness leads to a lack of safeguarding of these organizations from cybercrime and other cyber-related threats [3]. To date, systems that can protect themselves without involving the human element have not been realised, and consequently systems are prone to be threatened by human action (both intentionally and unintentionally. Therefore, there is a need to examine internal procedures and protection mechanisms to prevent cyberattacks related to the human aspects of these systems [4]. Building a cybersecurity culture has been argued by researchers to be essential in changing attitudes and perceptions as well as instilling good security behaviour in individuals [5].

The creation of a cybersecurity culture within an organisation is not an easy task, where a layered approach is required which includes aspects such as organisational and management support, policy, awareness and training, monitoring and auditing. It also requires aspects such as employee involvement and communication, learning from experience, shared responsibility, continuous learning and empowerment of employees [6]. One fundamental aspect to create such a culture is that employees must be empowered to understand cybersecurity vulnerabilities and the important role that they play in securing themselves and their organisation. This empowerment requires employees to have a certain level of cybersecurity awareness (CSA), be engaged in continuous training and communication. This paper aims to determine what knowledge employees are required to have to promote cybersecurity culture and awareness in the water sector.

To determine the answer, a systematic literature review was conducted with the objective to determine approaches to build the cybersecurity knowledge and awareness of a typical employee to support the creation of a cybersecurity culture within organisations in the water sector. The focus of this research was on water infrastructure and the sector-specific cybersecurity attacks but can be utilised in other critical infrastructure sectors as the results prove to be overarching and applicable to the wider critical infrastructure sector. This paper's arrangement begins with an introduction section stating the research goal. Section 2 describes the research approach, and Sect. 3 describes how the approach was carried out. Section 4 discusses the findings of the literature review. Section 5 of the paper concludes with recommendations for future research.

2 Research Methodology

The following procedure was developed by combining approaches from Xiao and Watson [7] and Shaffril [8] and is illustrated and summarized in Fig. 1 below.

- Planning the review: consist of two stages, the first step will be the identification of the need for a review followed by the development of the review protocol.
- Conducting the review: consist of five stages. The first stage will be the identification of research followed by selection of primary studies, study quality assessment, data extraction and data synthesis.
- Reporting the review: Reporting findings and data demonstration.

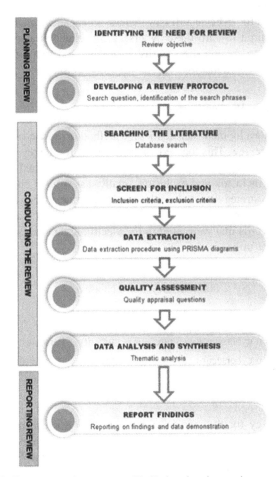

Fig. 1. Systematic literature review process [7, 9] the planning review stage of the systematic literature review is discussed in the subsection below.

3 Planning the Review

3.1 Identifying the Need for a Review

The objective of the systematic review in this research is to enable the answering of the research question as to *what knowledge is essential for typical employees in the water sector to support the creation of a cybersecurity culture within the organization.* The necessity for this systematic literature review comes as a result of the need to gather and summarize all the existing literature that will present evidence on existing and anticipated sector-specific cybersecurity awareness, where subsequently the knowledge and capabilities required to curb these cybersecurity related attacks will be outlined with the overall goal to create cybersecurity awareness and support the creation of a cybersecurity culture in organizations within the water sector.

3.2 Development of a Review Protocol

The review protocol development step defines the methods to be used for undertaking the systematic literature review. This focused on the rationale for the review, research question, search strategy including search terms, resources to be searched and the databases, selection criteria for inclusion and exclusion, quality assessment checklist and procedures, data extraction strategy and the synthesis of the extracted data [10]. The research question was structured and framed in terms of a modified PICO model to formulate a combination of keywords that were used in the electronic databases. Table 1 below is the key search phrases utilized;

Table 1. Key search phrases

Population	Intervention	Outcome
Employees	Support cybersecurity culture	Identify cybersecurity knowledge
	Support cybersecurity awareness	Identify cybersecurity education and training

The search strategy for the research made use of a Boolean operations to build up controlled vocabulary terms for acquiring articles through joining together the key search phrases with the Boolean "AND" operator. Following the Boolean operation, search strings were formulated as follows:

String 1:   *Employees **AND** Cybersecurity culture challenges **AND** Cybersecurity knowledge requirement **AND** Critical Infrastructure*

String 2:   *Employees **AND** Cybersecurity awareness **AND** Cybersecurity education and training **AND** Critical Infrastructure*

The results after the execution of the protocol are summarized in the next section.

4 Conducting the Review

4.1 Searching the Literature

The study put a limit on the search for review papers to peer-reviewed studies. The studies were acquired from a pre-selected list of databases that include ProQuest, IEEE, Emerald, Engineering Village, Wiley, and ScienceDirect were utilized.

4.2 Screening for Inclusion and Exclusion

To reduce the possibility of bias, the selection criteria were used to find studies that will provide evidence for the research question. The inclusion and exclusion criteria were defined for including studies and further selecting the most related studies. The inclusion criteria are prepared for identifying studies that are related to research questions [11]. Table 2 and Table 3 below illustrate the detailed inclusion and exclusion criteria.

Table 2. Inclusion criteria [11]

Language in article	To prevent compromising output quality, articles delivered in English will be used
Article is peer-reviewed	Only peer-reviewed papers will be used to ensure the study's quality
Article is in full text	To allow extensive reading, only full-text articles will be included
Type of article	The article can be comparative, action research, case study, survey, emphatical study
Article relation	The article is related to cybersecurity knowledge and awareness in the water sector
Article discussion	Articles explore the prerequisites for cybersecurity knowledge in order to raise awareness
Article Evaluation and analysis	The article evaluates and analyses existing cybersecurity knowledge of employees in the water sector

Table 3. Exclusion criteria [11]

Articles not matching criteria	Articles that do not comply with the inclusion criteria will be excluded
Articles not in English	Articles not written in English will be excluded, this may affect the accuracy of the research

(*continued*)

Table 3. (*continued*)

Unverified articles	To avoid misleading information, articles that are not peer-reviewed will be excluded
Duplicated articles	DOI numbers will be used to identify repeating articles from different databases
Unreliable sources	Unreliable sources such as Wikipedia, Ask.com, Encarta.msn.com, Answers.com will not be used

4.3 Data Extraction

Data extraction is referred to as the most challenging aspect of the systematic literature review given that the process involves going back to primary articles and highlighting the relevant information that will eventually answer the research question [12]. To ensure a transparent and complete reporting of the systematic review and meta-analysis [13], The Preferred Reporting Items for Systematic Reviews and Meta-analysis (PRISMA) approach was used for summarising aggregate data from the identified databases. Table 4 below shows the results.

Table 4. Summary of total reviewed document titles.

Database name	Initial search results	Retained articles after removing duplicates	Retained articles after screening using codes	Retained articles after 2nd screening
ProQuest	662	494	41	5
IEEE	309	206	28	8
Emerald	230	148	20	2
Engineering Village	445	266	59	11
Wiley Online	106	74	4	0
ScienceDirect	261	192	13	4
Total	**2013**	**1380**	**165**	**30**

Six databases were used in the identification phase to search for literature using the search strategy. The search strategy returned 2013 literature documents, 633 of which were identified duplicates as a result of searching multiple databases. The remaining 1380 literature documents were subjected to screening. The first screening procedure involved the use of codes to identify literature that will help answer the research question. The codes screening process resulted in the retention of 165 pieces of literature, which then went through the second screening process, which involved reading abstracts. The second screening process resulted in the retention of 30 pieces of literature for full-text assessment, where eligibility was checked based on the inclusion and exclusion criteria. The qualitative synthesis and analysis will be carried out in next section.

4.4 Screening for Eligibility

Screening articles for eligibility was done through full-text screening through the application of the inclusion criteria and the exclusion criteria. After downloading and reading the full text of the 30 articles, seven articles were found to be irrelevant and/or not applicable for this research. In the end, the seven articles were excluded and 23 studies from the literature were chosen for qualitative synthesis and analysis that will be covered in the next section.

4.5 Quality Assessment

The study quality assessment was used to assist in investigating whether quality differences explain differences in the study results. This was achieved through formulating questions to model the study quality assessment. The quality assessment model was adopted from Kitchenham [14]. Study quality appraisal was conducted in two stages. The first stage was, reading the article's summary or abstracts and conclusion in each study to assess relevancy. The second stage was quality appraisal through the 10 Critical Appraisal Skills Program (CASP) checklist of questioning, this provided for distinguishing issues in a systematic manner [15].

5 Data Analysis and Synthesis

The process of data synthesis involved the collating and summarising the results of the included primary studies to create a new understanding through comparing and analysing concepts and findings from the different sources that focused on the same topic of interest. Data synthesis requires transparency in the formulation process and requires authors to identify and extract evidence from the studies included to develop combined synthesized findings [16].

The thematic analysis process involved a constant back and forth movement between the data set, the coded extract and the analysis of the data being produced. The first step is familiarisation with the data, this step is necessary for the researcher to note initial ideas and transcribing the data from reading. The second step is generating initial codes where the author code interesting features in the data and collate relevant data before searching for themes, searching for themes is the third step where codes are then collated into potential themes. Themes are reviewed in the fourth stage by verifying if the theme works with the coded extract. Analysing and refining the specifics of each of them becomes the fifth stage before reporting on the analysis of selected extracts relating to the research question [17]. The five stages by Braun and Clarke [17] were followed and the outcome of each stage will be discussed in the sections below.

5.1 Familiarisation with the Data

The studies were read repeatedly for familiarisation. The studies consisted of 10 journal articles and 13 conference papers. The aim of grouping these studies is to assist in a better understanding of the data by grouping the studies.

5.2 Generating Initial Codes

At this stage, codes were developed through the process of forming categories based on elements shared within the data. The coding was developed with the consideration of the research question.

5.3 Searching for Themes

At this stage, themes for identifying the cybersecurity challenges and the corresponding themes for building cybersecurity knowledge emerged through the use of codes. Codes with common features were allocated to the appropriate and relevant themes. The theme aims to capture important details in the data with the research question to present patterned response or meaning in the data set [17].

Themes for Cybersecurity Challenges. Eight themes were identified for cybersecurity challenges. These themes assisted in identifying the blocks of knowledge that general employees should have to protect the critical infrastructure. The themes below were developed based on the codes retrieved from the 23 studies. The common types of cybersecurity threats indicated in each study were highlighted and allocated a single digit per study. Figure 2 below is the summary of different types of cyberattacks that are prevalent in critical infrastructure.

Themes for Methods of Mitigating Cybersecurity Threats. Four themes were identified for mitigating cyber threats. These themes assisted in identifying methods for mitigating cybersecurity threats as identified from the 23 collected studies from which a systematic literature review conducted. The common methods of building cybersecurity knowledge were allocated a single digit per study. Figure 3 below is the summary of different types of methods that can be used to build the cybersecurity knowledge of employees.

5.4 Reviewing the Themes

Internal Homogeneity: This criterion is concerned with the degree to which data belonging to a specific category or code holds together in a meaningful way [18]. In evaluating the internal homogeneity for cybersecurity challenges, the summary of themes and frequency of codes presented in the research were assessed.

External Heterogeneity: This criterion concerns for determining the degree to which differences between categories are clear and bold [18]. In evaluating the external heterogeneity, the chosen themes were found to be consistent with the supporting codes creating a unified pattern. The theme "cybersecurity culture" appeared less coherent as compared to the other themes.

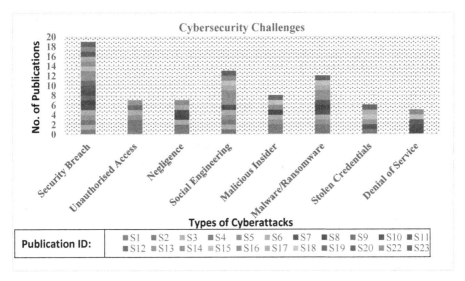

Fig. 2. Types of cybersecurity threats per study

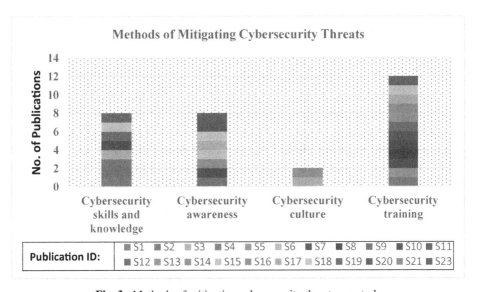

Fig. 3. Methods of mitigating cybersecurity threats per study

5.5 Reporting on Findings

Responding to security threats necessitates cybersecurity skill and knowledge training. It is critical to teach all employees and organizational leaders in cybersecurity skills so that they can better guard against and respond to cyber threats [19]. The detection and reaction to critical circumstances is a crucial component that companies should prioritize. These measures have the potential to dramatically decrease losses associated with cyber security breaches [20]. Employees' understanding of information security is seen as a protective element whereas a probable lack of awareness regarding security threats to which they may be exposed if not properly identified or detected in advance is regarded as a risk factor [21].

5.6   Framework for Defining the Cybersecurity Knowledge

A high-level approach leading towards building and identifying the cybersecurity knowledge required for a general employee is depicted in Fig. 4, where the basic Input Process Output (IPO) model was followed in building the framework illustrated in Fig. 5.

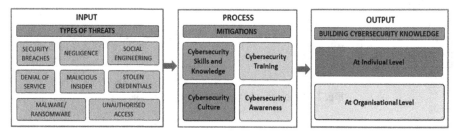

Fig. 4. IPO model for building cybersecurity knowledge

The study was approached from the angle of firstly determining the main threats which an organisation and its employees are generally faced with, marked at the input section of the model. The process section of the model relates to the various mitigation methods that can be employed by an organization in order to mitigate the threats listed in the input section. The output section relates to the actions stemming from the determined threats and various mitigation methodologies. As mentioned earlier in the document, the establishment of a cybersecurity culture within an organization must follow a layered approach which includes building cybersecurity knowledge at an individual level as well as an organizational level. These three sections were expanded to create the framework for identifying cybersecurity knowledge required for a general employee in the water sector, shown in Fig. 5 below.

The cyber threats identified in the input section of the model is considered the minimal knowledge that a typical general employee in the water sector should have. Data breaches, employee negligence, social engineering (phishing attacks), denial of service attacks, malicious insiders, malware/ransomware, stolen credentials and unauthorised access were recognized as eight risks that every general employee should be aware of as depicted in Fig. 5. It is acknowledged that there exist many other threats which can be included in employee training. The focus of this study was to determine the most general of these topics, limiting it to eight.

The literature studied listed four mitigation methods which can be employed both the individual and organizational levels to mitigate the vulnerabilities and hazards indicated as the minimal knowledge or capabilities. These methods are, cybersecurity skills and knowledge, cybersecurity awareness, cybersecurity training and cybersecurity culture.

The organisational level and individual levels depicted in the framework below ties back to the need for a layered approach to creating a cyber aware organisation.

At an organisational level, management support, inter-organisational knowledge sharing, awareness and training, policy, and monitoring is required. At the individual level, employees need to be supported and engage in continuous learning, knowledge sharing and must share the responsibility of cybersecurity in the organisation. It is imperative that employees must be supported by the organisation to improve their cybersecurity knowledge and skills through contextualisation, knowledge sharing and empowering of employees. These goals toward a cybersecurity culture in an organisation is frequently reflected in the knowledge and skills of its personnel [22]. A lack of cybersecurity knowledge and awareness can be one of the major causes of cyber-incidents, thus cybersecurity awareness in a company is important [23].

The literature studies gathered agree that a general employee in the water sector should be knowledgeable in at least the eight types of cybersecurity threats identified in the framework in Fig. 5. The protection of critical infrastructure can be assisted by building the knowledge of employees by employing mitigations methods by the organisations.

Building cybersecurity knowledge and skills at individual level requires employees to develop the capacity understand the context of cyberattacks and have the ability to recognise potential security threats, foreseeing the impact and initiating suitable responses. It is important that employees are knowledgeable on the different types of attackers, their motivation, resources and skills, which would further assist in gasping possible loopholes and risks. In an organisational setting, the cybersecurity knowledge and skills involve a joint organisational cybersecurity capability of the staff which include the ability to detect and respond in critical situations, sharing of knowledge amongst employees, and the development of policies aimed at making employees knowledgeable. The effort made by the organisation is critical in the support of individual knowledge and skills development.

Cybersecurity awareness requires employees to develop situational awareness that will enable them to be aware of potential cyberthreats. It is good practice to create awareness about topics such as the creation of strong passwords and keeping passwords safe. Employees can develop critical awareness based on experiences of co-workers, therefor information sharing is critical and must be supported by the organisation. Organisations should design and develop CSA for compliant behaviour to enable employees to identify cyber-risks in their specific work context. The security behaviour of employees must be in line with the organisation's security procedures and policies.

Cybersecurity training requires employees to build skills through developing abilities to manage incidents and reduce successful attacks. Through training, individuals can develop abilities to recognise threats and take appropriate action. The capability of spotting cyberthreats and the preparedness to respond in an adequate manner can be achieved through different training methods with the more hands-on skills training deemed crucial. Hands-on skills training includes methods such as gamification and cyber-ranges which must be conducted or supported by the organisation. Cybersecurity training entails building the team's capacity to detect and respond to attacks and the training must be such that it is tailored to meet the security policies of an organisation.

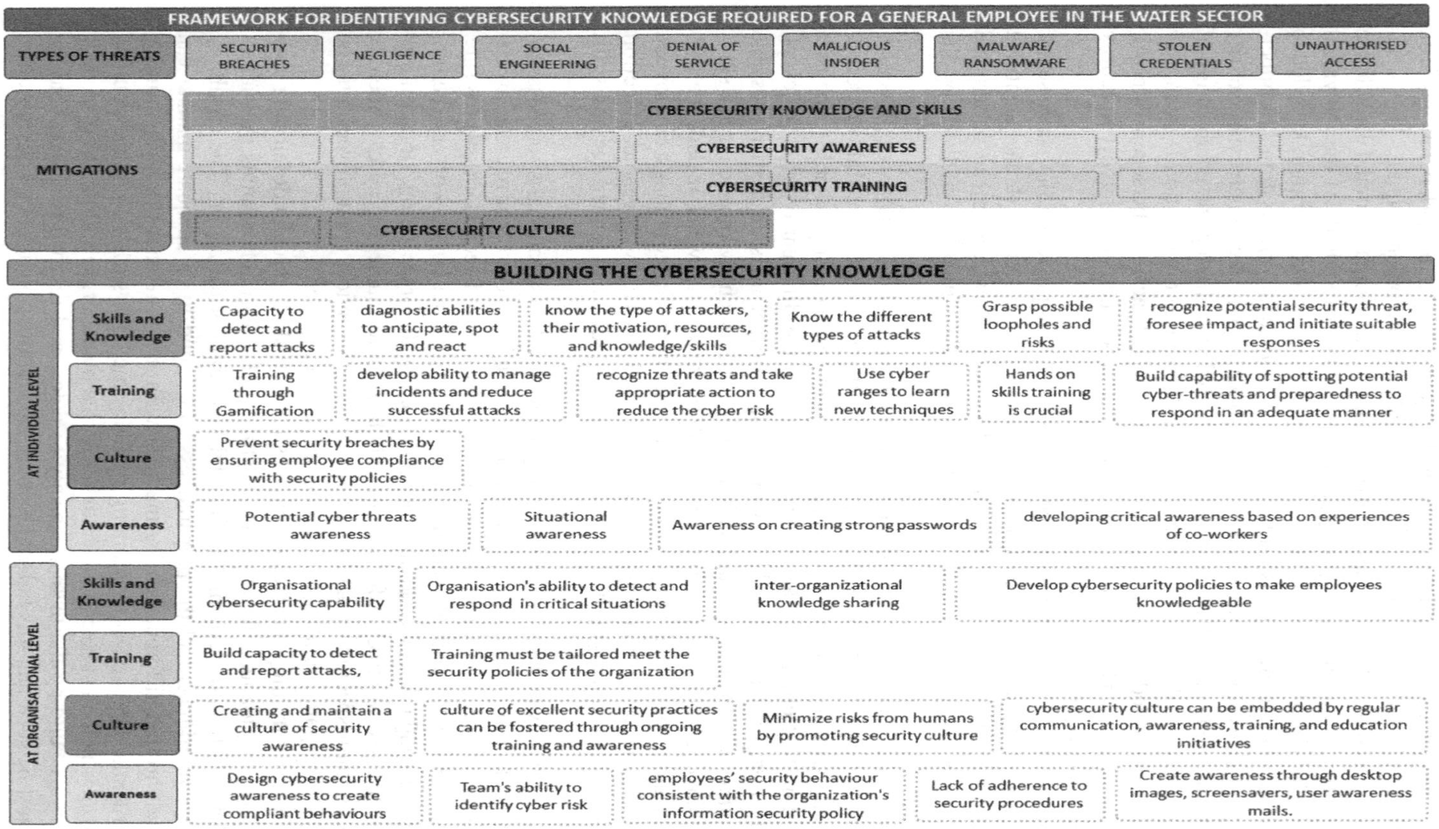

Fig. 5. Framework for identifying cybersecurity knowledge

The creation of a cybersecurity culture within the organisation should be an end goal. Cybersecurity culture should be embedded within organisations to reduce the occurrence of security breaches. This can be achieved by ensuring that a culture of CSA is created and maintained within the organisation, fostering excellent security practices through ongoing training and awareness. Regular communication is important to maintain the culture of safe practices; this can be achieved through several initiatives, including education and awareness, management support, policy, and information sharing.

6 Conclusion

The aim of this research was to develop approaches to follow in building the cybersecurity knowledge and awareness for a typical employee, to assist in the creation of a cybersecurity culture within organizations in the water sector. It is acknowledged that organisational resilience can only be achieved through a layered approach with a combination of technical, formal, and informal mitigation strategies and that cybersecurity knowledge alone will not be sufficient. The focus of this paper was to determine the general cybersecurity knowledge requirements which must be considered by organisations looking into promoting a cybersecurity culture.

The finding of the study was the identification of the different cyber threats that employees in the water sector must be aware of as well as the approaches that can be followed to build employees cybersecurity knowledge. Employees that are aware of the vulnerabilities are likely to distinguish possible security risks, predict their impact, and take appropriate action if the organisational structures are put in place to facilitate such actions.

6.1 Limitations and Future Research

This was limited to peer reviewed publications and was limited to six databases that include; ProQuest, IEEE, Emerald, Engineering Village, Wiley Online and ScienceDirect. This review has specifically targeted as an initial literature review relating to the critical infrastructure context. The findings of this initial study proved to mostly include general cybersecurity skills and knowledge which can be utilised in various sectors, not only limited to the water sector or the critical infrastructure sector. This paper will be extended in the future to include additional literature outside of the critical infrastructure context that could be applied in the water sector context which will assist in understanding the problem more thoroughly.

The study will serve as the foundation for future work, which will involve the expansion of the literature review and the development of the theoretical framework through feedback from water industry specialists. The finalized framework will guide the creation of instructional materials that will educate personnel in the industry on how to better safeguard infrastructure and foster a cybersecurity culture in the sector.

Acknowledgements. This research study was supported by the Water Research Commission (WRC) of South Africa, grant number 2021/2023-00354.

References

1. Panguluri, S., Phillips, W., Cusimano, J.: Protecting water and wastewater infrastructure from cyber attacks. Front. Earth Sci. **5**(4), 406–413 (2011)
2. Von Solms, R., Von Solms, B.: National cyber security in South Africa: a letter to the minister of cyber security. In: Proceedings of the 10th International Conference on Cyber Warfare and Security, ICCWS 2015, pp. 369–374 (2015)
3. Parker, A., Brown, I.: Skills requirements for cyber security professionals: a content analysis of job descriptions in South Africa. In: Venter, H., Loock, M., Coetzee, M., Eloff, M., Eloff, J. (eds.) ISSA 2018. CCIS, vol. 973, pp. 176–192. Springer, Cham (2019). https://doi.org/10.1007/978-3-030-11407-7_13
4. Burghouwt, P., Maris, M., Peski, S., Luiijf, E., Voorde, I., Spruit, M.: Cyber targets water management. In: Havarneanu, G., Setola, R., Nassopoulos, H., Wolthusen, S. (eds.) CRITIS 2016. LNCS, vol. 10242, pp. 38–49. Springer, Cham (2017). https://doi.org/10.1007/978-3-319-71368-7_4
5. Alshaikh, M.: Computers & security developing cybersecurity culture to influence employee behavior : a practice perspective. **98** (2020). https://doi.org/10.1016/j.cose.2020.102003
6. Reegård, K., Blackett, C., Katta, V.: The concept of cybersecurity culture. In: Proceedings of the 29th European Safety and Reliability Conference, pp. 4036–4043 (2019). https://doi.org/10.3850/978-981-11-2724-3_0761-cd
7. Xiao, Y., Watson, M.: Guidance on conducting a systematic literature review. J. Plan. Educ. Res. **39**(1), 93–112 (2019)
8. Mohamed Shaffril, H.A., Samsuddin, S.F., Abu Samah, A.: The ABC of systematic literature review: the basic methodological guidance for beginners. Qual. Quant. **55**(4), 1319–1346 (2020). https://doi.org/10.1007/s11135-020-01059-6
9. Kraus, S., Breier, M., Dasí-Rodríguez, S.: The art of crafting a systematic literature review in entrepreneurship research. Int. Entrepreneurship Manag. J. **16**(3), 1023–1042 (2020). https://doi.org/10.1007/s11365-020-00635-4
10. Tawfik, G.M., et al.: A step by step guide for conducting a systematic review and meta-analysis with simulation data. Trop. Med. Health **47**(1), 1–9 (2019)
11. Svahnberg, M., Gorschek, T., Feldt, R., Torkar, R., Saleem, S.B., Shafique, M.U.: A systematic review on strategic release planning models. Inf. Softw. Technol. **52**(3), 237–248 (2010)
12. Bettany-Saltikov, J.: How to do a systematic literature review in nursing. A step-by-step guide. Nurse Educ. Pract. **13**(3) (2012)
13. Liberati, A., et al.: The PRISMA statement for reporting systematic reviews and meta-analyses of studies that evaluate health care interventions: explanation and elaboration. J. Clin. Epidemiol. **62**(10), e1–e34 (2009). https://doi.org/10.1016/j.jclinepi.2009.06.006
14. Kitchenham, B.: A rare case of Erdheim-Chester disease in the breast. Proced. Perform. Syst. Rev. **37**(1), 79–83 (2004)
15. Panchal, K., Damodaran, M.: Computation of the flowfield in the vicinity of an electric vehicle platform. In: Saha, A.K., Das, D., Rajesh Srivastava, P.K., Panigrahi, K.M. (eds.) Fluid Mechanics and Fluid Power – Contemporary Research, pp. 333–341. Springer, New Delhi (2017). https://doi.org/10.1007/978-81-322-2743-4_32
16. Noyes, J., Popay, J., Pearson, A., Hannes, K., Booth, A.: Qualitative research and Cochrane reviews. In: Cochrane Handbook for Systematic Reviews of Interventions: Cochrane Book Series, October 2017, pp. 571–591 (2008)
17. Braun, V., Clarke, V.: Qualitative research in psychology using thematic analysis in psychology using thematic analysis in psychology (2006)
18. Patton, M.: Qualitative Research and Evaluation Methods, 4th edn., vol. 148 (2015)

19. Adams, M., Makramalla, M.: Paget's disease: another paramyxovirus in the archaeological record. cybersecurity skills training: an attacker-centric gamified approach. Technol. Innov. Manag. Rev. **5**(1) (2015). https://doi.org/10.15173/nexus.v12i1.150

20. Mishra, S., et al.: A modular approach to teaching critical infrastructure protection concepts to engineering, technology and computing students. In: Proceedings - Frontiers in Education Conference, FIE, 2016-Novem (2016). https://doi.org/10.1109/FIE.2016.7757367

21. Nagarajan, A., Allbeck, J.M., Sood, A., Janssen, T.L.: Exploring game design for cybersecurity training. In: Proceedings - 2012 IEEE International Conference on Cyber Technology in Automation, Control, and Intelligent Systems, CYBER 2012, pp. 256–262 (2012)

22. Daniel Ani, U.P., He, H.M., Tiwari, A.: Human capability evaluation approach for cyber security in critical industrial infrastructure. In: Nicholson, D. (ed.) Advances in Human Factors in Cybersecurity Advances in Intelligent Systems and Computing, vol. 501, pp. 267–277. Springer, Cham (2016). https://doi.org/10.1007/978-3-319-41932-9_14

23. Prins, S., Marnewick, A., von Solms, S.: Cybersecurity awareness in an industrial control systems company. In: European Conference on Information Warfare and Security, ECCWS, 2020-June, pp. 314–323 (2020)

CAP: Patching the Human Vulnerability

Thaddeus Eze[✉] and Neil Hawker

Computer Science Department, University of Chester, Chester, England
{t.eze,n.hawker}@chester.ac.uk

Abstract. Cyber threats to organisations across all industries are increasing in both volume and complexity, leading to significant, and sometimes severe, consequences. The common weakest link in organisations security is the human vulnerability. The sudden popularity of remote-working due to the Covid-19 pandemic opened organisations and their employees up to more risks, particularly as many workers believe that they are more distracted when at home. Existing cyber training using a 'one-size-fits-all' approach has been proven inefficient/ineffective and the need for a more fit-for-purpose training is required. When it comes to cyber training, we know that there is no single-training-fits-all solution – people have different technical skills, different prior knowledge and experience, are in different roles, exposed to different security risks, and require knowledge that is relevant to what they do. This study makes a case for tailored role-based cybersecurity training suitable for awareness within organisations across multiple industries. The study explores the strengths and weaknesses of existing cyber training and literature to make recommendations on efficient awareness and training programme strategies. The study carries out knowledge and task analysis of job roles to create profiles of skills and knowledge they require. These are grouped by topic and level to form scenario-based multiple-choice questions which are mapped to create a Cyber Awareness Platform (CAP). A CAP prototype is introduced as a flexible web-based system allowing users to assess their prior knowledge and skills personalised to their role. Knowledge gaps and training needs are identified, and recommendations are tailored to the individual. Initial analysis of CAP shows promising results, indicating that such role-sensitive solution would be highly beneficial to users. This offers further development opportunities in producing an all-in-one cyber assessment and training platform.

Keywords: Cyber Awareness Platform · Cybersecurity awareness · Role-based training · Human vulnerability · Tailored cybersecurity · Task analysis

1 Introduction

Businesses have been able to benefit significantly from developments in technology that allows them to interact with their customers, suppliers, and other businesses in the digital world. No longer are trading hours restricted to those of a physical store presence. Businesses can trade 24/7 using e-commerce, mobile apps, smart home digital assistants, and through social media channels. However, as these technologies are adopted, they

© IFIP International Federation for Information Processing 2022
Published by Springer Nature Switzerland AG 2022
N. Clarke and S. Furnell (Eds.): HAISA 2022, IFIP AICT 658, pp. 106–119, 2022.
https://doi.org/10.1007/978-3-031-12172-2_9

bring new security risks and challenges, leading to more attack surfaces. Bad actors take advantage of security vulnerabilities to attack business information systems which can lead to data breaches. Confidential data such as employees' logins, company secrets, and customer personal data are then at risk of being leaked, resulting in major reputational damage and serious ramifications that can be hard to recover from. A study by VMware Carbon Black [1] reported 70% of respondents had suffered from damages to their brand image following a data breach. Rankin [2] puts the average cost of a data breach at $141 for each record stolen while IBM [3] explains that an average breach involves 25,575 records. According to [3], the average time to identify and contain a breach is 279 days and the average cost of a data breach rose 12% between 2015 and 2020, costing about $3.92 million to correct.

The UK's Information Commissioners Office fined the University of Greenwich £120,000 in 2018 after multiple cyber-attacks on a legacy microsite resulted in around 20,000 people's personal data being breached [4]. The site that was to facilitate a conference in 2004 was not shutdown or maintained. This meant it was susceptible to SQL injection attacks in 2013 which led to further attacks in 2016 [4]. The 2017 WannaCry ransomware attack on the UK's National Health Service (NHS) was partly possible due to a significant number of machines within the NHS, at the time, running on older unpatched versions of Windows. In 2018, British Airways (BA) revealed it had been victim to a data breach leaking 380,000 customers personal and payment details [6]. The rogue code, a web-based card skimmer, used by the attackers sent personal and credit card information silently to a disguised, but legitimate looking domain '*baways.com*' once customers press the submit button. In 2015, a clinic staff in London accidentally leaked sensitive information of patients by using Cc (Copy) instead of Bcc (Blind Copy) in an email[1]. These, and most successful breaches, are due to human errors.

Human error is the weakest security link and continues to be the common reason for successful cyber-attacks and data breaches [7, 8]. A study by Hancock [9] to understand the impacts of human mistakes and vulnerabilities on cybersecurity found that 88% of data breaches are caused by human error. Common human errors causing successful cyber-attacks include system misconfiguration, poor patch management, use of default usernames/passwords and easily guessable passwords, loss of mobile devices, and disclosure of controlled information via email [7]. A major rise in cyber-attacks, targeting home workers since the Covid-19 pandemic, involving malicious emails attempting to steal employee credentials have been reported [10]. These phishing attempts involved tricking employees to use fake sign-in pages for systems they would regularly use. Employee's corporate accounts for VPNs and video conferencing accounts such as Zoom were frequently targeted. It is then evident that reducing the level of human errors will significantly improve cyber security posture. The best patch for human vulnerability has always been training, awareness, and education. With well-trained employees, organisations can be more prepared and protected from cyber-attacks. However, training needs to be fit-for-purpose.

The traditional cybersecurity training approaches are mostly ineffective in changing employees' behaviours. These behaviours have proven the human as the weakest link in cybersecurity. A usual practice, within organisations, is to have a generic training

---

[1] https://bit.ly/3qaQw83.

programme for everyone. So, if an organisation wishes to sign up for staff training, they choose a provider or a training course and lump everyone into it. However, when it comes to cyber training, we know that there is no *single-training-fits-all* solution – people have different technical skills, different prior knowledge and experience, are in different roles, exposed to different security risks (some more complex than others), require knowledge that is relevant to what they do etc.

An efficient solution would be a role-based tailored training approach that involves a generic classification of roles as well as a finer-grained classification that considers the individual's personal prior knowledge in addition to their role. There is an increase in recent studies recommending tailored training as against generic '*off the shelf*' packages [7, 8, 11]. Although role-based/tailored training is not new, it is not sufficient to consider the individual's role in determining their training requirement without also considering their prior knowledge. So, the question is whether we can come up with a tailored training system that appreciates people's prior knowledge and current role. A starting point is to design a system that can correctly determine one's relevant cyber-related knowledge and be able to recommend required role-based training. This will involve task analysis to be able to understand different roles in order to capture what is relevant to them in terms of cyber knowledge. This project attempts to answer the question; '*What is an appropriate cybersecurity training and/or body of knowledge for the particular individual*'? This involves thorough overview of existing approaches and articulation of a widely accepted solution. It is expected that the intended product, the CAP, would help companies organise efficient and fit-for-purpose cyber training.

With regards to training, the focus of our proposed solution is not on mode of delivery. Yes, nature/mode of delivery is an important aspect to consider as well as the content itself. However, the question that needs to be answered first is '*what (in terms of content) constitute an effective and efficient training for the individual (emphasis on personalised, role-based training)*'? This will need to explore/address a number of issues – task analysis, knowledge analysis, existing or new cybersecurity body of knowledge, understanding the individual's position on the knowledge spectrum etc. So, the proposed role-based tailored training is not limited to a generic classification of known role groups. It takes a finer-grained approach of determining role grouping and the consideration of prior and required knowledge within those groups.

2 Literature Review

The question of terminology needs to be addressed first. Cybersecurity awareness, training, and education all involve some level of learning that leads to changes in user behavior. Although they are sometimes used interchangeably, they do differ in meaning. Awareness establishes a generic foundation of security understanding and deals with security related issues that all users, regardless of job role, must be aware of. Training deals with teaching the user the dos and don'ts, while performing their tasks, in order to meet specific security requirements. Education is a more formal arrangement of pursuing a wider knowledge and usually offered by a third party. See [12] for more details. In the context of this paper, cyber awareness/training is where a person has both the knowledge and the understanding of the importance of information security to protect themselves and/or the organisation they work for from cyber-crime/attack [13, 14].

There are several existing cybersecurity awareness and training resources available, including research that identify recommendations for creating successful cyber training. While these are interesting materials, most are about modes or methods of training delivery and not about how to determine what training, in terms of content, is needed.

2.1 Existing Cyber Security Awareness and Training

The UK National Cyber Security Centre (NCSC)'s study [15] to understand training issues with small to medium sized enterprises (SMEs) highlighted key issues of organisations struggling to explain why cybersecurity is important and explained technical aspects that are relevant to employees. They produced two set of resource materials for users, depending on their technical knowledge. The *'Top Tips for Staff'* training package, covering defending against phishing, using strong passwords, securing devices, and reporting incidents with the premise *'if in doubt, call it out'* is aimed at those staff who have little to no technical knowledge. The *'10 Steps to Cyber Security'* guidance [11] helps security and technical staff within organisations manage their cybersecurity risks. These materials can be used as base layer of core cybersecurity skills required for training that are applicable to all employees within an organisation. NCSC [11], as well as [7, 8], recommend, and we agree, tailoring cybersecurity training to the needs of the organisation rather than having a generic *off-the-shelf* training package.

Regner *et al.* [8] proposed their 'Cybersecurity Awareness TRAining Model (CATRAM)' as a replacement for traditional cybersecurity training that have become ineffective in changing employee's behaviour. This is asserted from the fact that human error and actions continue to happen despite organisations having strong security controls in place. According to [8], CATRAM addresses the deficiencies in existing cyber awareness and training available. The model targets different levels of role within an organisation such as board level, executives, managers, and IT specialists. Each level has their own part to play in promoting and ensuring a consistent cyber aware approach to threats. Axelos [16] supports cyber specific training, tailored to employee roles that takes place on a regular basis. The CATRAM model is designed to be adapted and used across multiple industries and audiences, making it more flexible and effective than traditional cyber training programs [8]. The role-based tailored training proposed by [8] follows a generic classification of roles. Whereas this is an interesting solution, a more effective approach would consider the individual's personal prior knowledge in addition to their role. This new approach would start with role grouping and then move on to consider prior knowledge within those groups.

He and Zhang [7], in their study, 'Enterprise cybersecurity training and awareness programs: Recommendations for success', put forward a number of recommendations for a successful cybersecurity training. Two of the recommendations include *Personalisation* – using examples that help employees relate to the training and also instill the behaviour that cybersecurity risks are not just at work but at home too, and *Relevancy* – providing training that is tailored to roles and responsibilities.

The case can be made that tailored training, whether in delivery or determining need, is efficient and yields better result in the long-term. McCormac *et al.* [17] state that there is potential value in tailoring cybersecurity training to a person's personality and learning style, which could maximise participants learning outcomes. Pattinson *et al.*

[18] found that matching an individual's learning style to appropriate training improves the participants information security awareness (ISA) and that an individual's ISA score did not increase significantly when training regularity was increased, suggesting that an organisation may not need to increase their training budget but instead tailor training to the individual.

2.2 Related Studies

Shinoda *et al.* [19] propose their cybersecurity training framework CyTrONE, which uses classical training paradigm of scenario and topic-based questions along with practical exercises. This is an important means for assessing a person's competencies and weaknesses. Whilst [19] involves the creation of a practical training environment, which is beyond the scope for this study, it is still useful as it also deals with cybersecurity training content generation and environment setup tasks which is a focus and aspect considered by CAP. Lessons from CyTrONE will feed into CAP future research.

A study [20] for developing cyber education and training for the UK police forces focused on various roles within a police force and involved establishing responsibilities and role-based knowledge and skills profiles within that force. A web-based prototype tool was created to allow employees assess their individual cybercrime training needs [20]. The research links into this study as it involves assessing employee's cyber awareness and training needs whilst also considering their role and prior knowledge.

Oyinloye [21] also carried out a study to develop an application to determine an understanding of a user's cybersecurity awareness and make suggestions based on these outcomes. [21] is useful to draw lessons from as it found participants in awareness tests who scored high overall had weaknesses in other areas such as viruses and malware, so it is important to tailor training recommendations to individual responses.

Overall, the studies and works discussed in this review highlighted the need for a tailored cyber training solution over one-size-fits-all approaches for organisations. One key finding is that whilst there are examples of tailored training [8, 22], there is still a gap for taking employees existing knowledge into consideration as part of the tailored training. Skills frameworks, e.g., CIISec [23] and SFIA [24], can be used to inform this study's skills and roles mapping design. This is discussed further in the next section.

2.3 Assessing and Measuring Skills

Assessing a person's prior cybersecurity related knowledge and using that information to determine their training need is an important aspect of CAP. The ability to assess and measure an employee's skills is crucial to understanding their specific training needs. The Chartered Institute of Information Security (CIISec) Skills Framework [23] provides basis of what knowledge and skills are expected for 11 security disciplines – from level 1 (basic knowledge) to 6 (expert/lead practitioner) in each discipline. Figure 1 shows sections of the framework along with associated security disciplines.

The CIISec skills, knowledge, and role frameworks are a strong basis for developing assessment questions to assess a person's knowledge against a section. An example for a software developer could be testing section C level 3 (*C3 – Secure Development*) to see which level that particular employee meets. It would then be possible to identify

Fig. 1. CIISec framework skills areas and security disciplines [23].

appropriate training on a level-by-level basis for employees by role [23]. Watkins *et al.* [25] explain the methods available for carrying out needs assessments to make decisions. On a basic principle, the first steps to a need's assessment are to identify the gaps between the current state and desired state. In this study, it is the gaps in an employee's cyber awareness knowledge. Determining the employee's needs can be done by skills mapping to a framework such as [23]. Where the outcome is a lower skill level than desired, interventions can be put in place to highlight these and refer to suitable training.

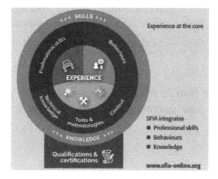

Fig. 2. SFIA diagram showing the elements that make up the competency framework [24].

Skills Framework for the Information Age (SFIA) is a not-for-profit organisation and model for managing skills and competencies for those working in IT and other digital disciplines. The elements that make up the framework are shown in Fig. 2. SFIA [26] state that everybody has information security responsibilities and should make it part of their day-to-day working. Each SFIA level increases in information security responsibilities as shown in Table 1. SFIA skills can be mapped to other frameworks such as NICE (National Initiative for Cybersecurity Education) work roles [27]. The framework is comprised of 7 high-level categories of common cybersecurity areas, 33 distinct areas of cybersecurity work and importantly 52 work roles. The work roles are in detailed groupings of what is expected in those roles made up of specific knowledge, skills, and abilities to perform tasks within that role [28]. Whereas the NICE framework's focus is cybersecurity roles, the SFIA framework is applicable to wider roles that interact with IT [24].

Table 1. SFIA Information security attributes in levels of responsibility [26].

SFIA level	Information security attributes and responsibilities
1 Follow	Understands and applies basic personal security practice
2 Assist	Is fully aware of and complies with essential organisational security practices expected of the individual
3 Apply	Understands how own role impacts security and demonstrates routine security practice and knowledge required for own work
4 Enable	Fully understands the importance of security to own work and the operation of the organisation. Seeks specialist security knowledge or advice when required to support own work or work of immediate colleagues
5 Ensure, Advise	Proactively ensures security is appropriately addressed within their area by self and others. Engages or works with security specialists as necessary. Contributes to the security culture of the organisation
6 Initiate, Influence	Takes a leading role in promoting security throughout own area of responsibilities and collectively in the organisations
7 Set Strategy, Inspire, Mobilise	Champions security within own area of work

These frameworks are instrumental in the classification of role-holder's knowledge and design of knowledge assessment for the Cyber Awareness Platform (CAP).

3   CAP Design

CAP is a tailored framework that helps us understand the cybersecurity need of an individual and identify a suitable training for that individual. The system can assess a person's cybersecurity knowledge and identify knowledge gaps whilst considering their role-profile and existing skills. Figure 3 shows the different components that make up the CAP framework. To efficiently recommend an appropriate training, the system considers two important aspects – *Knowledge* and *Task*. Knowledge Analysis (KA) establishes a mapping of recognised body of knowledge against which any claim of cybersecurity knowledge can be tested. This can feed from the CyBOK[2] knowledge areas [29] and/or any existing cybersecurity body of knowledge like the CIISec and SFIA frameworks discussed in Sect. 2. The vPK component identifies the user's cybersecurity knowledge with reference to the body of knowledge expressed in KA. KA's knowledge

---

[2] https://www.cybok.org/.

base provides a basis for developing assessment questions from which to assess a person's knowledge against different areas. This can test generic or specific knowledge, depending on implementation choice.

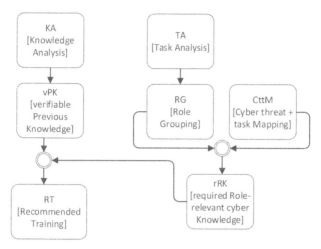

Fig. 3. CAP framework.

Task Analysis (TA) determines the tasks employees (users) are expected to undertake by role. The guide to task analysis in [30] is a good reference for conducting TA. The result here is an understanding of the relevant activities or tasks performed by a role which will help in determining the kind of cybersecurity risks the role faces. Job descriptions and person specifications are good sources of information here. This means that roles are coded into the system, making CAP adaptable, and for that to happen, roles need to be grouped. RG deals with classification of identified roles into groups of common themes, from cybersecurity viewpoint. These could be high-level or detailed groupings of roles with similar or overlapping requirements and tasks. This makes it easier to understand and define a set of cybersecurity threats associated to those task groups (CttM). So, the CttM component establishes the common cybersecurity threats associated to roles. Although there are generic security threats (e.g., human error), there are also threats that are unique to certain job roles (e.g., whaling). The outputs of RG and CttM are mapped to give an understanding of generic cybersecurity threats and those unique to particular role groups. This then informs the required cybersecurity knowledge relevant to those roles (rRK).

After establishing the user's existing cybersecurity knowledge (vPK) and their role-relevant knowledge (rRK), a kind of gap analysis is performed (mapping of vPK and rRK) to then identify knowledge gap and recommend required training (RT). It is important to note that each of the components in Fig. 3 could form a branch of research on its own. Figure 4 shows the general process of generating training recommendations.

The subprocesses referenced in Fig. 4 have been explained above but full details are omitted here. CAP uses a relational database which makes it flexible to be managed, allowing entities such as questions, topics, or roles to be amended quickly, through an admin panel, based on feedback, without a full rebuild and deployment of the system.

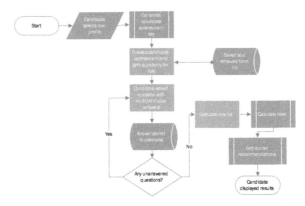

Fig. 4. User assessment flow diagram.

The design presented her is used to implement a web-based prototype in Sect. 4.

4 CAP Implementation and Analysis

CAP is implemented as a role-based assessment system that allows users to take a cybersecurity skills assessment based on their role. Following an assessment, users are recommended tailored training course(s) based on their level and performance. The prototype, presented here, provides the basis of a system that could be further developed into a product. It is web based and uses a database backend, along with an admin panel to allow configuration of user assessments, roles, courses, questions, topics, and levels.

For the prototype, and to manage the scope of the study, only two roles (*Data Analyst* and *Web Developer*) and three knowledge levels are used for proof of concept. The subset of topics and levels used are based on CIISec's framework sections [23]. The CAP levels are; Level 1 – Basic knowledge of principles, Level 2 – Working knowledge and understanding, and Level 3 – Expert. Questions around topics are written to be scenario and competency based, giving users four possible answers with one-best-answer. Four possible answers and a single correct response makes the probability of a user correctly guessing an answer 25% and incorrectly choosing a distractor 75% [31].

4.1 CAP – User Viewpoint and Admin Configuration

Figure 5 shows the prototype system's homepage. Job roles are displayed from the database job roles table, with an image relating to the role to make the system more visually appealing. This is where users first choose the role closest to their job to begin the assessment process. Once a role is selected, a pre-assessment screen that confirms the chosen role name along with a unique user assessment code is displayed. Users can use this code in future to continue an assessment or access their results, if they have already completed it, using the *Existing Assessment* menu page. Once the user starts the assessment, they are asked a series of multiple-choice questions. Only one question is asked at a time to not overwhelm the user and lower the user experience which could result in them performing less than they normally would [32].

Fig. 5. CAP prototype role selection homepage.

Once the user has finished answering all the questions required for their role, they are taken to the results page which is made up of several sections starting with their determined level followed by recommended cyber training courses based on their performance. Statistics are shown providing how long they took and how many questions they answered correct/incorrect as well as the total. A *Results* section lists the possible levels followed by their overall percentage and the determined level. A *Topic analysis* section shows a radar chart listing all the topic areas assessed and the user's performance for each out of 100%. This helps visualise the user's result which can be important for visual learners as one of the four perceptual preferences for input of information [33]. A *Scoring criteria and topic level analysis* card explains the scoring formula, followed by the percentage correct by topic at each level and level total. This provides a clear way to see which areas they performed well in and those that have room for improvement. If the user did not score 100% then an *Incorrectly answered questions* section is shown. The answer the user selected is marked as well as the correct response shown in green text. This allows the user to see where they went wrong and learn the correct answer.

The system can be configured using an administrator account through a secure area. Administrators can see attempted and/or completed assessments. There are also functions to delete and access the results or manually continue the assessment if it is not complete. When creating or editing a role, the topics that apply to that role can be assigned. This is how a candidate's assessment knows which questions to use as these are attached to topics and then to roles through the relational database design. One of the important parts of CAP is the ability for administrators to manage the question bank for assessments.

The flexibility of being able to amend questions and answers easily is important for CAP to be adaptable and user friendly.

Relevant security considerations are also made. For example, ASP.net Core's Identity package, currently considered one of the secure password hashing algorithms that makes it harder to brute force passwords [34], was used to implement the login functionality to secure the administrator area. The system also protects against cross-site request forgery (CSRF) by using ASP.net core's automatic forms protection for POST requests. This means a hard to guess verification token is generated by the server-side code that is tied to the user's session and placed in a hidden field as shown in Fig. 6. When the user submits the form, the code is validated to check if it is valid for that user, if it is not correct the form data is not processed, and an exception occurs. This protects both the application and the user from a malicious actor trying to post form data from third party web page [35].

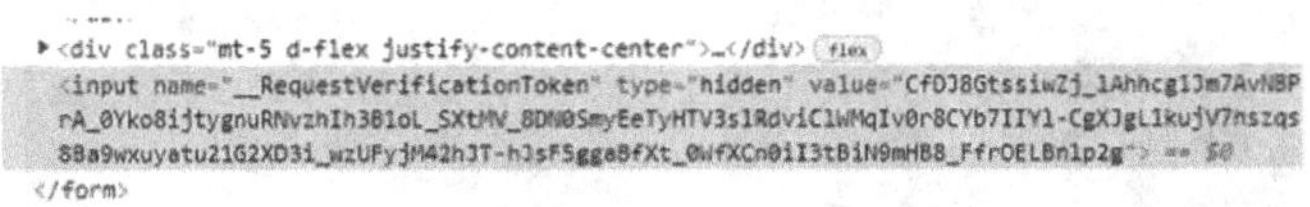

```
► <div class="mt-5 d-flex justify-content-center">_</div> (flex)
    <input name="__RequestVerificationToken" type="hidden" value="CfOJ8GtssiwZj_1Ahhcg1Jm7AvNBP
    rA_0Yko8ijtygnuRNvzhIh381oL_SXtMV_8DN0SmyEeTyHTV3s1RdviC1WMqIv0r8CYb7IIY1-CgXJgL1kujV7nszqs
    8Ba9wxuyatu21G2XD3i_wzUFyjM42h3T-h3sF5ggaBfXt_0WfXCn0iI3tBiN9mHB8_FfrOELBn1p2g"> == $0
    </form>
    </main>
```

Fig. 6. CAP CSRF protection showing the unique request token in the HTML source.

4.2 Testing, Results, and Analysis

As part of this study, a cyber awareness survey was conducted to gauge the current state of cyber awareness within organisations. This helped with making informed decisions about the design of CAP. 106 participants, from 30 different sectors (majority of 38% from higher education) responded to the survey. On the need for tailored versus generic cyber training, a strong 94% agreed that '*tailored cyber training that respects my current knowledge, skill set and role would be beneficial to me*'. Considering the sample size and spread of participants in this survey, this makes a reasonable case for CAP.

Three participants took part in testing the CAP prototype, of which two were Web Developers and one was a Data Analyst. All were employed in the higher education sector. Two participants had prior cyber training and all considered themselves cyber aware. Two participants felt that CAP provided an accurate representation of their knowledge and possible training solutions for their knowledge gaps. One participant felt it was unclear how the levels were determined and made suggestions that the system could explain the calculation and criteria for levels. Table 2 shows the post-assessment question findings which were mainly positive. Notably, all three participants agreed they can see the benefit of using such a system in the workplace. One of the web developers scored 91.7% in the assessment but was capped at level one because their data security score was 50%. As a result, they were recommended GDPR and Data Protection training. Additionally, a PCI DSS Awareness course was recommended for being at level two within the secure systems development topic area.

This is a limited result as we cannot draw conclusions from a test of just three participants. However, this is a meaningful proof of concept on which to build.

Table 2. CAP prototype participant post assessment question findings. Three participants in all.

Post assessment statement	Findings
I felt confident using the system	All agreed or strongly agreed
The system was user friendly and intuitive to use	All agreed or strongly agreed
The design (look and feel) of the system was appealing	2 agreed whilst 1 disagreed
I felt that the system was accessible	All agreed
I can see the benefit in CAP being used in the workplace	All agreed
Training courses suggested are of interest and relevance to my role	2 agreed whilst 1 disagreed

Following the feedback from participants, several improvements were made to the system. These include:

- design, colour, and styling improvements; displaying the scoring criteria with the topic/level breakdowns to help candidates understand their result further;
- adding incorrect questions to the results page highlighting the candidate's response and the correct answer;
- and promoting recommended training courses to the top of the results page, so it is clear what the candidate needs to 'do', followed by their assessment outcome showing 'how' they got those recommendations, and lastly the 'why' showing their incorrect responses.

Opportunities have been, and will continue to be, identified for future CAP improvements. This will include explanations for each wrong and correct answer to help educate the candidate on the reasoning. Also, future work will include surveying a larger and more represented potential user group and detailed usability test with significant number of participants. With such improvement, more accurate conclusions can be drawn.

5   Conclusion

This study was undertaken to contribute towards improving cyber awareness and training within organisations and therefore reduce successful cyber incidents. The aims include developing a system that can assess a person's cyber awareness knowledge and identify gaps whilst considering their role profile and pre-existing skills to help companies organise efficient and fit for purpose training recommendations replacing the '*one-size-fits-all*' approach as advocated by [9, 20]. The CAP prototype does this by allowing Web Developer and Data Analyst employees to be assessed and provided with links to suitable courses dependent on their assessment outcomes. In CAP, questions are tied to topics, levels, and roles which allows candidates to be assessed at a topic level and make training recommendations based on these. Whilst this study concentrated on two role-profiles, generic recommendations can be made that apply to all roles and should be considered in cyber awareness and training.

A key limitation of the work is the few roles available for assessment as well as the depth the role profiles go into. However, this study has put in place the fundamental mechanisms for future work to be carried out to build-up more role profiles as well as higher assessment levels. It is hoped that this study would further research in this area. With additional improvements to the CAP prototype system, and detailed test with more participants, we intend to develop an all-in-one product from assessment to training employees based on identified needs in future. As the COVID-19 pandemic has increased demand for remote working, it is vital that effective cyber training is delivered to protect organisations.

References

1. VMware Carbon Black. Global Threat Report (2020). https://bit.ly/3LJ9gnk. Accessed 05 Apr 2022
2. Rankin, B.: Examining the Total Cost of Ownership of a Network Intrusion Detection System (2018). https://bit.ly/3uae4MD. Accessed 05 Apr 2022
3. IBM. How much would a data breach cost your business? (2020). https://www.ibm.com/security/data-breach. Accessed 05 Apr 2022
4. Eckersley, S.: The University of Greenwich - Montetary Penalty Notice (2018). https://bit.ly/3uOR6cY. Accessed 05 Apr 2022
5. Department of Health & Social Care. Securing cyber resilience in health and care: Progress update October 2018 (2018). https://bit.ly/3LG8aZE. Accessed 05 Apr 2022
6. Klijnsma, Y.: Inside the Magecart Breach of British Airways: How 22 Lines of Code Claimed 380,000 Victims. RiskIQ, 11 September 2018. https://bit.ly/3j9JI6S
7. He, W., Zhang, Z.: Enterprise cybersecurity training and awareness programs: recommendations for success. J. Organ. Comput. Electron. Commer. **29**(4), 249–257 (2019). https://doi.org/10.1080/10919392.2019.1611528
8. Regner, S., Jordi, S.-R., Victor, C., Jeimy, J.C.M.: An effective cybersecurity training model to support an organizational awareness program: the cybersecurity awareness TRAining model (CATRAM). A case study in Canada. J. Cases Inf. Technol. (JCIT) **21**(3), 26–39 (2019). https://doi.org/10.4018/JCIT.2019070102
9. Hancock, J.: Psychology of Human Error: understand the mistakes that compromise your company's cybersecurity. Tessian Research (2020). https://bit.ly/3Lzn1Fg
10. Jolly, J.: Huge rise in hacking attacks on home workers during lockdown (2020). https://bit.ly/3NMq4vJ. Accessed 05 Apr 2022
11. NCSC. 10 steps to cyber security - Common cyber attacks - reducing the impact (2019). https://bit.ly/3LJK3cs. Accessed 05 Apr 2022
12. Chapple, M., Stewart, J., Gibson, D.: Certified Information Systems Security Professional Official Study Guide, 9th edn., pp 96–98. Wiley, Hoboekn (2021)
13. HM Government. National Cyber Security Strategy 2016–2021 (2016). https://bit.ly/3J5mI3r
14. Zwilling, M., Klien, G., Lesjak, D., Wiechetek, Ł., Cetin, F., Basim, H.N.: Cyber security awareness, knowledge and behavior: a comparative study. J. Comput. Inf. Syst. **62**, 82–97 (2020). https://doi.org/10.1080/08874417.2020.1712269
15. NCSC. NCSC's new cyber security training for staff now available. National Cyber Security Centre, 14 April 2021. https://bit.ly/3DHRlL6
16. Axelos. RESILIA® Cyber Resilience Best Practice. TSO (The Stationery Office) (2015)
17. McCormac, A., Zwaans, T., Parsons, K., Calic, D., Butavicius, M., Pattinson, M.: Individual differences and information security awareness. Comput. Hum. Behav. **69**, 151–156 (2017). https://doi.org/10.1016/j.chb.2016.11.065

18. Pattinson, M., et al.: Matching training to individual learning styles improves information security awareness. Inf. Comput. Secur. **28**(1), 1–14 (2019). https://doi.org/10.1108/ics-01-2019-0022

19. Shinoda, Y., Tan, Y., Chinen, K.-I., Tang, D., Pham, C., Beuran, R.: CyTrONE: an integrated cybersecurity training framework. In: Proceedings of the 3rd International Conference on Information Systems Security and Privacy (2017)

20. Elvey, C.A.: Policing the UK Cyber Threat: Developing Education and Training for the Front Line. University of Chester (2020)

21. Oyinloye, T.A.: Towards Cyber-User Awareness: Design and Evaluation. University of Chester (2019)

22. MITRE. Cybersecurity: Awareness & Training. The MITRE Corporation (2017). https://bit.ly/38joAbU. Accessed 05 Apr 2022

23. CIISec. CIISec Skills Framework (2018). https://www.ciisec.org/Skills_Framework

24. SFIA. Digital Transformation Skills in SFIA (n.d.-a). https://sfia-online.org/en/assets/documents/sfia-view-of-digital-transformation-skills.pdf. Accessed 05 Apr 2022

25. Watkins, R., West, M.M., Visser, Y.: Guide to assessing needs: Essential tools for collecting information, making decisions, and achieving development results. World Bank Publications (2012). https://ebookcentral.proquest.com/lib/uocuk/detail.action?docID=868308

26. SFIA. Everyone has information security responsibilities (n.d.-b). https://bit.ly/3r5sxrc. Accessed 05 Apr 2022

27. SFIA. Mapping SFIA skills to NICE work roles (n.d.-c). https://bit.ly/3j5l0Sr. Accessed 05 Apr 2022

28. NICCS. Workforce Framework for Cybersecurity (NICE Framework), 29 July 2021. https://bit.ly/35Gda10. Accessed 05 Apr 2022

29. Rashid, A., Chivers, H., Lupu, E., Martin, A., Schneider, S.: The Cyber Security Body of Knowledge, Version 1.1.0 (2021). https://www.cybok.org/media/downloads/CyBOK_v1.1.0.pdf

30. Kirwan, B., Ainsworth, L.K.: A Guide to Task Analysis: The Task Analysis Working Group. CRC Press (1992)

31. Hingorjo, M.R., Jaleel, F.: Analysis of one-best MCQs: the difficulty index, discrimination index and distractor efficiency. J. Pak. Med. Assoc. **62**(2), 142–147 (2012). https://www.ncbi.nlm.nih.gov/pubmed/22755376

32. Garrett, J.J.: Elements of User Experience, The User-Centered Design for the Web and Beyond. Pearson Education (2010)

33. Leite, W.L., Svinicki, M., Shi, Y.: Attempted validation of the scores of the VARK: learning styles inventory with multitrait-multimethod confirmatory factor analysis models. Educ. Psychol. Measur. **70**(2), 323–339 (2009). https://doi.org/10.1177/0013164409344507

34. 1Password, 12 August 2021. https://support.1password.com/pbkdf2/

35. Hasan, F., Anderson, R., Smith, S.: Prevent Cross-Site Request Forgery (XSRF/CSRF) attacks in ASP.NET Core. Microsoft (2022). https://bit.ly/3x6oLSc. Accessed 05 Apr 2022

A Novel Framework for the Development of Age Appropriate Information Security Serious Games

Rudi Serfontein[✉] [iD] and Riana Serfontein[iD]

North-West University, Potchefstroom, South Africa
Rudi.Serfontein@nwu.ac.za

Abstract. Serious games have been shown to be an effective tool when teaching information security concepts to children and adults alike. However, due to the different ways in which people learn during different stages of their life, developing effective games for children can be a non-trivial task. In this paper, a novel framework is introduced that aims to simplify the process of developing serious games for children by making use of well-known developmental psychology principles. The framework is based on Erikson's Theory of Psychosocial Development, as well as Bandura's Social Cognitive Theory. Both of these theories are well-known within the field of developmental psychology, and have been shown to be valid in prior studies. To validate the proposed framework, a number of existing serious games from the literature is used in order to determine if the framework could have been used to develop the extant games. The framework, developed from a psychological basis, matches the games found in the literature. This suggests that the framework is a valid approach when developing age appropriate information security games.

Keywords: Information security · Serious games · Developmental psychology

1 Introduction

It is well known that addressing the human aspect in information systems is crucial for effective information security risk management [1]. Sadly, many users of information systems still act as the greatest vulnerabilities to these systems as a result of unsafe or irresponsible behaviour [2]. Studies have shown that one of the most effective ways to reduce the risks associated with users is to improve their behaviour when it comes to interacting with these systems [2–4]. There are several methods that can be used in organisations to address this problem, such as clear and well-structured policies [5], but when it comes to improving information security behaviour outside of organisations different approaches are needed [6]. Two of the best known approaches are awareness programmes and education, both of which can also be used in organisations to improve information security in general [7, 8]. The difficulty with both of these approaches, however, is that they can be difficult to implement effectively, especially outside of

© IFIP International Federation for Information Processing 2022
Published by Springer Nature Switzerland AG 2022
N. Clarke and S. Furnell (Eds.): HAISA 2022, IFIP AICT 658, pp. 120–129, 2022.
https://doi.org/10.1007/978-3-031-12172-2_10

organisations: continuous awareness programmes could lead to information security fatigue if it is not managed correctly [9], whereas education requires structured courses presented by appropriately trained educators. This leads to the suggestion that using formal education to improve information security becomes more difficult when targeting larger, unstructured groups. There is also the risk that education courses might not be as effective as hoped [10]. One potential approach to improving the efficacy of information security education in a larger group, while also potentially improving the efficacy of the education course, is to use serious games. A serious game, in principle, is any game where the primary focus is on teaching or education, rather than amusement [11]. These games have been shown to be an effective way to improve education courses, and there are several serious games that have focussed specifically on information security concepts [12, 13]. These serious games do have limitations, however, one of which is that they can only target particular age groups due to the way in which education occurs at various stages in a person's life [14]. This highlights two important aspects that need to be taken into account when developing serious games: firstly, for a serious game to be effective, it needs to conform to the principles of effective education, and secondly, it needs to be appropriate for a specifically targeted age group. Addressing these factors could pose problems if a serious game developer is unfamiliar with the concepts of developmental psychology, and especially if the serious game being developed has a specialised focus like information security that also needs other areas of specialised knowledge.

In this paper, a novel framework will be introduced that aims to simplify the process of developing age appropriate information security serious games for children by making use of the principles of developmental psychology. Specifically, the framework incorporates Erikson's Theory of Psychosocial Development [15], which details the various developmental stages a human being goes through during their life, and Bandura's Social Cognitive Theory [16], developed from Bandura's Social Learning Theory [17], which explains how learning occurs. Both of these theories are well-known within the field of developmental psychology, and they have been shown to be valid in a number of studies over the years [18–21]. A serious game developed using a framework that incorporates these two theories could, therefore, be both age appropriate for the targeted age groups, as well as effective from an educational standpoint.

The remainder of the paper is structured in the following manner. In the next section, background is provided on the topics of developmental psychology, serious games, and information security in serious games. Then the proposed framework is introduced, followed by an evaluation of the validity of the framework using existing information security focussed serious games. The paper then concludes with a discussion of the results and potential further research.

2   Background

The purpose of the framework presented in this paper is to make it easier for developers to create age appropriate information security serious games. In this section, some of the background necessary for the development of such a framework is discussed. The section starts with an overview of Erikson's Theory of Psychosocial Development, followed by a brief discussion of Bandura's Social Cognitive Theory. The section concludes by considering serious games and, in particular, the information security concepts addressed in serious games.

2.1 Erikson's Stages of Psychosocial Development

Erik Erikson's theory on psychosocial development posits that there are eight stages of development [14, 15]. These stages are defined by specific crises that should be resolved during the stage so that the person can function successfully in life [14, 22]. The stages are presented in Table 1. The stages that will be focused on are the third through fifth stages: Initiative versus guilt; Industry versus inferiority and Identity versus role confusion. The reason for focussing on these three stages in the development of the framework proposed in this paper are twofold. Firstly, it is expected that younger children (under 3 years of age) would not be able to effectively learn from a serious game. Secondly, the purpose of this framework is specifically to aid in the development of age appropriate serious games aimed at improving information security skills among children, and thus the framework does not focus on adults.

Table 1. Erikson's stages of development [14, 23]

Period in life/age	Psychosocial stage	Challenge
Infancy (0–1)	Trust vs Mistrust	Develop trust in caregivers/world
Toddlerhood (1–3)	Autonomy vs Shame	Realise ability to make decisions
Preschool (3–6)	Initiative vs Guilt	Develop willingness to try new things and handle failure
Childhood (6-adolescence)	Industry vs Inferiority	Learn basic skills and how to work with others
Adolescence	Identity vs Role confusion	Develop a lasting, integrated sense of self
Young adulthood	Intimacy vs Isolation	Develop lasting relationships
Middle adulthood	Generativity vs Stagnation	Contribute to future generations and community
Late adulthood	Integrity vs Despair	View life as satisfactory with no regret

During the three stages that span the time between preschool and adolescence, children develop certain skills through play and observation [15, 16], as well as becoming more steadfast in the skills and habits that they have learned during the previous stages of development [15]. During the preschool phase (initiative vs guilt), a child should develop purpose, allowing the child to develop and realise goals as well as learn to handle failure and try new methods to solve a problem [14, 15, 23]. The childhood phase (industry vs inferiority) is where the child develops a sense of competence, learning what their strengths are and honing their skills [14, 15]. During this phase children start developing habits that will stay with them for the rest of their lives [24]. Finally, the third phase that will be focused on is the adolescence phase (identity vs role confusion), where fidelity is developed [14, 22], meaning that the child develops a strong sense of self and start to consider their meaning in life [14, 22]. In adolescence the person needs to develop their own value system, that they can be faithful to [23].

2.2 Bandura's Social Cognitive Theory

People learn certain behaviours, often through observation and experience [17]. By observing or experiencing certain consequences, certain behaviours are strengthened or discouraged [16, 17]. This process happens constantly throughout a person's life, as they learn more about themselves and the world around them [16, 17]. The process of observing consequences of behaviours and adjusting behaviour to get the desired consequence is not limited to the "real world", but is also valid within the world of games. Computer programs allow a person to test risky behaviours, without any real risk to themselves [16]. Behaviour is influenced by a person's expectations, experiences and environments. If a person expects a certain behaviour will have a rewarding effect (emotional or physical), they are more likely to perform that behaviour, than if they expect a punishment or negative effect. This behaviour can also be dependent on the environment as the expected effect might be different based on who the person is with, or where they are, for example a child might be more comfortable doing certain things at home, rather than at school [17].

2.3 Information Security Serious Games

Serious games are generally accepted to be games that have a serious or utilitarian focus, while still being fun [13]. These games have been shown to be effective in teaching information security concepts, and the targeted age ranges for these games span from preschool to adulthood. One such game, named CyberCIEGE, has been used in organisations in the past to teach information security concepts [12]. The topics covered in these games vary from game to game, but a non-exhaustive list of topics that are covered by some of these games are shown in Table 2.

Table 2. Information security serious games for children (adapted from [25])

Game name	Cybersecurity topics
Interland[a]	• Communicate responsibly • Know the signs of a potential scam • Create a strong password • Set an example and take action against inappropriate behaviour
Carnegie Cadets[b]	• Staying safe online • Protection against malware • Using social media responsibly

(continued)

Table 2. (*continued*)

Game name	Cybersecurity topics
CyberKids [26]	• Strong passwords • Vulnerability identification
PBS Cybersecurity Lab [27]	• Staying safe online • Spotting scams • Defending against cyber attacks
Wolf, Hyena, and Fox, and Happy Hippo [13, 25]	• Password complexity • Online bullying

[a]https://beinternetawesome.withgoogle.com/en_us/interland
[b]https://www.carnegiecyberacademy.com

As shown in Table 2, there are a variety of information security topics that can be covered in a serious game. Some of these topics might be too simple or too advanced when targeting a specific age group, however, so it is important to keep the developmental stage of the targeted group in mind when developing a serious game.

3 Method

In this section the proposed framework will be introduced. The framework has three main components that need to be addressed, namely the selection of an age group, the factors that the game will need to focus on as a result of the selected age group, and finally the structure of the overall game cycle. In this paper, the game cycle is defined as the basic flow of a game's events, such as the tasks and challenges that a player will need to complete in order to progress through the game.

The framework as presented in this paper is focussed on the development of serious games for children, and is therefore limited to the third, fourth, and fifth stages of development. The first step in utilising the framework is identifying which age group the game will target; this can be based purely on selecting an age group, but it should also be possible to select a developmental group based on the attributes of the group being targeted. For the second component of the framework, the challenges and developmental features of the targeted group are used to determine which skills or knowledge the game should focus on. During the third stage, Preschool, for instance, a child will be challenged to develop a willingness to try new things and learn to handle failure. This is, arguably, an ideal phase to introduce the foundational concepts of information security, such as the importance of remembering a password, or not sharing your password with others. This is also the stage where the child can be encouraged to determine why information security is important in a personal sense. During the fourth stage, when a child is challenged to develop basic skills, the game could focus on teaching simple information security skills, such as the creation of strong passwords, how to protect against malware, identifying obvious scams, etc. Finally, during the fifth stage, when a child is challenged to develop an integrated sense of self, the game could focus on helping to develop the player's way of thinking with regard to information security concepts. The game could also attempt to improve a player's overall security behaviours by helping them to develop a sense of value within this context, i.e. the conviction that safe behaviour is important and has personal value to the player.

The third component, namely the game cycle, is the core of what the game will be structured around. In order to determine how the game cycle should be structured, the pattern found in Bandura's Social Cognitive Theory, which is similar to the pattern commonly found in normal games, is considered. In normal games, this pattern is one of the more typical ways in which players are taught gameplay skills: a player will be taught the basics of the skill, be put into environments where the skills are used with increasing levels of difficulty, and then finally be confronted with problems that require the use of multiple combined skills [28]. This can also have a positive effect on physical skills in addition to cognitive skills, as players can be trained to have better visual skills through games [29]. In this framework, this pattern is used to inform the design of the game cycle. This cycle has four main stages as informed by Bandura's theory: the introduction of a new skill (or knowledge), the testing of that skill in a suitable game environment, challenging the skill via a more advanced set of tests, and finally the combination of the new skill with existing skills in order to solve more complex problems. Once these four stages have been completed, a new skill can be introduced. An example of how this cycle could be used to teach password safety is as follows. The basic rules of secure passwords are introduced in the first stage, and then used by the player in the second stage to create a secure password. This is repeated until the user can easily create simple secure password repeatedly, at which point the game transitions to the third stage. Here the user must then evaluate seemingly secure passwords and determine if they are, in fact secure. Upon completion of the third stage, the player could be expected to combine previously acquired knowledge on safe password use with the newly acquired knowledge on secure passwords to determine safe and unsafe situations in the fourth stage. The proposed framework, with all three components included, is presented graphically in Fig. 1.

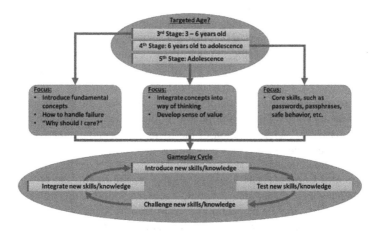

Fig. 1. The proposed serious game development framework

In the next section, the framework will be evaluated by using serious games from the literature and determining if those games could have been developed with the aid of this framework.

4   Framework Evaluation

While the framework presented in the previous section should be valid as it is based on accepted developmental psychology principles, it is important to confirm the validity of the framework by evaluating it against existing serious games. In this section this validation is accomplished by studying existing serious games literature, and comparing the patterns and topics covered in the literature to those contained in the framework. By demonstrating that the framework could have been used to develop extant serious games, it is reasoned that the framework may be considered valid within the context of the existing literature, and therefore could be used effectively to create new games.

4.1   3rd Stage: 3–6 Years Old

The game that is used to evaluate the 3rd stage (preschool) of the framework is the Wolf, Hyena, and Fox games, as well as the Happy Hippo game [13, 25]. These are two components of a single serious game that targets preschool children, and makes use of poems to teach information security concepts, at an appropriate level of difficulty, in order to spread awareness of digital wellness and information security concepts. The game touches on password complexity and good online behaviour, which are fundamental concepts in information security.

The game cycle starts by reading a poem to the player, and then asking a number of reflection questions about the contents of the poem after it has finished. After this, a quiz is opened to test the player's comprehension of the topics addressed in the selected poem, and a mini-game is launched once the quiz is over. Finally, at the end of the cycle, a message is shown to the player that shows whether they won or lost. The game does not place blocks on a player's progress if they get answers wrong during the game's quiz component; while the authors indicated that this was done because the game is meant as an awareness tool, it could also have the added benefit of teaching its players that failure is not a disaster, and that it is possible to recover and improve following failures. Based on these attributes of the game, it seems probable that the proposed framework could have been used to aid the development of this game had it been available. This conclusion is based on a consideration of the focus topics and content, as well as the design of the game cycle.

Focus Topics and Content: The game is targeted at children in the preschool stage of development, which means that it should focus on introducing fundamental concepts. It should also aim to help children learn how to handle failure. This game addresses both of these aspects in one way or another, as both password complexity and good online behaviour could be considered fundamental concepts when discussing information security education.

Game Cycle: This game has a game cycle that matches the cycle proposed in the framework. The game cycle starts by teaching a new skill or knowledge by means of a poem, and then transitions to a testing phase where the player must reflect on what they have learned. The quiz represents the challenge phase, where the player must use their new skills/knowledge in order to solve the quiz. During the integration phase, a mini-game is presented, where the player can engage in a fun activity where some of the content of the selected poem is coupled with gameplay skills (e.g. memory of tile locations). The game cycle therefore matches the pattern as presented in the framework.

In summary, the framework seems to be valid where the development of serious games targeted at preschool children is concerned.

4.2   4th Stage: 6 Years Old to Adolescence, and 5th Stage: Adolescence

For evaluating the 4th stage, the PBS Cybersecurity lab [27] that is targeted at school children is considered, and for the 5th stage the six games developed by Mostafa & Faragallah [30] for teaching undergraduate students is used. In both cases, the games match the framework.

Focus Topics and Content: The Cybersecurity lab, which is aimed at children from as young as 6th grade, has a focus on the development of skills, such as coding and password cracking. The six Mostafa & Faragallah games, meanwhile, are aimed at improving comprehension of the topics and the integration of these topics into real-world scenarios, and many of the games have the stated goal of helping students to understand particular concepts. This could help to incorporate these topics into a student's way of thinking, while also enforcing the idea that it has personal value to the individual.

Game Cycle: The game cycles also match those proposed in the framework. While the Cybersecurity lab does place a greater emphasis on teacher input during the process, the overall cycle is still the same. The six games developed by Mostafa & Faragallah also have this game cycle, in that these games all introduce a skill that has to be used, and then tests and challenges that skill.

In conclusion, the proposed framework should be useable in developing new games, as there are existing serious games that follow the principles incorporated into the framework.

5   Conclusion and Future Work

In this paper, a novel framework is introduced that aims to simplify the process of developing serious games for children. The framework is based on developmental psychology principles, and in particular makes use of Erikson and Bandura's theories in order to provide guidance when developing games for specific age groups. The framework was tested by comparing it to extant serious games, and it matches the games that were used in the evaluation. The framework has not yet been used directly to create a game, which is a limitation to the current research, but it is expected that this framework could be used to create effective age appropriate serious games that can be used to effectuate information security education, training, and awareness in future research.

References

1. Dang-Pham, D., Kautz, K., Hoang, A.-P., Pittayachawan, S.: Identifying information security opinion leaders in organizations: insights from the theory of social power bases and social network analysis. Comput. Secur. **112**, 102505 (2022)
2. McLeod, A., Dolezel, D.: Information security policy non-compliance: can capitulation theory explain user behaviors? Comput. Secur. **112**, 102526 (2022)
3. López, A.U., et al.: Analysis of computer user behavior, security incidents and fraud using self-organizing maps. Comput. Secur. **83**, 38–51 (2019)
4. Tsai, C.-Y., Shih, W.-L., Hsieh, F.-P., Chen, Y.-A., Lin, C.-L., Wu, H.-J.: Using the arcs model to improve undergraduates' perceived information security protection motivation and behavior. Comput. Educ. 104449 (2022)
5. Moody, G.D., Siponen, M., Pahnila, S.: Toward a unified model of information security policy compliance. MIS Q. **42**(1), 285–311 (2018)
6. Holgersson, J., Kävrestad, J., Nohlberg, M.: Cybersecurity and digital exclusion of seniors: what do they fear? In: International Symposium on Human Aspects of Information Security and Assurance, pp. 12–21, Springer (2021)
7. Kemper, G.: Improving employees' cyber security awareness. Comput. Fraud Secur. **2019**(8), 11–14 (2019)
8. Chen, Y.-T., Shih, W.-L., Lee, C.-H., Wu, P.-L., Tsai, C.-Y.: Relationships among undergraduates' problematic information security behavior, compulsive internet use, and mindful awareness in taiwan. Comput. Educ. **164**, 104131 (2021)
9. Furnell, S., Thomson, K.-L.: Recognising and addressing 'security fatigue.' Comput. Fraud Secur. **2009**(11), 7–11 (2009)
10. Bernard, L., Raina, S., Taylor, B., Kaza, S.: Minimizing cognitive overload in cybersecurity learning materials: an experimental study using eye-tracking. In: IFIP World Conference on Information Security Education, pp. 47–63, Springer (2021)
11. Jaffray, A., Finn, C., Nurse, J.R.: Sherlocked: a detective-themed serious game for cyber security education. In: International Symposium on Human Aspects of Information Security and Assurance, pp. 35–45, Springer (2021)
12. Cone, B.D., Irvine, C.E., Thompson, M.F., Nguyen, T.D.: A video game for cyber security training and awareness. Comput. Secur. **26**(1), 63–72 (2007)
13. Allers, J., Drevin, G., Snyman, D., Kruger, H., Drevin, L.: Children's awareness of digital wellness: a serious games approach. In: IFIP World Conference on Information Security Education, pp. 95–110, Springer (2021)
14. Dunkel, C.S., Harbke, C.: A review of measures of Erikson's stages of psychosocial development: evidence for a general factor. J. Adult Dev. **24**(1), 58–76 (2017)
15. Erikson, E.H.: Childhood and society. Paladin Grafton Books (1993)
16. Bandura, A.: Social cognitive theory: an agentic perspective. Asian J. Soc. Psychol. **2**(1), 21–41 (1999)
17. Bandura, A.: Social Learning Theory. Prentice Hall (1977)
18. Nwosu, H.E., Obidike, P.C., Ugwu, J.N., Udeze, C.C., Okolie, U.C.: Applying social cognitive theory to placement learning in business firms and students' entrepreneurial intentions. Int. J. Manag. Educ. **20**(1), 100602 (2022)
19. Woods, E.K., Fly, A.D., Dickinson, S.L., Chen, X.: P18 a test of social cognitive theory on fruit and vegetable intake in indiana high school students. J. Nutr. Educ. Behav. **53**(7), S32 (2021)
20. Maree, J.G.: The psychosocial development theory of Erik Erikson: critical overview. Early Child Dev. Care **191**(7–8), 1107–1121 (2021)

21. McGaw, J., Vance, A., White, S., Mongta, S.: Whose place? Lessons from a case study of a guardianship determination for an Australian indigenous child. Health Place **73**, 102739 (2022)
22. Sokol, J.T.: Identity development throughout the lifetime: an examination of Eriksonian theory. Graduate J. Counsel. Psychol. **1**(2), 1–10 (2009)
23. Louw, D., Louw, A.: Child and Adolescent Development. Psychology publications (2014)
24. Blake, S., Winsor, D.L., Allen, L.: Child Development and the Use of Technology: Perspectives, Applications and Experiences. Information Science Reference (2011)
25. Snyman, D.P., Drevin, G.R., Kruger, H.A., Drevin, L., Allers, J.: A wolf, hyena, and fox game to raise cybersecurity awareness among pre-school children. In: International Symposium on Human Aspects of Information Security and Assurance, pp. 91–101, Springer (2021)
26. Pérez, J., Torres, R., Brand, S.V.: Cyberkids: video game for raising cyber security awareness in children. In: 2020 39th International Conference of the Chilean Computer Science Society (SCCC), pp. 1–8 (2020)
27. Pbs.Org: The cybersecurity lab – educator guide I nova labs I pbs. https://www.pbs.org/wgbh/nova/labs/about-cyber-lab/educator-guide/. Accessed 6 Apr 2022
28. Rogers, S.: Level Up! The Guide to Great Video Game Design. John Wiley & Sons (2014)
29. Green, C.S., Bavelier, D.: Action video game modifies visual selective attention. Nature **423**(6939), 534–537 (2003)
30. Mostafa, M., Faragallah, O.S.: Development of serious games for teaching information security courses. IEEE Access **7**, 169293–169305 (2019)

Cyber Security Culture

Security Culture in Industrial Control Systems Organisations: A Literature Review

Stefanos Evripidou[1]([✉]), Uchenna D. Ani[2], Jeremy D McK. Watson[3], and Stephen Hailes[4]

[1] Centre for Doctoral Training in Cybersecurity, University College London, London, UK
stefanos.evripidou.16@ucl.ac.uk
[2] School of Computing and Mathematics, Keele University, Keele, UK
[3] Department of Science Technology Engineering and Public Policy, University College London, London, UK
[4] Department of Computer Science, University College London, London, UK

Abstract. Industrial control systems (ICS) are a key element of a country's critical infrastructure, which includes industries like energy, water, and transport. In recent years, an increased convergence of operational and information technology has been taking place in these systems, increasing their cyber risks, and making security a necessity. People are often described as one of the biggest security risks in ICS, and historic attacks have demonstrated their role in facilitating or deterring them. One approach to enhance the security of organisations using ICS is the development of a security culture aiming to positively influence employees' security perceptions, knowledge, and ultimately, behaviours. Accordingly, this work aims to review the security culture literature in organisations which use ICS and the factors that affect it, to provide a summary of the field. We conclude that the factors which affect security culture in ICS organisations are in line with the factors discussed in the general literature, such as security policies and management support. Additional factors related to ICS, such as safety culture, are also highlighted. Gaps are identified, with the limited research coverage being the most prominent. As such, proposals for future research are offered, including the need to conduct research with employees whose roles are not security related.

Keywords: Industrial control systems · ICS · Cybersecurity · Security culture · Critical infrastructure · Human factors · Operational technologies · OT

1 Introduction

Industrial Control Systems (ICS) are systems that manage, monitor, and control industrial processes [1]. Among those, ICS are used to operate critical infrastructure (CI) in sectors like energy, water, and transport, and are essential for a country's security, economy, and safety [2]. A convergence between information technology (IT) and operational technology (OT) has been increasingly taking place in ICS, further widening their attack

© IFIP International Federation for Information Processing 2022
Published by Springer Nature Switzerland AG 2022
N. Clarke and S. Furnell (Eds.): HAISA 2022, IFIP AICT 658, pp. 133–146, 2022.
https://doi.org/10.1007/978-3-031-12172-2_11

surface [3]. Given the potential catastrophic impact of a cyber-attack which could include injury and loss of life or property, there is an increasing need to secure these systems.

Typically, three core interacting elements can be found in an ICS environment: people, processes, and technology. As such, to effectively control the vulnerabilities and threats in ICS, all three elements must be incorporated into holistic security solutions [3]. Additionally, from a socio-technical perspective, successful system performance is achieved by the 'joint optimization' of both the social and technical elements of a system [4]. Technology-based security solutions [5], as well as security processes (e.g., security assessment [6], risk management [7]), have been extensively researched for ICS. In contrast, the 'human factor' in ICS security has been relatively under-researched.

Some studies have shown that people pose a significant security risk in ICS. Namely, respondents in the 2019 SANS OT/ICS Cybersecurity survey [8] ranked people as the greatest risk to a control system compromise (62.3%), followed by technology (21.8%) and processes (14%). According to Kaspersky [9], social engineering is the most widely used method to gain initial access to these systems. Miller et al. [10], having extensively reviewed past ICS attacks, similarly state that attackers have relied on social engineering techniques such as spear-phishing to obtain access to ICS, especially in the last decade.

Some of the attacks where the human factor played a significant role include Stuxnet, believed to have been delivered to the Natanz nuclear facilities by removable media [10]. Additionally, the 2015–16 attacks on Ukrainian power stations, which resulted in widespread power outages, were initiated via spear-phishing [10]. More recently, intruders attempted to remotely change the levels of lye in the supply of a water treatment facility in Florida. Fortunately, an operator detected and reversed this action [11]. While technical safeguards were in place to prevent damage even if the change was undetected by an operator, this incident highlights the importance of users in enhancing ICS security.

One approach that aims to reduce the human factor risk and improve an organisation's security is the cultivation of an organisational security culture. Developing and strengthening a security culture aims to increase security awareness, as well as influence the security attitudes and behaviours of employees [12]. As such, academics [10], security agencies [13], and governmental bodies [14] have called for the development of an enhanced security culture in organisations using ICS.

Currently, few works have investigated security culture in such organisations, with most research conducted in the IT domain. However, organisations using ICS differ from IT organisations. For example, they have a wider diversity of user roles compared to 'end-users' in IT systems, including operators, technicians, and engineers [15]. Moreover, while research in security culture has been influenced by the safety culture literature [16], safety culture is not as prominent in IT organisations, and the two cultures have rarely been studied together. Organisations using ICS, however, have developed a strong safety culture over the years due to the nature of their physical operations. Accordingly, they foster an environment where both cultures co-exist. Employees' safety perceptions, or processes to ensure safety, might also enhance or obstruct the security culture in ICS.

Thus, this work aims to provide an overview of the literature, answering the following research questions:

1) What is the scope and level of maturity of the security culture research in ICS environments?

2) Which constituents of security culture have been examined in an ICS context?
3) Which factors affect the security culture of organisations using ICS and how do they align with the factors described in the general security culture literature?

Providing clear answers to the above research questions can help industrial organisations to identify and understand relevant factors and attributes that can help improve their organisational security culture. In turn, an enhanced security culture can improve the security and resilience levels of their business and operational environments.

The remainder of this work is presented as follows; Sect. 2 provides an overview of the literature on security culture, followed by the methodology in Sect. 3. Accordingly, the selected works are presented in Sect. 4 and a discussion of the findings, research gaps, and potential future research is provided in Sect. 5. Finally, Sect. 6 provides the conclusion.

2 Background on Security Culture

Security culture research has been heavily influenced by the organisational and safety culture literature. It aims to examine how organisational procedures can affect employees' security perceptions and behaviours and to propose better ways to manage security [17]. Defining security culture has been an ongoing process with a variety of definitions presented in the literature [18], leading some academics to describe it as an ill-defined problem [19]. However, despite the multitude of definitions, the majority assert that security culture is constituted by cognitive-related attributes such as the knowledge, attitudes, perceptions, values, beliefs, and behaviours of employees. Accordingly, this work defines the security culture of organisations using ICS as 'the collective perceptions, attitudes, beliefs, and knowledge of users, and subsequently how they are manifested in their security behaviours in an ICS context'.

The constituent elements of an organisation's security culture can be influenced by a variety of factors, internal or external to an organisation, and several reviews have collated these factors [16, 20]. In their systematic review, Uchendu et al. [21], have identified 19 factors, including rewards and sanctions. Da Veiga et al. [18], having integrated academic and industrial perspectives, proposed a model with 25 factors, including trust between employees and change management. Another internal factor is the provision of education, training, and awareness (ETA) programmes to employees [16]. Employees' security perceptions can also be affected by the actions of their co-workers or managers [22]. Oftentimes, security tasks may conflict with every-day tasks, which also negatively affects employees' attitudes towards security [23]. External factors include national culture, i.e., the different security values and beliefs of each nation [21]. Additionally, security legislation and regulation, such as the General Data Protection Regulation (GDPR) and the changes it has introduced, such as mandatory reporting along with substantial fines, can also affect an organisation's security culture [18].

Calls have been made for these factors to be standardised to enable practitioners and researchers to work with common models and to allow research findings to be generalisable [24]. However, given that each organisation is different in terms of size, function, and regulations among others, this seems infeasible, as the candidate factors are potentially limitless. Moreover, these factors affect each organisation differently. For example, research into small and medium sized enterprises (SMEs) has validated some of the factors in the extant literature [21]. However, tools or frameworks developed for larger organisations can be unusable by SMEs due to their complexity. Additionally, resources are much more limited in SMEs, making change initiatives harder to implement. Consequentially, different, custom-built approaches may be needed to influence their security culture [21].

The way these factors affect organisations differently motivates our research in ICS. As already stated, ICS organisations have many differences compared to IT organisations where most security culture research has taken place. These range from the lifecycle and heterogeneity of their system components [3] to the variety of operating roles [15]. As such, research is needed to identify the most impactful factors and how they affect ICS security culture, to efficiently enhance it.

3   Methodology

A narrative literature review was conducted, with Scopus and Web of Science being the main research indexes used. This is due to their reputation for maintaining high-impact and quality research and the relevancy of their results as they encompass works from popular scientific databases such as IEEE, ACM, Springer etc. This minimises the chances of missing out relevant works.

As a starting point, the following query was used: ('security culture' AND ('industrial control systems' OR 'critical infrastructure' OR ICS)), returning 17 distinct results. Accordingly, three modifications were made on the base query to increase the number of results. The following keywords were added to the second part of the query: water, energy, oil, gas, transport, and nuclear, representing different industrial sectors that operate ICS. Additionally, another search was conducted with 'security culture' broken down into two keywords (security AND culture). Finally, to broaden the scope and capture studies related to the attributes making up security culture, such as knowledge or attitudes, the first part of the base query was reformulated to ('human factors' AND security). In total, 407 results were identified. Accordingly, titles and abstracts were scanned, and works were excluded based on the following criteria:

a) Works before 2010 were excluded, as the issues around security culture in ICS organisations were not common and were not considered by research prior to this time. For example, security could signify security of supply, without incorporating cybersecurity.
b) If the study had vaguely used the term critical infrastructure without making any distinction between ICS or other OT systems and IT systems, or critical infrastructure referred to sectors like finance who do not typically use ICS.
c) If security culture or any of the constituents of security culture (i.e., perceptions, attitudes, knowledge etc.) were not the focus, or examined in detail as part of the study.

As such, 9 works were selected. Supplementary searches were also conducted through Google Scholar, as well as by looking into other publications by the identified authors. Finally, selected works were also backwards and forwards reference searched [25]. This step produced another 3 works. Overall, works which were judged to sufficiently touch upon security culture, or at least one aspect of it such as employees' security perceptions, were selected. In total, 12 works were included to be reviewed. Figure 1 details the literature selection process.

Fig. 1. Literature selection process

The factors that affect security culture as identified by the reviews in Sect. 2 were aggregated and synthesised to develop a collection of themes to analyse the selected works [16, 18, 20, 21]. Namely, different terms that referred to the same underlying factor, such as leadership involvement or top management support, were grouped under a common theme. The most prominent factors with respect to their frequency were selected. These factors were security training, security awareness, communication, management and leadership, and security policies and procedures. While no factors were outright excluded, some factors such as change management and national culture were not identified in the literature.

4 Results

Regarding the constituent elements of security culture, personnel security perceptions have been the focus of some works. Namely, Frey et al. [15], analysed six historical ICS incidents to understand the factors that affect ICS security, concluding that operators' perception errors, such as those about their system's boundaries, had played a significant role in them. However, it was emphasised that latent design conditions like the lack of fail-safe mechanisms had fundamentally affected these perceptions, challenging the idea that humans are the weakest link in a system's security.

Small scale surveys were also used to capture employees' security perceptions and beliefs. Green et al. [26], examined how employees in an ICS organisation prioritise each dimension of the confidentiality, integrity, availability (CIA) triad, to obtain insights into how security perspectives were formed in the organisation. Their results demonstrated discrepancies across both ICS levels and operational roles (operators and support/maintenance). For example, operators were prioritising availability and/or integrity before confidentiality which was not the case for support/maintenance staff, indicating the effect that ICS level and role can have in the formation and prioritisation of security perceptions. As such, to prevent fragmented approaches to security, the need for effective and coherent messaging from an organisation to its employees was highlighted.

Madnick et al. [27], presented a methodology to measure employees' perceptions on eight security constructs, including security culture. Participants came from two renewable energy companies, and similar perception discrepancies between different stakeholders were highlighted. OT personnel had the biggest gaps between their perceived assessment and the ideal level of importance across all constructs, with policy and procedures having the biggest difference compared to personnel from other functional areas, such as IT.

In an analysis of 25 interviews with ICS personnel having security-related roles, including control engineers, managers, and IT staff, Zanutto et al. concluded that security is a grey area, shaped by the multitude of demands of its stakeholders [28]. Oftentimes, organisations prescribed a top-down approach to security, which was not always compatible with everyday practices. Moreover, security was seen as a concern to be handled by a specific team rather than a problem to be tackled by every employee, with the authors highlighting that this perception was maintained by the lack of organisational commitment towards the management and communication of security. Besides, security practices did not always align with employees' practices and expected workload, creating tensions, as they necessitated a change in their habits. Generally, the many obstacles arising from organisational divisions, and the lack of guidance security personnel faced, have led the authors to describe them as "shadow warriors".

Reflecting the cyber-physical nature of ICS, employees' different roles and functional areas translated to different operational priorities. Discussing these, OT engineers in the water sector would refer to the safety, reliability, and availability (SRA) triad as being representative of their systems' priorities [29]. Contrastingly, interviewees working in IT were more concerned about the security and accuracy of their data. These differences in ICS security perceptions were highlighted in a variety of practices like patch management, access privileges, and backups, indicating how differing priorities arising from each role also affect personnel's security perceptions.

Shapira et al. [30], reported on the findings of an active workshop which elicited cybersecurity perspectives from stakeholders in the Israeli water sector. The lack of both professional security knowledge and organisational awareness of cybersecurity risks were identified as the sector's two biggest gaps. Consequently, comprehensive security policies, together with education, awareness and training campaigns were recommended to solve the lack of awareness. Skotnes [31], also revealed similar practices while studying ICS owners and suppliers in the Norwegian electric power supply industry to understand the division of cybersecurity responsibilities between them. ICS owners appeared to have limited awareness of cybersecurity threats and relied heavily on their suppliers and their technical solutions for improving their systems' security, which resulted in a weakly focused organisational security culture.

A couple studies have proposed more holistic and validated approaches to measure aspects of security culture. Ani et al. [1], presented a methodology to assess the cybersecurity capabilities of workers in ICS, measured with respect to their knowledge and skills. Recognising that many studies had focused on the perceptions and behaviours of individuals, the authors state that knowledge and skills underpin and influence the two former attributes. Accordingly, their survey consisted of scenario-based questions tailored to ICS environments in areas like patch management and removable media protection, demonstrating the effectiveness of their approach in assessing individual employee cybersecurity capabilities.

Nævestad et al. [32], evaluated the information security culture of a Norwegian critical infrastructure organisation. The GAIN scale, originally developed to measure safety culture was used, supplemented with security knowledge and attitude questions. This allowed for comparisons to be made between organisational departments concerning topics such as reporting culture. Additionally, security culture was found to be the most significant predictor of security behaviour. A follow-up study was conducted with the same organisation two years later, comparing the security culture before and after the organisation's attempts to enhance it [33]. The results suggest that security culture had improved, which was attributed to the measures taken by the organisation's management. Unfortunately, these measures were not discussed in depth, but stronger password practices and improved security consultations between each department's supervisor and their team were highlighted.

Safety culture and its relationship to security culture was also discussed in a few works. Piggin and Boyes [34], in their 2015 article, stated that security culture was not yet on the same level as safety culture. Moreover, security was still not viewed as business as usual in most ICS. On the other hand, safety was given top priority with recurrent lesson sharing and the disobedience of safety guidance was not tolerated, especially in high hazard environments. This organisational lack of commitment towards security could also influence employees' perceptions. While physical security and safety risks could easily be appreciated due to their tangible impacts, this was not the case for cybersecurity risks.

More recently, Dewey et al. [35] conducted four case studies with UK nuclear organisations on the status and challenges of security culture. In one of their case studies, the authors reported that staff were more aware of issues concerning safety than security. Moreover, the security team was viewed as an obstacle by employees, as they were seen to be limiting business development. From their viewpoint, the security team reported that they had to compete for employees' time and attention with issues related to safety. However, the organisations studied had taken a variety of measures to improve their security culture. These ranged from awareness campaigns and training, to appointing a security culture manager. Moreover, security assessment procedures were put in place, enabling the benchmarking of security culture and comparisons over time.

5   Discussion

The number of reviewed works indicate that research in security culture, and more generally human factor security in ICS, is limited. However, research in ICS security culture is emerging, as most of the reviewed articles were published from 2017 onwards. This can be partly attributed to the fact that cybersecurity concerns are relatively recent in ICS. Moreover, the wider cybersecurity literature had for years not given strong attention to human-factor security, compared to technical security solutions. A similar trend can be observed for ICS, where technical research appears to be outnumbering people-centric security research.

Regarding their scope, some works were quite narrow such as [26] where employees' perceptions of the confidentiality, integrity, and availability (CIA) attributes were specifically explored, or were pilot studies [27]. One work had relied on the authors' knowledge as practitioners to discuss security culture in ICS, without providing any empirical evidence, thus raising concerns about its external validity [34]. Moreover, while the ability of the employee security evaluations methodology in identifying variations in the capabilities of industrial personnel was demonstrated [1], participants did not originate from a single organisation. Applying similar evaluation methodologies in partnership with a particular organisation could lead to more significant results, such as highlighting differences between organisational departments [36], or gaps in their security culture [37]. However, it should be noted that collaboration with industrial partners was limited. Only two works had an industry co-author, but none were industry-led. Similar trends have been described in prior research, where no industry-led works were identified in a systematic review of the state of cybersecurity research in the water sector [38]. Security is a multi-disciplinary field, which increasingly requires collaboration between academia and industry. Additionally, partnership with industrial organisations can lead to richer insights and improve the validity of research findings.

As for application areas, studies have been conducted in various critical infrastructure sectors, including water, energy, transport and nuclear. Among those, the cases studies conducted in nuclear organisations indicate that despite the challenges, these organisations appear to be making good efforts to establish and maintain a strong security culture. Overall, the nuclear sector appears to be more mature with respect to security culture compared to other critical infrastructure sectors. This is unsurprising, given that the International Atomic Energy Agency (IAEA) released a security culture implementation guide more than a decade ago [39], and a self-assessment security culture guide in 2017 [40], whereas other industrial sectors lack similar guidelines.

Overall, a few works have presented methodologies to evaluate specific constituents of security culture, including security perceptions, knowledge and skills, and attitudes. Different perceptions were highlighted between functional areas such as IT and OT, as well as between OT roles, which could translate into different security practices and introduce security blind spots and vulnerabilities. Indeed, OT operators' perception errors regarding the observability and controllability of their systems were shown to be detrimental in past ICS attacks. Nevertheless, there is still room for research when it comes to incorporating these constituent attributes into more holistic evaluation approaches and systems viewpoints, as well as research with additional organisations using ICS to increase the validity of existing findings.

Regarding the factors that impact the security culture of organisations using ICS, the lack of awareness and subsequently of security initiatives from the top management was often highlighted. Skotnes [33], asserted that due to their limited security awareness and involvement, ICS owners were placing too much trust on their suppliers, who could only provide security assurances for their products but not entire systems. Green et al. [26], also emphasised the importance of coherent messaging from an organisation's management, to address potential risks arising from varied security perceptions between roles or departments. However, the top management's involvement may not always prove beneficial. For example, excessively strict policies and procedures set from the top of the organisation can prove unpopular with staff as they often exert constraints on operational practices. This can put security personnel at an uneasy position, as they must act as enforcers by trying to negotiate the uptake of security with operational staff [28]. Some studies recommended proper framing of security in terms of risk management and business losses to persuade the buy-in for security initiatives from senior management [28, 35].

Insufficient employee training, and the lack of security awareness and knowledge also emerged as key factors influencing security culture. It was observed that important security information such as the threat landscape or previous ICS attacks were not disseminated across organisations and were not reaching OT personnel, leading to flawed security perceptions. This was part of a general trend where organisation-wide security training and awareness initiatives were found to be insufficient [28]. Another study also highlighted that OT personnel had the biggest gaps on policy as well as security awareness, reaffirming the inadequacy of organisational security guidance [27].

Latent design conditions can also affect operators' security perceptions and lead to security incidents [15]. For example, weaknesses in an intrusion detection system may lead an operator to form inaccurate assumptions about the observability of their system and induce a false sense of security. Broadly, technical and other factors related to a system's design have not been studied in the context of ICS security culture as much as people-centric factors such as security training or policy. This generally extends to the wider security culture literature, where technology aspects and their influence on security culture have had limited attention [41]. However, the unique operational nature of ICS, where patching is harder to implement, or passwords frequently need to be shared [29], often contrasts general security practices. As such, security staff should recognize and resolve such issues, as insisting on unworkable security practices can negatively influence the attitudes of OT personnel towards security.

Security culture research has been heavily influenced by safety culture, and safety culture approaches to study security culture were utilised [22, 32]. As such, it was expected that more works would have investigated security along with, or in relation to safety perceptions in ICS environments. However, only three works had explicitly acknowledged the existence of a safety culture in ICS and only one had provided evidence on the state of the two cultures, with the authors of [35] positing that security culture was still not on the level of safety culture in their study organisations. Nevertheless, the factors that affect security and safety culture are quite similar. As such, there is potential value into research that aims to establish how the challenges and achievements of establishing a safety culture can be incorporated to enhance security culture.

Nonetheless, constructive security practices that strengthened security culture also emerged in the literature. The importance of factors such as communication, which should be two-way and active between all levels was stressed [35]. Training programs, which should be varied and interactive to stimulate participants were also highlighted as a good practice, along with establishing procedures for the continuous assessment of security culture. One study clearly asserted that the improvements in security culture in the study organisation could be attributed to the initiatives taken by the top management, such as improved training and additional middle management support [35].

Generally, the works reviewed highlighted that operational personnel's practices and everyday tasks would often clash with security requirements. This can be partially attributed to their differing operational priorities such as the safety, availability, and functionality of their systems [28]. One example was the dissatisfaction OT engineers expressed with requests for stricter access permissions and log-in auditing as these security measures would add to their routine workload. The human-factors security literature has proposed that employees have a compliance threshold, which once exceeded, results in non-compliance towards security [23]. Alternatively, employees may result in 'shadow security' practices to resolve these tensions [42]. Improving the security attitudes and perceptions of operational personnel is then paramount to ensure that employees behave securely.

While the reviewed studies had considered various ICS stakeholders, OT employees were generally underrepresented. For example, two works had focused on personnel with security roles [28, 29] and one had focused on system owners and suppliers [31]. However, no study has examined the perspectives of employees whose main roles and responsibilities do not revolve around security, such as operators or maintenance staff. As such, a gap currently exists in the literature that needs to be addressed, to better understand how to improve security from the OT viewpoint. Further research with operational personnel is warranted, to investigate their attitudes and perceptions towards the security of their systems.

Overall, a range of high-level factors that affect the security culture of ICS organisations across the span of critical infrastructure sectors were identified, as shown in Fig. 2. These include the top management and their role in promoting security throughout the organisation, and middle management, which as the employees' reporting line should also be involved in security. Additionally, security policies and the need to minimise their conflict with every-day working practices was highlighted. The need for security communication between departments, the security team and employees, as well as efficient security messaging from the top to the whole organisation was also discussed. Security awareness and training were also found to be lacking on all levels of the organisation, from the senior management to OT operators, leading to inadequate knowledge. Finally, two factors more closely linked to ICS environments which have not been the focus of the wider security culture literature were identified; latent design conditions and their effect on operators' perceptions, and safety culture and how its prevalence in ICS organisations can affect security perceptions and attitudes.

However, the degree to which each of these factors can affect security culture is still not clearly understood. Factors which were identified in the wider literature, such as rewards and sanctions, have not been examined in ICS contexts. As such, further research is needed with organisations that use ICS to examine the state of their security culture along with their current practices. Additionally, it is crucial for organisations to identify the most important factors that influence security culture, to develop appropriate measures towards enhancing it, and ultimately improve their security. Our ongoing research is focused on these objectives, by collaborating with industrial practitioners in ICS organisations through surveys and one-to-one interviews.

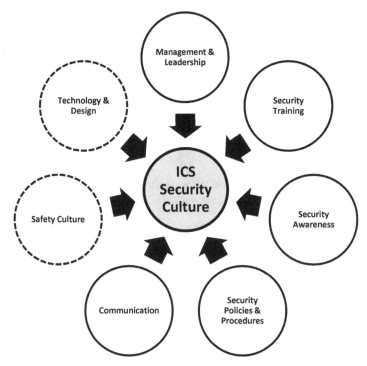

Fig. 2. Factors that affect security culture in organisations using ICS

6 Conclusion

This work has reviewed the literature on the security culture of organisations using ICS, with a focus on two areas: the constituent elements of security culture such as attitudes and beliefs, and the factors that affect it. Studies have examined the various attributes that make up security culture, indicating differences in perceptions and attitudes between roles and departments, which partially stem from employees' different operational priorities. It was also demonstrated that the factors that affect security culture in the broader security culture literature also apply to ICS organisations and their security culture. These include management and their leadership, training and awareness, and security communication among others. Two additional factors, closely related to ICS, have also been identified: safety culture and technology and system design.

Overall, the literature is limited but emerging. However, there is a clear lack of research with operational personnel whose roles are not security-related, with most works having focused on employees with security roles. Additional research with operational personnel would enable a better understanding of their views on security and how it affects their work. Finally, there is a lack of research looking into safety culture and its relationship with security culture. Potential future research could examine how safety culture was cultivated and maintained in organisations using ICS, and how these lessons can be used to enhance their security culture.

Nevertheless, ICS organisations should take steps to improve their security, with security culture being one such socio-technical approach. Treating personnel as the 'weakest-link' or confining them to unworkable policies has been demonstrated to be a bad approach. As such, future research should aim to propose better ways to positively influence personnel's security attitudes and perceptions along with making organisational security procedures workable to employees, thus fostering a strong and beneficial security culture in organisations using ICS.

References

1. Ani, U.D., He, H., Tiwari, A.: Human factor security: evaluating the cybersecurity capacity of the industrial workforce. J. Syst. Info. Tech. **21**(1), 2–35 (2019). https://doi.org/10.1108/JSIT-02-2018-0028
2. Critical Infrastructure Sectors | CISA: https://www.cisa.gov/critical-infrastructure-sectors . Accessed 27 Nov 2021
3. Ani, U.P.D., He, H., Tiwari, A.: Review of cybersecurity issues in industrial critical infrastructure: manufacturing in perspective. J. Cyber Security Technol. **1**(1), 32–74 (2017). https://doi.org/10.1080/23742917.2016.1252211.
4. Walker, G.H., Stanton, N.A., Salmon, P.M., Jenkins, D.P.: A review of sociotechnical systems theory: a classic concept for new command and control paradigms. Theor. Issues Ergon. Sci. **9**(6), 479–499 (2008). https://doi.org/10.1080/14639220701635470
5. Suaboot, J., et al.: A taxonomy of supervised learning for IDSs in SCADA environments. ACM Comput. Surv. **53**(2), 40:1–40:37 (2020). https://doi.org/10.1145/3379499
6. Qassim, Q.S., Jamil, N., Daud, M., Patel, A., Ja'affar, N.: A review of security assessment methodologies in industrial control systems. ICS **27**(1), 47–61 (2019). https://doi.org/10.1108/ICS-04-2018-0048
7. Cherdantseva, Y., et al.: A review of cyber security risk assessment methods for SCADA systems. Comput. Secur. **56**, 1–27 (2016). https://doi.org/10.1016/j.cose.2015.09.009
8. SANS 2019 State of OT/ICS Cybersecurity Survey | SANS Institute. https://www.sans.org/white-papers/38995/. Accessed 23 Jul 2021
9. APT attacks on industrial organizations in H1 2021 | Kaspersky ICS CERT: Kaspersky ICS CERT | Kaspersky Industrial Control Systems Cyber Emergency Response Team, 26 Oct 2021. https://ics-cert.kaspersky.com/reports/2021/10/26/apt-attacks-on-industrial-organizations-in-h1-2021/. Accessed 27 Nov 2021
10. Miller, T., Staves, A., Maesschalck, S., Sturdee, M., Green, B.: Looking back to look forward: lessons learnt from cyber-attacks on industrial control systems. Int. J. Crit. Infrastruct. Prot. **35**, 100464 (2021). https://doi.org/10.1016/j.ijcip.2021.100464
11. Florida Hack Exposes Danger to Water Systems | The Pew Charitable Trusts. https://www.pewtrusts.org/en/research-and-analysis/blogs/stateline/2021/03/10/florida-hack-exposes-danger-to-water-systems. Accessed 2 Aug 2021
12. ENISA: Cyber Security Culture in organisations. https://www.enisa.europa.eu/publications/cyber-security-culture-in-organisations. Accessed 31 May 2021
13. NCSC: A positive security culture. https://www.ncsc.gov.uk/collection/you-shape-security/a-positive-security-culture. Accessed 27 Nov 2021
14. DCMS: Water Sector Cyber Security Strategy, p. 12
15. Frey, S., Rashid, A., Zanutto, A., Busby, J., Follis, K.: On the role of latent design conditions in cyber-physical systems security. In: 2016 IEEE/ACM 2nd International Workshop on Software Engineering for Smart Cyber-Physical Systems (SEsCPS), May 2016, pp. 43–46. https://doi.org/10.1109/SEsCPS.2016.015.

16. Reegård, K., Blackett, C., Katta, V.: The concept of cybersecurity. Culture (2019). https://doi.org/10.3850/978-981-11-2724-3_0761-cd

17. Ruighaver, A.B., Maynard, S.B., Chang, S.: Organisational security culture: extending the end-user perspective. Comput. Secur. **26**(1), 56–62 (2007). https://doi.org/10.1016/j.cose.2006.10.008

18. da Veiga, A., Astakhova, L.V., Botha, A., Herselman, M.: Defining organisational information security culture—Perspectives from academia and industry. Comput. Secur. **92**, 101713 (2020). https://doi.org/10.1016/j.cose.2020.101713

19. Gcaza, N., Solms, R.: Cybersecurity culture: an ill-defined problem, p. 109 (2017). https://doi.org/10.1007/978-3-319-58553-6_9

20. Glaspie, H.W., Karwowski, W.: Human factors in information security culture: a literature review. In: Advances in Human Factors in Cybersecurity, Cham, pp. 269–280 (2018). https://doi.org/10.1007/978-3-319-60585-2_25

21. Uchendu, B., Nurse, J.R.C., Bada, M., Furnell, S.: Developing a cyber security culture: current practices and future needs. Comput. Secur. **109**, 102387 (2021). https://doi.org/10.1016/j.cose.2021.102387

22. Chan, M., Woon, I., Kankanhalli, A.: Perceptions of information security in the workplace: linking information security climate to compliant behavior. J. Inf. Priv. Secur. **1**(3), 18–41 (2005). https://doi.org/10.1080/15536548.2005.10855772

23. Beautement, A., Sasse, A., Wonham, M.: The compliance budget: managing security behaviour in organisations, Jan 2008. https://doi.org/10.1145/1595676.1595684

24. Nasir, A., Arshah, R.A., Hamid, M.R.A., Fahmy, S.: An analysis on the dimensions of information security culture concept: a review. J. Inf. Secur. Appl. **44**, 12–22 (2019). https://doi.org/10.1016/j.jisa.2018.11.003

25. Levy, Y., Ellis, T.J.: A systems approach to conduct an effective literature review in support of information systems research. InformingSciJ **9**, 181–212 (2006). https://doi.org/10.28945/479

26. Green, B., Prince, D., Roedig, U., Busby, J., Hutchison, D.: Socio-technical security analysis of Industrial Control Systems (ICS). In: Presented at the 2nd International Symposium for ICS & SCADA Cyber Security Research 2014, Sep 2014. https://doi.org/10.14236/ewic/ics-csr2014.2

27. Madnick, S., et al.: Measuring stakeholders' perceptions of cybersecurity for renewable energy systems. In: Data Analytics for Renewable Energy Integration, Cham, 2017, pp. 67–77. https://doi.org/10.1007/978-3-319-50947-1_7

28. Zanutto, A., Shreeve, B., Follis, K., Busby, J., Rashid, A.: The Shadow Warriors: in the no man's land between industrial control systems and enterprise IT systems, p. 6 (2017)

29. Michalec, O., Milyaeva, S., Rashid, A.: Reconfiguring governance: how cyber security regulations are reconfiguring water governance. Regul. Gov. https://doi.org/10.1111/rego.12423.

30. Shapira, N., Ayalon, O., Ostfeld, A., Farber, Y., Housh, M.: Cybersecurity in water sector: stakeholders perspective. J. Water Resour. Plann. Manage. **147**(8), (ASCE)WR.1943-5452.0001400, 05021008 (2021). https://doi.org/10.1061/(ASCE)WR.1943-5452.0001400

31. Skotnes, R.: Division of cyber safety and security responsibilities between control system owners and suppliers. In: Critical Infrastructure Protection X, Cham, 2016, pp. 131–146. https://doi.org/10.1007/978-3-319-48737-3_8

32. Nævestad, T.O., Meyer, S.F., Honerud, J.H.: Organizational information security culture in critical infrastructure: developing and testing a scale and its relationships to other measures of information security. In: Safety and Reliability – Safe Societies in a Changing World. CRC Press (2018)

33. Nævestad, T.O., Honerud, J.H., Meyer, S.F.: How can we explain improvements in organizational information security culture in an organization providing critical infrastructure? In: Safety and Reliability – Safe Societies in a Changing World. CRC Press (2018)

34. Piggin, R.S.H., Boyes, H.A.: Safety and security — a story of interdependence. In: 10th IET System Safety and Cyber-Security Conference 2015, Oct 2015, pp. 1–6. https://doi.org/10.1049/cp.2015.0292

35. Dewey, K., Foster, G., Hobbs, C., Salisbury, D.D.: Nuclear security culture in practice, p. 46 (2021)

36. Beautement, A., Becker, I., Parkin, S., Krol, K., Sasse, A.: Productive security: a scalable methodology for analysing employee security behaviours, pp. 253–270 (2016) [Online]. Available: https://www.usenix.org/conference/soups2016/technical-sessions/presentation/beautement

37. Da Veiga, A.: Comparing the information security culture of employees who had read the information security policy and those who had not: Illustrated through an empirical study. Inf. Comput. Secur. **24**(2), 139–151 (2016). https://doi.org/10.1108/ICS-12-2015-0048

38. Tuptuk, N., Hazell, P., Watson, J., Hailes, S.: A systematic review of the state of cyber-security in water systems. Water **13**(1) 1 (2021). https://doi.org/10.3390/w13010081

39. IAEA: Nuclear Security Culture (2008). https://www.iaea.org/publications/7977/nuclear-security-culture. Accessed 27 Nov 2021

40. IAEA: Self-assessment of nuclear security culture in facilities and activities (2017). https://www.iaea.org/publications/10983/self-assessment-of-nuclear-security-culture-in-facilities-and-activities. Accessed 27 Nov 2021

41. Ocloo, C.M., da Veiga, A., Kroeze, J.: A conceptual information security culture framework for higher learning institutions. In: Human Aspects of Information Security and Assurance, pp. 63–80, Cham, 2021. https://doi.org/10.1007/978-3-030-81111-2_6

42. Kirlappos, I., Parkin, S., Sasse, A.: Learning from "shadow security:" why understanding non-compliant behaviors provides the basis for effective security, Feb 2014. https://doi.org/10.14722/usec.2014.23007

Systematic Review of Factors that Influence the Cybersecurity Culture

Emilia N. Mwim[1(✉)] and Jabu Mtsweni[2]

[1] Department of Information System, School of Computing, College of Science Engineering and Technology, Unisa, Florida, South Africa
mwimen@unisa.ac.za
[2] Head of Information and Cyber Security Centre, CSIR, Pretoria, South Africa
jmtsweni@csir.co.za

Abstract. There is a need to shift from a purely technological approach in addressing cybersecurity threats to a more human inclusive method. As a result, cybersecurity culture is gaining momentum in research as an approach in addressing cybersecurity challenges due to human related issues. To develop a better understanding of cybersecurity culture, this paper presents a comprehensive view of cybersecurity culture (CSC) factors. These holistic cybersecurity culture factors have been developed by conducting a detailed review of literature. A total of 539 records were initially identified from seven different databases and via other sources, from which 58 records were finally selected using focused inclusion and exclusion criteria. The review identified a total of 29 cybersecurity culture factors, with security education, training, and awareness (SETA), and top management or leadership support appearing among the 10 dominant factors. The researchers produced a consolidated list of factors for CSC that can guide future researchers in this research area.

Keywords: Cybersecurity · Cybersecurity culture · Cybersecurity culture factor

1 Introduction

Cyber threats are considered a global concern across all levels of society [1, 2]. To minimise cyber-threats and their associated challenges, various technological and non-technological solutions have been applied [3, 4]. Examples of efforts focused on developing cybersecurity regulations and legislation are the development of the Health Insurance Portability and Accountability Act (HIPAA) of 1996 [104–191], the Protection of Personal Information (POPI) Act, the International Organization for Standardization (ISO), and the National Institute of Standards and Technology Cybersecurity Framework (NIST) [5–9]. The non-regulatory measures include the development and use of anti-virus software, firewall protection, encryption, and the development of policies and standards [10–14].

© IFIP International Federation for Information Processing 2022
Published by Springer Nature Switzerland AG 2022
N. Clarke and S. Furnell (Eds.): HAISA 2022, IFIP AICT 658, pp. 147–172, 2022.
https://doi.org/10.1007/978-3-031-12172-2_12

Despite all these efforts, however, cyber threats and challenges continue to increase [14]. It is argued that the core reason for the increase is that all the efforts have focused predominantly on technological solutions which on their own cannot minimise cybersecurity threats due to the element of human vulnerabilities [14]. Solving cybersecurity problems requires more than technical controls, as the human factor in security is becoming increasingly prominent, alongside technical issues [15–17]. According to research, the appropriate approach to address the human factor problem of information security is the cultivation of an information security culture [15, 17]. Similarly, to solve the human factor problem in cybersecurity, it is argued that the solution should focus on human factors by cultivating a cybersecurity culture [17]. Cybersecurity culture is still an emerging research field, which has not been well researched [17–20]. To contribute to the body of knowledge, the researchers in this study tried to provide a consolidated and holistic list of cybersecurity culture factors by conducting a systematic review. As an emerging research area, the identified factors in this research will future serve as a point of reference for fellow researchers in this area.

2   Research Aims

In this research, a systematic literature review process [21] was applied using the Preferred Reporting Items for Systematic Reviews and Meta-Analyses (PRISMA) method to develop a comprehensive list of cybersecurity culture factors that can be used as a basis for researchers working in the field of cybersecurity culture. The objective of this paper is to provide a holistic review of literature that is specific to the cybersecurity culture.

The results are combined and synthesised to develop a consolidated list of cybersecurity culture factors that can be used as a point of reference for cybersecurity culture research in the future.

3   Background

During the review, the researchers came across different definitions and description of cybersecurity culture that exist in literature [10, 17, 22–25]. The elements that emerge out very strongly in the existing definitions of cybersecurity culture include human characteristics, context and SETA. The definition of cybersecurity culture in this research is informed by the existing definitions.

"Cybersecurity culture" is defined in this research as a measure used as a performance tool by management (guided by policies and procedures) to change human characteristics and their socio-cultural measures (e.g. attitudes, assumptions, beliefs, norms, knowledge, perceptions, skills, behaviours and practices) to achieve cybersecurity at all levels of cybersecurity culture (i.e. international, national and organizational) to hinder intentional and unintentional cyber-harms.

Significant efforts have been made in addressing cybersecurity challenges, but there is a concern that the majority of the efforts have focused predominately on technological solutions [10, 14, 26], which on their own have proven insufficient in addressing cybersecurity problems because of threats emerging from human related problems [14, 16, 20, 26, 27]. This calls for the establishment of measures that will incorporate human factor elements (non-technical solutions) and cybersecurity culture is one such measures.

Up until now, the work done in the area of cybersecurity and information security culture: has (1) focused predominately on information Security culture (ISC) [2, 28–30] and (2) the reviews on CSC have not been sufficiently comprehensive as they have focused only on cybersecurity culture at a specific level (either at the international, national or organisational levels) [31, 32]; as such, there is no consolidated and comprehensive list of cybersecurity culture factors. Consequently, the majority of cybersecurity culture factors consolidated in most reviews are factors that influence the cultivation of cybersecurity culture at the organisational level and there is no consolidated and comprehensive list of factors that influences cybersecurity culture in literature. This is a major limitation in research, which intensifies the need to take a more comprehensive approach in identifying holistic and all-inclusive factors of cybersecurity culture.

4 Information Security and Cybersecurity

Over the years researchers have considered information security and cybersecurity to be the same hence the terms are used interchangeably [33–35]. Research has argued that using the terms synonymously confuses research communities and security practitioners thereby obscuring the main difference between the two concepts and that extends to information security culture and cybersecurity culture [20]. Although in most cases the information security and cybersecurity are used interchangeably, a profound difference exist between them according to literature [17, 19, 36, 37]. In addition to other differences between the terms, the critical distinction between them is based on the fact that information security focuses on the protection of information within the organizational context while cybersecurity extends to the outside borders of the organization since cyberspace allows the sharing of information outside the borders of the organization [17]. The same approach applies to information security culture and cybersecurity culture. The two concepts both refer to culture as it relates to security with the main difference being in the context they are applied. On this ground, this research finds it needful to review literature specifically on cybersecurity culture to help consolidate list of factors that are associated with cybersecurity culture.

5 Research Method

The paper followed a systematic literature review method using the PRISMA technique [38]. The PRISMA guideline for performing systematic reviews makes use of cautiously designed methods that enables the selection and review of relevant records and an analysis of the findings that emerge from the literature.

This review used four phases, as contained in the PRISMA diagram. The following study selection steps were taken in this research:

- Publications in the academic databases and non-academic databases were searched. The focus of the retrieved literature related to cybersecurity culture at all levels (international, national and organisational).
- After reviewing the title and abstract, duplicates articles were removed.
- The remaining records (after the removal of duplicates) were saved on the researchers computers and from there, imported into ATLAS.ti for final review.
- During the review, other articles were removed either because the content covered in the article was not predominantly focused on cybersecurity culture or because the paper used the concept of information security culture as a synonym for cybersecurity culture. Lastly, a few more articles were added from the references of the reviewed articles.

5.1 Data Sources and Selection Criteria

The researchers conducted a search of peer-reviewed literature through the databases depicted in Fig. 1.

Cybersecurity is a broad and multi-disciplinary research area that cuts across various industrial sectors. To ensure a rigorous search for the systematic review on cybersecurity culture, the literature search included both computing and non-computing databases. The search included peer-reviewed academic publications and a few other non-academic publications, which were included to accommodate industry, business and experts' writings on the topic of cybersecurity culture. The search was conducted between December 2010 and March 2021 and the following key words were used in the search:

"cybersecurity culture" OR "cyber security culture".

"cybersecurity cultur*" OR "cyber security culture*".

After the search, alerts were also set up for the keywords to identify any important literature that might be published after the search so that these sources could be added during the review.

The searched databases, together with the number of retrieved records, is depicted in Fig. 1.

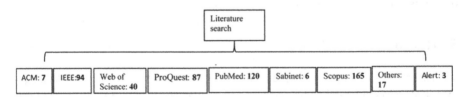

Fig. 1. Systematic review search database

The following inclusion criteria (IC) were used:

IC1 - the year range- (e.g. papers published between 2010 and 2021)

IC2 - only articles published in English

IC3 - published work in the form of journal articles, conference proceedings, policy documents, book chapters, theses, reports and/or statistics

IC4 - cybersecurity culture studies conducted at all levels of cybersecurity culture (where available, that included cybersecurity culture research done at international, national and organisational levels)

The review excluded (EX) any of the following papers:

EX1 - those that fell outside the stipulated year range (2010 – 2021)

EX2 - those not published in English

EX3 - those whose content was not predominantly cybersecurity culture

EX4 - those that covered predominantly information security culture.

5.2 Results

The keyword search yielded a total of 539 articles. After all the retrieved articles were assembled, 39 duplicates were removed. Upon review of the titles and abstracts, a further 423 records were removed because they were either irrelevant or included editor's notes. A total of 77 articles were retained for full-text review. Thereafter, 19 records were removed when the last inclusion criteria (IC) criteria was applied, which excluded those sources where cybersecurity culture was not the focus of the research, the concept was mentioned only in passing or it was an information security paper. After all these exclusions, a total of 58 records were deemed relevant for inclusion in the review to address the main research objective, which was to identify holistic factors that influence cybersecurity culture. Figure 2 depicts the PRISMA method used.

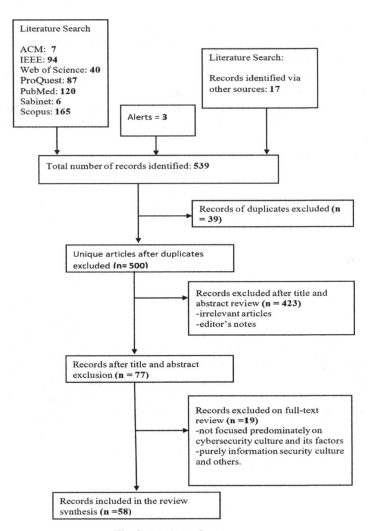

Fig. 2. PRISMA flow process

Table 1 presents the full list of all the documents reviewed and their references, as organised in ATLAS.ti.

Table 1. List of reviewed documents and their references

Document #	Author/s & year	Document #	Author/s & year
D1	Abeyratne, 2016 [23]	D35	Pătrascu, 2019 [64]
D2	Alshaikh, 2020 [40]	D36	Paul & Porche, 2012 [65]
D3	Bounas et al., 2020 [76]	D37	Pavlova, 2020 [48]
D4	Cardoso et al., 2017 [44]	D38	Ramluckan et al., 2020 [78]
D5	Ciuperca et al., 2019 [24]	D39	Reegård et al., 2019 [43]
D6	Clark et al., 2017 [52]	D40	Reid & Van Niekerk, 2014a [15]
D7	Saigushev et al., 2020 [25]	D41	Reid & Van Niekerk, 2014b [17]
D8	Corradini, 2020 [22]	D42	Reid & Van Niekerk, 2015 [72]
D9	Da Veiga, 2016 [80]	D43	Ribeiro, 2019 [75]
D10	Simona, 2019 [54]	D44	Trim & Upton, 2016 [71]
D11	ENISA, 2017 [10]	D45	Wierzynski, 2019 [66]
D12	Gcaza & Von Solms, 2017a [19]	D46	Van't Wout, 2019 [14]
D13	Gcaza et al., 2017 [20]	D47	Lewis, 2020 [67]
D14	Gcaza, 2017 [18]	D48	Rinchi, 2021 [68]
D15	Gcaza & Von Solms, 2017b [39]	D49	Marotta & Pearlson, 2019 [27]
D16	Aiken, 2019 [50]	D50	Gcaza et al., 2015 [11]
D17	Georgiadou et al., 2020 [53]	D51	Da Veiga, 2018 [47]
D18	Georgiadou et al., 2020 [73]	D52	Ronchi, 2019 [69]
D19	Georgiadou et al., 2021 [74]	D53	Branley-bell et al., 2021 [41]
D20	Ghernaouti et al., 2019 [79]	D54	Uchendu et al., 2021 [31]
D21	Ghernouti-Hélie, 2010 [56]	D55	Alvarez-Dionisi & Urrego-Baquero, 2019 [70]
D22	Gundu et al., 2019 [32]	D56	Malmedal & Roislien, 2016 [49]
D23	Gupta & Bajramovic, 2017 [57]	D57	Huang & Pearlson, 2019 [36]
D24	Holdsworth & Apeh, 2017 [12]	D58	Ogden, 2021 [42]
D25	Ioannou et al., 2019 [58]		
D26	ISACA, 2018a [77]		
D27	ISACA, 2018b [46]		

(*continued*)

Table 1. (*continued*)

Document #	Author/s & year	Document #	Author/s & year
D28	Leenen & Van Vuuren, 2019 [45]		
D29	Kortjan & Von Solms, 2014 [1]		
D30	Leenen et al., 2018 [59]		
D31	Loică, 2017 [60]		
D32	Mills, 2018 [61]		
D33	Malyuk & Miloslavskaya, 2016 [62]		
D34	Sousane, 2018 [63]		

The identified CSC factors have been found to be critical in the development, recommendations for, maintenance, best practices or framework of cybersecurity culture [10, 22, 39–45]. Therefore, the identified factors are not only elements or factors that constitute CSC; they can also be considered factors that characterize, challenge, influence, and are used in the development of CSC. The absence of these factors are (1) regarded as challenges that inhibit the cultivation and improvement of cybersecurity culture [39, 46] and (2) are considered critical source factors for developing and strengthening CSC [32, 46].

After working through years of publications, 29 factors were identified as the cybersecurity culture factors. These factors are depicted using the ATLAS.ti network diagram in Fig. 3. Among the identified CSC factors, the top 10 include training and education; awareness; top management or leadership support; human behaviour; organisational culture; cybersecurity policy and procedures; cybersecurity champions; budget and resources; knowledge; and engagement, encouragement and cooperation. Other identified factors of cybersecurity culture include cybersecurity strategy; commitment; information sharing; accountability; a cybersecurity hub; national culture; role and responsibility; compliance; ethical conduct; security audit; change management; measure of effectiveness; trust; rewards and sanctions; collectivism; physical security; collaboration; governance and control (legal and regulatory); and a business continuity plan.

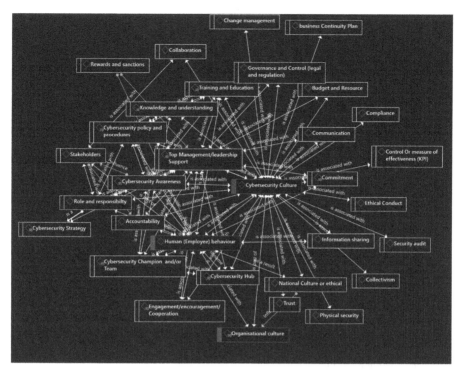

Fig. 3. Network diagram of the identified cybersecurity culture factors

5.3 Cybersecurity Culture Factors

The identified cybersecurity culture factors are summarised below according to their order of importance in the review. See APPENDIX A for the full table with factors, the number of literature sources that highlighted the factors and their literature references.

#	Cybersecurity culture factors
1.	**Cybersecurity training and education**: This factor deals with providing members of the organisations, communities and societal groups with the necessary, essential and appropriate training and education on cybersecurity. The combination of training and education emerged as the dominant factor of CSC, with 43 records highlighting this aspect during the review
2.	**Cybersecurity awareness:** This factor deals with making members and employees aware of security-related issues and maintaining their consciousness on security obligations within their organisations. Awareness was overwhelmingly highlighted as the greatest and essential factor for the cultivation and achievement of CSC. A total of 38 out of 58 reviewed records highlighted awareness a as a factor in cybersecurity culture

(continued)

(continued)

#	Cybersecurity culture factors
3.	**Top management support:** This factor also referred to as leadership support and executive buy-in, clarifies the type of support that management provides for the cultivation and implementation of CSC. Top management support assumes different forms, starting with developing cybersecurity policy; defining clear goals for the management of security; endorsement of security requirements; the willingness to commit by providing financial resources to support the implementation of cybersecurity requirements and support cybersecurity; and organising and following up on cybersecurity activities such as education, skills and awareness programmes within the organisation. This factor emerged as the third most dominant factor and was contained in 21 records
4.	**Cybersecurity policy and procedures:** This factor deals with the definition, clarification and management of cybersecurity policies and procedures that are fundamental for the achievement of CSC. Cybersecurity policy is indicated in the literature as a foundational factor for the achievement of cybersecurity culture; hence it ranked number 4 among the top factors of CSC, with 17 records testifying to this
5.	**Human behaviour:** This factor entails developing an understanding of human attributes in terms of their beliefs, values, perceptions, attitudes and emotions. Security culture should mirror people's behaviour so that security culture becomes their natural form of behaviour and CSC should shape and reshape human behaviours. These human factors are essential for the cultivation and integration of successful CSC. 14 articles signified the importance of this factor
6.	**Knowledge and understanding:** This factor relates to acquiring facts and information about the organisation upon which CSC will be built. Such knowledge assists in comprehending the diversity of groups within the organisation (e.g. educational level, age group gender group, and departmental level) and will assist the security team in making well-informed security-related decisions accommodate different groups. This factor also relates to equipping the members of the organisation with the necessary cybersecurity knowledge (e.g. on security policies and procedures) that should inform their actions regarding cybersecurity-related issues, thereby helping to create a culture of security [47]
7.	**Cybersecurity champions or a team:** This factor refers to the appointment and management of authorities in the form of individuals (e.g. chief security officers) or teams that champion cybersecurity and are responsible for ensuring a secure system, the development of awareness and training activities and consistency across organisational efforts regarding the creation and management of CSC [36]
8.	**Organisational culture:** This factor refers to the components of belief systems that form collective action, values that indicate what is considered important and artifacts that comprise the visible technology and behavioural patterns that form the bases of cybersecurity culture layers and factors

(continued)

(continued)

#	Cybersecurity culture factors
9.	**Engagement, encouragement and cooperation:** This factor addresses and manages how members of an organisation or community are involved in cybersecurity-related activities such as decision making and strategy development, are motivated to adhere to the security regulations/guidelines and how teams work collaboratively to achieve a culture of security. The importance of these factors was highlighted in 11 of the reviewed records
10.	**Budget and resources:** This factor refers to the financial and non-financial commitment and support provided for the development and maintenance of CSC
11.	**Cybersecurity strategy:** This factor addresses the strategies that guide cybersecurity practices that underlies any cybersecurity culture development. 11 articles identified the existence of cybersecurity strategy as a cybersecurity culture factor
12.	**Collaboration:** This factor deals with how collaborative efforts are initiated and strengthened by and between members (leaders and employees) and across different sectors of the organisation to confront the challenges to cybersecurity [27, 48]
13.	**Commitment:** This factor relates to assessing executive management and employee commitment to support CSC and it is evidence of the kind of relationship that exists between the organisation, management and the users. Commitment also relates to the actions that guarantee adherence to policy and foster a solid security culture [31]
14.	**Role and responsibility:** This factor deals with people's (and groups, teams, sections and levels') expectations in terms of their roles and responsibilities in achieving cybersecurity culture. 8 records indicated this as an influential factor of CSC
15.	**Risk and change management:** Risk management deals with assessing the security culture of an organisation to identify security vulnerabilities and understand their security condition for effective and improved achievement of cybersecurity [48]. Change management relates to efforts in getting members of the organisation to comprehend and accept changes related to security to prevent employee resistance to change [27, 47]
16.	**Trust:** This factor refers to the relationship that exists between the top management and employees of the organisation in relation to compliance with security policies. The factor of trust also relates to confidence in employees' actions and intentions, as well as in management's transparency and communication within the organisation [31, 49]
17.	**Communication:** This factor deals with discussions and providing feedback to the role-players that have security responsibilities. It also entails circulation of best security practices, policies and procedures to the stakeholders
18.	**Information sharing:** This factor is associated with communication that contributes to achieving CSC. It deals with sharing of security knowledge and known or potential cyber threats and vulnerabilities through formal security structures and a steering committee with the stakeholders
19.	**Rewards and sanctions:** This factor deals with the principles of rewarding good and acceptable behaviors and punishing unacceptable and non-compliant behaviours. Rewards also refer to the element of incentives in relation to cybersecurity compliance

(continued)

(*continued*)

#	Cybersecurity culture factors
20.	**Governance and control (legal and regulatory):** This factor relates to the views concerning how a group of people should be regulated and legally guided on cybersecurity issues and who should regulate them. It draws attention to the question of responsibility regarding online safety
21.	**Compliance:** This factor relates to the importance of ensuring and encouraging adherence to security policies, procedures, standards, and regulations among all organisational members. It highlights the relationship between organisational security behaviour and the organisation's existing security policies and standards
22.	**Measure of effectiveness:** This factor refers to the key performance indicators (KPIs) and controls established in the organisation for baseline measurement in evaluating the effectiveness and efficiency of their security controls. The KPIs help organisations to track any improvements
23.	**National culture:** This factor refers to national differences that determine and influence people's attitudes, beliefs, values and assumptions about CSC and the use of technologies in general
24.	**Ethical conduct:** This factor refers to the codes of ethics that guide the organisation and its members, as well as the influences of workforce perceptions and attitudes on the achievement of acceptable ethical conduct in relation to cybersecurity. This factor can help with the categorisation of attitudes and perceptions that are not consistent with the code of ethics of the organisation
25.	**Business continuity plan:** This factor relates to organisational plans of recovery and continuity in the event of threats
26.	**Collectivism:** According to this factor, individuals relate to the collective and, as a result, individual behaviours are formed by the collective shared norms and behaviours [49]
27.	**Cybersecurity hub:** As with a cybersecurity champion, this factor deals with the establishment and existence of cybersecurity centres that play a role in achieving a culture of cybersecurity
28.	**Security audit:** This factor relates to the actions of institutions to test their implemented security controls [44]
29.	**Physical security:** This factor refers to ensuring a secure location, placing physical equipment such as routers and servers in locked places, having access control and conducting background investigations on new employees and visitors, when necessary [50]

6 Discussion and Contribution

Although research has recently worked to aggregate various components (factors and metrics) that are essential (core) for the achievement of cybersecurity culture [31], the current research produced a more comprehensive list of factors of cybersecurity culture, as it focused on understanding and consolidating factors across all levels of cybersecurity culture. Moreover, there are a few additional factors that might not be considered essential (core), but their significance should not be underestimated as they might/could emerge as factors that contribute to the achievement of cybersecurity culture at a particular level or in a different context, since cybersecurity culture is not a one size fits-all but is greatly influenced by contextual factors. In conducting this review, 11 factors were identified as additional cybersecurity culture factors that are missing from recent review by [31]. These factors include cybersecurity strategy; budget and resources; organisational culture; human behavior; collectivism; a cybersecurity hub; a business continuity plan; physical security; information sharing; a security audit; and measure of effectiveness.

Among all the identified factors, fulfilling the three elements of providing security education, training and awareness, together with having the support of top management, ensuring a sound policy that promotes cybersecurity, understanding human factors, acquiring knowledge and understanding of the organization, establishing cybersecurity champions and understanding organizational culture, appeared as the leading cybersecurity culture factors. A significant number of the reviewed articles indicated in one way or another the importance of these factors in the development, maintenance, best practices, recommendations for and framework of cybersecurity culture. These factors are considered the top factors, not necessarily because of their number of occurrences in the literature, but because of their level of significance in the cultivation, implementation and maintenance of cybersecurity culture, as well as in the level of association and relationship that they have with other factors.

Some of the top cybersecurity culture factors identified in this review are inconsistent with top factors identified in other reviews, for instance top management support, awareness, training, policy, knowledge, role and responsibility. However, some of the top factors identified in this review, such as organisational culture, human factors and budget and resources, are not even recognised as cybersecurity factors in a recent review conducted by [31].

7   Limitations and Future Work

A possible limitation of this paper is that it included a few sources of literature on security culture in the reviewed records. Since this paper is part of a bigger research, the identified factors are still to be validated. In future studies, the researchers plan to provide a detailed comparison between cybersecurity culture and information security culture factors (to identify factors that are specific to each of these types of security culture). Also, part of the future research would involve mapping and categorising the identified CSC factors according to the human factor domain [51].

8   Conclusion

The study developed a comprehensive list of cybersecurity culture factors by broadening the search scope and the review to include cybersecurity culture studies conducted at all levels of cybersecurity culture, not just those specific to the organisational level. This helped the researchers to consolidate factors of cybersecurity culture that are spread across all levels. Such consolidation will help future researchers in the field and can also help in the development and maintenance of cybersecurity culture as the developers would be able to consider factor/s that are level specific but might contribute to building a cybersecurity culture at a different level. During the review, a broad list of 29 factors, summarised in Table 1, were consolidated as the cybersecurity culture factors that can be added to the body of knowledge in this fast-emerging field of research.

Appendix

#	Cybersecurity culture factors	# of literature sources and their references
1.	**Cybersecurity training and education**: This factor deals with providing members of the organisations, communities and societal groups with the necessary, essential and appropriate training and education on cybersecurity. The combination of training and education emerged as the dominant factor of CSC, with 43 records highlighting this aspect during the review	The 43 records are – [1, 10, 11, 15, 18–20, 22–25, 27, 31, 32, 36, 39–41, 44–48, 52–54, 56–72]
2.	**Cybersecurity awareness**: This factor deals with making members and employees aware of security-related issues and maintaining their consciousness on security obligations within their organisations. Awareness was overwhelmingly highlighted as the greatest and essential factor for the cultivation and achievement of CSC. A total of 38 out of 58 reviewed records highlighted awareness a as a factor in cybersecurity culture	The 38 records are – [1, 10–12, 17–20, 22, 23, 27, 31, 32, 36, 39–45, 47, 48, 54, 56–61, 64, 66–70, 73, 74]

(continued)

(*continued*)

#	Cybersecurity culture factors	# of literature sources and their references
3.	**Top management support:** This factor also referred to as leadership support and executive buy-in, clarifies the type of support that management provides for the cultivation and implementation of CSC. Top management support assumes different forms, starting with developing cybersecurity policy; defining clear goals for the management of security; endorsement of security requirements; the willingness to commit by providing financial resources to support the implementation of cybersecurity requirements and support cybersecurity; and organising and following up on cybersecurity activities such as education, skills and awareness programmes within the organisation. This factor emerged as the third most dominant factor and was contained in 21 records	21 records are – [10, 19, 22, 31, 32, 36, 39, 40, 42–44, 46, 47, 50, 52, 58, 65, 67, 70, 74, 75]
4.	**Cybersecurity policy and procedures:** This factor deals with the definition, clarification and management of cybersecurity policies and procedures that are fundamental for the achievement of CSC. Cybersecurity policy is indicated in the literature as a foundational factor for the achievement of cybersecurity culture; hence it ranked number 4 among the top factors of CSC, with 17 records testifying to this	The 17 records are – [18, 19, 31, 32, 39, 41, 43–47, 52, 58, 62, 65, 71, 76]

(*continued*)

(continued)

#	Cybersecurity culture factors	# of literature sources and their references
5.	**Human behaviour:** This factor entails developing an understanding of human attributes in terms of their beliefs, values, perceptions, attitudes and emotions. Security culture should mirror people's behaviour so that security culture becomes their natural form of behaviour and CSC should shape and reshape human behaviours. These human factors are essential for the cultivation and integration of successful CSC. 14 articles signified the importance of this factor	The 14 records are – [10, 14, 17, 19, 22, 24, 31, 32, 36, 40, 41, 43, 45, 49]
6.	**Knowledge and understanding:** This factor relates to acquiring facts and information about the organisation upon which CSC will be built. Such knowledge assists in comprehending the diversity of groups within the organisation (e.g. educational level, age group gender group, and departmental level) and will assist the security team in making well-informed security-related decisions accommodate different groups. This factor also relates to equipping the members of the organisation with the necessary cybersecurity knowledge (e.g. on security policies and procedures) that should inform their actions regarding cybersecurity-related issues, thereby helping to create a culture of security [47]	The 14 records are – [10, 22, 24, 25, 36, 39, 41, 44, 46–48, 57, 61, 65]

(continued)

(continued)

#	Cybersecurity culture factors	# of literature sources and their references
7.	**Cybersecurity champions or a team:** This factor refers to the appointment and management of authorities in the form of individuals (e.g. chief security officers) or teams that champion cybersecurity and are responsible for ensuring a secure system, the development of awareness and training activities and consistency across organisational efforts regarding the creation and management of CSC [36]	The 13 records are – [14, 22, 31, 36, 39, 40, 42, 44, 46, 52, 58, 59, 66]
8.	**Organisational culture:** This factor refers to the components of belief systems that form collective action, values that indicate what is considered important and artifacts that comprise the visible technology and behavioural patterns that form the bases of cybersecurity culture layers and factors	The 12 records are – [10, 17, 22, 27, 32, 41, 43, 45, 48, 59, 63, 74]
9.	**Engagement, encouragement and cooperation:** This factor addresses and manages how members of an organisation or community are involved in cybersecurity-related activities such as decision making and strategy development, are motivated to adhere to the security regulations/guidelines and how teams work collaboratively to achieve a culture of security. The importance of these factors was highlighted in 11 of the reviewed records	The 11 records are – [10, 14, 22, 27, 31, 39, 43, 46, 58, 61, 77]

(continued)

(continued)

#	Cybersecurity culture factors	# of literature sources and their references
10.	**Budget and resources:** This factor refers to the financial and non-financial commitment and support provided for the development and maintenance of CSC	The 11records are – [11, 20, 22, 36, 39, 44, 46, 52, 66, 66]
11.	**Cybersecurity strategy:** This factor addresses the strategies that guide cybersecurity practices that underlies any cybersecurity culture development. 11 articles identified the existence of cybersecurity strategy as a cybersecurity culture factor	The 11 records are – [10, 19, 22, 24, 25, 36, 44, 46, 56, 62, 63]
12.	**Collaboration:** This factor deals with how collaborative efforts are initiated and strengthened by and between members (leaders and employees) and across different sectors of the organisation to confront the challenges to cybersecurity [27, 48]	The 10 records are – [10, 18, 19, 23, 36, 40, 45, 46, 57–59]
13.	**Commitment:** This factor relates to assessing executive management and employee commitment to support CSC and it is evidence of the kind of relationship that exists between the organisation, management and the users. Commitment also relates to the actions that guarantee adherence to policy and foster a solid security culture [31]	The 9 records are – [10, 11, 22, 27, 31, 36, 46, 57, 65]
14.	**Role and responsibility:** This factor deals with people's (and groups, teams, sections and levels') expectations in terms of their roles and responsibilities in achieving cybersecurity culture. 8 records indicated this as an influential factor of CSC	The 8 records are – [17, 20, 27, 31, 42, 46, 47, 57]

(continued)

(*continued*)

#	Cybersecurity culture factors	# of literature sources and their references
15.	**Risk and change management:** Risk management deals with assessing the security culture of an organisation to identify security vulnerabilities and understand their security condition for effective and improved achievement of cybersecurity [48]. Change management relates to efforts in getting members of the organisation to comprehend and accept changes related to security to prevent employee resistance to change [27, 47]	The 8 records are – [14, 27, 31, 32, 47, 65, 74, 78]
16.	**Trust:** This factor refers to the relationship that exists between the top management and employees of the organisation in relation to compliance with security policies. The factor of trust also relates to confidence in employees' actions and intentions, as well as in management's transparency and communication within the organisation [31, 49]	The 7 records are – [31, 41, 47, 49, 53, 58, 73]
17.	**Communication:** This factor deals with discussions and providing feedback to the role-players that have security responsibilities. It also entails circulation of best security practices, policies and procedures to the stakeholders	The 6 records are – [36, 42, 46, 58, 67, 74]

(*continued*)

(continued)

#	Cybersecurity culture factors	# of literature sources and their references
18.	**Information sharing:** This factor is associated with communication that contributes to achieving CSC. It deals with sharing of security knowledge and known or potential cyber threats and vulnerabilities through formal security structures and a steering committee with the stakeholders	The 5 records are – [23, 45, 46, 58, 79]
19.	**Rewards and sanctions:** This factor deals with the principles of rewarding good and acceptable behaviors and punishing unacceptable and non-compliant behaviours. Rewards also refer to the element of incentives in relation to cybersecurity compliance	The 5 records are – [31, 36, 46, 65, 67]
20.	**Governance and control (legal and regulatory):** This factor relates to the views concerning how a group of people should be regulated and legally guided on cybersecurity issues and who should regulate them. It draws attention to the question of responsibility regarding online safety	The 5 records are – [10, 39, 49, 53, 73]
21.	**Compliance:** This factor relates to the importance of ensuring and encouraging adherence to security policies, procedures, standards, and regulations among all organisational members. It highlights the relationship between organisational security behaviour and the organisation's existing security policies and standards	The 5 records are – [23, 31, 41, 65, 74]

(continued)

(*continued*)

#	Cybersecurity culture factors	# of literature sources and their references
22.	**Measure of effectiveness:** This factor refers to the key performance indicators (KPIs) and controls established in the organisation for baseline measurement in evaluating the effectiveness and efficiency of their security controls. The KPIs help organisations to track any improvements	The 4 records are – [32, 45, 46, 58]
23.	**National culture:** This factor refers to national differences that determine and influence people's attitudes, beliefs, values and assumptions about CSC and the use of technologies in general	The 4 records are – [10, 22, 31, 32]
24.	**Ethical conduct:** This factor refers to the codes of ethics that guide the organisation and its members, as well as the influences of workforce perceptions and attitudes on the achievement of acceptable ethical conduct in relation to cybersecurity. This factor can help with the categorisation of attitudes and perceptions that are not consistent with the code of ethics of the organisation	The 4 records are – [31, 45, 47, 62]
25.	**Business continuity plan:** This factor relates to organisational plans of recovery and continuity in the event of threats	The 4 report are – [50, 53, 73, 74]
26.	**Collectivism:** According to this factor, individuals relate to the collective and, as a result, individual behaviours are formed by the collective shared norms and behaviours [49]	The 3 records are – [40, 45, 49]

(*continued*)

(continued)

#	Cybersecurity culture factors	# of literature sources and their references
27.	**Cybersecurity hub:** As with a cybersecurity champion, this factor deals with the establishment and existence of cybersecurity centres that play a role in achieving a culture of cybersecurity	The 3 records are – [40, 44, 59]
28.	**Security audit:** This factor relates to the actions of institutions to test their implemented security controls [44]	The 2 records are – [44, 50]
29.	**Physical security:** This factor refers to ensuring a secure location, placing physical equipment such as routers and servers in locked places, having access control and conducting background investigations on new employees and visitors, when necessary [50]	The only 1 record is – [50]

References

1. Kortjan, N., Vson Solms, R.: A conceptual framework for cyber-security awareness and education in SA. South African Computer Journal **52**, 29–41 (2014). https://doi.org/10.18489/sacj.v52i0.201
2. Hassan, N.H., Maarop, N., Ismail, Z., Abidin, W.Z.: Information security culture in health informatics environment: A qualitative approach. In: 2017 International Conference on Research and Innovation in Information Systems (ICRIIS), pp, 1–6 (2017). https://doi.org/10.1109/ICRIIS.2017.8002450
3. Harries, D., Yellowless, P.M.: Cyberterrorism: Is the U.S. Healthcare System Safe? Telemedicine and e-Health **19**(1), 61–66 (2013)
4. Rengamani, H., Upadhyaya, S., Rao, H.R., Kumaraguru, P.: Protecting senior citizens from cyber security attacks in the e-health scenario: an international perspective. In: Proceedings of the Sixth Annual Workshop on Cyber Security and Information Intelligence Research - CSIIRW '10, pp, 1–4 (2010)
5. Jalali, M.S., Kaiser, J.P.: Cybersecurity in hospitals: a systematic, organizational perspective. J. Med. Internet Res. **20**(5), e10059 (2018). https://doi.org/10.2196/10059
6. U.S. PUBLIC LAW: Health Insurance Portability and Accountability Act of 1996 (1996)
7. National Institute of Standards and Technology: Framework for Improving Critical Infrastructure Cybersecurity. Version 1.1, April 16 (2018)
8. Information Regulator (South Africa): Protection of Personal Information Act, 2013. Act No. 4 (2013)

9. ISO 27799:2016 - Health informatics — Information security management in health using ISO/IEC 27002. In: International. Organisation for Standardization (2016). https://www.iso.org/standard/62777.html

10. European Union Agency for Network and Information Security (ENISA): Cyber Security Culture in Organisations (2017). www.enisa.europa.eu

11. Gcaza, N., Von Solms, R., Van Vuuren, J.J.: An ontology for a national cyber-security culture environment. In: Proceedings of the Ninth International Symposium on Human Aspects of Information Security & Assurance (HAISA 2015), pp, 1–10 (2015)

12. Holdsworth, J., Apeh, E.: An effective immersive cyber security awareness learning platform for businesses in the hospitality sector. In: Proceedings of 2017 IEEE 25th International Requirements Engineering Conference Workshops, REW 2017, pp, 111–117 (2017). https://doi.org/10.1109/REW.2017.47

13. Pfleeger, S.L., Caputo, D.D.: Leveraging behavioral science to mitigate cyber security risk. Computers and Security **31**(4), 597–611 (2012). https://doi.org/10.1016/j.cose.2011.12.010

14. Van' 't Wout, C.: Develop and maintain a cybersecurity organisational culture. In: 14th International Conference on Cyber Warfare and Security (ICCWS 2019), pp, 457–466 (2019)

15. Reid, R., Van Niekerk, J.: Towards an education campaign for fostering a societal, cyber security culture. In: 8th International Symposium on Human Aspects of Information Security & Assurance (HAISA 2014), pp, 174–184 (2014)

16. Ponemon Institute: The Rise of Ransomware. Ponemon Institute LLC, January (2017)

17. Reid, R., Van Niekerk, J.: From information security to cyber security cultures. In: 2014 Information Security for South Africa - Proceedings of the ISSA 2014 Conference, pp, 1–7 (2014)

18. Gcaza, N.: A National Strategy towards Cultivating a Cybersecurity Culture in South Africa. PhD thesis, 1–380. Nelson Mandela Metropolitan University Port Elizabeth, South Africa (2017)

19. Gcaza, N., von Solms, R.: Cybersecurity Culture: An Ill-Defined Problem. In: Bishop, M., Futcher, L., Miloslavskaya, N., Theocharidou, M. (eds.) WISE 2017. IAICT, vol. 503, pp. 98–109. Springer, Cham (2017). https://doi.org/10.1007/978-3-319-58553-6_9

20. Gcaza, N., Von Solms, R., Grobler, M.M., Van Vuuren, J.J.: A general morphological analysis: Delineating a cyber-security culture. Information & Computer Security **25**(3), 259–278 (2017). https://doi.org/10.1108/ICS-12-2015-0046

21. Xiao, Y., Watson, M.: Guidance on conducting a systematic literature review. J. Plan. Educ. Res. **39**(1), 93–112 (2019). https://doi.org/10.1177/0739456X17723971

22. Corradini, I.: Building a cybersecurity culture. In: Building a Cybersecurity Culture in Organizations, pp. 63–86. Springer International Publishing, Berlin/Heidelberg, Germany (2020). https://doi.org/10.1007/978-3-030-43999-6_4

23. Abeyratne, R.: Rulemaking in air transport: a deconstructive analysis, p. 252. Springer International publishing, Switzerland (2016). https://doi.org/10.1007/978-3-319-44657-8

24. Ciuperca, E.M., Vevera, V., Cirnu, C.: Social variables of cyber security educational programmes. In: In The 15th International Scientific Conference eLearning and Software for Education Bucharest, pp. 190–194. Bucharest (2019)

25. Saigushev, N.Y., Vedeneeva, O.A., Melekhova, Y.B., Tsaran, A.A.: Cooperation of future automated machinery specialists in informational context as a means of communication during vocational training process. In: 7th International Conference on Actual Problems in Machine Building IOP Conference Series: Materials Science and Engineering, p. 843 (2020). https://doi.org/10.1088/1757-899X/843/1/012002

26. Gcaza, N., Von Solms, R., Van Vuuren, J.: An ontology for a national cyber-security culture environment. In: Proceedings of the Ninth International Symposium on Human Aspects of Information Security & Assurance (HAISA 2015), pp. 1–10 (2015)

27. Marotta, A., Pearlson, K.: A culture of cybersecurity at banca popolare di sondrio. In: 25th Americas Conference on Information Systems (AMCIS 2019), pp. 1–10 (2019)
28. Da Veiga, A., Eloff, J.H.P.: A framework and assessment instrument for information security culture. Comput. Secur. 29(2), 196–207 (2010). https://doi.org/10.1016/j.cose.2009.09.002
29. Da Veiga, A., Martins, N.: Improving the information security culture through monitoring and implementation actions illustrated through a case study. Comput. Secur. 49, 162–176 (2015). https://doi.org/10.1016/j.cose.2014.12.006
30. Thomson, K.L., Von Solms, R., Louw, L.: Cultivating an organizational information security culture. Computer Fraud Security 7–11 (2006). https://doi.org/10.1016/S1361-3723(06)704 30-4
31. Uchendu, B., Nurse, J.R.C., Bada, M., Furnell, S.: Developing a cyber security culture: current practices and future needs. Computer & Security 109, 102387 (2021). https://doi.org/10.1016/j.cose.2021.102387
32. Gundu, T., Maronga, M.I, Boucher, D.: Industry 4. 0 business perspective: fostering a cyber security culture in a culturally diverse workplace. In: Proceedings of 4th International Conference on the Internet, Cyber Security and Information Systems, pp. 85–94. Kalpa Publication in Computing (2019)
33. Astakhova, L.V.: The concept of the information-security culture. Sci. Tech. Inf. Process. 41(1), 22–28 (2014). https://doi.org/10.3103/S0147688214010067
34. Ghernaouti-Hélie, S.: An inclusive information society needs a global approach of information security. In: Proceedings of International Conference on Availability, Reliability Security, pp. 658–662 (2009). https://doi.org/10.1109/ARES.2009.127
35. Republic of Uganda Republic of Uganda Ministry of Information and Communications Technology (Niss Final Draft), pp. 1–54 (2011)
36. Huang, K., Pearlson, K.: for what technology can' t fix: building a model of organizational cybersecurity culture. In: Proceeding of the 52nd Hawaii International Conference on System Sciences, pp. 6398–6407 (2019)
37. van Solms, R., van Niekerk, J.: From information security to cyber security. Computer Security 38, 97–102 (2013). https://doi.org/10.1016/j.cose.2013.04.004
38. Moher, D., Liberati, A., Tetzlaff, J., Altman, D.G., Group, P.: Preferred reporting items for systematic reviews and meta-analyses: the PRISMA statement. Annuls of Internal Medicine 151(4), 264–270 (2009)
39. Gcaza, N., Von Solms, R.: A strategy for a cybersecurity culture: a south african perspective. Ele. J. Info. Sys. Develop. Countries 80(1), 1–17 (2017). https://doi.org/10.1002/j.1681-4835.2017.tb00590.x
40. Alshaikh, M.: Developing cybersecurity culture to influence employee behavior: a practice perspective. Computers & Security 98 (2020). https://doi.org/10.1016/j.cose.2020.102003
41. Branley-bell, D., Coventry, L., Sillence, E.: Promoting cybersecurity culture change in health-care. In: The 14th PErvasive Technologies Related to Assistive Environments Conference, pp, 544–549 (2021)
42. Ogden, S.E.: Cybersecurity: creating a cybersecurity culture. Master thesis. California State University, San Bernardino (2021)
43. Reegård, K., Blackett, C., Katta, V.: The concept of cybersecurity culture. In: 29th European Safety and Reliability Conference, pp. 4036–4043 (2019)
44. Cardoso, G.M.S., Laureano, R.D., Serrao, C.: Cybersecurity culture in portuguese organizations: an exploratory analysis. In: Iberian Conference on Information Systems and Technologies (CISTI), pp. 7–12 (2017). https://doi.org/10.23919/CISTI.2017.7976008
45. Leenen, L., van Vuuren, J.C.J.: Framework for the cultivation of a military cybersecurity culture. In: 14th International Conference on Cyber Warfare and Security (ICCWS 2019), pp. 212–220 (2019)

46. Information Systems Audit and Control Association (ISACA).: Narrowing the Culture Gap for Better. ISACA, pp. 1–11 (2018)
47. Da Veiga, A.: Achieving a security culture. In: Cybersecurity Education for Awareness and Compliance, pp. 72–100. IGI Global (2018)
48. Pavlova, E.: Enhancing the organisational culture related to cyber security during the university digital transformation. Information & Security **46**(3), 239–249 (2020). https://doi.org/10.11610/isij.4617
49. Malmedal, B., Roislien, H.E.: The Norwegian Cyber Security Culture. Norwegian Centre for Information Security (NorSIS) (2016)
50. Aiken, G.M.: Cybersecurity and productivity: has a cybersecurity culture gone too far? In: ASBBS Proceedings of the 26th Annual Conference, pp. 13–23. American Society of Business and Behavioral Sciences, San Diego (2019)
51. Alhogail, A., Mirza, A., Bakry, S.H.: A comprehensive human factor framework for information security in organizations. J. Theor. Appl. Inf. Technol. **78**(2), 201–211 (2015)
52. Clark, R.M., Panguluri, S., Nelson, T.D., Wyman, R.P.: Protecting drinking water utilities from cyberthreats. J. Am. Water Works Assoc. **109**(2), 50–58 (2017). https://doi.org/10.5942/jawwa.2017.109.0021
53. Georgiadou, A., Mouzakitis, S., Bounas, K., Askounis, D.: A cyber-security culture framework for assessing organization readiness. J. Comp. Info. Sys. 1–11 (2020). https://doi.org/10.1080/08874417.2020.1845583
54. Simona, E.: The concept of cybersecurity culture. In: The Fourth Annual Conference of the National Defency College Romania in the New International Security Dynamics, pp. 176–4191. Carol I National Defence University Publishing House (2019)
55. Ghernouti-Hélie, S.A.: National strategy for an effective cybersecurity approach and culture. In: ARES 2010 - 5th International Conference on Availability, Reliability, and Security, pp. 370–373 (2010). https://doi.org/10.1109/ARES.2010.119
56. Gupta, D., Bajramovic, E.: Security culture for nuclear facilities. In: AIP Conference Proceeding 1799, p. 050014 (2017). https://doi.org/10.1063/1.4972948
57. Ioannou, M., Stavrou, E., Bada, M.: Cybersecurity culture in computer security incident response teams: Investigating difficulties in communication and coordination. In: 2019 International Conference Cyber Security Protection of Digital Services Cyber Security, pp. 1–4 (2019). https://doi.org/10.1109/CyberSecPODS.2019.8885240
58. Leenen, L., Aschman, M., Grobler, M., van Heerden, A.: Facing the culture gap in operationalising cyber within a military context. In: Proceedings of the 13th International Conference on Cyber Warfare and Security, pp. 387–394 (2018)
59. Loică, M.F.: Genesis of cyber security culture – an important component of education for a modern society. In: International Scientific Conference "Strategies XXI", pp. 387–397 (2017)
60. Mills, R.R.: The current state of insider threat awareness and readiness in corporate cyber security - an analysis of definitions, prevention, detection and mitigation. Utica College, pp. 1–68 (2018)
61. Malyuk, A., Miloslavskaya, N.: Cybersecurity culture as an element of IT professional training. In: 2016 3rd International Conference on Digital Information Processing, Data Mining, Wireless Communication (DIPDMWC 2016), pp. 205–210 (2016). https://doi.org/10.1109/DIPDMWC.2016.7529390
62. Sousane, R.J.: Understanding federal cybersecurity culture: an expert perspective on current and ideal state. PhD Theses, pp. 1–185. George Washington University (2018)
63. Pătrascu, P.: Promoting cybersecurity culture through education. In: 15th International Scientific Conference on eLearning and Software for Education, pp. 273–279 (2019)
64. Paul, C., Porche, I.R.: Toward a U.S. army cyber security culture. Int. J. Cyber Warfare and Terrorism **1**(3), 70–80 (2012). https://doi.org/10.4018/ijcwt.2011070105

65. Wierzynski, A.J.: The Vulnerabilities of Autonomous Vehicles. Master Thesis, 125. Utica college (2019)
66. Lewis, J.: What is cybersecurity culture, and how do you build it? a strong cybersecurity culture can help keep your organization safe—and your employees engaged. Cira (2021). https://www.cira.ca/blog/cybersecurity/what-cybersecurity-culture-and-how-do-you-build-it
67. Rinchi.: How to create cybersecurity culture according to an SMS scheduling feature. In: TECHINAFRICA (2021). https://www.techinafrica.com/create-cyber-security-culture-according-professional/. Accessed 15 May 2021
68. Ronchi, A.M.: Fostering the culture of cyber security. IST-Africa 2019 conference Proceedings (IST-Africa 2019), pp. 1–10 (2019). https://doi.org/10.23919/ISTAFRICA.2019.8764870
69. Alvarez-Dionisi, L.E., Urrego-Baquero, N.: Implementing a cybersecurity culture. Isaca Journal **2**, 1–6 (2019)
70. Trim, P., Upton, D.: Cyber Security Culture: Counteracting Cyber Threats through Organizational Learning and Training. Routledge, New York (2016)
71. Reid, R., Van Niekerk, J.: A cyber security culture fostering campaign through the lens of active audience theory. In: Proceeding of the 9th International Symposium on Human Aspects of Information Security and Assurance (HAISA 2015), pp. 34–44 (2015)
72. Georgiadou, A., Mouzakitis, S., Askounis, D.: Towards assessing critical infrastructures' cyber-security culture during COVID-19 crisis: a tailor-made survey. In: Wyld, D.C., et al. (eds.) CSEA, DMDBS, NSEC, NETWORKS, Fuzzy, NATL, SIGEM – 2020, pp. 71–80 (2020). https://doi.org/10.5121/csit.2020.101806
73. Georgiadou, A., Mouzakitis, S., Askounis, D.: Designing a cyber-security culture assessment survey targeting critical infrastructures during covid-19 crisis. Int. J. Netw. Secu. ITs Appli. **13**(1), 33–50 (2021). https://doi.org/10.5121/ijnsa.2021.13103
74. Ribeiro, L.G.: Understanding Phishing Mitigation Strategies in the U.S. Federal Government: a Qualitative Multiple Descriptive Case Study. Phd Thesis. Capella University (2019)
75. Bounas, K., Georgiadou, A., Kontoulis, M., Mouzakitis, S., Askounis, D.: Towards a cyber-security culture tool through a holistic, multi-dimensional assessment framework. In: Proceedings of the 13th IADIS International Conference Information Systems 2020 (IS 2020). pp. 135–139 (2020). https://doi.org/10.33965/is2020_202006c016
76. Information Systems Audit and Control Association (ISACA).: The Business Impact of a Cybersecurity Culture. ISACA (2018)
77. Ramluckan, T., van Niekerk, B., Martins, I.: A change management perspective to implementing a cyber security culture. In: European Conference on Information Warfare Security (ECCWS), pp. 442–448 (2020). https://doi.org/10.34190/EWS.20.059
78. Ghernaouti, S., Cellier, L., Wanner, B.: Information sharing in cybersecurity: enhancing security, trust and privacy by capacity building. In: 2019 3rd Cyber Security in Networking Conference (CSNet 2019), pp. 58–62 (2019). https://doi.org/10.1109/CSNet47905.2019.9108944
79. Da Veiga, A.: A cybersecurity culture research philosophy and approach to develop a valid and reliable measuring instrument. In: Proceedings of 2016 SAI Computing Conference (SAI 2016), pp. 1006–1015 (2016). https://doi.org/10.1109/SAI.2016.7556102

Cyber4Dev Security Culture Model for African Countries

Victor Reppoh[1,2(✉)] ⓘ and Adéle da Veiga[1] ⓘ

[1] School of Computing, College of Science, Engineering and Technology, University of South Africa (UNISA), Florida Campus, Johannesburg, South Africa
`reppohv@who.int, dveiga@unisa.ac.za`
[2] Information Technology Management (ITM), World Health Organization – Zimbabwe, Harare, Zimbabwe

Abstract. Creating a good information security culture among employees within organizations is the cornerstone for a safe and robust cyberspace. Furthermore, a strong information security culture within organizations will assist in reducing the effects of human habits that lead to data breaches. This article seeks to conduct a scoping review of the scholarly literature on Cyber Resilience for Development (Cyber4Dev) security culture within the context of African countries. With limited scholarly articles available for Cyber4Dev, the review will focus on information security culture to adapt it to a Cyber4Dev security culture that organizations in Africa can replicate. Using the Preferred Reporting Items for Systematic Reviews and Meta-Analyses (PRISMA) for the scoping review, this paper analysed 40 scholarly articles on information security culture to propose a Cyber4Dev security culture model for organizations applicable within an African context. Economic, social-culture and trust were identified as some of the factors to consider in an African context to promote an information security culture. Organisations can consider these factors as part of their information security programs. The model serves as reference for further research to explore the influence of the identified factors in an African context.

Keywords: Information security culture · Cyber4Dev · Cyber security · Cyber resilience · Developing

1 Introduction

With the rapid expansion of the internet and its dependent technologies like cloud computing, cyber security threats have also grown exponentially [1]. Developing countries, especially those in Africa, are highly susceptible to these threats due to a myriad of challenges, including inadequate technological infrastructure, low literacy rates, and poverty, which harm cyber security awareness. As a result, Africa is a soft target for cybercriminals [2]. With these pitfalls in mind, Cyber Resilience for Development (Cyber4Dev), a European Union project, seeks to ensure that developing countries enjoy a digital environment that is open, irrepressible, and secure [3]. Unfortunately, under the African

© IFIP International Federation for Information Processing 2022
Published by Springer Nature Switzerland AG 2022
N. Clarke and S. Furnell (Eds.): HAISA 2022, IFIP AICT 658, pp. 173–185, 2022.
https://doi.org/10.1007/978-3-031-12172-2_13

Union (AU) banner, African countries have not fully complied with their own African Union Convention on Cyber Security and Personal Data Protection due to innumerable challenges faced on the continent [4].

This paper seeks to conduct a scoping literature review of the scholarly literature on Cyber Resilience for Development (Cyber4Dev) security culture within the context of African countries. The Cyber4Dev project is a relatively new concept and thus still has limited available literature. Therefore, the authors reviewed the literature on the broad concept of information security culture with a bias towards African countries due to their unique governance, poverty, infrastructure, and literacy challenges, which hamper efficient and effective cyber security culture development [5]. The authors reviewed and consolidated information from 40 articles on information security culture and proposed a Cyber4Dev Security Culture Model for use by organizations in Africa.

2 Research Problem and Research Questions

Cyber4Dev security culture is a new concept with very little scholarly literature available for review or study. Consequently, research material on this European Union project is scarce with its website positing its objective for international cooperation to bring about adequate capacity in cyber security [6]. However, many scholarly articles on information security culture need contextualizing into an African perspective. With their litany of difficulties curbing cybercrimes, including inadequate legal frameworks, technological inadequacies, lack of requisite human resource skills and security, African countries have unique information security challenges [7]. Many African internet users are not technically skilled, with a large percentage of them having restricted access to computers and the internet [8]. In Mozambique, for example, there is a scarcity of cyber security awareness programs, skills development, and cyber security training and education [8]. In Gambia by September 2020, there were no national cybersecurity awareness programs initiated by the government to raise awareness on the pitfalls of insecure cyberspace practices [9]. Even though South Africa is one of the few African countries having a national cybersecurity policy framework addressing the cybersecurity environment, little is known about this policy and information on safeguarding cyberspace [9]. Literature on information security culture is abounding, but there is limited focus to adapt and implement it in an African context.

This paper aims to define Cyber4Dev security culture from an African perspective and contribute to this area's limited body of knowledge. In line with achieving this objective, the author formulated the following research questions:

- Which are the models or frameworks developed for the Cyber4Dev security culture?
- What factors should be considered when creating a Cyber4Dev security culture model?

3 Background

3.1 Defining Information Security Culture and Cyber4Dev Security Culture

The assumptions, ethics, and attitudes that employees share about the safety of institutional data are defined as the information security culture. This culture is a sub-culture of the organizational culture that encompasses the employees' everyday responsibilities, guidelines, activities, and practices that should assist them in protecting the firm's information assets [9]. The rapid development of new technologies in the information and communication technology (ICT) industry has also led to exponential growth in information security risks [10]. Information security culture helps to secure security risks within organizations by promoting safe cyber practices by individuals [11, 12]. However, more researchers have posited that solving information security risks and threats cannot purely be from a technological perspective [13]. Human capital plays a crucial role in securing organizations from these cyber threats; humans being viewed as the weakest link in information security terms [13, 14]. Any institutional interventions to curb cyber threats or risks which fail to consider the human element dismally fall short of the requisite expectations [15]. Employees, for example, need to act and manipulate institutional information in a consistent manner compliant with the organization's information security policy [16]. Social and national cultures like obedience to authority, can impact an individual's attitudes and assumptions, and thus shape an information security culture [17]. Furthermore, information security culture is dynamic and ever-changing, and thus, a balance between stability and constant evolution is needed to ensure that organizations adequately protect their information systems.

Cybersecurity culture is a subset of information security culture that describes how users protect data in cyberspace. On the other hand, the entire lifecycle of information (in its various formats) within organizations, as well as the safeguards that users employ to protect it, is the focus of an information security culture [18]. A Cyber4Dev security culture likewise can be defined as people-driven, cyber-safe actions and behaviors that protect organizations' information assets in developing countries. This culture takes cognizance of the shared assumptions, ethics, and attitudes, of employees in African organizations towards the protection information assets. Adopting a Cyber4Dev security culture will ensure that employee interactions with information resources will not harm the institutions via the information superhighway [19]. Employees, when adequately trained, can become an organization's most vital link when it comes to the security of information resources [20]. A Cyber4Dev security culture will ensure that individuals within African organizations make accountable decisions and take responsible actions that safeguard organizations' information assets.

3.2   Cyber Security Challenges in Africa

The term "cyber security" refers to the protection of computer systems from theft, damage, or manipulation of their hardware, software, or data. In Africa, technology adoption is increasing at an exponential rate, with mobile smart device ownership, social media usage, and the Internet of Things (IoT) becoming a reality. Even the most pessimistic data suggest that Africa is on course to make considerable progress and contribute to global growth. However, with increased affluence come new dangers and vulnerabilities that may jeopardize development [21]. Africa is exposed to cyber threats and possible harms due to limitless cyberspace, which does not recognize borders, inadequate information security funding, and weak legislation [22]. Therefore, information security is a critical economic and national security concern that requires careful definition and context. According to the United Nations Economic Commission for Africa [23], and various surveys, Africa is vulnerable to cyber-threats because of its many domains and poor network and information security. According to estimates, cybercrime costs the African economy $895 million each year [24, 25].

Many developing countries lack the resources and capabilities of industrialized countries, making cyber security a major concern for businesses in sub-Saharan Africa. [22]. In many African countries, cyber security is still seen as a luxury rather than a need with firms' cyber security budgets being less than 1%, and many organizations have no cyber security budget at all according to the World Bank's 2016/17 Global Cybersecurity Report [8]. There is a low rate of Information Communication Technology (ICT) literacy [26]. As a result, ICT users in Africa are inexperienced and technologically illiterate. Most are also illiterate in English, which is critical because most security product information is only in English [8]. In addition, basic requirements such as housing, food, health, and education frequently take precedence over the adoption of ICT [27].

3.3 Cyber Awareness in Africa

Cyber awareness is described as employees' understanding toward the security of the organization's information assets. Being security-conscious entails being aware of the risks associated with an organization's information assets and how to protect them [28]. Unfortunately, the lack of understanding within Africa about the risks of accessing cyberspace contributes to a permissive climate for cybercrime. African countries' digital infrastructure development level harms their security position, with cybercriminals taking advantage of poor security habits [29]. The significance of information security awareness in reducing the risks associated with data security breaches cannot be overstated [30]. Policymakers need to develop strong legislation and awareness programs to stem the rising flood of cyber risks in Africa [31]. Several organizations, like the African Information Society Initiative (UNECA/AISI), have previously emphasized the importance of continental collaboration and increased cyber security awareness [26].

3.4 Why Promote a Cyber4Dev Security Culture?

According to the Ernest and Young Global Information Security Survey (GISS) [32], the number of damaging attacks against organizations increased dramatically during 2019, with 59 percent of them reporting severe security breaches. In addition, the number of employee error-related breaches increased six-fold [33]. Africa could benefit immensely from guidelines to promote a security culture that is adaptable to the African context. A Cyber4Dev security culture would encourage governments, employees, and individuals to take the lead in combating cyber-security threats through awareness-raising, legislation, and performing cyber-safe practices. This paper will focus on Cyber4Dev security culture in Africa, a continent with a population with insufficient cyber skills, limited security awareness, inadequate infrastructure, and few training institutions that focus on cyber awareness [34].

4 Research Method

Scoping reviews give a broad overview of a specific topic without much regard for the quality of the study [35]. This paper utilizes the Preferred Reporting Items for Systematic Reviews and Meta-Analyses (PRISMA) method [35]. This methodology has two components, namely a systematic review and a meta-analysis. Its main objective is to ensure that literature reviews are conducted transparently and produce repeatable results [21].

4.1 Information Sources

The author selected four electronic databases. Each database had unique filtering tools to screen the large number of papers obtained from the initial search. Table 1 lists the databases and search strings (keywords) used in each for the initial broad searches conducted by the author.

Table 1. Search strings that were used in each database.

Database	Search String (Keywords)
Association of Computing Machinery (ACM)	[[[Abstract: security] AND [Abstract: information] AND [Abstract: security] AND [Abstract: culture]]] AND [[[Publication Title: security] AND [Publication Title: culture]]] AND [[[Full Text: security] AND [Full Text: culture]] OR [[Full text: information] AND [Full Text: security] AND [Full text: security] AND [Full Text: culture]] OR [[Ful Text: information] AND [Full text: security] AND [Full Text: culture]]] AND [Publication Date: (01/01/2015 TO 08/31/2021)]
Electrical and Electronic Engineers (IEEE)	("Document Title": security AND "Document Title": Culture OR "Document Title": Information AND "Document Title": Security AND "Document Title": Culture) OR ("Abstract": security AND "Abstract": Culture OR "Abstract": Information AND "Abstract": Security AND "Abstract": Culture) OR ("Index Terms": Security AND "Index Terms": Culture OR "Index Terms": Information AND "Index Terms": Security AND "Index Terms": Culture)

(*continued*)

Table 1. (*continued*)

Database	Search String (Keywords)
Scopus	TITLE-ABS-KEY (security AND culture OR information AND security AND culture) AND (LIMIT-TO (PUBYEAR, 2021) OR LIMIT-TO (PUBYEAR, 2020) OR LIMIT-TO (OR LIMIT-TO (PUBYEAR, 2016) OR LIMIT-TO (PUBYEAR, 2015)) AND (LIMIT-TO (SUBAREA, "COMP")) AND (LIMIT-TO (LANGUAGE, "English"))
Web of Science	((((TS = (Security AND Culture OR Information AND Security AND Culture)) AND AB = (Security AND Culture OR Information AND Security And Culture)) AND TI = (Security AND Culture OR Information AND Security And Culture)) AND PY = (2015 OR 2016 OR 2017 OR 2018 OR 2019 OR 2020 or 2021)) AND AK = (Security AND Culture OR Information AND Security And Culture)

4.2 Eligibility Criteria

The articles had to meet specific criteria. Firstly, all papers should be from published journals and conference papers. Secondly, the papers should be written in English between 2015 and 2021. Thirdly, the subject areas were limited to Computer Science and Engineering, and finally, the country/regions were restricted to countries in Africa.

4.3 Data Collection

After searching within the databases, the article title, article abstract, author name(s), the journal name, keywords, and the publication year of the identified articles then exported as a CSV file into a Microsoft Excel spreadsheet; the authors then screened the selected papers by going through the article abstracts and keywords. From the 925 articles retrieved from the databases, 797 were discarded based on abstract review and duplicate removal. After a full text review of the articles a further 88 articles were discarded leaving 40 articles used in this study.

5 Results

5.1 Synthesis of the Results

Of the chosen articles, twenty-one (21) were journal articles and nineteen (19) were from conference papers. Many of these articles were published in 2015 (14) with the

Table 2. Summary of publication types and years they were published.

	2015	2016	2017	2018	2019	2020	2021
Journals	5	2	2	2	4	2	4
Conference Papers	9	2	3	1	3	1	0

least number published in 2018 (3) and 2020 (3). The summary of the publication types and the year in which the papers were published is represented in Table 2.

The bulk of the analyzed articles (29) had a clear definition of information security culture or security culture. The rest of the papers (11) did not give a definitive definition for either security culture or information security culture although the terms were used copiously within the articles. In summary, a Cyber4Dev security culture was defined as people-driven, cyber-safe activities and behaviors that protect developing-country organizations' information assets. The definition highlighted the important role of people in the success of an information security culture within African organizations.

Most publications (28) examined created conceptual models or based their studies on a specific framework or model. The Information Security Culture Framework (ISCF) (7) [36–42], was the most often used or altered framework/model in the publications reviewed. Other identified models included the Organizational Security Culture Model [43], Information Security Shared Tacit Espoused Values (MISSTEV) model [44, 45], STOPE (Strategy; Technology; Organization; People; and Environment) Framework [10], and the TOE (Technology, Organization, and Environment) model [46]. The bulk of publications (32) included information security cultural factors. Table 3 summarizes the factors considered vital in developing an information security culture from these articles. Only factors with more than 10 citations were included.

Table 3. Important information security culture factors.

Factors	Total	Papers
Information security training	10	[12, 15, 16, 19, 36, 38, 44, 47–49]
Compliance and trust	11	[12, 36, 37, 39, 41, 43, 46–48, 50, 51]
Information security policy/regulations	16	[10, 11, 15, 19, 21, 36–38, 41, 45–48, 50–52]
Top management/leadership support	18	[10, 11, 15, 19, 21, 36–39, 43, 46–48, 50, 51, 53–55]
Information security awareness and sharing	20	[36, 47, 48], [11, 15, 16, 19, 21, 37–39, 41, 44–46, 51–55]

Employees gain information security knowledge and skills they need to navigate cyberspace through information security training. Information security policies guide the security culture within organizations and direct employee behavior for compliance with information security policies. Compliance and by-in to these policies promote a positive information security culture [37]. Top management defines the strategies that ensure a cyber-secure work environment. These factors are also relevant to African countries as they form the pillars in successfully implementation of cyber-safe practices within organizations and thus are utilized in the proposed Cyber4Dev Security Culture Model.

5.2 The African Perspective

In total, thirteen papers [11, 16, 20, 37, 38, 41, 44–46, 49, 50, 56, 57] were retrieved with an African perspective. Information security training (8) was the most significant component influencing a healthy information security culture in African organizations, which is in line with the work of the African Information Society and other related organisation's who emphasized the importance of information security training [26]. African organizations can utilize information security training to avoid and mitigate user risk by helping users and employees understand their role in preventing and mitigating information security breaches [15], whilst also ensuring that it is presented in African languages. Information security policy/regulations (7) are a set of rules and standards that govern the usage, management, and protection of information technology assets and resources [19]. African countries fall short in cyber-safe policy formulation and implementation thus exposing organizations to innumerable cyber threats. Economic (3), technological (3), and social-cultural/environmental (3) factors were prominently highlighted by African authors. Economic factors refer to financial/monetary conditions within these African countries that affect the organizations' ability to implement effective information security practices. The technology factors in the context of Africa encompass the numerous infrastructural and technical requirements for the effective protection of organizational information assets. The social-cultural and environmental factors are the forces inside societies that shape people's views, beliefs, and behaviors. These influences have a bearing on how individuals perceive the importance of cyber-safe practices and organizational information assets. Table 4, summarizes the main factors affecting African organizations in instilling good information security cultures.

Table 4. Important information security culture factors from an African perspective.

Factors	Total	Papers
Information security training	8	[11, 37, 38, 41, 44, 45, 49, 50]
Information security policy/regulations	7	[14, 16, 37, 38, 41, 45, 50],
Economic factors	3	[37, 44, 50]
Technological factors	3	[37, 46, 50]
Social-cultural/environmental factors	3	[44, 46, 50]

6   Cyber4Dev Security Culture Model

From the analysis of the thirteen (13) papers written by African authors or with an African perspective on information security culture, five factors were identified as the most influential to instilling a good information security culture within organizations in Africa, derived from Table 4. Compliance and trust, top management support and information security awareness and sharing factors from Table 3 were also incorporated to define the proposed model. Figure 1 depicts the proposed Cyber4Dev Security Culture Model, with the eight factors. According to the model, the information security culture influencing factors on the left and right have a beneficial impact on instituting an information security culture within organizations in Africa. Information security training, information security awareness and sharing, information security policy and regulations, and top management support (factors on the right) were most influential according to authors, in promoting an ideal information security culture in organizations. The interplay of these eight components can contribute to foster an information security culture that could be of benefit to African countries.

Fig. 1. The Cyber4Dev security culture model

The first request question aimed to identify existing models of frameworks for Cyber4Dev security culture, which was found to be lacking based on the literature review. Figure 1 answers the second research question by proposing a Cyber4Dev security culture model, being a novel model in the cyber for development context. Organisations can consider these factors as part of their information security programs and governments can incorporate it in their cyber resilience programs. The model serves as reference for further research to explore the influence of the identified factors in an African context.

7   Conclusion and Future Work

The Cyber4Dev Security Culture Model proposed in this paper provides a foundation for African countries and organizations to build a successful information security culture to secure information assets. The model's application to any African business would enhance its employees' awareness of and interactions with information assets, resulting in a positive impact and protection against numerous information security dangers posed by insiders. A Cyber4Dev security culture would encourage governments, employees, and individuals to take the lead in combating information security threats through awareness-raising, legislation, and performing cyber-safe practices. A limitation of the study is that the model is conceptual. Future work will aim to validate the model with cyber security experts from Africa using a qualitative method and to further expand the model for implementation as part of a case study to test it. Furthermore in future work the literature review could cover more than the five year period covered in this paper and include other domains in information security culture.

References

1. Sas, M., Hardyns, W., van Nunen, K., Reniers, G., Ponnet, K.: Measuring the security culture in organizations: a systematic overview of existing tools. Secur. J. **34**(2), 340–357 (2021). https://doi.org/10.1057/s41284-020-00228-4. Palgrave Macmillan UK
2. Kurebwa, J., Magumise, E.: The effectiveness of cyber security frameworks in combating terrorism in Zimbabwe. Int. J. Cyber Res. Educ. **2**, 1–16 (2019). https://doi.org/10.4018/ijcre.2020010101
3. Cyber4Dev: Project objectives – Cyber4d – Cyber Resilience for Development. https://cyber4dev.eu/project-activities/
4. Abdulrauf, L.A.: Giving 'teeth' to the African Union towards advancing compliance with data privacy norms. Inf. Commun. Technol. Law. **30**, 87–107 (2021). https://doi.org/10.1080/13600834.2021.1849953
5. Obuhuma, J., Zivuku, S.: Social engineering based cyber-attacks in kenya. In: 2020 IST-Africa Conf. IST-Africa 2020, pp. 1–9 (2020)
6. Campbell, M.: What's in a project name? - Cyber Resilience for Development [Cyber4Dev] (2019)
7. ITU: Global Cybersecurity Index, 2017. ITU Publications (2019)
8. Kshetri, N.: Cybercrime and cybersecurity in Africa. J. Glob. Inf. Technol. Manag. **22**, 77–81 (2019). https://doi.org/10.1080/1097198X.2019.1603527
9. Nagyfejeo, E., Solms, B. Von: Why do national cybersecurity awareness programmes often fail? Int. J. Inf. Secur. Cybercrime. **9**, 18–27 (2020). https://doi.org/10.19107/ijisc.2020.02.03
10. Alhogail, A.: Design and validation of information security culture framework. Comput. Human Behav. **49**, 567–575 (2015). https://doi.org/10.1016/j.chb.2015.03.054
11. Da Veiga, A., Martins, N.: Information security culture and information protection culture: a validated assessment instrument. Comput. Law Secur. Rev. **31**, 243–256 (2015). https://doi.org/10.1016/j.clsr.2015.01.005
12. Nasir, A., Arshah, R.A., Hamid, M.R.A., Fahmy, S.: An analysis on the dimensions of information security culture concept: a review. J. Inf. Secur. Appl. **44**, 12–22 (2019). https://doi.org/10.1016/j.jisa.2018.11.003
13. Orehek, Š, Petrič, G.: A systematic review of scales for measuring information security culture. Inf. Comput. Secur. **29**, 133–158 (2020). https://doi.org/10.1108/ICS-12-2019-0140
14. Da Veiga, A.: An approach to information security culture change combining ADKAR and the ISCA questionnaire to aid transition to the desired culture. Inf. Comput. Secur. **26**, 584–612 (2018). https://doi.org/10.1108/ICS-08-2017-0056
15. Alnatheer, M.A.: Information security culture critical success factors. In: Proc. - 12th Int. Conf. Inf. Technol. New Gener. ITNG 2015, pp. 731–735 (2015). https://doi.org/10.1109/ITNG.2015.124

16. Da Veiga, A., Martins, N.: Improving the information security culture through monitoring and implementation actions illustrated through a case study. Comput. Secur. **49**, 162–176 (2015). https://doi.org/10.1016/j.cose.2014.12.006
17. Connolly, L.Y., Lang, M., Wall, D.S.: Information security behavior: a cross-cultural comparison of irish and US employees. Inf. Syst. Manag. **36**, 306–322 (2019). https://doi.org/10.1080/10580530.2019.1651113
18. Da Veiga, A.: Achieving a Security Culture, pp. 72–100 (2019). https://doi.org/10.4018/978-1-5225-7847-5.ch005
19. Mousavi, M.Z., Kumar, S.: Analysis of key factors for organization information security. In: Proc. Int. Conf. Mach. Learn. Big Data, Cloud Parallel Comput. Trends, Prespectives Prospect. Com. 2019, pp. 514–518 (2019). https://doi.org/10.1109/COMITCon.2019.8862191
20. Nel, F., Drevin, L.: Key elements of an information security culture in organisations. Inf. Comput. Secur. **27**, 146–164 (2019). https://doi.org/10.1108/ICS-12-2016-0095
21. Mahfuth, A., Yussof, S., Baker, A.A., Ali, N.: A systematic literature review: Information security culture. Int. Conf. Res. Innov. Inf. Syst. ICRIIS. 1–6 (2017). https://doi.org/10.1109/ICRIIS.2017.8002442
22. Schia, N.N.: The cyber frontier and digital pitfalls in the Global South. Third World Q. **39**, 821–837 (2018). https://doi.org/10.1080/01436597.2017.1408403
23. United Nations Economic Commission for Africa: Policy Brief Tackling the challenges of cybersecurity in Africa. www.economist.com/. (2014)
24. KnowBe4: African Cybersecurity Research Report. 1–8 (2019)
25. Check Point Research: Cyber Security Report 2020. Security **7**, 1–15 (2020)
26. Bada, M., von Solms, B., Agrafiotis, I.: Reviewing national cybersecurity awareness in africa: an empirical study. In: Third Int. Conf. Cyber-Technologies Cyber-Systems, CYBER 2018, pp. 78–83 (2018)
27. Schelenz, L., Schopp, K.: Digitalization in Africa: interdisciplinary perspectives on technology, development, and justice. Int. J. Digit. Soc. **9**, 1412–1420 (2018). https://doi.org/10.20533/ijds.2040.2570.2018.0175
28. Amankwa, E., Loock, M., Kritzinger, E.: Enhancing information security education and awareness: proposed characteristics for a model. In: 2nd Int. Conf. Inf. Secur. Cyber Forensics, InfoSec 2015, pp. 72–77 (2016). https://doi.org/10.1109/InfoSec.2015.7435509
29. Von Solms, B., Bada, M., Agrafiotis, I.: Reviewing national cybersecurity awareness for users and executives in Africa. Int. J. Adv. Secur. **12**, 108–118 (2019)
30. Ndiege, J.R., Okello, G.: Towards information security savvy students in institutions of higher learning in Africa: a case of a university in Kenya. In: 2018 IST-Africa Week Conf. IST-Africa 2018, pp. 1–8 (2018)
31. Devi, A.: Cyber Crime and Cyber Security: Trends in Africa, pp. 160–171 (2017). https://doi.org/10.4018/978-1-5225-2154-9.ch011
32. EY: EY Global Information Security Survey 2020. How does security evolve from bolted on to built-in? (2020)
33. Nathan, A.J., Scobell, A.: 2020 Data Breach Investigations Report. Verizon (2020)
34. Malatji, M., Marnewick, A.L., von Solms, S.: Cybersecurity policy and the legislative context of the water and wastewater sector in South Africa. Sustain. **13**, 1–33 (2021). https://doi.org/10.3390/su13010291
35. Tricco, A.C., et al.: A scoping review on the conduct and reporting of scoping reviews. BMC Med. Res. Methodol. **16**, 1 (2016). https://doi.org/10.1186/s12874-016-0116-4
36. Tolah, A., Furnell, S.M., Papadaki, M.: An empirical analysis of the information security culture key factors framework. Comput. Secur. **108**, 102354 (2021). https://doi.org/10.1016/j.cose.2021.102354

37. Woretaw, A., Lessa, L., Negash, S.: Factors hindering full-fledged information security in banking sector in Ethiopia: Emphasis on information security culture. In: 25th Am. Conf. Inf. Syst. AMCIS 2019. (2019)

38. da Veiga, A., Martins, N.: Defining and identifying dominant information security cultures and subcultures. Comput. Secur. **70**, 72–94 (2017). https://doi.org/10.1016/j.cose.2017.05.002

39. Nasir, A., Arshah, R.A., Ab Hamid, M.R.: Information security policy compliance behavior based on comprehensive dimensions of information security culture: A conceptual framework. ACM Int. Conf. Proceeding Ser. Part **F1282**, 56–60 (2017). https://doi.org/10.1145/3077584. 3077593

40. Chen, Y., Ramamurthy, K., Wen, K.W.: Impacts of comprehensive information security programs on information security culture. J. Comput. Inf. Syst. **55**, 11–19 (2015). https://doi.org/10.1080/08874417.2015.11645767

41. Martins, N., Da Veiga, A.: An Information security culture model validated with structural equation modelling. In: Proc. 9th Int. Symp. Hum. Asp. Inf. Secur. Assur. HAISA 2015, pp. 11–21 (2015)

42. Hogail, A. Al: Cultivating and assessing an organizational information security culture; an empirical study. Int. J. Secur. its Appl. **9**, 163–178 (2015). https://doi.org/10.14257/ijsia.2015. 9.7.15

43. Dang-Pham, D., Pittayachawan, S., Bruno, V.: Investigating the formation of information security climate perceptions with social network analysis: A research proposal. In: Pacific Asia Conf. Inf. Syst. PACIS 2015 - Proc. (2015)

44. Da Veiga, A.: Comparing the information security culture of employees who had read the information security policy and those who had not Illustrated through an empirical study. Inf. Comput. Secur. **24**, 139–151 (2016). https://doi.org/10.1108/ICS-12-2015-0048

45. Da Veiga, A.: The influence of information security policies on information security culture: Illustrated through a case study. In: Proc. 9th Int. Symp. Hum. Asp. Inf. Secur. Assur. HAISA 2015, pp. 22–33 (2015)

46. Mokwetli, M., Zuva, T.: Adoption of the ICT security culture in SMME's in the gauteng province, South Africa. In: 2018 Int. Conf. Adv. Big Data, Comput. Data Commun. Syst. icABCD 2018. (2018). https://doi.org/10.1109/ICABCD.2018.8465139

47. Uchendu, B., Nurse, J.R.C., Bada, M., Furnell, S.: Developing a cyber security culture: current practices and future needs. Comput. Secur. **109**, 102387 (2021). https://doi.org/10.1016/j.cose. 2021.102387

48. Arbanas, K., Spremic, M., Zajdela Hrustek, N.: Holistic framework for evaluating and improving information security culture. Aslib J. Inf. Manag. **73**, 699–719 (2021). https://doi.org/10. 1108/AJIM-02-2021-0037

49. Da Veiga, A.: An information security training and awareness approach (ISTAAP) to instil an information security-positive culture. In: Proc. 9th Int. Symp. Hum. Asp. Inf. Secur. Assur. HAISA 2015, pp. 95–107 (2015)

50. Da Veiga, A., Astakhova, L.V., Botha, A., Herselman, M.: Defining organisational information security culture—Perspectives from academia and industry. Comput. Secur. **92**, 101713 (2020). https://doi.org/10.1016/j.cose.2020.101713

51. Nasir, A., Abdullah Arshah, R., Ab Hamid, M.R.: A dimension-based information security culture model and its relationship with employees' security behavior: A case study in Malaysian higher educational institutions. Inf. Secur. J. **28**, 55–80 (2019). https://doi.org/10. 1080/19393555.2019.1643956

52. Tang, A., Han, J., Chen, P.: A comparative analysis of architecture frameworks. In: Proc. - Asia-Pacific Softw. Eng. Conf. APSEC, pp. 640–647 (2004). https://doi.org/10.1109/APSEC. 2004.2

53. Hassan, N.H., Maarop, N., Ismail, Z., Abidin, W.Z.: Information security culture in health informatics environment: A qualitative approach. Int. Conf. Res. Innov. Inf. Syst. ICRIIS. 1–6 (2017). https://doi.org/10.1109/ICRIIS.2017.8002450

54. AlKalbani, A., Deng, H., Kam, B.: Organisational security culture and information security compliance for e-government development: The moderating effect of social pressure (2015)

55. Nasir, A., Arshah, R.A., Hamid, M.R.A.: Information security culture for guiding employee's security behaviour: a pilot study. In: 2020 6th IEEE Int. Conf. Inf. Manag. ICIM 2020, pp. 205–209 (2020). https://doi.org/10.1109/ICIM49319.2020.244699

56. DaVeiga, A.: An approach to information security culture change combining ADKAR and the ISCA questionnaire to aid transition to the desired culture. Inf. Comput. Secur. **26**, 584–612 (2018). https://doi.org/10.1108/ICS-08-2017-0056

57. Govender, S., Kritzinger, E., Loock, M.: The influence of national culture on information security culture. In: 2016 IST-Africa Conf. IST-Africa 2016, pp. 1–9 (2016). https://doi.org/10.1109/ISTAFRICA.2016.7530607

A Model for Information Security Culture with Innovation and Creativity as Enablers

Adéle da Veiga[(⊠)] [iD]

School of Computing, College of Science, Engineering and Technology, University of South
Africa (UNISA), Florida Campus, Johannesburg, South Africa
dveiga@unisa.ac.za

Abstract. This research aims to elicit a conceptual understanding of creativity
and innovation to enable a totally aligned information security culture. Stimulating the creativity and innovation of employees in an organisation can help to solve
information security problems and to create a culture where information security
issues are addressed and resolved, as opposed to being introduced by end-users.
The study applied a theoretical approach with a scoping literature review using the
PRISMA method to derive traits and programmes that organisations can implement to stimulate creativity and innovation as part of the organisational culture.
A model for engendering employee creativity and innovation as part of the information security culture is proposed, through the lens of the three levels of organisational culture. This study both offers novel insights for managerial practice and
serves as a point of reference for further academic research about the influence of
creativity and innovation in information security culture.

Keywords: Information security culture · Creativity · Innovation · Model

1 Introduction

Creativity is critical for organisational success [1], while innovation is regarded as a
driver for organisational growth, resilience [2], sustainability [3], performance [4] and
competitiveness [5]. Creativity and innovation are becoming a core part of organisational
strategies to achieve success and to incorporate technology changes [6], these being key
factors that can aid organisations to adapt in a world where there is an accelerated
pace of change [7]. Creativity and innovation will play a critical role in equipping
organisations to become cyber resilient, to manage through the change brought about
by the fourth industrial revolution [8], and to enhance organisational effectiveness by
also applying innovation in information systems security [9]. Research has shown that
eighty-eight per cent of board members are concerned about cyber threats [10], affecting
the confidentiality, integrity and availability of information and information systems.
With increasing numbers of cyber-attacks and data breaches, organisations need to be
creative and innovative if they are to combat threats and become cyber resilient. The
human element is still a key target in attacks and often part of the threat [11, 12]. Phishing

© IFIP International Federation for Information Processing 2022
Published by Springer Nature Switzerland AG 2022
N. Clarke and S. Furnell (Eds.): HAISA 2022, IFIP AICT 658, pp. 186–196, 2022.
https://doi.org/10.1007/978-3-031-12172-2_14

attacks accounted for the majority of data breaches in 2021, with 96% occurring via e-mails targeting end-users [10]. Information security challenges, especially those related to end-users, require organisations to develop an information security culture where creativity and innovation are encouraged so as to protect information and information systems.

Organisational culture is seen as an enabler to facilitate creativity and innovation in an organisation [2, 5, 7, 13]. Organisational culture can be explained as the assumptions, beliefs, values and norms that are shared by employees [14] and that distinguish the organisation from other organisations [3]. Values, beliefs, and knowledge of employees influence the organisational culture, but they also shape the employee's cognition, motivation, and problem solving [15] that is visible in the employee behaviour. This behaviour of employees should be shaped to be in line with the information security policies of the organisation where compliance behaviour is required. In an organisation where there is a supportive organisational culture for creativity and innovation, employees will be equipped to solve information security issues and problems [15]. Creativity on the part of individual employees extends to problem solving and competency in information security and individuals require it to address security issues that occur in their daily work [15]. Innovation and creativity could therefore play an additional role in aiding with problem solving to combat cyber-attacks and data breaches and to encourage employee behaviour that mitigates risks to information protection.

Information security culture research has shown that a strong information security culture can aid in protecting information and in minimising employee behaviour that results in information security risk or data breaches [11, 12, 16]. The factors that influence information security culture have been defined and investigated in numerous studies [12, 16, 17]. To date, however, there has not been a study that has considered creativity and innovation to strengthen the information security culture. Nonetheless, numerous research studies have been conducted about the role of creativity and innovation in an organisational culture [1, 2, 5, 18] and these studies can be leveraged in an information security context.

The objective of this paper is to propose a conceptual model whereby creativity and innovation are applied to strengthen an information security culture. This study is conducted by applying a scoping literature review and building on research in the organisational culture domain. The research question that has guided this research is, "What would an information security culture model comprise where innovation and creativity are used as enablers?".

It is envisaged that such a model can be applied in organisations to stimulate creativity and innovation as traits of an information security culture and with the aim of mitigating security risks and threats from a human perspective. The model will serve as a point of reference for further academic work to investigate the influence of creativity and innovation on the information security culture.

2 Background

2.1 Information Security Culture

An information security culture is a subculture of the organisational culture [19–21]. In line with Schein's [14] definition of organisational culture, the information security culture also comprises assumptions, values, beliefs and attitudes [21, 22] of employees toward information security. These influence the employee behaviour when employees interact with information and information systems and, over time, become the way things are done in the organisation to protect information and information systems, that will be visible in behaviour and artifacts in the organisation [23, 24]. It is critical that the way things are done in an organisation is in line with the information security policy of the organisation and that employees share the same values and beliefs to protect information. In order to secure and protect information effectively, a strong information security culture is required [11]. The organisation should aim for a totally aligned information security culture where the strategy of the organisation, as well as employee behaviour and values, are both in support of the protection of information [24]. A strong information security culture will enable employee behaviour, thereby leading to fewer security incidents and data breaches arising from end user threats due to error or negligent behaviour [24]. Information security should be part of the organisational strategy and vision and should be seen as a strategic advantage, as opposed to a hindrance. In an organisational culture where information security is valued, one would observe compliant behaviour which is strengthened through positive reinforcement and proactive interventions such as awareness, education and training of employees.

2.2 Creativity and Innovation in an Organisation

The terms "creativity" and "innovation" are used interchangeably and together in literature [18, 25]. Creativity is part of the innovation processes, with innovation resulting after creativity [6, 26] as part of a routine process. Creativity is seen by some researchers as a subset of innovation [27] whereby new ways to resolve a problem are expected. Creativity is regarded as a requirement for innovation; however, authors agree that creativity does not always result in innovation [27]. Willingness and creativity (which relates to intrinsic motivation) lead to the generation of new ideas, resulting in turn in knowledge creation when applied in a work situation [25]. To encourage innovation in an organisation, a bottom-up approach can be followed, with ideas emanating from employees, or a top-down approach can be taken, with the organisation driving creativity through its vision and strategy [26]. Creativity in an organisation can also be achieved by encouraging creativity in individual employees in three areas, namely, "expertise, creative thinking skills and intrinsic task motivation" [3] Creative ideas from individuals and groups lead to new approaches, solutions [28] and problem solving. These, as part of a dynamic process in an organisation, will result in knowledge creation. The organisational culture can be conducive to creativity and innovation or hinder them. In either case, there is an impact on creativity and innovation through basic values, assumptions and beliefs which are translated into artifacts such as the information security policy and management processes [7]. When management provides employees with resources to develop new ideas or to solve problems they will perceive it as valuable, which will influence how they behave [7].

2.3 Applying Creativity and Innovation in Information Security Culture

An information security culture is required where innovation for information security is supported and where the employees of the organisation feel encouraged to support information security but also to partake in the day-to-day implementation thereof [9]. Employees of an organisation will be more committed to innovation in information security, as well as more committed to implementing and upholding it, in an organisational culture where flexibility is promoted and where such organisational culture is conducive to information system security innovation [9]. One of the cultures that are found to be supportive of innovation in information security is the open culture, where employees are seen as flexible with a focus on the future [9]. Hwang and Choi state, for "ISS to be effective, a culture that facilitates information security and supports information systems security innovation is crucial for encouraging members to support information systems security and actively participate in its implementation" [9]. The behaviour of each employee in the organisation impacts on the effectiveness of information security, which means that their behaviour should be in line with the policies, standards, procedures and required practices of the organisation, as directed by the organisation's management and leadership [9]. In the study of [9], it is argued that there is a dependency on every employee to implement information system security policies in order for information system security to be effective. However, they also emphasise that there should be a culture in the organisation that supports information system security innovation, as promoted by the leaders of the organisation, in order for the employees to adopt the culture and for their own values and belief to be aligned to that culture. There is, however, no guidance on how management should foster an information security culture that is enabled through creativity and innovation.

3 Research Methodology

The literature review study was conducted using a scoping literature review approach to identify the extent of research published focusing on creativity and innovation in an information security culture context [29]. The PRISMA (Preferred Reporting Items for Systematic reviews and Meta-Analyses) method was applied to systematically gather, screen and review the retrieved research papers [30].

Two literature searches were conducted in the Emerald, Science Direct, Scopus and Web of Science databases. The first search used the keywords: (title: Information security culture) AND (abstract: Innovation OR Creativity) in the abstract, between the years 2011–2022, and in English. Only two papers from Web of Science, [9, 15] were extracted. Due to the limited research previously carried out on creativity and innovation in information security culture, a second literature search was conducted to identify studies where creativity and innovation were considered as part of organisational culture. Table 1 outlines the results of the second literature search. A total of 18 papers were included in the full-text review. The next section provides a summary of the eligible papers.

Table 1. PRISMA approach for literature search

Databases	(title: "organisational culture") AND (title Innovation OR Creativity) in abstract, 2011–2022, English				
	#Records identified through database searching	#Records after duplicates removed	#Records screened	#Records excluded (exclusion/inclusion criteria)	#Full-text articles assessed for eligibility
Emerald	1	1	1	0	1
Science Direct	6	6	6	1	5
Scopus	21	21	21	15	6
WoS	18	17	17	11	6

4 Results

4.1 Creativity and Innovation in the Information Security Culture Context

Hwang et al. [9] conducted a study in the e-government sector to investigate innovation in information systems security. They argued that increased organisational effectiveness can be established if there is a culture for information systems security innovation. The participating organisation fostered an information systems security innovative-support culture, which incorporated an information security culture. Some of the key factors focused on to facilitate this were formal and information communication and education, as well as training programmes on the organisational, group and interpersonal levels. They also introduced an artifact creation programme to aid in shifting security attitudes to information systems. They used the example of symbols or mottos about information systems security aspects which can be shown on end users' computer screens.

Individual creativity was emphasised as an important factor to facilitate problem solving concerned with information security issues at work [15]. The authors refer to the work of Ambile [31] in which creativity is portrayed as task motivation, domain-relevant skills and creativity-relevant processes. Task motivation relates to intrinsic (internally motivated, "inherently interesting or enjoyable" [32]) as well as extrinsic motivation (such as rewards for compliance, leading to an outcome [32]). Intrinsic motivation is linked with commitment, which, in turn, is associated with task completion at work and can aid in the completion of information security tasks and problem solving. The implementation of security awareness and training in organisations aids in developing the domain-relevant skills that it is necessary for employees to apply in their work. These skills are a prerequisite to facilitating creativity in information security problem solving. This supports research that showed if employees are trained they are five times more likely to identify and avoid clicking on malicious links [10]. Lin and Wittmer [15] argued that creativity-relevant processes, which are the manner or pathways in which a solution is derived, are required for problem solving in information security management.

4.2 Creativity and Innovation in an Organisational Culture Context

Martins [33] conducted a study to investigate aspects of organisational culture and behaviour that influence knowledge retention in an organisation. The paper refers to creativity, but not in the context of an innovation culture. Earlier work of Martins [7, 18] focused on the development of a model for the Influence of Organisational Culture on Creativity and Innovation, using determinants of organisational culture that promote creativity and innovation, these being: strategy of the organisation, with a vision and mission that supports creativity and innovation; purposefulness (vision and mission understanding); trust relationships (trust and support for change); behaviour that encourages innovation (idea generation, risk taking, decision making); working environment (goals and objectives, conflict handling, cooperative teams, participation, control of own work); customer orientation (flexibility & improvement in service, understanding needs); and management support (open communication, availability of resources, tolerance of mistakes, adaption of rules and regulations).

Other aspects that support creativity and innovation in an organisation are the organisational structure being non-hierarchical, autonomy, working in teams, freedom, being flexible; support mechanisms (e.g. rewards and recognition, use of technology, recruitment of certain types of employees valuing diversity, energetic, with knowledge, inquisitiveness); behaviour (e.g. tolerance of mistakes, taking risks and experimenting, as long as it does not harm the organisation, support for change); and communication (open and transparent) [7]. The study of Martins et al. did not focus on what type of organisational culture promotes creativity and innovation but rather defined the elements that could determine or encourage creativity and innovation as part of an organisational culture.

The Competing Values Framework of [34, 35] is used to measure organisational culture in four distinct quadrants, namely, Hierarchy, Market (Rational), Clan (Group) or Adhocracy (Developmental) through the evaluation of two dimensions. The first dimension considers internal focus and integration versus external focus and differentiation. The second dimension focuses on flexibility and discretion versus stability and control. Choo [36] applied the Competing Values Framework to an information culture and postulated that an organisation might have one or two dominant information cultures while also valuing other cultures to varying degrees. While this profile was not tested empirically, it provides a visual representation of an information culture, which is valuable both in contextualising the culture and directing change.

The clan culture has, based on a study in Serbia, been found to be one of the cultures that lead to innovation being encouraged in an organisation [37]. Some of the reasons for this are related to knowledge sharing and communication, both of which are pertinent in the clan culture [37], and there is also a link to domain-relevant skills, which are required for creativity. Innovation is applied to identify and solve new information security problems are the solutions are then shared with the group as part of knowledge sharing and communication. A further study in Brazil also found the clan culture, as well as the adhocracy culture, to be conducive to innovation and creativity, whereas the hierarchical type culture did not have an influence on innovation [13]. The adhocracy culture was also found to have the most impact on innovativeness in universities [38]. This is supported by the work of Makumbe [8] in Zimbabwe. Ogbeibu et al. [28] also proposed that the clan and adhocracy organisational cultures might positively influence employee creativity, but found in a further study in a manufacturing organisation that clan and rational organisational culture have a negative effect on employee creativity, while the hierarchy organisational culture has no effect [39]. The flexibility and external orientation traits of the adhocracy organisational culture favour innovation. Cameron et al. [35] explain that the adhocracy culture supports the generation of new ideas, innovation and creativity. However, in a study in Brazil conducted in the T-Kibs organisations, it was found that the market culture supports innovation, whereas the clan, adhocracy and hierarchical organisational cultures did not have an influence on innovation in this study [5]. Further research confirmed that the clan and rational culture have a positive influence on creativity; however, it was also established that the influence of the clan culture on creativity did not appear to be affected as a result of whether computer-mediated communication or face-to-face communication was used. Nonetheless, the rational culture was influenced positively [27]. The culture that supports creativity and innovation therefore varies, based on the industry or type of organisation being researched. However, group and adhocracy cultures seem to mostly support creativity and innovation.

A study in Pakistan measured the influence of five constructs. i.e. external orientation, organisational climate, flexibility to change, teamwork, and employee empowerment, on innovation performance in an organisation and found that all five constructs positively correlate with innovation performance [6]. They concluded that an organisation should aim to promote research and development activities to contribute to innovation.

Kashan et al., [2] identified 12 innovation values (risk tolerance, creativity, trust, empowerment, flexibility, teamwork and collaboration, employee recognition, diversity, external orientation, learning, continuous development and proactivity) with 33 underlying cultural dimensions that that can positively contribute to an innovation culture. These factors were identified through a literature review and interviews with experts in the mining industry in Australia. While the findings are specific to the mining industry, with its unique culture of risk and rigid structures, the findings can still be applicable to relevant contexts to drive innovation as part of the organisational culture [2]. The authors also use the organisational cultural levels of Schein and explain that a culture of innovation will be perceived at an abstract, values-and-belief level and that such a culture is "built, promoted, reinforced and communicated through behaviours, practices and artefacts [2]. Employee creativity can be positively influenced when knowledge sharing is taking place and if employees are motivated [1]. A further study, conducted in Romania, found that employees consider autonomy as a positive contributor to being creative [26] and that innovation supports risk-taking while also enabling trust in organisations [9]. Table 2 outlines the elements, extracted and summarised from the literature, that can stimulate creativity and innovation as part of the organisational culture.

4.3 Conceptual Model

The information security culture model, enabled through creativity and innovation, is depicted in Fig. 1. The concepts applied in the model were derived from the literature review summary in Table 2, grouped according to either organisational traits or programmes that the organisation can implement to stimulate creativity and innovation. The model displays that organisations can implement certain organisational traits to stimulate creativity and innovation. For some organisational cultures, such as the clan or group

Table 2. Stimulating creativity and innovation elements

Elements that can stimulate creativity and innovation as part of the organisational culture	
Artifact program [9]	Knowledge sharing [2, 37]
Autonomy [2, 18, 26]	Leaders who challenge, support and empower staff to generate new ideas [18]
Awareness, training and education on organisational, group and levels [9, 15]	Research and development activities [6]
Continuous learning and development [2]	Resources [18]
Creativity-relevant processes and behaviour [18]	Risk tolerance [2, 6, 18]
Communication: formal and informal communication [9, 37]; value free, open and transparent [18]	Strategy that support creativity and innovation [18]
Conflict handling [18]	Support change, flexible [2, 6, 18]
Diversity [2, 18]	Task motivation: extrinsic (reward and recognition) [2, 15, 18, 31, 32] and intrinsic motivation [15, 31, 32]
Domain-relevant skills [31, 37]	Teamwork and collaboration [2, 6, 18]
Employee empowerment [2, 6]	Tolerate mistakes [18]
External orientation [2, 6]	Trust [2, 18]
Freedom and discretion [18]	

culture, certain traits – for instance, open communication or teamwork – will already be part of the organisational culture. Creativity and innovation are an output that is applied in the context of information security within the organisation. The information security programme block in the model refers to the people, process, technology, governance and regulatory aspects of information security within the organisation, encapsulating all aspects of information and cyber security. These could relate to applying creativity to the manner in which information security policies are written, an innovative approach for information security awareness, innovative solutions to aid employees in combating phishing attacks and encouraging employees to apply creative thinking to resolve security issues and problems, as examples.

The model depicts that creativity and innovation stimulate a totally aligned information security culture whereby security is part of the organisation's strategy and vision, employees display compliant behaviour and adapt their behaviour in creative and innovative manners to combat security threats, whereby information security is regarded as a strategic advantage resulting in minimised security incidents, especially from a human perspective, as stimulated through creative and innovative problem solving by employees. Risk mitigation is part of such a culture, with proactive management, problem solving and monitoring of information security. The model postulates that, if creativity and innovation can be stimulated in an organisation as part of the organisational culture

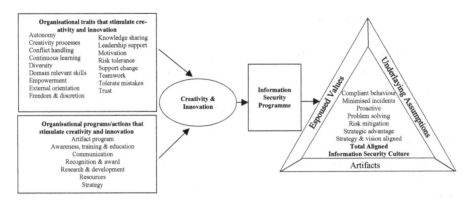

Fig. 1. Information security culture enabled through creativity and innovation

and specifically translated to the information security culture, it will aid in establishing a strong and totally aligned security culture, on a values, assumptions and artifact level – one where the risk of the human element is minimised and converted to become a contributing element in combatting security risks and threats through creativity and innovation.

5   Conclusion and Future Work

An investigation was conducted into what an information security culture model would be comprised of where innovation and creativity are used as enablers. The study provided a foundation to propose a conceptual model whereby information security culture is enabled through creativity and innovation. Key traits to stimulate creativity and innovation were identified, such as support for change, diversity, autonomy, teamwork and trust, that can stimulate creativity and innovation in an organisation. Certain organisational programmes also enable creativity and innovation, such as an artifact programme, education, training and awareness, communication and recognition and rewards. These traits can be applied to stimulate a creative and innovative-friendly security culture in organisations. A limitation of the paper is that the model is conceptual in nature and has not been validated. Future research will employ a qualitative research method to validate the model using an expert panel and to further explore the implementation of the model in organisations with different types of organisational cultures.

References

1. Andleeb, N., Ahmad, M.F., Hassan, M.F., Rahman, N.A.A., Abdullah, A.S., Nawi, M.N.M.: Linkage of knowledge sharing, organizational culture, supply chain strategies towards employee creativity in manufacturing organizations. Int. J. Supply Chain Manage. **9**, 132–140 (2020)
2. Javanmardi Kashan, A., Wiewiora, A., Mohannak, K.: Unpacking organisational culture for innovation in Australian mining industry. Resour. Policy **73**, 1021249 (2021). https://doi.org/10.1016/j.resourpol.2021.102149

3. Robbins, S.P., Judge, T.A., Odendaal, A., Roodt, G.: Organisational behaviour - Global and Southern African Perspectives, 3rd edn. Pearson Holdings South Africa, Cape Town (2018)
4. Strychalska-Rudzewicz, A., Rudzewicz, A.: The impact of organizational innovativeness on Ffirm performance in Poland. The moderating role of innovation culture. European Research Studies Journal. **XXIV**, 130–148 (2021)
5. Bianchi, C.E., Tontini, G., Gomes, G.: Relationship between subjective well-being, perceived organisational culture and individual propension to innovation. European J. Innova. Manage. ahead-of-print, 1460–1060 (2021). https://doi.org/10.1108/EJIM-01-2021-0045
6. Shahzad, F., Xiu, G.Y., Shahbaz, M.: Organizational culture and innovation performance in Pakistan's software industry. Technol. Soc. **51**, 66–73 (2017). https://doi.org/10.1016/j.tec hsoc.2017.08.002
7. Martins, E.C., Terblanche, F.: Building organisational culture that stimulates creativity and innovation. Eur. J. Innov. Manag. **6**, 64–74 (2003). https://doi.org/10.1108/146010603104 56337
8. Makumbe, W.: The impact of organizational culture on employee creativity amongst Zimbabwean academics. African J. Sci. Technol.Innova. Develo. (2021). https://doi.org/10.1080/ 20421338.2020.1864882
9. Hwang, K., Choi, M.: Effects of innovation-supportive culture and organizational citizenship behavior on e-government information system security stemming from mimetic isomorphism. Gov. Inf. Q. **34**, 183–198 (2017)
10. Mimecast: Confronting the new wave of cyberattacks - The State of Email Security 2022 (2022)
11. ENISA: Cyber Security Culture in organisations. European Union Agency for Network and Information Security (ENISA) (2017)
12. Da Veiga, A., Astakhova, L. V., Botha, A., Herselman, M.: Defining organisational information security culture—perspectives from academia and industry. Computers and Security **92** (2020). https://doi.org/10.1016/j.cose.2020.101713
13. Scaliza, J.A.A., et al.: Relationships among organizational culture, open innovation, innovative ecosystems, and performance of firms. J. Bus. Res. **140**, 264–279 (2022). https://doi.org/ 10.1016/j.jbusres.2021.10.065
14. Schein, E.H.: Organizational culture and leadership. Jossey-Bass, San Francisco (1985)
15. Lin, C., Wittmer, J.L.S.: Proactive information security behavior and individual creativity: effects of group culture and decentralized IT governance. In: IEEE International Conference on Intelligence and Security Informatics: Security and Big Data, pp. 1–6. IEEE International Conference on Intelligence and Security Informatics: Security and Big Data (2017)
16. Tolah, A., Furnell, S.M., Papadaki, M.: An empirical analysis of the information security culture key factors framework. Computers & Security **108** (2021). https://doi.org/10.1016/j. cose.2021.102354
17. AlHogail, A.: Design and validation of information security culture framework. Comput. Hum. Behav. **49**, 567–575 (2015). https://doi.org/10.1016/j.chb.2015.03.054
18. Martins, E.C., Martins, N., Terblanche, F.: An organisational culture model to stimulate creativity and innovation in a university library. Advances in Library Administration and Organization **21**, 83–130 (2004). https://doi.org/10.1016/S0732-0671(04)21003-3
19. Hayden, L.: People-centric security Transforming your enterprise security culture. McGraw-Hill Education, New York (2016)
20. Van Niekerk, J., Von Solms, R.: A holistic framework for the fostering of an information security sub-culture in organizations. In: Proceedings of the Information Security South Africa Conference, pp. 1–13 (2005)
21. Schlienger, T., Teufel, S.: Information security culture: the socio-cultural dimension in information security management. In: Proceedings of the IFIP TC11 17th International Conference on Information Security: Visions and Perspectives, pp. 191–202 (2002)

22. Von Solms, R., Van Niekerk, J.: From information security to cyber security. Comput. Secur. **38**, 97–102 (2013). https://doi.org/10.1016/j.cose.2013.04.004

23. Da Veiga, A.: Information Security Culture. In: Encyclopedia of Cryptography, Security and Privacy, pp. 1–4. Springer Berlin Heidelberg (2021). https://doi.org/10.1007/978-3-642-277 39-9

24. Da Veiga, A.: Achieving a Security Culture. In: Cybersecurity Education for Awareness and Compliance, pp. 72–100. IGI Global, Hershey PA, USA (2019). https://doi.org/10.4018/978-1-5225-7847-5.ch005

25. Auernhammer, J., Hall, H.: Organizational culture in knowledge creation, creativity and innovation: towards the Freiraum model. J. Inf. Sci. **40**, 154–166 (2014). https://doi.org/10.1177/0165551513508356

26. Ciuciu, R.A., Mateescu, V., Ciuciu, I.: Organizational Culture and Innovation: An Industrial Case Study. In: Meersman, R., et al. (eds.) OTM 2014. LNCS, vol. 8842, pp. 514–518. Springer, Heidelberg (2014). https://doi.org/10.1007/978-3-662-45550-0_52

27. Scheibe, K.P., Gupta, M.: The effect of socializing via computer-mediated communication on the relationship between organizational culture and organizational creativity. Commu. Associ. Info. Sys. **40**, 294–314 (2017). https://doi.org/10.17705/1cais.04013

28. Ogbeibu, S., Senadjki, A., Luen Peng, T.: An organisational culture and trustworthiness multidimensional model to engender employee creativity. American Journal of Business. **33**, 179–202 (2018). https://doi.org/10.1108/ajb-12-2017-0043

29. Grant, M.J., Booth, A., Centre, S.: A typology of reviews: an analysis of 14 review types and associated methodologies. Health Info. Libr. J. **26**, 91–108 (2009). https://doi.org/10.1111/j.1471-1842.2009.00848.x

30. Moher, D., Liberati, A., Tetzlaff, J., Altman, D.G., Group, P.: Preferred reporting items for systematic reviews and meta-analyses: The PRISMA statement. Annuls of Internal Medicine **151**(4), 264-270 (2009)

31. Ambile, T.M.: Creativity in context. Westview Press, Boulder, CO (1996)

32. Padayachee, K.: Taxonomy of compliant information security behavior. Comput. Secur. **31**, 673–680 (2012). https://doi.org/10.1016/j.cose.2012.04.004

33. Martins, E.C., Meyer, H.W.J.: Organizational and behavioral factors that influence knowledge retention. J. Knowl. Manag. **16**, 77–96 (2012). https://doi.org/10.1108/13673271211198954

34. Quinn, R.E., Rohrbaugh, J.: A spatial model of effectiveness criteria - towards a competing values approach to organizational analysis. Manage. Sci. **29**, 363–377 (1983)

35. Cameron, K.S., Quinn, R.E.: Diagnosing and changing organizational culture: Based on the competing values framework. Jossey-Bass, San Francisco, CA (2011)

36. Choo, C.W.: Information culture and organizational effectiveness. Int. J. Inf. Manage. **33**, 775–779 (2013). https://doi.org/10.1016/j.ijinfomgt.2013.05.009

37. Colovic, A., Williams, C.: Group culture, gender diversity and organizational innovativeness: Evidence from Serbia. J. Bus. Res. **110**, 282–291 (2020). https://doi.org/10.1016/j.jbusres.2019.12.046

38. Gorzelany, J., et al.: Finding links between organisation's culture and innovation. The impact of organisational culture on university innovativeness. Plos ONE. **16** (2021). https://doi.org/10.1371/journal.pone.0257962

39. Ogbeibu, S., Senadjki, A., Gaskin, J.: The moderating effect of benevolence on the impact of organisational culture on employee creativity. J. Bus. Res. **90**, 334–346 (2018). https://doi.org/10.1016/j.jbusres.2018.05.032

Understanding Phishing in Mobile Instant Messaging: A Study into User Behaviour Toward Shared Links

Rufai Ahmad$^{(\boxtimes)}$ (iD) and Sotirios Terzis (iD)

Department of Computer and Information Sciences, University of Strathclyde, Glasgow, UK
{rufai.ahmad,sotirios.terzis}@strath.ac.uk

Abstract. In recent years, users of Mobile Instant Messaging (MIM) apps like WhatsApp and Telegram are being targeted by phishing attacks. While user susceptibility to phishing in other media is well studied, the literature currently lacks studies on phishing susceptibility in MIM apps. This paper presents a study that offers the first insights into the susceptibility of users of MIM apps to phishing by investigating their behaviour towards shared links. Using an online survey, we collected data from 111 users of MIM apps and found that participants frequently click and forward links during instant messaging, while factors such as the user's relationship with the sender and the group context of the communication influence these behaviours. The results show that behaviours of most users towards shared links try to reduce their risk to phishing by trusting their friends, family and colleagues to protect them. This raises some interesting questions for further research on the effectiveness and reliability of their strategy.

Keywords: Mobile Instant Messaging · Phishing · Mobile phishing

1 Introduction

Phishing is an attempt to obtain sensitive information from internet users by tricking them into visiting fraudulent websites or downloading malware [1]. According to the Anti-Phishing Working Group (APWG), phishing attacks have tripled since early 2020, with the number of unique phishing URLs detected in the last quarter of 2021 increasing to 316,747 from 260,642 in the third quarter of 2021 [2]. A recent report by Kaspersky shows that phishing is moving to Mobile Instant Messaging (MIM) apps, with a significant share of phishing links on android smartphones between December 2020 and May 2021 distributed through WhatsApp (89.6%), Telegram (5.6%) and Viber (4.7%) [3]. This is not surprising considering the popularity of these apps, with recent data showing that 3.09B mobile phone users communicated using these apps in 2021 [4]. The lack of countermeasures to protect MIM app users from phishing [5] and functions like sharing and forwarding links, creating and joining private and public groups advertised online actually facilitate phishing. The small screen size of mobile devices and the fact that users are likely to check messages while engaged in other activities may also affect users'

N. Clarke and S. Furnell (Eds.): HAISA 2022, IFIP AICT 658, pp. 197–206, 2022.
https://doi.org/10.1007/978-3-031-12172-2_15

ability to assess message validity and spot phishing thus increasing their susceptibility. As a result, phishing in MIM apps is a concern in need of attention.

To date there has been little research on how best to address phishing in MIM apps. A key step in this respect is to understand to what extent users engage in behaviours in MIM apps that put them at risk of phishing. This paper aims to fill this gap by answering the following research questions:

RQ1: How frequently do users click and forward links shared in MIM apps?
RQ2: Do factors such as the communicating parties and group context influence users' behaviours towards links shared in MIM apps?

To address these questions, we conducted an online survey about the behaviours of MIM app users towards shared links. The survey targeted MIM app users aged 18 and above. Our findings show that 1) many participants frequently click and share links; 2) participants click links from friends, family, and work colleagues more frequently than other communicating parties; and 3) although participants are as likely to click links in one-to-one and group communication, they are more likely to share links they receive in private rather than public groups. Although these results are encouraging in that they show users take some care to reduce their risk to phishing, they also show that users tend to put their trust on friends, family and work colleagues to protect them from phishing raising some interesting questions on the reliability and effectiveness of this strategy that deserve further research.

We begin the paper with a review of related literature before we focus on the design of our study, the presentation of its results, and a discussion of the result implications and study limitations. We conclude the paper by identifying directions for future work.

2 Literature Review

Research on phishing tends to fall into four categories: (1) solutions that detect and block phishing links and content with minimum or no user intervention [6, 7]; (2) phishing awareness/training approaches that aim to equip users with the required knowledge to defend themselves [8, 9]; (3) approaches that support users to detect phishing attacks by providing security cues [10]; and (4) studies that aim to determine user susceptibility to phishing by analysing their behaviours [11]. Our work falls within the scope of the latter, so this section will provide an overview of research in this area, focusing on the mobile context. However, it is interesting to note that MIM apps do not provide any automated means for detecting and blocking links [5].

Most studies on user susceptibility to phishing focus on fixed devices such as desktop computers and tend to look into phishing emails [12–14], phishing web pages [11] and phishing URLs [15]. The main conclusion from these studies is that users do not use the right cues when deciding the legitimacy of emails or URLs and this makes them susceptible to phishing attacks. Moreover, research shows that trust is a significant predictor of phishing susceptibility [16, 17], with trust being the willingness to be vulnerable to others because we expect them to act according to our expectations [17]. This is because the user tendency to trust others is often exploited in phishing attacks. Finally, the study in [18] found that respondents were more likely to respond to phishing emails when the sender was their friend. These findings are likely to be relevant for MIM apps where communication tends to be between known contacts [19].

Research on the susceptibility of mobile device users to phishing is limited. Motivated by the need to understand the impact of mobile device limitations, like smaller screen size compared to desktop computers, in [20] researchers studied mobile phone users to determine which indicators they used when deciding the legitimacy of a webpage. They found that (>90%) of the participants rely on the website's design, content, and functionality to decide its legitimacy. Participants who used URL and other browser security indicators performed better than those who didn't. There was no correlation between participants' scores and their age, technical proficiency, or time spent on a smartphone. Participants also reported being confused with the HTTPS and green padlock in safari. These findings are similar to those found for desktop computers.

In [21], the cybersecurity knowledge and attitudes of 206 mobile phone users from Japan (n = 106) and Tanzania (n = 100) were assessed. In addition, to lacking knowledge about phishing, 58% of respondents from Tanzania were likely to open a link in an email from an unknown sender. Participants from Japan had higher awareness of the risk as only 38% were likely to do so.

In [22] the authors assessed the susceptibility of mobile phone users to phishing through Quick Response (QR) codes. Their findings show that 225 users visited obscured URLs attached to QR codes placed in public places, with only 58% reading the URLs before visiting, while 36% visited the URLs without checking them.

Despite evidence of phishing in MIM apps, the literature currently offers no insights into users' susceptibility to phishing in them. The popularity of these apps, combined with many features they provide, such as the ability to receive messages from strangers during group-based communication; privately message members of groups; share and forward links; and use of link previews, can facilitate phishing attacks. These features, combined with the lack of automated solutions to detect and block phishing URLs, make investigating user susceptibility to phishing in this context timely and worthwhile.

3 Methodology

This study used a web-based survey to collect data from MIM apps users above 18 years. The survey focused on user behaviour towards links shared through MIM apps both during one-to-one and group communication. Our departmental ethics committee approved the study.

We limited our respondents to those using Signal, Slack, Telegram, Viber, Line, and WhatsApp because of their popularity and the features that they provide, such as group communication, link previews, link sharing, messages/links forwarding, and the ability to join public groups via links shared by group admins online, which can increase the phishing susceptibility of their users.

All questions in the survey were based on either a Likert-scale or multiple choice answers. More specifically, the survey includes four demographic questions relating to age, gender, education and country of residence, one device usage question, one question on what MIM apps respondents use, seventeen Likert-type questions relating to the behaviour of the participants during one-to-one and group communication, and six questions on link forwarding behaviours.

We recruited participants using an approach that combines snowball sampling and social media. Snowball sampling is a non-random sampling method appropriate for recruiting research participants that are hard to reach or unknown [23]. The process for recruiting participants involves three steps: (1) the first author used the contact list of all the mobile messaging apps he currently uses to advertise the survey; (2) we identified and posted the survey on various social media groups, including r/SampleSize on Reddit, samplesize on Facebook and SurveyCycle; and (3) we emailed our colleagues asking them to take part and forward the survey to others. At each stage, we asked participants to invite others to participate in the study by sharing the link to the survey with them. Data collection began on Oct. 12 2021, and ended on Nov. 5 2021.

The data collected from the survey was purely nominal or ordinal. We used frequencies and percentages of each response and present the data visually using frequency graphs. Where a test of significance was required, we used non-parametric tests like Wilcoxon signed-rank and Friedman test, as they are considered appropriate for this type of data [24]. However, we acknowledge that the discussion on the appropriateness of either parametric or non-parametric tests is ongoing [25]. All follow-up pairwise comparisons were conducted using Dunn-Bonferroni posthoc tests. All survey questions were optional. Therefore, missing values may exist, but we excluded them from the analysis, in which case, the actual number of participants used is reported. We used SPSS software for the statistical analysis.

4 Results

A total of 129 participants accessed the online survey. After data cleaning, we excluded 18 participants for failing to meet our screening criteria. The participants were skewed with respect to gender (73, 65.8%) male, (37, 33.3%) female, and one participant preferred not to disclose their gender. The highest age group in the sample was 18–30 (54, 48.6%), followed by 31–45 (51, 45.9%) and 46+ (6, 5.4%). Most of the participants have a postgraduate qualification (60, 54.1%), followed by undergraduate (33, 29.7%), further education (13, 11.7%), and secondary education (5, 4.5%). Many participants resided in the UK (64, 58.7%) when they accessed the survey, followed by Nigeria (18, 16.5%), and (29, 26.1%) other countries, including Germany, Canada, the USA, Malaysia, the Netherlands, France, Singapore, Saudi Arabia, Finland, Russia and Libya.

All participants used mobile phones daily (n = 111). The highest used MIM app by the participants was WhatsApp (106, 95.5%), followed by Telegram (40, 36.0%), Signal (19, 17.1%), Slack (13, 11.7%), Viber (6, 5.4%) and Line (4, 3.6%). We are not surprised by this, considering that WhatsApp and Telegram are among the most popular messenger apps globally [26]. Figure 1 shows that many participants use MIM apps to communicate with friends (97, 87.4%), family (92, 82.9%) and work colleagues (80, 72.1%). This confirmed earlier findings that showed instant messaging is mainly between friends or family [27]. Most participants are currently members of MIM app groups (103, 92.7%), but when asked whether they know the types of groups, only (71, 68.9%) said yes. We asked this because groups in MIM apps can be public or private, with public groups exposing users to higher phishing risks as they are open to anyone.

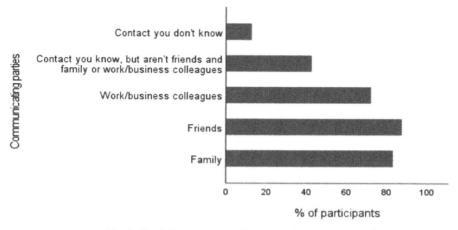

Fig. 1. Participants communicating parties (n = 111)

To answer RQ1, we first asked the participants to indicate how frequently they click on links during communication in MIM Apps. We followed up with another question regarding their frequency of clicking links shared in groups. We wanted to check if there was any difference in the participants' behaviour across these two conditions. Figure 2 shows that most participants sometimes click on links in both conditions (52, 51%) for general click frequency and (47, 46.1%) for group communication. The figure also shows that a high percentage of the participants tend to engage in these behaviours frequently. We noticed a slight difference in the frequency of clicking shared links in general and during group communication. To test whether this difference is significant, we conducted Wilcoxon signed-rank test. The test results in a Z statistics of -0.394, and a p-value of .680, implying that this difference is not statistically significant. Thus, we cannot reject the null hypothesis of equal medians for the two variables. To measure the participants' link forwarding behaviour, we asked them to indicate the frequency they engage in this behaviour. Out of 105 responses (n = 42) indicated that they sometimes forward links to others, as indicated by a median value (Mdn = 3). Some participants (n = 18) indicated that they often do so, while (n = 31) said they rarely do so.

To answer RQ2, we first looked into how frequently users click on links from different communicating parties. Due to the design of the questionnaire, questions relating to the frequency of clicking links from communicating parties were only displayed to participants if they had previously indicated to communicate with them. As a result, there were many combinations. Our findings revealed that most participants (n = 30) used MIM apps to talk with four different types of people, typically friends, family, work colleagues, and other known contacts, followed by those with three types (n = 28) typically friends, family and work colleagues, and those with two (n = 13) typically family and friends. Some participants (n = 10) indicated they communicate with all five types of people listed in Fig. 1, while others (n = 17) said they communicate with only one type of people, typically friends (n = 7), family (n = 4), or work colleagues (n = 4). Since we aim to find the difference in user click behaviour based on two or more conditions, our analysis focused only on participants that communicate with more

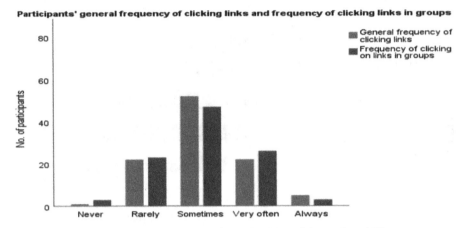

Fig. 2. Frequency of clicking links by the participants (n = 102)

than one type of user. Furthermore, we only report cases where we found a statistically significant difference.

Table 1. Count of participants that selected four types of users with the frequency level

Communicating party	Never	Rarely	Sometimes	Very often	Always	Medians
Friends	0	2	13	8	7	3.5
Family	0	4	10	10	6	4.0
Work colleagues	0	1	12	14	3	4.0
Other known contacts	6	18	4	1	1	2.0

For the participants that selected four communicating parties (n = 30), our analysis revealed that many of them rarely (n = 18) or never (n = 6) clicked on links from contacts they did not know (see Table 1). Clicking links from family and work colleagues received the highest frequency ratings, as indicated by each having a median of (Mdn = 4), followed by friends (Mdn = 3.50). The frequency of clicking links from contacts who are not family, friends or work colleagues has the lowest rating (Mdn = 2). A Friedman test showed a significant difference in the median ratings across the four communicating parties, χ^2 (3) = 59.416, p < .001. Post hoc tests indicate a significant difference between the first three communicating parties and contacts the participants know but are not friends, family or business colleagues (p < .001).

Some participants (n = 10) indicated that they communicate with all the five types of communicating parties. Table 2 shows the number of participants for each frequency level based on communicating parties. Links from friends, family and work colleagues received the highest ratings, with a median (Mdn = 3.50) for each. Other communicating parties received lower ratings (Mdn = 2.50) for known contacts but not friends, family or work colleagues, and (Mdn = 2) for unknown contacts. A Friedman test showed a significant difference in the median ratings across the four communicating parties, χ^2 (4) = 25,638, p < .001. Post hoc tests indicate a significant difference between the participants' frequency of clicking links from work colleagues and contacts not known (p = .007).

Table 2. Count of participants that selected five types of users with the frequency level

Communicating party	Never	Rarely	Sometimes	Very often	Always	Medians
Friends	0	3	2	4	1	3.50
Family	0	2	3	4	1	3.50
Work colleagues	0	1	4	3	2	3.50
Other known contacts	0	5	4	1	0	2.50
Strangers	3	5	2	0	0	2.00

We examined the impact of group type on the participants' link forwarding behaviour by requesting them to indicate how frequently they forward links shared in public or private groups. Figure 3 shows that the frequency of forwarding links received in private groups received the highest ratings, as indicated by the median (Mdn = 3) compared to (Mdn = 2) for public groups. A related sample test using the Wilcoxon Signed-Rank test was performed. The outcome revealed a statistically significant difference between the medians of the two behaviours z = 4.884, p < .001.

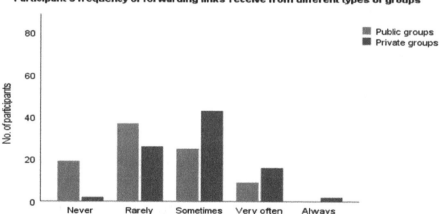

Fig. 3. Participants' frequency of forwarding links received from different types of groups

5   Discussion and Limitations

Our study results show that many participants click and forward links shared in MIM apps. A number of them do so not only in one-to-one but also group communication, as we found no statistically significant difference in the frequency of clicking links shared in the both. While it is okay to do so, it becomes a problem when such behaviour becomes habitual since this can affect how users process information [28]. With evidence of phishing in MIM apps, habitual clickers and forwarders are likely to put themselves and others at risk. However, our findings reveal that participants' behaviour is more nuanced, as they are more likely to click on links shared by their friends, family or work colleagues. Moreover, they are more likely to forward links they receive in private rather than in public groups, most likely because private groups comprise known contacts, like friends, family and work colleagues. However, worryingly some users are not aware what types of groups they actually use.

Although the reasons behind these behaviours are not known, trust is likely to be a factor, with participants implicitly or explicitly relying on people in their social circle to protect them from phishing. However, it is unclear whether this reliance is justified. Phishers can abuse people's trust in their social circle. In fact, there is evidence that in the context of phishing emails, trust makes users more susceptible to phishing.

One limitation of this study is that our sample size is relatively small. In addition to this, the use of snowball sampling, despite being powerful, often results in participants with higher interconnectivity than would be seen in the general population, and has introduced some biases in our participant population. Our survey participants are highly educated, as evidenced by the majority having an undergraduate or postgraduate education, which may have an impact on the measured behaviours. Moreover, they are predominantly male, but the effect of gender on user security behaviour has been inconsistent in the literature. They also tend to be younger in age with few of them in the 46+ age groups, but this may reflect the higher popularity of MIM app use in younger ages. Our participants are mostly resident in the UK with some in Nigeria, which may have also an impact on the measured behaviours. Thus, generalising our findings to the whole MIM app large and diverse userbase carries certain risks. Finally, our study relies on self-reported behaviours, as such the data may not be an accurate reflection of how users behave towards links in real-life.

6 Conclusions

MIM apps with billions of people using them to communicate with friends, family, and others have drawn the attention of phishers. The functionalities of these apps, such as the ability to share links or join groups, including public ones, enable easy access to a large pool of users, making these apps an attractive medium for phishing attacks. Despite that, little research to date has focused on phishing in MIM apps.

In this paper, we offer the first insights into the behaviours of users of MIM apps towards shared links. Our online survey study found that participants frequently click and forward shared links, and they do so both in one-to-one and group communication, potentially exposing them to the risk of phishing. However, we also found that participants try to protect themselves from phishing by being less likely to click links that are shared by those that aren't their friends, family and work colleagues. They are also less likely to forward links shared in public rather than private groups. So, most participants appear to trust their friends, family and work colleagues to protect them from phishing.

It is unclear how reliable and effective this strategy is. Research on email phishing indicates that it may be neither reliable nor effective, but further research is required to determine whether this is the case in MIM. In addition to this, future research could also investigate whether technical skills and phishing efficacy influence users' behaviours towards shared links in MIM apps with the aim to establish whether such behaviours differ from those in other media, like email.

References

1. NCSC: Phishing attacks: defending your organisation. https://www.ncsc.gov.uk/guidance/phishing (2018). Accessed 25 Jan 2021
2. APWG: Phishing Activity Trend Report (4th Quarter 2021). https://docs.apwg.org/reports/apwg_trends_report_q4_2021.pdf?_ga=2.172997153.361044271.1647946096-199395 7391.1647946096&_gl=1*1c9f67o*_ga*MTk5Mzk1NzM5MS4xNjQ3OTQ2MDk2*_ga_ 55RF0RHXSR*MTY0Nzk0NjA5NS4xLjEuMTY0Nzk0NzU0MC4w (2022)
3. Kaspersky: "Phishing in messenger apps – what's new?". https://www.kaspersky.com/about/press-releases/2021_phishing-in-messenger-apps-whats-new (2021). Accessed 4 Jan 2022
4. Statista: Number of mobile phone messaging app users worldwide from 2018 to 2022. https://www.statista.com/statistics/483255/number-of-mobile-messaging-users-worldwide/ (2021). Accessed 13 Apr 2021
5. Stivala, G., Pellegrino, G.: Deceptive previews: a study of the link preview trustworthiness in social platforms (2020)
6. Medvet, E., Kirda, E., Kruegel, C.: Visual-similarity-based phishing detection. In: Proceedings of the 4th international conference on Security and privacy in communication netowrks (SecureComm '08). Association for Computing Machinery, Article 22, pp. 1–6. New York, NY, USA (2008). https://doi.org/10.1145/1460877.1460905
7. Zhang, Y., Hong, J.I., Cranor, L.F.: Cantina: A content-based approach to detecting phishing web sites. In: Proceedings of the 16th International Conference on World Wide Web (WWW '07). Association for Computing Machinery, pp. 639–648. New York, NY, USA (2007). https://doi.org/10.1145/1242572.1242659
8. Kumaraguru, P., et al.: School of phish: A real-world evaluation of anti-phishing training. In: Proceedings of the 5th Symposium on Usable Privacy and Security (SOUPS '09). Association for Computing Machinery, Article 3, pp. 1–12. New York, NY, USA (2009). https://doi.org/10.1145/1572532.1572536
9. N. A. G. Arachchilage and M. Cole, "Design a mobile game for home computer users to prevent from "phishing attacks". In: International Conference on Information Society (i-Society 2011), pp. 485–489 (2011). https://doi.org/10.1109/i-society18435.2011.5978543
10. Volkamer, M., Renaud, K., Reinheimer, B.: Torpedo: tooltip-powered phishing email detection. In: Hoepman, J.-H., Katzenbeisser, S. (eds.) ICT Systems Security and Privacy Protection: 31st IFIP TC 11 International Conference, SEC 2016, Ghent, Belgium, May 30 - June 1, 2016, Proceedings, pp. 161–175. Springer International Publishing, Cham (2016). https://doi.org/10.1007/978-3-319-33630-5_12
11. Alsharnouby, M., Alaca, F., Chiasson, S.: Why phishing still works: user strategies for combating phishing attacks. Int. J. Hum. Comput. Stud. **82**, 69–82 (2015). https://doi.org/10.1016/j.ijhcs.2015.05.005
12. Jayatilaka, A., Arachchilage, N.A.G., Babar, M.A.: Falling for phishing: an empirical investigation into people's email response behaviors. arXiv Prepr. arXiv:2108.04766 (2021)
13. Parsons, K., Butavicius, M., Pattinson, M., Calic, D., Mccormac, A., Jerram, C.: Do users focus on the correct cues to differentiate between phishing and genuine emails? arXiv Prepr. arXiv:1605.04717 (2016)

14. Parsons, K., Butavicius, M., Delfabbro, P., Lillie, M.: Predicting susceptibility to social influence in phishing emails. Int. J. Hum. Comput. Stud. **128**, 17–26 (2019)
15. Albakry, S., Vaniea, K., Wolters, M.K.: What is this URL's destination? empirical evaluation of users' URL reading. In: Proceedings of the 2020 CHI Conference on Human Factors in Computing Systems. Association for Computing Machinery, pp. 1–12. New York, NY, USA (2020). https://doi.org/10.1145/3313831.3376168
16. Workman, M.: Wisecrackers: A theory-grounded investigation of phishing and pretext social engineering threats to information security. J. Am. Soc. Inf. Sci. Technol. **59**(4), 662–674 (2008)
17. Moody, G.D., Galletta, D.F., Dunn, B.K.: Which phish get caught? an exploratory study of individuals' susceptibility to phishing. Eur. J. Inf. Syst. **26**(6), 564–584 (2017)
18. Jagatic, T.N., Johnson, N.A., Jakobsson, M., Menczer, F.: Social phishing. Commun. ACM **50**(10), 94–100 (2007)
19. Church, K., De Oliveira, R.: What's up with WhatsApp? Comparing mobile instant messaging behaviors with traditional SMS. In: Proceedings of the 15th International Conference on Human-computer interaction with mobile devices and services (MobileHCI '13), pp. 352–361. Association for Computing Machinery, New York, NY, USA (2013). https://doi.org/10.1145/2493190.2493225
20. Loxdal, J., Andersson, M., Hacks, S., Lagerström, R.: Why phishing works on smartphones: a preliminary study. In: HICSS, pp. 1–10 (2021)
21. Ndibwile, J.D., Luhanga, E.T., Fall, D., Miyamoto, D., Kadobayashi, Y.: A comparative study of smartphone-user security perception and preference towards redesigned security notifications. In: Proceedings of the Second African Conference for Human Computer Interaction: Thriving Communities, pp. 1–6 (2018)
22. Vidas, T., Owusu, E., Wang, S., Zeng, C., Cranor, L.F., Christin, N.: QRishing: The susceptibility of smartphone users to QR code phishing attacks. In: Adams, A.A., Brenner, M., Smith, M. (eds.) FC 2013. LNCS, vol. 7862, pp. 52–69. Springer, Heidelberg (2013). https://doi.org/10.1007/978-3-642-41320-9_4
23. Rashidi, Y., Vaniea, K., Camp, L.J.: Understanding Saudis' privacy concerns when using WhatsApp. In: Proceedings of the Workshop on Usable Security (USEC'16), pp. 1–8 (2016)
24. Jamieson, S.: Likert scales: How to (ab) use them? Med. Educ. **38**(12), 1217–1218 (2004)
25. Norman, G.: Likert scales, levels of measurement and the 'laws' of statistics. Adv. Heal. Sci. Educ. **15**(5), 625–632 (2010)
26. Tankovska, H.: Most popular global mobile messenger apps as of January 2021, based on number of monthly active users. https://www.statista.com/statistics/258749/most-popular-global-mobile-messenger-apps/ (2021). Accessed 11 Apr 2021
27. Sultan, A.J.: Addiction to mobile text messaging applications is nothing to 'lol' about. Soc. Sci. J. **S1**, 57–69 (2014). https://doi.org/10.1016/j.soscij.2013.09.003
28. Frauenstein, E.D., Flowerday, S.V.: Social network phishing: Becoming habituated to clicks and ignorant to threats? In 2016 Information Security for South Africa (ISSA), pp. 98–105 (2016)

Privacy

How Privacy Concerns Impact Swedish Citizens' Willingness to Report Crimes

Gunnar Lindqvist and Joakim Kävrestad(✉)

University of Skövde, Skövde, Sweden
{gunnar.lindqvist,joakim.kavrestad}@his.se

Abstract. In today's information technology-driven world, most criminal acts leave digital evidence. In such cases, cooperation through the handover of digital devices such as mobile phones from victims is a success factor that enables evidence-seeking through digital forensics. Unfortunately, forensic examinations of devices can become an additional negative consequence due to privacy invasion. Privacy invasion can make crime victims less cooperative and less willing to report crimes. To address this problem, we surveyed 400 Swedish adults to identify their hypothetical willingness to report certain crimes. The survey examined the impact a mobile phone handover made on the willingness to report a crime. Our findings demonstrate that mobile phone handover resulted in a significantly lower willingness to report crimes. However, the data could not show privacy as a common tendency cause. The presented results can be used as a reference for further research on attitudes and behaviours regarding the subject.

Keywords: Crime · Digital forensics · Mobile phone

1 Introduction

From the traditional criminal process, where only physical traces of crime have been vital evidence, digital evidence has also become a prominent part of criminal prosecutions. It is challenging to commit a crime without leaving digital evidence in today's technology-driven society [1]. Consequently, most crimes are committed connected to information technology (IT), making them IT-related [2]. Digital forensics (DF) is a well-used process to collect pieces of evidence from digital devices in IT-related crime investigations [3–5]. The information-packed mobile phone is a prominent source of such evidence, arguably the most personal device [6]. Fundamentally, crime reports are essential for criminals to take responsibility for their actions and not expose more people to crimes. Crime victims can facilitate investigations and increase the probability of prosecution through cooperation by deposing their mobile phones to the police's forensic unit. However, an additional negative consequence for those exposed to crime is the invasion of privacy, a severe challenge in digital investigations [7]. The potentially harmful effect of privacy violations can influence people's willingness to report crimes to the police [8]. Such violations can impact people's "privacy attitudes", referring to their stance on privacy

© IFIP International Federation for Information Processing 2022
Published by Springer Nature Switzerland AG 2022
N. Clarke and S. Furnell (Eds.): HAISA 2022, IFIP AICT 658, pp. 209–217, 2022.
https://doi.org/10.1007/978-3-031-12172-2_16

[9]. A reduced number of crime reports leads to a "dark figure" of crime, making it challenging to determine the extent to which crime occurs. Lack of crime reports results in criminals not being held accountable for their actions. Allowing them to continue with their illegal activities [10].

Previous research has raised several crime investigation challenges when utilising mobile phones for identifying evidence through DF. It has been argued that DF and privacy confront one another [11]. The confrontation is primarily due to technical and legal challenges such as encryption and preserving crime victims' privacy in criminal investigations [11–13]. Researchers have also examined people's privacy attitudes, which indicated that people could be divided into groups with similar attitudes regarding privacy [9, 14]. Furthermore, research has shown that IT-related crimes are reported to a lesser extent. The reason is a lower belief in the likelihood that the police will succeed in arresting the criminal who committed the crime [15]. Lastly, research authors have argued that it is crucial to conduct criminal investigations properly. The held argument is that IT-related crimes' severe impact on the victims goes further than the monetary loss [16]. Therefore, the approach of criminal investigations must be considered where privacy is one of the aspects.

This work explores the possible problem of how privacy concerns affect the willingness to hand in mobile phones for crime investigations. The work aimed to address whether privacy concerns impact the willingness to provide a mobile phone as evidence. Additionally, expand the knowledge of human behaviour and attitudes regarding crime reports.

Our results suggest that the handover of a mobile phone reduces the willingness to report crimes which, in turn, increases the dark figure of crime. The collected data indicates a weak correlation between the influence of privacy concerns when handing in a mobile phone is necessary when reporting a crime. This research contributes to continued research to understand why the willingness to report crimes is reduced when the victim needs to provide their mobile phone for forensic analysis.

2 Methodology

The aim of the study was met by distributing a quantitative mobile phone survey directed to Swedish citizens over the age of 18. A pilot test was implemented before the final questionnaire was sent out to ensure the quality of the survey, as suggested by [17]. The pilot test was distributed through convenience sampling with 24 respondents. The collected data helped clarify the text and assess the time needed to complete the survey.

The data was collected in March 2022 via Pollfish, a research platform that distributes mobile phone surveys. Pollfish relies on Random Device Engagement (RDE) and uses organic non-probability sampling [18]. Pollfish allows the selection of a specific population, and the target group was specified as Swedish citizens of the age above 18. Four hundred responses were bought at a rate of 0.95$ per completed survey [19]. The survey was additionally distributed through Reddit. The intention of the second sample was to validate the results of the first sample. This data collection served as a means of triangulation, as described by [20]. As argued by [21], Reddit is a beneficial tool for inexpensive and reliable data collection. The survey had 76 respondents, and two subreddits were used to gather respondents. Posts were published on the survey recruitment

/r/SampleSize [22] and the dedicated Swedish survey thread for the /r/Sweddit [23]. The posts briefly described the study, its purpose and a link to the survey.

Based on previous research recommendations, the questions were designed as a 7-point Likert scale [24–26]. A non-response option was offered to avoid opinion or attitude enforcement [24]. The survey questions were based on Sweden's four most common types of reported crimes in 2021 [27] and the Swedish police description [28]. The privacy-oriented statements were based on Solove's taxonomy of four types of activities [29]. The survey had the four following questions:

- Q1: The following statements describe criminal incidents. If you were the victim of one of these crimes, how likely is it that you would make a police report?
- Q2: The following questions describe criminal incidents. If you were the victim of one of these crimes, how likely will you make a police report if you are required to submit your mobile phone as evidence? Assume that your phone will remain with the police for two days.
- Q3: If you submitted your mobile phone to the police as evidence for a crime you have reported, how would then these statements fit into you?
- Q4: How do these statements fit into you?

The likeliness of reporting a crime had the anchors 1 (*Very Unlikely*) and 7 (*Very Likely*). In contrast, the attitude towards the police and mobile phone applications was 1 (*Very Inaccurate*) and 7 (*Very Accurate*), measuring people's attitudes toward the statements of Q3 and Q4. Table 1 below shows the survey's four questions with corresponding statements that were answered through the previously referenced Likert scales. Q1 and Q2 had the same statements to indifferently measure if there was an impact on the handover of the mobile phone.

Data analysis was conducted using inferential statistics to answer the hypothesis of whether privacy correlates to handing in mobile phones as evidence to the police [30, 31]. Cronbach's Alpha was used to measure the internal consistency of each scale, and the statements in each scale were used to compute an index value [32]. The index value was calculated as the mean answer value ((statement1 + statement2 + … statement 8)/8). We analysed if handing over a mobile phone impacted significantly using a paired t-test. The privacy magnitude was calculated using Pearson correlation using each question's mean [30]. Due to the unequal sample size, Welch's t-test was conducted to test the data quality [33]. The analysis allowed conclusions from the sample data to be generalised to the population on a probabilistic basis [34]. The non-response answers were excluded from the data analysis. The conventional significance level of 95% was used in this research.

Table 1. Set of questions with corresponding statements. 1 EUR = ~10 SEK at the time of writing

Q1 and Q2	Q3	Q4
Someone steals your wallet at an ATM	I would be worried that things would disappear on my cell phone	I would allow mobile applications to collect my contacts for backup so that they can be restored
Someone steals your motor vehicle	I would be worried that my personal information would be spread outside the police	I would allow mobile applications to collect my location, to let me see my site history
Someone sends you an unwanted nude photo via social media	I would be worried about damage to my mobile phone	I would allow personalised advertising based on my mobile purchases for the grocery store I shop at
Someone sexually abuses you	I would be worried because I do not know what the police would do with my mobile phone	I would allow my site history to be used to get restaurant suggestions
Someone writes graffiti on your motor vehicle	I would be worried because I do not trust the police	I would allow my information, such as my customer information, to be shared between telephone operators for a more effortless number transfer
Someone writes graffiti on your home	I would be worried about being without my mobile phone because I need it	I would allow you to get personalised offers based on my mobile purchases for the clothing stores I shop at
Someone defrauds you with a scam invoice of 500 SEK	I would be worried that the police would lose my mobile phone	I would allow receiving emails with surveys and competitions
Someone defrauds you with a scam invoice of 5.000 SEK	I would be worried that the police would see my messages, pictures or contacts	I would allow telemarketers to call me for offers

3 Results

The survey was conducted in March 2022 and resulted in 400 people responding, of whom 42% were females, and 58% were males. The four survey scales resulted in acceptable consistency, Q1 ($\alpha = .913$), Q2 ($\alpha = .921$), Q3 ($\alpha = .891$) and Q4 ($\alpha = .823$) [35]. Thus, all statements were included in the indexes and were used for the remainder of the analysis. The index value for each scale were, Q1 ($M = 4.81$), Q2 ($M = 4.57$), Q3 ($M = 3.88$) and Q4 ($M = 3.93$),

The paired t-test between Q1 and Q2 resulted in a significant difference $t(343) = 4.01, p < .001$ [30]. As such, the identified difference between Q1 and Q2 is statistically significant. In other words, participants are less likely to report crimes if they have to submit their cellphone for forensic analysis.

Correlation analysis was used to analyze if privacy concerns or attitudes towards the police correlate with willingness to report crimes. The correlation coefficients of willingness to report when handing in a mobile phone against mobile privacy and police worry attitudes are illustrated in Table 2. While the correlation tests are significant, the coefficients are too low to be considered meaningful [30].

Table 2. Correlation coefficients of question indexes

	Q3	Q4
Q2	−.055	+.157

3.1 Analysis of the Results

Contrary to our expectations, the data did not support the hypothesis that privacy concerns affect handing a mobile phone to the police's DF in combination with a crime report. The result was unexpected because the idea that the mobile phone containing a considerable amount of personal information would impact the willingness to report and show a correlation that privacy concerns influence. The concern of privacy intrusion indicates no common correlation that creates a lower willingness to cooperate with mobile phones. However, the result may indicate a diverse perception of privacy. As shown by [9, 14], people perceive privacy differently; thus, the relationship between privacy and evidence provided by mobile phones may vary. A possible explanation of this finding is the high variation in the relationship between crime report intents, mobile phone privacy attitudes, and people's attitudes towards the police.

The results further indicate that people's attitudes and behaviour regarding integrity, on average, are not so strong-willed. The reason is that the data from the survey questions tended to be close to the midpoint value. As long as the reason to share personal information with companies and authorities is for self-gain, information sharing may seem reasonable. The statements presented possible benefits to gain by sharing personal information. Furthermore, the company that collected information could have given a more targeted result as there are general attitudes towards varying companies. No specific company was therefore mentioned. The result does not automatically indicate that privacy and police attitudes are generally low. As explained above, people arguably differ in perceiving privacy. The mean value is close to the median value for the Likert scale and may result from polarized opinions. Possibly people can either be opinionated or careless regarding privacy.

Although the willingness to report a crime was significantly lower when the mobile phone was involved, the meaning of handing over the mobile phone can influence it. For example, data in the survey showed a higher willingness to report crimes when IT was the means. The finding could be that people perceive benefit from handing over their mobile phones for such crimes. The description of the crime was "Someone sends you an unwanted nude photo via social media", and it resulted in $(M = 3.48)$ and $(M = 3.81)$. Similar to how people may surrender parts of their integrity in trade for other benefits, similar reasoning can be given for evidence.

Our findings can be compared to the results of earlier studies that reporting intentions increase with the severity of the crime [15], both for regular crime reports and crime reports with mobile phones as a requirement for evidence. The most apparent evidence of this claim is the significant difference in the monetary value of a scam invoice. A paired t-test between the loss of 500 and 5.000 Swedish kronor resulted in Q1 $t(392) = -5.9$, p $< .001$, and for Q2 $t(382) = -7.26$, p $< .001$, which provides strong evidence that the severity of the crime impact significantly. As seen in Table 1, the likelihood of reporting a crime was relatively low $(M = 4.81)$, where $5 =$ "quite likely". Similarly, Q2 was close to "quite likely" $(M = 4.57)$. Nonetheless, we find a significant difference in the likelihood of reporting a crime, concluding that handing in a mobile phone impacts.

3.2 Discussion of the Results

This paper reports whether privacy concerns influence the willingness to report a crime when handing in a mobile phone for evidence to Swedish DF is necessary. The study surveyed 400 Swedish adults as the primary data source through a mobile phone survey. In order to test the data quality of the collected responses, the survey was also distributed through Reddit, an Internet website for social forums. As shown below in Table 3, the two samples did not significantly differ regarding willingness to report crime when handing over the mobile phone to the police (Q2) $t(111.23) = 1.19$, p $= .24$, or privacy attitudes regarding the mobile phone (Q3) $t(92.15) = 1.71$, p $= .09$. A significant difference was shown between willingness to report crimes (Q1) $t(198.09) = -4.28$, p $< .001$, and worry concerning handing over the mobile phone to the police (Q4) $t(111.77) = 4.64$, p $< .001$. A possible explanation for this finding could be that Reddit mainly consists of young male users [36]. It is, therefore, not fully equal to the Pollfish sample.

The sample from Reddit indicated a similar correlational coefficient between Q2 and Q3 $(-.176)$. The data from the study indicate that different groups may differ in attitudes and behaviours regarding privacy and the police, as argued in the analysis. However, it was beyond the scope of this article to explore groupings of people regarding privacy and police attitudes.

Research ethics unavoidably play a role when involving humans as subjects, enforcing the obligation to consider ethical treatment [17, 37]. The involvement may inadvertently harm them, not solely physically, by embarrassing them, violating their privacy and other undesirable harmful effects. Those undesirable effects are essential to keep in mind when conducting research. However, implementing an adequate quantitative survey when a platform is used as a distribution method is cumbersome because it is beyond the control of how the company operates. Pollfish complies with applicable GDPR and allows respondents to opt out [38]. The respondents received compensation for their time in carrying out the study, and the purpose of the study was to benefit the judiciary.

As for the limitations, it can be assumed that most respondents have never been in a position where they had to decide whether to submit their mobile phones for a

Table 3. Descriptive statistics and Welch's *t*-test

	Pollfish			Reddit			Welch's t-test		
	N	*M*	*SD*	*N*	*M*	*SD*	*t*	*df*	*p*
Q1	367	4.81	1.69	73	5.39	0.87	−4.28	198.09	< .001
Q2	359	4.57	1.76	71	4.33	1.51	1.19	111.23	.24
Q3	363	3.88	1.54	76	3.59	1.69	1.71	92.15	.09
Q4	361	3.93	1.21	73	3.10	1.27	4.64	111.77	< .001

crime report or not. Most participants would likely give an opinion without having complete insight into the scenario and thus affect the non-generalisable situation. Another limitation was that users registered with Pollfish only had the opportunity to participate in the study, excluding people without the service. However, the use of Pollfish verified that respondents owned a mobile phone. Additionally, participants that are particularly interested in the topic take the time and trouble to respond. In contrast, uninterested may avoid the trouble of conducting the survey and thus, it is challenging to understand respondent bias [39].

The result of not proving that privacy is a prominent factor that influences attitudes and behaviour regarding the handover of evidence suggests not automatically an absent contribution. On the contrary, the study indicates that further research is needed. As a result, it shows a lower willingness to report crimes when handing over a personal mobile phone, revealing a real negatively impacting problem.

4   Conclusions

This paper aimed to see if there was a difference in the tendency to report a crime when the handover of a mobile phone was necessary as evidence. If that was the case, the paper further aimed to investigate if privacy concerns caused that difference. By distributing a mobile phone survey to Swedish adults, attitudes and behaviours were measured through Likert scales. The results were then analysed using inferential statistics, which identified a significantly lower willingness to report crime when the handover of a mobile phone is necessary. However, the statistical analysis identified no meaningful correlation between privacy attitudes and willingness to report crime when the handover of a mobile phone is necessary. Furthermore, the study found no direct correlation between several reasons for concern if the police obtained the mobile phone.

This paper's contribution explores attitudes and behaviours regarding the combination of privacy, DF, mobile phones and crime reportage. The research addresses that the willingness to report crimes contributes to a dark figure in statistics and explores possible reasons for the phenomenon. The results and methodology can support future studies by providing an insight into what the results can yield and how research can be done. Subsequently, this paper can help create new ways and ideas for conducting research in this field of research within different demographics or aims.

Future studies will have to investigate further how privacy influences behaviour and attitudes. More rigorous research can be conducted with a larger data sample to strengthen the findings of this research. Another direction for future work is investigating people's attitudes toward the providence of digital evidence to DF. Research can also assess the extent to which other digital devices and scenarios differentiate. Further, another possible direction is measuring the privacy concerns and exploring the differences between ages or other types of subgroups. Nonetheless, this paper's results indicate ambiguities that can be answered with further research.

References

1. Marshall, A.: Digital Forensics: Digital Evidence in Criminal Investigations, 1st edn. Wiley-Blackwell, New Jersey (2008)
2. Andersson, F., Nelander Hedqvist, K., Ring, J., Skarp, A.: It-inslag i brottsligheten och rättsväsendets förmåga att hantera dem. Stockholm (2016)
3. Garfinkel, S.: Digital forensics research: the next 10 years. Digit. Investig. **7**, 64–73 (2010)
4. Salamh, F., Mirza, M., Hutchinson, S., Yoon, Y., Karabiyik, U.: What's on the horizon? an in-depth forensic analysis of android and iOS applications. IEEE Access **9**, 99421–99454 (2021)
5. Kävrestad, J.: Fundamentals of Digital Forensics, 2nd edn. Springer, Cham (2020)
6. Tamma, R., Skulkin, O., Mahalik, H., Bommisetty, S.: Practical Mobile Forensics, 4th edn. Packt Publishing, Birmingham (2020)
7. Nickson, K., Hein, V.: Taxonomy of challenges for digital forensics. J. Forensic Sci. **60**(4), 885–893 (2015)
8. Felson, R., Messner, S., Hoskin, A., Deane, G.: Reasons for reporting and not reporting domestic violence to the police. Criminology **40**(3), 617–648 (2002)
9. Demertzis, N., Mandenaki, K., Tsekeris, C.: Privacy attitudes and behaviors in the age of post-privacy: an empirical approach. J. Digital Soc. Res. **3**(1), 119–152 (2021)
10. Biderman, A., Reiss, A.: On exploring the "dark figure" of crime. Ann. Am. Acad. Pol. Soc. Sci. **374**(1), 1–15 (1967)
11. Nieto, A., Rios, R., Lopez, J.: IoT-forensics meets privacy: towards cooperative digital investigations. Sensors **18**(2), 492 (2018)
12. Javed, A., Jalil, Z., Zehra, W., Gadekallu, T., Suh, D., Piran, M.: A comprehensive survey on digital video forensics: taxonomy, challenges, and future directions. Eng. Appl. Artif. Intell. **106**, 104456 (2021)
13. Halboob, W., Mahmoda, R., Udzira, N., Abdullaha, M.: Privacy levels for computer forensics: toward a more efficient privacy-preserving investigation. Procedia Comput. Sci. **56**, 370–375 (2015)
14. Chignell, M., Quan-Haase, A., Gwizdka, J.: The privacy attitudes questionnaire (PAQ): initial development and validation. Proc. Hum. Factors Ergon. Soc. Annu. Meet. **47**(11), 1326–1330 (2003)
15. Graham, A., Kulig, T., Cullen, F.: Willingness to report crime to the police: traditional crime, cybercrime, and procedural justice. Policing: An Int. J. **43**(1), 1–16 (2020)
16. Jansen, J., Leukfeldt, R.: Coping with cybercrime victimization: an exploratory study into the impact and change. J. Qual. Crim. Justice Criminol. **6**(2), 1–29 (2017)
17. Gillespie, B., Ruel, E., Wagner, W., III.: The Practice of Survey Research: Theory and Applications, 1st edn. SAGE Publications Inc, New York (2016)

18. Rothschild, D., Konitzer, T.: Random Device Engagement and Organic Sampling. https:// resources.pollfish.com/market-research/random-device-engagement-and-organic-sampling/. Accessed 2020
19. Pollfish, Inc: Buy Survey Responses With a DIY Market Research Platform. https://res ources.pollfish.com/market-research/buy-survey-responses-with-a-diy-market-research-pla tform/. Accessed 21 Feb 2022
20. Lincoln, Y., Guba, E.: Naturalistic Inquiry, 1st edn. SAGE Publications Inc, New York (1985)
21. Jamnik, M., David, J.L.: The use of reddit as an inexpensive source for high-quality data. Pract. Assess. Res. Eval. **22**(5), 5 (2017)
22. Reddit: SampleSize (2012). https://www.reddit.com/r/SampleSize/
23. Reddit: Sweddit (2008). https://www.reddit.com/r/sweden/. Accessed 1 Apr 2022
24. Alwin, D.: Margins of Error: A Study of Reliability in Survey Measurement. Wiley, New York (2007)
25. Lavrakas, P.: Encyclopedia of Survey Research Methods 1–0. Sage Publications Inc, Thousand Oaks (2008)
26. Menold, N.: Rating-scale labeling in online surveys: an experimental comparison of verbal and numeric rating scales with respect to measurement quality and respondents' cognitive processes. Sociol. Methods Res. **49**(1), 79–107 (2020)
27. Brå: Anmälda brott 2021 Prelimär statistik. Brottsförebyggande rådet, Stockholm (2022)
28. Polisen: Olika typer av brott A-Ö. https://polisen.se/utsatt-for-brott/olika-typer-av-brott/
29. Solove, D.: A Taxonomy of Privacy. Univ. Pa. Law Rev. **154**(3), 477–564 (2006)
30. Jackson, S.L.: Research Methods and Statistics: A Critical Thinking Approach, 5th edn. Cengage Learning, Boston (2015)
31. Sahu, P., Pal, S., Das, A.: Estimation and Inferential Statistics, 1st edn. Springer, New Delhi (2015)
32. Cronbach, L.: Coefficient alpha and the internal structure of tests. Psychometrika **16**(3), 297–334 (1951)
33. Welch, B.L.: The generalization of 'student's' problem when several different population variances are involved. Biometrika **34**(1/2), 28–35 (1947)
34. Robson, C.: Real World Research: A Resource for Social Scientists and Practitioner-Researchers, 2nd edn. Wiley-Blackwell, New Jersey (2002)
35. Tavakol, M., Dennick, R.: Making sense of Cronbach's alpha. Int. J. Med. Educ. **2**, 54–55 (2011)
36. Proferes, N., Jones, N., Gilbert, S., Fiesler, C., Zimmer, M.: Studying reddit: a systematic overview of disciplines, approaches, methods, and ethics. Soc. Media + Society **7**(2), 1–14 (2021)
37. Fowler, F.J.: Survey Research Methods, 5th edn. SAGE Publications Inc, New York (2013)
38. Pollfish: Your Data. Your Call. https://www.pollfish.com/gdpr/. Accessed 2022
39. Andrade, C.: The limitations of online surveys. Indian J. Psychol. Med. **42**(6), 575–576 (2020)

"Your Cookie Disclaimer is Not in Line with the Ideas of the GDPR. Why?"

Anne Hennig[1]([✉])[iD], Heike Dietmann[1], Franz Lehr[2], Miriam Mutter[1],
Melanie Volkamer[1][iD], and Peter Mayer[1][iD]

[1] Karlsruhe Institute of Technology, Karlsruhe, Germany
{anne.hennig,heike.dietmann,miriam.mutter,melanie.volkamer,
peter.mayer}@kit.edu
[2] Technische Universität Dresden, Dresden, Germany
franz.lehr@tu-dresden.de

Abstract. Cookie disclaimers are omnipresent since the GDPR went into effect in 2018. By far not all disclaimers are designed in a way that they are aligned with the ideas of the GDPR, some are even clearly violating the regulation. We wanted to understand how websites justify the use of those cookie disclaimers and what needs to happen for them to change the design of their cookie disclaimers. We, therefore, notified 147 websites (out of the top 500 Alexa German webpages) that their cookie disclaimers are (potentially) not GDPR compliant and asked for their motivation to use specific designs. We also monitored changes at the websites' cookie disclaimers.

Keywords: Cookie disclaimer · Vulnerability notification · GDPR · EU privacy directive · Web security and privacy

1 Introduction

Since the EU's General Data Protection Regulation (GDPR) went into effect in 2018, the use of cookie disclaimers got under close scrutiny. If cookies that are not strictly technically necessary are stored or accessed, the EU's ePrivacy Directive (ePD) requires the consent of the users concerned. The design of the consent mechanism must be in accordance with the provisions of the GDPR.

The authors of [4] examined the cookie disclaimers of the Alexa Top 500 websites in Germany regarding their GDPR compliance. While they identified six categories and various sub-categories of cookie disclaimers, we focused only on two aspects for this study : (1) so-called opt-out procedures which is clearly against the law and (2) highlighting of the *Accept All* option which is nudging users towards accepting all cookies and is legally disputed. Furthermore, we only considered websites that provided the possibility to decline optional cookies. A total of 150 websites of all 500 websites studied in [4] met these characteristics.

© IFIP International Federation for Information Processing 2022
Published by Springer Nature Switzerland AG 2022
N. Clarke and S. Furnell (Eds.): HAISA 2022, IFIP AICT 658, pp. 218–227, 2022.
https://doi.org/10.1007/978-3-031-12172-2_17

The goal of our research was to understand how websites justify the use of non-compliant cookie disclaimers. And – if they indicated that they would not change the current design of their cookie disclaimers – what would need to happen for them, to change the design to a more privacy-friendly one. Understanding the company's justification processes helps to understand what (still) needs to be done to improve current legislation.

To answer our questions, we contacted the data protection officers of the corresponding websites via email. We developed two types of emails: For those using opt-out procedure, we explained that this is clearly not GDPR compliant and cited corresponding European Court of Justice (ECJ) case law. For those using highlighting, we explained that their cookie disclaimers are not privacy-friendly and might potentially be not GDPR compliant. The design of our email is based on [9]: We used a legal framing and named a researcher from a computer science and a researcher from a legal research group as senders.

We describe related work in Sect. 2. Section 3 gives an overview of the legal background. The study and the results are described in Sect. 4 and 5 respectively. We reflecting on our results and propose directions for future research in Sect. 6. Section 7 concludes our paper.

2   Related Work

There is already quite some research done on how to best inform website operators about security and privacy issues on their websites. While some details are still unclear, it is evident that notifying a website operator about the problem increases remediation rates compared to not notifying them [2,5,10,11,14,15]. Besides technical factors like reaching out to a valid email address or passing spam filters by either the mail provider or the company itself, raising awareness is an important parameter for a successful notification campaign [10]. Awareness can be raised by getting the recipient to trust the message and by motivating the recipient to consider the reported misconfiguration as serious [10].

Maass et al. [9] found that trust in notifications can be established by a variety of formal and content-related factors. The authors asked 460 website operators, which previously had received a notification about a GDPR-compliance misconfiguration, in an online survey whether they agree that the type of notification they received made a trustworthy impression. Participants were then asked to determine factors that led them to trust or distrust the messages. The answers were grouped into three categories:

- **Formal aspects:** The right choice of the sender seems to be a huge trust-promoting factor. The authors did not specify which aspects of the sender the participants deemed trustworthy, but hinted at further trust-promoting aspects like providing a logo, letterhead or signature. Furthermore, correct spelling was deemed trust-promoting.
- **Content-related aspects:** The participants named an accurate and detailed description of the problem as well as a clear motivation that is not attached to financial demands of the sender as trust-promoting factors.

- **Verifiability aspects:** Further trust-promoting factors are providing possibilities to verify the sender, for example by providing contact information or - if applicable - providing the possibility to verify the problem. As stated in [3], verification possibilities are the most important factors.

The right framing of the message can have a large impact on the effectiveness of a notification as well. Especially providing external incentives can drive remediation rates [3]. Incentives can be of technical nature, for example when search engines stop referring traffic to compromised websites [12] or browsers flag warnings on websites [13]. Providing legal incentives is also suggested as a possible solution. Letters sent out by a university law group with a framing that imposes possible legal consequences if the misconfiguration is not solved, showed the highest remediation rates in a notification experiment by [9]. In the following study we adapted both the study design and the design of a vulnerability notification from [9].

3   Background

Our focus is on two aspects of cookie disclaimers, which are *opt-out* and *highlighting*. In the following, we define both aspects according to [4].

Cookie disclaimers are defined as using *opt-out* when users have to actively deselect optional cookies. For example, when a check-box is shown, where at least one more checkbox than *only technically necessary cookies* is pre-selected. If the user wants to allow as few cookies as possible, the pre-selected check-boxes have to be deactivated, to allow only technically necessary cookies.

Highlighting occurs when the *Accept all* button is highlighted or emphasized compared to the other button(s), for example, the *Decline* or *Preferences* buttons. *Highlighting* also applies when only the *Accept all* option is visible as a button and the options to decline are integrated in the disclaimer text.

According to the ECJ's "Planet49" decision (judgment of 1.10.2019 - C-673/17), consent to the setting of cookies is not effective if this was given using an opt-out design, i.e. via pre-selected buttons. Pre-selecting cookies other than technically necessary cookies forces the user to actively deactivate unwanted tracking and is, therefore, not GDPR compliant. In addition, according to the "Orange Romania" decision of the ECJ (judgment of 11.11.2020 - C-61/19), the free decision of users is disproportionately constrained if the refusal of consent represents a greater effort than the granting of consent.

Highlighting heavily nudges users to accept all cookies. The compliance of such designs with the GDPR is disputed. There are first judgments that require an equivalent design of buttons for an effective consent as well as corresponding assessments of data protection authorities that require an equivalent communication effect of presented options. Therefore, it can be interpreted, that a cookie disclaimer violates the GDPR when the option to allow only technically necessary cookies is not equivalent in design to the *Accept all* button. As there is no final judgment, we consider *Highlighting* as potentially not GDPR compliant.

In this paper, we name cookie disclaimers that use only highlighting but no opt-out *Highlighted Only*. All cookie disclaimers that use highlighting and the opt-out procedure are called *Highlighted and Opt-Out Procedure*. Krisam et al. [4] found no website that used an opt-out procedure without highlighting the *Accept all* option. So, we did not considered this for our research either.

4   Methodology

4.1   Design Decisions for Communication

Our methodological design is mainly based on the findings of [9]. For our communication, we also chose a privacy issue that can be tied to a GDPR violation, i.e. privacy-intrusive cookie disclaimers. Note, we talk in the following paragraphs about notifications as this is the common term in the related work – while we do not only notify our recipients about our findings with their cookie disclaimer, but also invited them to answer our questions.

Recipient and Communication Channel. As described in [8], it is necessary to find the appropriate responsible party for a notification on security or privacy issues. In this study, we defined the data protection officers as the responsible party for our notification. Therefore, we gathered the contact information of the data protection officers for the websites in our sample. We considered sending emails as the most practical way for the amount of websites. Correspondingly, we searched for the email address of the data protection officer, but considered universal email addresses of the company (e.g. info@domain.de), contact forms on the websites and postal addresses as possible alternatives. We manually searched for this information in the imprint or on the websites of the corresponding websites. For the *Highlighted Only* - group we collected 123 email addresses (114 of these were from data protection officers and the remaining addresses were general ones), 12 online contact forms and three postal addresses. In the *Highlighted and Opt-Out Procedure* - group we found 11 email addresses (9 from data protection officers), one online contact form and no postal address.

Sender of the Notification. Maass et al. [9] suggest, that legal experts as senders increase the likelihood that the notification is considered serious enough to react on it. Therefore, the notification mentions that this email is sent as part of a cooperation between a computer science and legal research group. A researcher of both groups 'signed' the email (signing in terms of were mentioned as sender). The email as such was sent from the member of the computer science group.

Content of the Notification. We designed our notifications according the best practices for vulnerability notifications as described in [3,8,9]. We used good use of language with respect to correct spelling; we provided a clear motivation and a detailed description of the problem; we provided contact possibilities via telephone and email; and we used a proper signature.

Each email included a short text to provide some information about the research project in general. Then we explained our motivation. Explaining the motivation for a notification and providing detailed information on the problem is considered as a major trust-promoting factor [3]. Since the legal framing turned out to be most effective in [9], our notifications had a legal framing as well. Both groups received the legal information on highlighting, while the *Highlighting and Opt-out Procedure* group received additional information on the opt-out procedure. We referred to the court decisions described in Sect. 3.

Furthermore, we asked the recipients to answer some questions within the next four weeks. We ensured that the answers are analyzed anonymously. We provided the researchers' contact information, in case of questions, and to give the recipients the possibility to verify our notification, as suggested in [3].

Survey Questions. To provide a low threshold for the responses, we included our questions at the end of our email. We used mainly closed-ended questions, and participants could add comments, if wanted. We asked why they used highlighting and (if applicable) opt-out procedures (questions 1 and 2). Possible answers were "not intended", "taken over by default", "intended" or "Other" – while in the last case, they were asked to name the reason. Afterwards, we asked, if they were previously informed about the issue with their cookie disclaimer (question 3). Possible answers were "yes, I was informed", "I was just informed about...", "No, I was not informed" or "Other" – while in the last case, they were asked to describe the situation. Then, we asked whether the data protection officers were involved in the development process of the cookie disclaimer (question 4). Possible answers were "Yes, I was involved as data protection officer", "No, I was not involved" or "Other". Question 5 was an open-ended question, where participants were asked to explain the motivation why highlighting (or highlighting and an opt-out procedure) was applied. Finally, we asked for the future plans (question 6), i.e. whether they are planning to change the cookie disclaimers. Email texts and survey questions are available at [redacted for anonymous review].

4.2   Procedure

An overview of the study procedure is provided in Fig. 1. We considered two groups of cookie disclaimers from Krisam et al. [4]. The first group, *Highlighted Only*, includes 138 websites from the sample considered in [4]. The second group, *Highlighted and Opt-Out Procedure*, includes 12 websites. There were no websites which used the opt-out procedure but did not highlight the accept-all option.

Notifications were sent as an email or via the online contact form in June 2021 with a request for response within four weeks. We excluded the three postal addresses, as we considered it too difficult to guarantee the same level of anonymity for their answers. Consistent with [8], data protection officers managing several websites were only contacted once for all the websites they are in charge of.

Thus, in total, 147 of the 150 websites that showed *Highlighted Only* or *Highlighted and Opt-Out Procedure* were notified. Before sending out the notifications,

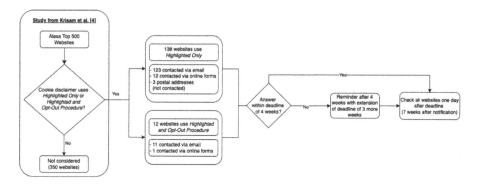

Fig. 1. Description of the methodology

the cookie disclaimers of all 150 websites were analyzed again to make sure they were still in the same category.

Just before the end of the deadline of four weeks, we contacted the contact persons of the websites again in July 2021. We did not put further pressure on the recipients, but rather offered that the deadline could be extended for 3 more weeks, if needed. One day after the end of the extended deadline, all notified websites were manually visited again in private mode to check whether the websites had changed their cookie disclaimers with regard to highlighting. And for the 12 which used opt-out procedures whether they still do so.

5   Results

Table 1 shows the responses to our notification of both groups (*Highlighted Only* and *Highlighted and Opt-Out Procedure*) as well as the number of websites which changed their cookie disclaimers after our notification.

16 contacted persons wrote that they refuse to answer. Five said they will forward the email to the person in charge, but in the end no one answered. Only from seven of 147 contacted websites we received responses to our questions, although some only partial: Only one person answered all survey questions. They noted that the highlighting was not intended and that they were notified about this before. They were not involved in the design process and they wrote that the reasons for the highlighting were unknown to them. They further answered that it is planned to change the current design of the cookie disclaimer and explained the changes the company is going to make. One person answered that their company is currently re-designing the cookie disclaimer and modifications "in several directions" are planned. One person just answered that they were informed about the design process but did not answer any of the other questions. One person said, they cannot tell anything about the process how the cookie disclaimer was created, "because we have no influence on the visual presentation [of the cookie disclaimer]". One person wrote that highlighting and using an opt-out procedure is intended and that they were involved in the design process.

They did not answer the question whether there are plans to change the current design in the future. But they explained that the current design was created with the help of the state data protection authority and is, therefore, compliant with current regulations. Two others also defended their company's decisions and stated that the design was used on purpose: While the current design is not unlawful, it, instead, allows the companies to collect valuable user data.

Table 1. Responses to our notifications in the *Highlighted Only* and *Highlighted and Opt-Out Procedure* groups and results of the comparisons of the cookie disclaimers

	Highlighted only		Highlighted and Opt-Out procedure	
	Emails (n = 123)	Online-forms (n = 12)	Emails (n = 11)	Online-forms (n = 1)
Responses with (partial) answers to the questions	6	0	1	0
Emails of refusal	13	3	0	0
Websites that eliminated highlighting and the opt-out procedure after notification	5	0	2	0

One day after the extended deadline ended in August 2021, we visited all 147 notified websites again and took screenshots of their cookie disclaimer. Then we compared those screenshots to the ones we took before we sent out the notifications. We only considered cookie disclaimers to have changed, if they either changed the highlighting and made *accept all* and *deny* buttons similar in design; or if they used an opt-in procedure instead of the opt-out procedure.

We could observe that of the 12 websites notified for using both, highlighting and the opt-out procedure, seven websites changed their cookie disclaimer. Five of those seven websites did not use the opt-out procedure anymore, but kept the highlighting. And two websites changed both, the highlighting and the opt-out procedure. Of the 135 notified websites that only used highlighting to emphasize the *Accept All* button, five websites changed their cookie disclaimers and made both the *Accept All* and the *Deny All* button equivalent in design.

In total, only seven of 147 websites changed the design of their cookie disclaimers to a more privacy friendly option and eliminated both: highlighting **and** the opt-out procedure. Furthermore, we could also observe quite the opposite: Three websites who used *Highlighted Only* before, now used the *Highlighted and Opt-Out Procedure* and, therefore, got even less privacy friendly.

We could also observe that our notification were only partially successful: From the three websites where the cookie disclaimers got less privacy friendly after our notification, two answered our email, but refused to answer our questions. And one did not answer at all. From the seven websites that got more privacy friendly, two websites (partially) answered our questions (one website was from the *Highlighted and Opt-Out Procedure* group, one was from the *Highlighted Only* group). One answered that the email will be forwarded, but no one got in contact with us afterwards. One website only sent an auto-reply. Furthermore, five websites answered our questions at least partially, but did not change the design of their cookie disclaimers.

6   Discussion

We notified 147 websites – 135 using *Highlighted Only* and 12 using *Highlighted and Opt-Out Procedure* – about the (potential) GDPR non-compliance of their cookie disclaimers and asked for their motivations to use such a design. Yet, we only got very few reactions from the recipients of our notifications (response rate to our questions was 4.67%) and the majority of websites did not change their cookie disclaimers towards a more compliant one.

A possible explanation for the little feedback is that the data protection officers might have not received our notification or the email was considered as spam, as this is a common problem with vulnerability notifications [3]. It is also likely that company's are not willing to share information on privacy and security issues. Response rates in studies with similar topics were low as well [1,6,9,10,14]. According to [7], sending letters could increase response rates. However, sending e-mails is still the most (cost-) efficient way for large-scale notification campaigns [10]. Also, we could have asked for answers via alternative channels, like phone. This had been proven successful in [3,10]. Unfortunately, most of the websites did not provide contact information other than email for their data protection officers. Due to our limited resources, we discarded this option.

We also decided against a framing with tougher legal incentives – a solution that has been suggested in [8]. We explicitly stated the legal problems with the current designs and did not feel responsible for pressing further legal charges. Additionally, expressing legal consequences would have even more diminished our chances to receive answers to our survey questions.

Since we considered the most visited websites in Germany, it is likely that we addressed comparatively big companies. Those companies actually benefit monetarily from the data collected through the cookies, and, furthermore, probably have a team of people handling various data protection topics. According to the careful answers we received, it is likely that the companies we contacted applied a risk-benefit analyses. With the result that the current design of the cookie disclaimers provides low risk of legal consequences, while it increases the likelihood to collect valuable data. This might be one reason for the low compliance rate.

Another reason might be that many websites, including governmental websites, highlight the *Accept all* option in their cookie disclaimers. Also, some websites might use pre-designed templates for their cookie disclaimers where the *Accept all* options are highlighted. Thus, data protection officers and/or chief information officers in companies may come to the conclusion that their cookie disclaimer in place is legally admissible.

It should also be admitted that a data protection officer has to ensure legally compliant data collection, rather than protecting users' privacy. Furthermore, data protection officers might not be used and/or entitled to answer surveys. Thus, future studies should reach out to the management level instead.

After we conducted our study, the conference of German data protection supervisory authorities published guidelines that clarified the requirements for legally compliant usage of cookies, including the design of cookie disclaimers, in December 2021. The guidelines confirmed the need for opt-in procedures as well as for equally designed decline options. Although not binding, the guidelines may have affected the design choices of website operators.

Therefore, we checked the cookie disclaimers of all 150 websites again in March 2022 to find out if the new regulations had any effect. We found that 130 of 147 websites still use highlighting. Compared to August 2021, where 140 websites still used highlighting, 10 additional website changed the design and made both options equal in design. Within the *Highlighted and Opt-Out Procedure* group, one website did neither use highlighting, nor the opt-out procedure anymore. Another website discarded only the opt-out procedure. Thus, from 130 websites which use highlighting in March 2022, only six websites still use highlighting *and* opt-out procedure, compared to eight websites which used both in August 2021.

We could also observe that some companies are modifying their cookie disclaimers over time – potentially to find those designs that increase the consent rates without violating current regulations. Still, further research is needed to get a real understanding how websites justify the use of non-compliant cookie disclaimers. With our study we provided possible improvements.

7   Conclusion

With the EU's General Data Protection Regulation (GDPR) being in effect since 2018, more and more privacy invasive techniques on the web had to be disabled. But the legal situation regarding cookie disclaimers is still a legal gray area.

The goal of our research was to understand how websites justify the design of their cookie disclaimers that either use (1) opt-out procedures which is against the law or (2) highlighting, which is at least against the idea of the GDPR, as one could argue that highlighting is nudging users towards accepting all cookies.

We notified 147 German websites of the Alexa Top 500 that used either *Highlighted Only* or *Highlighted and Opt-Out Procedure* (cf. Sect. 3), that their cookie disclaimers are (potentially) violating the GDPR. Furthermore, we included a short survey to find out how the websites justify the current design and what would need to happen for them to change the design to a more privacy-friendly one. Unfortunately, we got little feedback.

After our reminder deadline ended, 142 websites still used highlighting and 8 of those 142 also used the opt-out procedure. In the end, only seven websites got less privacy intrusive. We checked all cookie disclaimers again in March 2022 and found that 130 websites still used highlighting in their cookie disclaimers, while six of those 130 also used an opt-out procedure. Thus, in the end, 17 out of 147 websites chose for a more privacy friendly design of their cookie-disclaimers.

One possible reason is that the websites weighted the risks for potential penalties – which are rather low, considering the controversial legal situation – against the benefits they have from collecting valuable user data.

Thus, further clarifying case law and a clear positioning of the supervisory authorities is needed to provide unambiguous guidelines for website operators. The recent guidelines on dark patterns in social media platform interfaces by the European Data Protection Board are a step in the right direction.

Acknowledgement. This research is supported by the German Ministry of Education and Research (BMBF), as part of the INSPECTION project (Zuwendungsnummer 16KIS1113), and the Helmholtz Association (HGF) through the subtopic Engineering Secure Systems (ESS). The project was funded by the ministry of Science, Research and the Arts Baden-Württemberg as part of the DIGILOG@BW joint research project with funds from the digilog@bw State Digitization Strategy.

References

1. Ahrend, J.M., Jirotka, M., Jones, K.: On the collaborative practices of cyber threat intelligence analysts to develop and utilize tacit threat and defence knowledge. In: CyberSA (2016)
2. Durumeric, Z., et al.: The matter of heartbleed. In: IMC 2014 (2014)
3. Hennig, A., Neusser, F., Pawelek, A., Herrmann, D., Mayer, P.: Standing out among the daily spam: how to catch website owners attention by means of vulnerability notifications. In: CHI 2022 (2022)
4. Krisam, C., Dietmann, H., Volkamer, M., Kulyk, O.: Dark patterns in the wild: review of cookie disclaimer designs on top 500 German websites. In: EuroUSEC 2021 (2021)
5. Kührer, M., Hupperich, T., Rossow, C., Holz, T.: Exit from hell? Reducing the impact of amplification DDoS attacks. In: USENIX Security 2014 (2014)
6. Li, F., et al.: You've got vulnerability: exploring effective vulnerability notifications. In: USENIX Security 2016 (2016)
7. Maass, M., Clement, M.P., Hollick, M.: Snail mail beats email any day: on effective operator security notifications in the internet. In: ARES 2021 (2021)
8. Maaß, M., Pridöhl, H., Herrmann, D., Hollick, M.: Best practices for notification studies for security and privacy issues on the internet. In: ARES 2021 (2021)
9. Maass, M., et al.: Effective notification campaigns on the web: a matter of trust framing and support. In: USENIX Security 2021 (2021)
10. Stock, B., Pellegrino, G., Li, F., Backes, M., Rossow, C.: Didn't you hear me? - towards more successful web vulnerability notifications. In: NDSS 2018 (2018)
11. Stock, B., Pellegrino, G., Rossow, C., Johns, M., Backes, M.: Hey, you have a problem: on the feasibility of large-scale web vulnerability notification. In: USENIX Security 2016 (2016)
12. Vasek, M., Moore, T.: Do malware reports expedite cleanup? An experimental study. In: CSET 2012 (2012)
13. Zeng, E., Li, F., Stark, E., Felt, A.P., Tabriz, P.: Fixing HTTPS misconfigurations at scale: an experiment with security notifications. In: WEIS 2019 (2019)
14. Çetin, F.O., Ganan, C.H., Korczynski, M.T., Eeten, M.J.G.V.: Make notifications great again: learning how to notify in the age of large-scale vulnerability scanning. In: WEIS 2017 (2017)
15. Çetin, O., Jhaveri, M.H., Gañán, C., Eeten, M.V., Moore, T.: Understanding the role of sender reputation in abuse reporting and cleanup. J. Cybersecur. **2**, 83–98 (2016)

A Survey of Australian Attitudes Towards Privacy: Some Preliminary Results

Leah Shanley[(✉)] [iD], Michael N. Johnstone [iD], Patryk Szewczyk [iD], and Michael Crowley

Edith Cowan University, Perth, WA, Australia
{a.shanley,m.johnstone,p.szewczyk,m.crowley}@ecu.edu.au

Abstract. The challenge of meeting security requirements (of a nation-state) and the privacy needs of citizens is perhaps a political goal, but it is enabled by technology. Attacks on citizens tend to move the balance towards security, whilst civil liberties groups often act as a counter to not over-correct security, so as to guarantee privacy. This paper explores Australian attitudes towards privacy and surveillance during the pandemic. We consider a fundamental question: Has the pandemic changed the perception of Australian citizens with regard to their fundamental right to privacy? We surveyed Australian attitudes to privacy in the light of the COVID-19 pandemic and report on some interesting results.

Keywords: Privacy · Surveillance · Security · Public attitudes · COVID-19

1 Introduction

The notion of justifiably using privacy-invasive technologies to counteract crime, terrorism or cyber threats has evolved in line with the challenge of predicting increasing numbers of unlawful acts. Terrorism incidents such as the attacks in the United States of America on September 11, 2001 and the Bali bombings in 2002, among others, have highlighted the requirements for surveillance technologies to be used in private and public sectors (Mann and Smith 2017). Surveillance technologies, whilst perceived as beneficial in counteracting unlawful acts, raise questions regarding privacy of individuals and data protection. The advent of smart cities (Baig et al. 2017) with their plethora of devices (including, for example, CCTV cameras) all transmitting or sharing data, has not improved the situation. This is not a new issue. In 1928, Associate Justice Louis Brandeis (Supreme Court of the United States) highlighted his concerns with technology enabling governments to covertly invade one's privacy "by means far more effective than stretching upon the rack to obtain disclosure in court what is whispered in the closet" (Skala 1977). This concern is particularly evident in the circumstances brought about by the COVID-19 pandemic.

The COVID-19 pandemic has resulted in an abundance of active and archived tracking technologies created and deployed by governments and private entities (Ahmed et al. 2020). The use of tracking technologies raises the question of how health authorities and

© IFIP International Federation for Information Processing 2022
Published by Springer Nature Switzerland AG 2022
N. Clarke and S. Furnell (Eds.): HAISA 2022, IFIP AICT 658, pp. 228–239, 2022.
https://doi.org/10.1007/978-3-031-12172-2_18

governments can balance the need for privacy and efficient tracking during a pandemic (Amann et al. 2021). Highly transmissible strains of COVID-19, i.e., Omicron, prompted concerns as to whether it is feasible to track and trace people (Hannam 2021). Effective contact tracing is reliant upon the uptake of a technology and the willingness of citizens to proactively engage in a registration process at venues visited. When concern for civil liberties and privacy intersect, this combination will result in a lack of confidence that undoubtedly impacts attitudes towards privacy.

The freedom to move and travel within Australia has been regulated and restricted since 2020 as a result of the pandemic. Restrictions have curtailed civil liberties and encroached upon privacy supported by advancements in surveillance activities promoted by governments. Domestic and international vaccine passports have implications for freedom of association, privacy autonomy and access to goods and services (Australian Human Rights Commission 2021).

This paper examines the attitudes and perceptions of citizens who undertook a national survey to evaluate the changing nature of privacy in a pandemic world. First, we explore tolerance towards pandemic-related surveillance practices and whether public trust has eroded. Second, we test awareness of surveillance and whether citizens have adopted different behavior. Finally, we explore perceived control surrounding information collected and surveillance. According to a report by Australia's Chief Scientist, people have become less trusting of institutions over the last decade. Any major data breach that involves COVID-19 tracking data could see Australians lose confidence in government that will be extremely difficult to recover (Finkel 2020).

2 Related Work

Goggin et al. (2017) surveyed 1,600 Australians, exploring the nature of digital rights. The survey focused on four key issues, (1) privacy surrounding data profiling and analytics, (2) government data matching and surveillance, (3) digital privacy relating to the workplace, and (4) freedom of expression (speech) in online digital platforms. Goggin found that Australians are concerned about online privacy. The survey revealed 65% of participants felt they had nothing to hide, 67% took steps to protect their privacy online, 57% agreed that corporations are an ongoing threat to privacy.

Turning to government data matching and surveillance, 47% indicated concerns regarding government violations of privacy. However, 47% are in favour of law enforcement or security agencies accessing metadata, when framed as an anti-terrorism measure (Goggin et al. 2017). The change in attitudes suggests that personal views towards privacy vary depending on the context, highlighting the complexity of the issue. In a later survey on Australian attitudes towards privacy conducted by the Office of the Australian Information Commissioner (OAIC), 92% of respondents reported that they do not want their personal data sent and stored overseas (Office of the Australian Information Commissioner 2020).

More extensive studies relating to public perceptions of privacy and surveillance have been undertaken in the European Union. For example, the Privacy and Security Mirrors (PRISMS) project, analysed the trade-off model between privacy and security. Broek et al. pointed out that an increase in security often comes at the expense of privacy (Broek et al. 2017). The project found that attitudes towards privacy depend on the security issue presented, in other words, citizens are more likely to accept security practices when they understand the reasons and are convinced that a security measure is necessary for the safety and benefit of the public, consistent with Goggin et al. (2017), that context is a determining factor. Privacy, security, and liberty are concepts that undergo continuous change (Büscher et al. 2014), consequently, governments are confronted with managing the delicate balance that must exist for society to remain free and democratic. In late 2020, the Rapid Research Information Forum, chaired by Australia's Chief Scientist Dr Alan Finkel, was tasked by government to answer the question:

"Has COVID-19 had an impact on public sentiment in relation to privacy and the widespread use of data and technology by government in responding to the public health crisis, be it through tracing, compliance or enforcement?" (Australian Chief Scientist 2020).

The findings highlight the dynamic nature of opinion associated with privacy and the widespread use of surveillance. They found that trust towards government agencies increased during early stages of the pandemic; however, the majority (50%) remained concerned about management of personal data. Australians indicated strong concern surrounding opt-in arrangements, consent and the reasons for data and technology surveillance. In addition to voluntary data collection activities, i.e., contact tracing, involuntary data collection present indirect but significant risk to public sentiment towards government (Finkel 2020).

3   Method

Data collection occurred between February and September, 2021 using a cross-sectional, 40-question survey, containing a number of self-assessment questions. Solicitation first occurred via a University Facebook campaign, LinkedIn posts and word of mouth. To maximize responses a survey recruitment service provider was engaged resulting in 1135 responses and a sample size of 915 post-cleaning. Australian citizenship and age (18+) were the screening criteria. Information relating to the purpose and research objectives was provided together with informed consent prior to commencement of the survey. Survey questions were derived from past research and literature. The questions examined here are: (1) What are Australian's attitudes to privacy through the lens of trust? and (2) Has this attitude been affected by the impact of COVID-19?

Attitudes were explored from three perspectives, (1) trust in institutions, (2) control over surveillance in society and, (3) knowledge pertaining to information collection. Response categories were primarily 5-point Likert scales in combination with binary-response questions. Two important design considerations were factored into the survey. First, contextual framing of privacy and security concepts in attitudinal surveys and second, interpretation of survey data. To support the design objectives, anchoring vignettes were introduced, Anchoring vignettes are a psychometric approach used when dealing with complex concepts to be examined, such as privacy and security, or when there is a risk that respondents may unintentionally interpret questions differently. Anchoring vignettes translate theoretical concepts into hypothetical, authentic scenarios and the short narratives or storylines help position respondents in an unbiased way.

The theory of reasoned action that underpins this research, seeks to understand the relationship between attitudes and behaviours within human action (Fishbein and Ajzen 2009). The theory suggests that attitudes are event based (attitude-to-behaviour), or reasonably deliberated based on existing knowledge of the topic (reasoned action). Knowledge and awareness constitute what people assume they know and understand about surveillance devices, and knowledge relating to integrated data collection and handling practices. The research sought to investigate whether knowledge and awareness, perceived or otherwise, plays a role in the acceptance of said practices. Hypothetically, the more knowledge and awareness citizens possess relating to surveillance and associated data management practices, the less likely they are to support surveillance programs unless they can rationalise the necessity for it. Porcedda (2017) asserts that citizens are more concerned about the application of the technology and not the technology itself.

4 Results and Discussion

4.1 Trust

Watson et al. (2017) found in their analysis of public opinion surveys that the impact of public trust towards surveillance technologies is not always adequately addressed. In this paper the concept of trust is operationalised using three formative constructs comprised of twelve trust indicators. In formative constructs each indicator conveys information about its relative contribution to the construct (Avila et al. 2015). Each construct focused on a particular variation of trust that shifted focus to a unique classification, namely, (1) trust institutions will follow legislative requirements, (2) trust institutions will not sell or misuse information, and (3) trust institutions will adequately protect information from cybercrime. Each classification contained the same twelve indicators (institutions) verbatim. To calculate an overall Trust Summary Score (TSS), each of the three trust classifications (trust components) were analysed using Principal Component Analysis (PCA) to obtain factor scores to preserve the contribution and aspects of the indicators when measuring latent constructs (Avila et al. 2015). Trust component scores (TCS) were summed to form an overall trust summary score (TSS).

The first variation, trust institutions will follow legislative requirements, revealed that trust in federal government, state police and local council (71.8%, 73%, 70.2% respectively) is relatively high, indicating that government entities are perceived as being more trustworthy than private actors (Fig. 1). In contrast, social media (19.5%) and private business (37.9%) are perceived to be less trustworthy than most entities. The second variation, sale or misuse of information, is remarkable with only 7.8% of those surveyed, trusting social media companies to not sell or misuse information, suggesting minimal trust. With respect to the third variation, protection of information, 13.4% trust the social media industry. Private business entities show similar results. This trend is common for example, the OAIC survey on Australian attitudes toward privacy revealed 70% of Australians trust health service providers and government departments (51%) as compared to the social media industry whereby only 12% trust that personal information is adequately protected (OAIC 2020).

Hypothetically, 'More trust in public institutions the more likely people are to accept surveillance', In other words higher TSS means people are less concerned about surveillance.

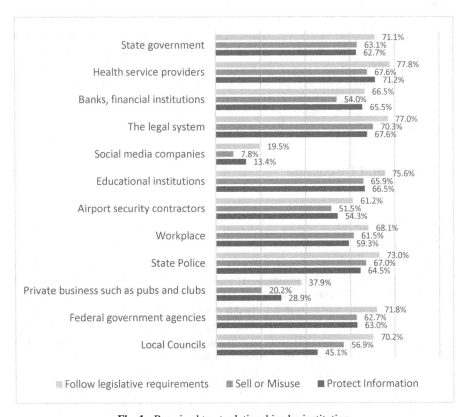

Fig. 1. Perceived trust relationships by institution.

Spearman's correlation was calculated to examine the relationship between TSS and surveillance concern within public and private spaces. We found a negative correlation for both variables, public spaces ($r_s = -.41$, $p < .001$) and private spaces. ($r_s = -.389$, $p < .001$). We then performed an ANOVA to further explore the relationship between a person's trust in institutions and concern towards surveillance or spread thereof (in public and private spaces). The higher the TSS, the less concern there should be regarding surveillance monitoring (or vice versa). The two independent variables were concern of surveillance in 1) public spaces and 2) private spaces. The variables were measured on a 5-point Likert scale (-2: Not at all concerned to $+2$: Very concerned).

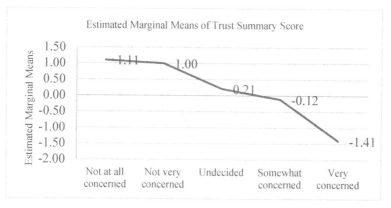

Fig. 2. Trust score - concern over surveillance in public spaces

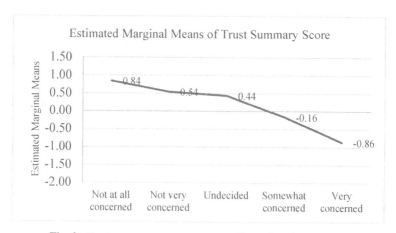

Fig. 3. Trust score - concern over surveillance in private spaces

Figure 2 and Fig. 3 depict the direction of the relationship. The higher the TSS the less concern there is about surveillance in public spaces. It could be postulated that trust is irrelevant with respect to private places given the trust indicators are largely trustworthy. In contrast, public spaces are perceived to be under control of the more trustworthy entities, i.e., the police and state government, consequently trust is a factor.

4.2 Behaviour

We sought to discover if participants alter their behaviour whilst under surveillance. To test this theory, we introduced an anchoring vignette (a small hypothetical scenario) that described two shopping precincts. One precinct operates a CCTV network, and the alternate, a precinct that does not operate CCTV surveillance. Participants were asked in which precinct they would prefer to shop, assuming equal travelling distance. 68.6%

preferred to visit the precinct that was convenient, thus surveillance did not influence their choice. We introduced the idea of the capture and upload of facial images to a national database, which would acquire images from multiple sources, including the aforementioned CCTV system. To see if behaviour would change the first vignette was reintroduced. We found that 68% of respondents would not change their original response while 27.1% would visit the precinct that does not use the CCTV system. The results suggest that participants do not mind their images being captured by CCTV, but they are concerned about being identified (which represents a change in the original use of the data).

4.3 Control

Control of the information environment, that is, the control (perceived or otherwise) people think they have over surveillance of themselves or their environment, is one factor often neglected in attitudinal surveys. The relevance for this research is to discover whether Australians accept surveillance practices due to an inability to opt out, or perceive they have no control or say as to whether these practices are implemented. In support of Hallinan et al. (2012) for most people data processing is invisible and likely involuntary, information processing activities are mostly not understood. Citizens feel they have lost control over their data and data collection practices.

Continuing with CCTV surveillance, the survey went on to question whether people felt they had a say in the collection of CCTV images about themselves. The majority, 69%, felt they had no say at all. Participants were asked if they would like more control over who collects the CCTV images-79.9% indicated they would like more say, control or the opportunity to opt out.

4.4 Awareness and Knowledge

In the context of this research, knowledge and awareness constitutes what a person assumes they know and understand about surveillance and associated activities, more importantly however, is knowledge relating to integrated data handling practices. The research sought to investigate whether knowledge and awareness, perceived or otherwise, plays a role in the acceptance of said practices. Hypothetically, the more knowledge and awareness citizens have relating to surveillance and associated data management practices, the less likely they are to support surveillance programs unless they can rationalise the necessity for it.

As part of the survey, we presented a news article informing participants of proposed legislation regarding surveillance. The news article outlined the State Government's intention to upload driver's license images to a federal government identity matching database, known as the National Facial Recognition Biometric Matching Capability (NFRBMC). The article provided reliable information relating to the associated legislation, and an application overview of the technology and its use. Notwithstanding the detail presented in the news article, 72% of participants agreed they still do not have sufficient knowledge to make an informed decision about the acceptance of the national facial recognition database. This suggests that citizens are struggling to grasp the data relationships that are formed by these systems, the consequences of such relationships and complexity of the environment. 53.9%, say they do not know who is collecting information about them and would like to know more about who is collecting and for what reasons.

We then shifted our approach and presented a range of surveillance technologies i.e., drones, facial recognition, CCTV and asked participants how knowledgeable they are (or perceive to be) about each item. The purpose was to gain insight into perceived knowledge and awareness relating to the knowledge indicators. The 5-point Likert scale was coded as: Very knowledgeable = 2, Somewhat knowledgeable = 1, Not sure = 0, Not very knowledgeable = -1, Not at all knowledgeable = -2. Scores were summed on a continuum to form a summary knowledge score (M = 3.5, Min -22, Max 22).

Figure 4 shows a summary composition of knowledge indicators, for example 60.16% say they are very or somewhat knowledgeable about contact tracing and 46.75% say they are very or somewhat knowledgeable about GPS ankle bracelets.

A discrepancy between participants desire for more information about who is collecting information about them using surveillance devices (53.3%) vs. perceived knowledge of technology, supports Porcedda's assertion that citizens are concerned about the application of the technology rather than the technology itself. A higher knowledge score does not necessarily indicate participants are aware of data handling practices regarding a particular technology. 51.5% say they are somewhat or very knowledgeable with data mining activities but are not automatically aware of what happens to data collected about them. Perceived knowledge also begs the question whether or not citizens feel they have lost control over opinions and data. For example, citizens value privacy, and consider themselves reasonably knowledgeable with respect to the technology items presented, however, in a related question about control over surveillance, 79.9% reported they would like more control and say over the technology.

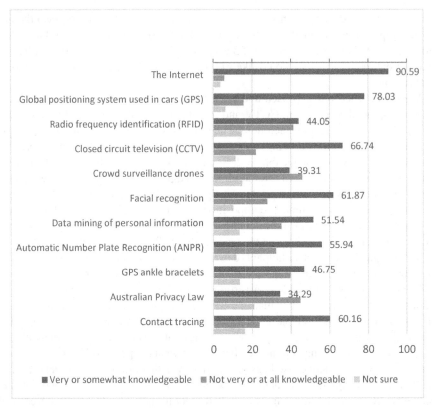

Fig. 4. Responses to knowledge indicators (%)

5   The COVID-19 Effect

During data collection, the Australian public had undergone numerous state-specific lockdowns causing discourse over government policy. Attitudes toward contact tracing had started to shift among the population, with some becoming complacent, others felt unconvinced of the need to continue the practice while others raising concerns. In the interim, independent State COVID apps emerged, thus, the public transitioned from the Federal COVIDSafe app to state-run apps. State and Federal legislation are unique to each jurisdiction; however, knowledge of the differences is not well-understood. Media attention centered around the Federal app, Australians were for the most part, under the impression the same laws apply to the States. Participants were asked a consecutive set of statements relating to COVIDSafe apps to generalise the use of contact tracing apps rather than isolating a particular State or Federal app.

Despite trust in the Government, Table 1 indicates that Australians have concerns regarding the protection and privacy of data collected. 62.2% of those surveyed are concerned about the tracking of movements for other purposes not related to the pandemic and 70.3% are concerned the data collected will not be deleted after the COVID pandemic ends.

Table 1. COVID-19 app privacy concern

	Very or somewhat concerned	Not very or at all concerned	Undecided
The tracking of your movements for purposes other than COVID-19	62.2%	29.7%	8.1%%
Monitor the movement of yourself or others in the community to ensure group gatherings are restricted (due to COVID-19)	37.8%	49.4%	13.0%
Share your captured information with government agencies for crime or terror related incidents	45.3%	42.1%	13.1%
Share your information with contractors, for example data storage providers, security companies or software providers	72.0%	16.5%	11.5%
Store your captured information overseas	76.3%	15.4%	8.3%
Share your captured information with foreign governments	74.9%	16.8%	8.3%
Protection of your captured information from Cyber crime	63.2%	22.1%	14.7%
Access to other information on your phone, for example, location information	72.4%	18.9%	8.7%
Your data not being deleted after the COVID-19 crisis ends	70.3%	22.0%	7.7%
Contact tracing surveillance becoming permanent regardless of the pandemic	68.1%	21.2%	10.7%

66.4% supported the rollout of the Federal COVIDSafe app. These finding support the OAIC report (2020) whereby 60% agreed that concessions must be made for the greater good but should not be made permanent. This suggests that Australians are somewhat hesitant with respect to data handling practices, albeit supporting the app rollout for health and safety. Trust that these measures will be rolled back after the pandemic has potential to become problematic with 40% expressing distrust. Notwithstanding earlier data that showed 71.8% trusted the Government will follow legislative requirements and protect their information (63%).

The West Australian Police admitted accessing the COVID check-in repository nine days after its release while refusing state government requests to cease data access requests. According to the police, the information was accessed as part of an investigation into two serious crimes (Hendry 2021). Consequently, these events forced the West Australian State Government to introduce specific data protection legislation surrounding the check-in repository as it was seen as a breach of trust by the public.

Function creep and data misuse emerged as a major concern with respect to the National Facial Recognition Database. Whilst not explicitly framed in relation to COVID app data stores, 73.5% agree the technology could be repurposed and 89% are concerned about misuse. There is some evidence that the same level of concern exists in relation to COVID app data given 83% expressed concern regarding the increase of surveillance monitoring.

6 Conclusion

The contact tracing technologies deployed by various state governments have enabled health authorities to advise the public of the dates and times of infectious locations. Despite the perceived positive response about government actions, individuals remain cautious and concerned about the data being collected. The COVID-19 pandemic has demonstrated that individuals have a desire to maintain their personal privacy, but are first to voice concerns, when others do not comply with contact tracing technologies.

In a state government context, the onus was placed on individuals to actively scan QR codes that were printed by all businesses and placed at store fronts, a practice that appeared to be accepted by the public. Nonetheless, the tension between security and privacy remains, even in a post-pandemic world, therefore we consider that the results presented here, whilst interesting, are preliminary, and will be analysed further.

References

Ahmed, N., et al.: A survey of COVID-19 contact tracing apps. IEEE Access 8, 134577–134601 (2020)

Amann, J., Sleigh, J., Vayena, E.: Digital contact-tracing during the Covid-19 pandemic: an analysis of newspaper coverage in Germany, Austria, and Switzerland. PLoS One 16, e0246524 (2021). https://doi.org/10.1371/journal.pone.0246524

Australian Chief Scientist: Changes in public sentiment in relation to data privacy during COVID-19. Australian Government Retrieved from https://www.chiefscientist.gov.au/sites/default/files/2020-12/Q13_RRIF_data_privacy_30112020.pdf (2020)

Australian Human Rights Commission: Human rights considerations for vaccine passports and certificates. https://humanrights.gov.au/our-work/rights-and-freedoms/human-rights-considerations-vaccine-passports-and-certificates (2021)

Avila, M.L., Stinson, J., Kiss, A., Brandão, L.R., Uleryk, E., Feldman, B.M.: A critical review of scoring options for clinical measurement tools. BMC. Res. Notes 8(1), 612 (2015). https://doi.org/10.1186/s13104-015-1561-6

Baig, Z.A., et al.: Future challenges for smart cities: cyber-security and digital forensics. Digit. Investig. **22**, 3–13 (2017). https://doi.org/10.1016/j.diin.2017.06.015

van den Broek, T., Ooms, M., Friedewald, M., van Lieshout, M., Rung, S.: Privacy and security: citizens' desires for an equal footing. In: Friedewald, M., Burgess, J.P., Cas, J., Peissl, W., Bellanova, R. (eds.) Surveillance, Privacy and Security: Citizens' Perspectives, pp. 15–35. Taylor & Francis (2017)

Büscher, M., Perng, S.-Y., Liegl, M.: Privacy, security, and liberty: ICT in crises. Int. J. Inform. Syst. Crisis Response Manag. **6**, 76–92 (2014). https://doi.org/10.4018/IJISCRAM.2014100106

Finkel, A.: Changes in public sentiment in relation to data privacy during COVID-19. https://www.chiefscientist.gov.au/sites/default/files/2020-12/Q13_RRIF_data_privacy_3 0112020.pdf (2020)

Fishbein, M., Ajzen, I.: Predicting and Changing Behavior: The Reasoned Action Approach. Taylor & Francis. http://www.123library.org/book_details/?id=74927 (2009)

Goggin, G., Vromen, A., Weatherall, K., Martin, F., Webb, A., Sunman, L., Bailo, F.: Digital Rights in Australia. U. o. Sydney. https://ses.library.usyd.edu.au//bitstream/2123/17587/7/USYDDigit alRightsAustraliareport.pdf (2017)

Hallinan, D., Friedewald, M., McCarthy, P.: Citizens' perceptions of data protection and privacy in Europe. Comput. Law Secur. Rev. **28**(3), 263–272 (2012). https://doi.org/10.1016/j.clsr.2012. 03.005

Hannam, P.: NSW scales back Covid contact tracing as health system faces Omicron strain. In: The Guardian. https://www.theguardian.com/australia-news/2021/dec/29/nsw-scales-back-covid-contact-tracing-as-health-system-faces-omicron-strain (2021)

Hendry, J.: WA Police refused request to stop accessing COVID check-in app data. https://www. itnews.com.au/news/wa-police-refused-request-to-stop-accessing-covid-check-in-app-data-566033 (2021)

Mann, M., Smith, M.: Automated facial recognition technology: recent developments and approaches to oversight. Univ. New South Wales Law J. **40**(1), 121–145 (2017)

Office of the Australian Information Commissioner: Australian Community Attitudes to Privacy Survey 2020. A. Government. https://www.oaic.gov.au/engage-with-us/research/australian-community-attitudes-to-privacy-survey-2020-landing-page/2020-australian-community-attitu des-to-privacy-survey/ (2020)

Porcedda, M.G.: The manifold significance of citizens' legal recommendations on privacy, security and surveillance 1. In: Surveillance, Privacy and Security: Citizens' Perspectives, pp. 191–211. Routledge, Abingdon, Oxon; New York, NY (2017). https://doi.org/10.4324/978131561930 9-12

Skala, S.: Is there a legal right to privacy. U. Queensland LJ **10**, 127 (1977)

Watson, H., Finn, R.L., Barnard-Wills, D.: A gap in the market: the conceptualisation of surveillance, security, privacy and trust in public opinion surveys. Surveill. Soc. **15**(2), 269–285 (2017). https://doi.org/10.24908/ss.v15i2.5324

Designing and Evaluating a Prototype for Data-Related Privacy Controls in a Smart Home

Chola Chhetri[✉] and Vivian Motti

George Mason University, Fairfax, VA 22030, USA
{cchhetri,vmotti}@gmu.edu

Abstract. The privacy concerns of home Internet of Things (IoT) device users and experts have been widely studied, but the designs of privacy controls addressing those concerns are sparse. Literature shows a significant body of research uncovering design factors for privacy controls in smart home devices, but fewer studies have translated those design recommendations into design and evaluated the designs. To fill this gap, we designed a prototype user interface implementing the design recommendations of data-related privacy controls based on prior work and evaluated the prototype for user experience, usability, perceived information control, user satisfaction, and intention to use. The results of interviews (n = 10) critique the proposed design and the survey results (n = 105) show that the prototype design provides positive evaluation for perceived information control, user satisfaction and intention to use. Based on findings, we discuss design recommendations for further improvements. Thus, this paper contributes to the design of data-related privacy controls for user interfaces of home IoT devices and applications.

Keywords: Prototype · Smart home devices · Privacy · Interface

1 Introduction

Researchers and security experts have identified vulnerabilities and concerns in smart home devices (SHDs) or home Internet of Things (IoT) devices [3,8]. Although users are known to have inadequate and inaccurate mental models of smart device risks [25], they have expressed concerns [6]. Privacy has been identified as one of the primary reasons for non-use of SHDs [4,25].

Researchers have further identified privacy concerns of users and made design recommendations for the development of privacy controls [22–24]. However, few studies have translated those design recommendations and needs into user interface designs that can address the privacy concerns.

To fill this gap, we designed a prototype of a user interface implementing the design factors elicited from prior literature. For the prototype design, we

© IFIP International Federation for Information Processing 2022
Published by Springer Nature Switzerland AG 2022
N. Clarke and S. Furnell (Eds.): HAISA 2022, IFIP AICT 658, pp. 240–250, 2022.
https://doi.org/10.1007/978-3-031-12172-2_19

followed an iterative approach. We evaluated the prototype for user experience, usability, perceived information control, user satisfaction and intention to use. Evaluation user studies included interviews (n = 10) and survey (n = 105). For the purpose of this study, we framed the prototype as an app for camera. However, the proposed design may serve as a design pattern for other home IoT systems.

We contribute the design of data-related privacy controls for home IoT systems and recommendations for further improvement to the design.

2   Background

2.1   Privacy Control Design Factors and Sub-factors

Researchers have identified privacy concerns and provided design recommendations for smart home designers and developers [7,10,21–23]. In [5], researchers empirically identified seven design factors for implementing privacy controls in smart home designs: data-related controls, device controls, transparency, multi-user, central interface, support and security controls. We summarize the design factors in the form of a graphic in Fig. 1a. The vertical bars represent constructs that affect all factors in horizontal bars.

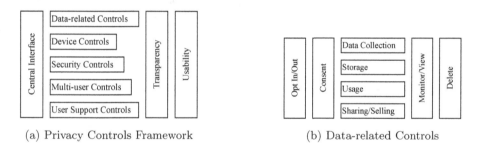

(a) Privacy Controls Framework   (b) Data-related Controls

Fig. 1. Privacy controls from literature and our research approach

2.2   Translating Privacy Control Design Factors into Design

Transparency with regard to online privacy has been widely investigated with one popular approach being privacy labels. There has been research about online privacy labels [8,11], which has even recently been adopted by Apple[1] and Google[2] in their app stores. Examples of privacy label work include privacy nutrition label [11], GDPR-based privacy label for IoT devices OnLITE [14], and security and privacy label with device factors [17]. Similarly, prior work has investigated the designs of user notifications to enhance transparency [13].

---

[1] apple.com.
[2] google.com.

Prior work has explored the design of *multi-user* controls. In [24], researchers developed and evaluated multi-user settings for a smart home app. In [9], authors proposed a design space for privacy choices and use-case design of a privacy choice platform app IOTAssistant.

While designs towards *transparency, multi-user settings,* d*evice controls,* and notice and choice have been explored, designs of *data-related controls* are sparse. So, this paper focuses on the design of data-related privacy controls using the design factors from Sect. 2.1 as a foundation. For this purpose, we drew from literature [5] the following data-related privacy control *requirements* : Opt-in (or out), Consent, Data collection, Storage, Usage, Sharing or selling, Monitor or view, and Delete [9,10,21–25]. We illustrate these requirements in Fig. 1b.

3   Method

We designed a prototype to implement the user requirements of data-related privacy controls. Then, we conducted user studies to evaluate the prototype and gain insights into design improvements. Figure 2 visualizes our research approach.

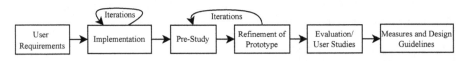

Fig. 2. Research approach

3.1   Stimulus (Prototype App)

We designed a prototype implementing the data-related privacy controls requirements using Mockplus[3]. The initial design was a result of a brainstorming session in our lab among multiple researchers involved in interface design and a feedback session involving designers working in our lab. We followed multiple design iterations of the prototype by reviewing the design among researchers and developers in our laboratory. We used the final iteration in user studies.

The prototype app, called MyCam, consisted of three pages: MyCam Home, Privacy Settings, and Data Dashboard. The home page contained the app logo, a view of the camera footage, a brief explanation that user can control the camera and manage privacy settings, and a continue button to navigate to the privacy settings page (See Fig. 3a). The privacy settings page consisted of data-related controls: opt-in to data collection, control what data type is collected, allow (or disallow) sending/sharing/selling of data, choose who data are shared with, and a link to data dashboard for viewing and managing data (See Fig. 3b). The data dashboard page displayed all audio, video and other activity files with options to view and delete the data individually or all-at-once (See Fig. 3c). In addition, each page contained a horizontal navigation bar with three buttons at the top.

---

[3] mockplus.com.

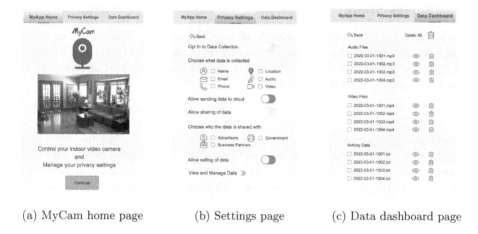

(a) MyCam home page   (b) Settings page   (c) Data dashboard page

Fig. 3. Home, settings, and dashboard pages of the MyCam prototype app.

3.2 Pre-study

We conducted a pre-study with four lab members to elicit feedback on the prototype design and to pilot test the user studies (interview and survey). We used the feedback to improve the prototype and user study protocols. The results of pilot user studies are not included in the analyses.

3.3 Interview Study

We conducted semi-structured interviews with 10 participants recruited via twitter. Interview protocol was reviewed by George Mason University's institutional review board (IRB). Interview protocol included demographics and prototype evaluation questions. We have shared the entire study in [2].

Participants were given 5–10 min to familiarize with the app. We gave them nine tasks to complete. Then, we asked them questions about their perception of the prototype: like, dislike, challenge, gaps, effectiveness (whether it meets privacy requirements) and improvements. Finally, we debriefed and thanked the participants. Participants were compensated with a gift card of US$25 for their participation in the interview. Average interview time was 45 min.

We qualitatively analyzed the interviews. We did not perform quantitative analysis on interview data due to the small sample size. Interviews allowed us to probe deeper into the perceptions of participants and understand the problems that participants experienced while using the prototype. We analyzed the interview transcripts for recurring patterns or themes.

Participants. Of the 10 participants, 5 were male and 5 were female. Four were 25–34 years of age, 4 were 35–44 years and 2 were 18–24 years. Three were Hispanic, 3 were Asian, 2 were African-American and 2 were White.

3.4   Survey Study

To reach a large and diverse sample of participants, we designed a survey in which we embedded the app and requested participants' opinions and feedback on the app. We designed the evaluation questions from standard instruments or psychometrically validated Likert scales.

Measurements. We used the User Experience Questionnaire (UEQ) scale (26 items) to measure user experience [15]. To measure usability, we used the System Usability Scale (SUS) scale (10 items, 5-point Likert) [1]. We measured user satisfaction using a 4-item scale adapted from [16]. We adapted perceived information control scale (5 items) from [20] and intention-to-use scale (3 items) from [19]. Unless otherwise noted, we designed all items as 7-point Likert items.

Procedure. We advertised the study as an evaluation of a prototype app. The study was approved by our university's Institutional Review Board (IRB) prior to the survey. We recruited participants using the crowd-sourcing platform Mechanical Turk (MTurk), which is widely used by researchers to conduct security and privacy studies. We screened out participants to ensure good quality responses. Participants were adults living in the United States, had an approval rating of 95%, completed 100 MTurk tasks, and used at least one SHD. Research shows that MTurk sample is diverse and its perception is US representative [18].

   Participants were presented with the informed consent. If they agreed to participate, they received demographics questions followed by the prototype embedded in the survey with an external link in case the embed failed. Participants performed a set of nine tasks and reported completion status. After that, they received open-ended questions on feedback and improvement and closed-ended measurement questions. Finally, we debriefed and thanked the participants.

Interface Interaction/Task Selection. We asked the participants to perform the following tasks in the prototype app and report completion status:

- TASK1 Click Continue on MyCam Home page to go to privacy settings page.
- TASK2 Turn on Opt In to Data Collection.
- TASK3 Select the data you would allow MyCam to collect about you.
- TASK4 Turn off Allow sending of data to the cloud.
- TASK5 Turn on Allow sharing of data.
- TASK6 Choose who you would allow the company to share the data with.
- TASK7 Turn on (or off) Allow selling of data.
- TASK8 Delete the fist audio file 2022-03-01-1001.mp3.
- TASK9 Go to the MyCam Home page.

Participants. A total of 120 participants completed the survey and were compensated US$1.50 for completing the survey. With an average completion time of 7 min, the rate averaged about $12.85 an hour. We excluded 15 responses that (a) did not pass the attention check questions, (b) contained copy-paste answers for an open-ended question, (c) had patterned or lined-up answers, or (d) had extremely low survey completion time resulting in low quality responses. We included the remaining 105 responses in the analysis.

Among 105 participants, 59% were male and 41% were female. Most of the participants were 25–34 years (48%), followed by 35–44 years (30%), 45–54 years (11%), 18–24 years (5%) and 55+ years (6%). About 94% were employed full-time and rest were part-time or unemployed.

4   Results

In this section, we describe the results of our evaluation studies.

4.1   Task Accuracy

Most survey participants reported completion of the given tasks. The accuracy of tasks 1 to 7 ranged from 93% to 98% (See Table 1). The low accuracy of task 8 (73%) is likely due to the lack of interactive functionality of the delete button. Similarly, the low accuracy of task 9 (52%) is likely due to the lack of *back-to-home* button on the dashboard and our reliance on the top navigation bar to return to home.

Table 1. Task accuracy (n = 105).

Task#	TASK1	TASK2	TASK3	TASK4	TASK5	TASK6	TASK7	TASK8	TASK9
Accuracy	0.981	0.952	0.971	0.962	0.943	0.971	0.933	0.733	0.524

4.2   User Experience

The UEQ instrument measures six dimensions of user experience: attractiveness, perspicuity, efficiency, dependability, stimulation, and novelty. Mean score below -0.8 is negative, between -0.8 and 0.8 is neutral, and above 0.8 is positive evaluation. Our prototype was evaluated *positive* for attractiveness (Mean μ = 0.91 and Variance σ^2 = 1.44), perspicuity (μ = 1.02, σ^2 = 1.58), efficiency (μ = 0.82, σ^2 = 1.42), and dependability (μ = 0.83, σ^2 = 1.08). It was evaluated *neutral* for stimulation (μ = 0.65, σ^2 = 1.38) and novelty (μ = 0.07, σ^2 = 0.95) (see Fig. 4).

4.3   Usability

We used the SUS scale to measure the usability of the prototype. The average overall SUS score from survey participants (n = 105) was 62.5 (Min = 37.5, Max = 100) which is about average [12]. The benchmark average SUS score for a website is 68; we were unable to find a benchmark for home IoT apps. The SUS scores of MyCam show that MyCam has room for improvement in usability.

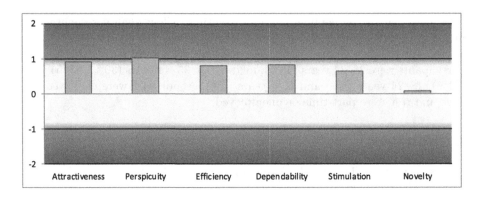

Fig. 4. Results showing scores for the six dimensions of the UEQ scale.

4.4   Perceived Information Control

Survey participants found MyCam's perceived information control to be above average ($\mu = 4.37$, $\sigma = 1.28$) and the scale demonstrated good internal consistency ($\alpha = 0.88$) (See Table 2).

Table 2. Scale statistics (n = 105)

Scale	Number of items	Mean (μ)	SD (σ)	Cronbach's alpha
Perceived information control	5	4.37	1.28	0.88
User satisfaction	4	5.14	1.46	0.91
Behavioral intention to use	3	5.40	1.28	0.85

4.5   User Satisfaction

The satisfaction scale scores of survey participants for MyCam were good ($\mu = 5.14$, $\sigma = 1.46$). The scale showed good internal consistency ($\alpha = 0.91$).

4.6   Behavioral Intention to Use

Most survey participants reported an intention to use a privacy control system similar to MyCam. The 3-item intention-to-use scale was rated good ($\mu = 5.40$, $\sigma = 1.28$) and showed good internal consistency ($\alpha = 0.85$).

4.7   User Feedback

We qualitatively analysed feedback from interview participants. We do not report the findings quantitatively due to the small sample size (n = 10). We found three areas of concern in our prototype design from thematic analysis of the interviews:

Lack of Transparency and the State of Confusion. Since MyCam app did not present information on what information is collected, used, shared or sold, participants stated confusion on how to decide on what privacy settings may be appropriate for their needs. They also stated confusion on how much they could trust these settings would actually be honored by the company.

Overwhelming and Burdensome. Participants mentioned that providing too many options to choose from can easily overwhelm them and create a sense of burden.

Colors and Beautification. Users suggested that the app looks old-fashioned and conventional, which is also highlighted by the UEQ scale results of the survey. They suggested using a theme color to identify the app uniquely.

5 Discussion

Results of users studies show that our prototype was perceived by participants with good perceived information control, user satisfaction, and intention to use. The usability and user experience scores were satisfactory but there is room for improvement. Thus, based on the findings, we discuss some design recommendations for improvement to MyCam's usability and user experience.

5.1 Design Recommendations

Complement Data-Related Controls with Transparency Features. In order to address the lack of transparency as stated in Sect. 4.7, we suggest that transparency mechanisms be utilized in conjunction with data related controls. A combination of our design with notice and choice designs presented in [9] may be useful in this regard. Improvements can also include integration of labels [11] and notifications [13] with the data-related privacy designs.

Tiered Privacy Approach for Managing User Burden. The provision of large number of privacy controls may give users a sense of control but it lowers usability. In [25], authors call for reducing burden of privacy on users. Thus, we recommend a balanced approach to reduce the user burden while providing privacy control. In this regard, we suggest a tiered privacy settings approach involving three preset options: high privacy, medium privacy, and low privacy. Each of these privacy presets will achieve privacy that is equivalent to many user clicks. For example:

High privacy: Collection OFF, sharing OFF, communication ENCRYPTED.

Medium privacy: Collection ON, sharing OFF, communication ENCRYPTED.

Low privacy: Collection ON, sharing ON, communication ENCRYPTED.

Usability. Although we envision our prototype to be useful to the design community as a reusable design pattern for privacy settings of home IoT and potentially other devices, it should be enhanced with an accessible color theme.

5.2   Limitations and Future Work

While a large body of privacy research utilizes MTurk, the representation has been debated. Recent literature shows that MTurk sample may not be US representative but its perceptions may be representative [18]. Thus, we utilized a mixed-methods approach to enhance the validity of findings. Another limitation is that the user studies' results may not be generalizable to non-US populations.

In our future work, we aim to improve the design of MyCam by implementing the above design guidelines and evaluate how they meet the user needs. We also aim to implement the data-related privacy controls designs in the context of other SHDs, such as voice speakers, baby monitors, thermostats, etc.

6   Conclusion

We proposed the design of privacy settings for home IoT devices based on user requirements of data-related privacy controls from prior work. We implemented a prototype and evaluated various aspects of it through qualitative and quantitative user studies. User studies showed that the prototype provided good perceived information control, user satisfaction and intention-to-use. We identified that the prototype can be improved to provide better user experience. We also discussed some design recommendations to further improve its usability.

Acknowledgement. We thank our lab members for their input and anonymous reviewers for their comments. We are grateful to the interview and survey participants. This research was funded in part by 4-VA, a collaborative partnership for advancing the Commonwealth of Virginia, and Commonwealth Cyber Initiative (CCI). Any opinions expressed in this article are those of the authors and do not necessarily reflect the views of our research sponsors.

References

1. Brooke, J.: SUS: a 'quick and dirty' usability scale. Usabil. Eval. Ind. 189–194 (1996)
2. Chhetri, C.: Study protocols for evaluation of MyCam app, June 2022. https://osf.io/zfvmx
3. Chhetri, C., Motti, V.: Identifying vulnerabilities in security and privacy of smart home devices. In: Choo, K.-K.R., Morris, T., Peterson, G.L., Imsand, E. (eds.) NCS 2020. AISC, vol. 1271, pp. 211–231. Springer, Cham (2021). https://doi.org/10.1007/978-3-030-58703-1_13
4. Chhetri, C., Motti, V.: Privacy concerns about smart home devices: a comparative analysis between non-users and users. In: Human Factors in Cybersecurity, vol. 53, pp. 1–9. AHFE International (2022)

5. Chhetri, C., Motti, V.G.: User centric privacy controls for smart home. Proc. ACM Hum.-Comput. Interact. **6**(CSCW2) (2022). In Press
6. Chhetri, C., Motti, V.G.: Eliciting privacy concerns for smart home devices from a user centered perspective. In: Taylor, N.G., Christian-Lamb, C., Martin, M.H., Nardi, B. (eds.) iConference 2019. LNCS, vol. 11420, pp. 91–101. Springer, Cham (2019). https://doi.org/10.1007/978-3-030-15742-5_8
7. Emami-Naeini, P.: Privacy and security nutrition labels to inform IoT consumers. USENIX Association, February 2021
8. Emami-Naeini, P., Agarwal, Y., Cranor, L.F., Hibshi, H.: Ask the experts: what should be on an IoT privacy and security label? In: 2020 IEEE Symposium on Security and Privacy (SP), pp. 447–464. IEEE (2020)
9. Feng, Y., Yao, Y., Sadeh, N.: A design space for privacy choices: towards meaningful privacy control in the internet of things. In: Proceedings of the 2021 CHI Conference on Human Factors in Computing Systems, pp. 1–16 (2021)
10. Haney, J.M., Furman, S.M., Acar, Y.: Smart home security and privacy mitigations: consumer perceptions, practices, and challenges. In: Moallem, A. (ed.) HCII 2020. LNCS, vol. 12210, pp. 393–411. Springer, Cham (2020). https://doi.org/10.1007/978-3-030-50309-3_26
11. Kelley, P.G., Bresee, J., Cranor, L.F., Reeder, R.W.: A "nutrition label" for privacy. In: Proceedings of 5th Symposium on Usable Privacy and Security, pp. 1–12 (2009)
12. Lewis, J.R.: The system usability scale: past, present, and future. Int. J. Hum.-Comput. Interact. **34**(7), 577–590 (2018)
13. Murmann, P., Karegar, F.: From design requirements to effective privacy notifications: empowering users of online services to make informed decisions. Int. J. Hum.-Comput. Interact. **37**(19), 1823–1848 (2021)
14. Railean, A., Reinhardt, D.: OnLITE: on-line label for IoT transparency enhancement. In: Asplund, M., Nadjm-Tehrani, S. (eds.) NordSec 2020. LNCS, vol. 12556, pp. 229–245. Springer, Cham (2021). https://doi.org/10.1007/978-3-030-70852-8_14
15. Schrepp, M., Hinderks, A., Thomaschewski, J.: Design and evaluation of a short version of the user experience questionnaire (UEQ-S). Int. J. Interact. Multimed. Artif. Intell. **4**(6), 103–108 (2017)
16. Seddon, P., Kiew, M.Y.: A partial test and development of Delone and McLean's model of is success. Aust. J. Inf. Syst. **4**(1), 90–109 (1996)
17. Shen, Y., Vervier, P.-A.: IoT security and privacy labels. In: Naldi, M., Italiano, G.F., Rannenberg, K., Medina, M., Bourka, A. (eds.) APF 2019. LNCS, vol. 11498, pp. 136–147. Springer, Cham (2019). https://doi.org/10.1007/978-3-030-21752-5_9
18. Tang, J., Birrell, E., Lerner, A.: How well do my results generalize now? The external validity of online privacy and security surveys. arXiv preprint arXiv:2202.14036 (2022)
19. Venkatesh, V., Morris, M.G., Davis, G.B., Davis, F.D.: User acceptance of information technology: toward a unified view. MIS Q. **27**(3), 425–478 (2003)
20. Xu, H.: The effects of self-construal and perceived control on privacy concerns (2007)
21. Yang, H., Lee, W., Lee, H.: IoT smart home adoption: the importance of proper level automation. J. Sens. **2018**, 1–11 (2018)
22. Yao, Y., Basdeo, J.R., Kaushik, S., Wang, Y.: Defending My castle: a co-design study of privacy mechanisms for smart homes. In: Proceedings of the 2019 CHI Conference on Human Factors in Computing Systems, CHI 2019, pp. 198:1–198:12. ACM, New York (2019). https://doi.org/10.1145/3290605.3300428

23. Yao, Y., Basdeo, J.R., Mcdonough, O.R., Wang, Y.: Privacy perceptions and designs of bystanders in smart homes. Proc. ACM Hum.-Comput. Interact. **3**(CSCW) (2019). https://doi.org/10.1145/3359161
24. Zeng, E., Roesner, F.: Understanding and improving security and privacy in {Multi-User} smart homes: a design exploration and {In-Home} user study. In: 28th USENIX Security Symposium (USENIX Security 2019), pp. 159–176 (2019)
25. Zheng, S., Apthorpe, N., Chetty, M., Feamster, N.: User perceptions of smart home IoT privacy. Proc. ACM Hum.-Comput. Interact. **2**(CSCW), 1–20 (2018)

Cyber Security Management

An Exploratory Factor Analysis of Personality Factors: An Insider Threat Perspective

Keshnee Padayachee[✉]

College of Science, Engineering and Technology, University of South Africa,
Pretoria, South Africa
padayk@unisa.ac.za

Abstract. This study used an exploratory factor analysis to examine the factors underlying personality traits that influence the constructs of information security compliance. Studies of this nature could be germane to organisations grappling with the insider threat problem. The current study, which is situated within the socio-technical realm and considers the human element within the information security domain, concludes by providing a conceptual model that could be useful to both researchers and practitioners.

Keywords: Insider threat · Personality traits · HEXACO

1 Introduction

The study in hand focuses on malicious insiders who misuse their legitimate access to an organisation's Information Technology (IT) infrastructure to intentionally thwart the confidentiality, integrity, and availability of the organisation's IT assets [1]. This type of crime is termed the insider threat problem as it is challenging to contain a threat that occurs within an organisation's security perimeter [2]. The insider threat problem ostensibly extends beyond the technological domain and considering its behavioural and psychological characteristics may also be valuable in the detection and prevention of cybercrime [3]. Detecting whether an event emanated from an insider threat is ranked as one of the most challenging issues in recent times [4]. It is purported that current anomalies in insider threat detection systems have propelled the exploration of psychological profiling and the understanding of attack motivations [5]. This study aims to delve deeper into the underlying factors that may regulate these aspects, such as personality.

Although personality mediates our compliance and our assessment of risk in information security, personality research in information security is scarce [6] and personality profiles constitute an under-examined area in the IT domain [7]. Therefore, researchers should continue to investigate various personality traits in order to understand the precursors to maleficence within the information security domain [8].

The current study involves understanding the influence of insider personality traits within the domain of information security compliance intention. The study culminates in the framing of a conceptual model that may support cybersecurity practitioners in accounting for personality factors in order to contain insider threats.

© IFIP International Federation for Information Processing 2022
Published by Springer Nature Switzerland AG 2022
N. Clarke and S. Furnell (Eds.): HAISA 2022, IFIP AICT 658, pp. 253–264, 2022.
https://doi.org/10.1007/978-3-031-12172-2_20

2 Related Work

Researchers consider both OCEAN (i.e. openness, conscientiousness, extraversion, agreeableness, and neuroticism) traits and the Dark Triad of personality traits (i.e. narcissism, Machiavellianism, and psychopathy) as being relevant to insider threat research.

Some researchers propose the Dark Triad of personality traits as being most relevant to the insider threat problem, given its association with socially aversive behaviour (see [9, 10]). However, Ong and Chong [11] considered the OCEAN traits as being most pertinent for security studies as the traits pervade over cultures and are generalisable across disciplines. Several studies considered the relationship between an insider's personality in terms of the OCEAN personality traits [3, 7, 12], while in some spheres researchers considered both types of traits simultaneously. Nurse et al. [13] developed a framework for characterising insider threats based on real-world cases, where they argued that personality characteristics are 'central' to understanding the insider threat. They found that the Dark Triad of traits and the OCEAN traits such as agreeableness and openness relate to an insider's susceptibility to scams. Simola et al. [6] found that low openness and high neuroticism and Machiavellianism were related to the need for insiders to rationalise their security misbehaviour.

Several studies are linked to general deterrence. Johnston et al. [14] found that insiders with a strong stability meta-trait (i.e., conscientiousness, agreeableness, and emotional stability (the reverse of neuroticism)) were more risk-averse and avoided risks and sanctions – in contrast to individuals with a strong plasticity meta-trait (i.e., dominant openness and extraversion traits). McBride et al. [15] found that 'extroverted' individuals with a low sense of 'sanction severity' are less likely to be non-compliant, while 'agreeable' individuals with a low sense of 'sanction certainty' are more likely to be non-compliant. They concluded that there may be other situational factors in combination with sanctions that will be valuable in controlling insider threats. This is an important caveat to consider in respect of personality-related studies.

3 Theoretical Framing

The Theory of Planned Behaviour (TPB) developed by Ajzen [16], considers the constructs of attitude, subjective norms and perceived behavioural control, which shape an individual's behavioural intentions and the resultant (actual) behaviour, has been previously leveraged in security-related studies [17, 18]. Studies show that there may be "stable individual differences that influence the relative weights of the different predictors in the TPB" [19] and that the TPB is thus amenable to the inclusion of other variables [16]. Therefore, this study includes personality constructs in addition to the existing theoretical TPB constructs. It is furthermore argued that the HEXACO model is suitable to crime research as it can be used in the "operationalisation of the trait component of the trait-state model of criminal decision making" [20]. The HEXACO model captures greater variance than the other five-dimensional models such as the OCEAN model [21]. The dimensions of the scale are the following: Honesty-Humility (**H**), Emotionality (**E**), Extraversion (**X**), Agreeableness (**A**), Conscientiousness (**C**) and Openness to experience (**O**) [22]. The research model conceptualised in this paper considered positive compliance attributes with respect to the components of the TPB, while the personality dimensions of the HEXACO model acted as antecedents to the TPB components.

4 Research Methodology

The data described in this paper was collected via an online quantitative survey conducted in 2021. The preliminary study involved considering the relationship between personality and situational prevention factors that affect insider compliance. The paper in hand focuses on the personality factors only, since the scarcity of research with respect to personality factors in information security justifies the relevance of this secondary data analysis.

The primary study involved non-probability purposive sampling. The sample was drawn from the researcher's LinkedIn connections which had been accumulated over several years. It was a representative sample of working professionals, which was the first criterion for inclusion. The insider threat is a crime of occupation as it is committed during the course of the insider's typical duties at work [1]. The second criterion was that the participants must have a basic understanding of working within a framework of organisational information security policies, as the insider is an element of an "organisation's security perimeter" [2]. Compliance with this criterion was determined within the survey, and those individuals who indicated that they did not have the required experience were requested to exit the survey. Using this process to recruit research participants does admittedly have limitations, since individuals with similar backgrounds and interests usually connect on social media platforms. Furthermore, it is possible that individuals who join a professional network may be imbued with traits of conscientiousness and agreeableness.

A large cohort of potential respondents (N = 2193) who had contactable email addresses and were not affiliated with the researcher were invited to participate. This sample was mostly unknown to the researcher and no incentives were provided. Initially, 196 individuals responded, but some respondents who were deemed unsuitable for the study were eliminated and consequently 186 responses were analysed. The sample consisted of professionals from several levels of engagement in security. The job profiles with respect to cybersecurity were as follows - High Level Engagement (n = 71), Mid-Level Engagement (n = 53), Entry Level Engagement (n = 8), End User Engagement (n = 39) and Other (n = 15). Most of the participants were South Africans (**92.94%**).

The personality scale and the constructs for compliant insider behaviour couched within the TPB were replicated and adapted from Ashton and Lee [23] and Safa et al. [24] respectively. The instrument had been validated by these previous studies. The individual constructs of the personality scale all showed Cronbach alpha coefficients above a tolerable level of 0.6. The preliminary results revealed that there was a moderate relationship with the traits of honesty-humility and conscientiousness and compliance intention. The remainder of the personality constructs appeared to be inconsequential, which led the researcher to speculate on whether the personality scale was indeed suitable to the context. Therefore, the researcher conducted an exploratory factor analysis to further refine the scale and explore its underlying facets with respect to information security compliance.

5 Data Analysis

An exploratory factor analysis with principal axis factoring extraction and quartimin rotation was executed. Initially, 21 factors were suggested by the eigen values greater than 1, which accounted for 67.882% of the variance. However, this resulted in a highly dispersed scale. Next, 11 factors were considered, but the resultant scale was not interpretable. Several options were attempted, and the analysis established that seven factors were found to be interpretable, which accounted for 35.947% of the overall variance in evaluation of personality. The results of the Bartlett Test of sphericity were ($\chi 2 = 440.676$, df = 1770.000, p < .001) and the value for the Kaiser-Meyer-Oklin was determined at 0.584, which is acceptable for exploratory factor analysis. An inspection of the items that loaded on each factor (factor loadings > |.32|) was considered without cross loadings. (The factor loadings are depicted in Appendix A.)

Factor 1 mostly reflected facets of *Honesty-Humility** (items 6, 12R, 24R, 30R, 48R, 54, 60R). This trait is characterised by facets of 'modesty', 'sincerity', and 'fairness'. Factor 2 mostly reflected the facets of *Agreeableness**. The items were loaded on two distinct traits – agreeableness (items 9R, 15R, 21R, 57R) and extraversion (items 4, 22, 52R). Considering the items related to 'extraversion' suggested an optimistic outlook. The trait of agreeableness suggests a person who is considerate, friendly and generous, with an optimistic view of human nature [25]. Therefore, this factor mostly describes an agreeable persona with facets of flexibility, patience, and optimism. Factor 3 mostly reflected facets of *Extraversion** (items 10R, 16, 34, 40, 58), a trait characterised by facets of 'social boldness' and 'sociability'. Factor 4 mostly reflected the facets of *Openness to Experience** (items 1R, 13, 25, 49R, 55R) and is indicative of facets of 'creativity' and 'aesthetic appreciation'. Item 55R was related to the facet of 'unconventionality'; however, it is more befitting to relabel this facet as 'contemplative'. Factor 5, which mostly reflected the facets of *Emotionality** (items 11, 17, 23, 29, 35R, 41R, 47, 59R), is representative of the facets of 'anxiety', 'sentimentality', 'dependence' and 'fearfulness'. Factor 6 mostly reflected the facets of *Conscientiousness** (items 2, 8, 14R). Item 19R suggests an attribute of tolerance of unconventional viewpoints. A persona with conscientiousness is deemed thoughtful during decision making and not inclined to avoid 'challenging goals' [23]. Therefore, it is possible that people who are conscientious may also accept views that are challenging in order to function better at their jobs. Descriptors such as 'organisation', 'diligence', 'perfectionism', and 'tolerance' describe this factor. Factor 7 loaded on only two traits –and was eliminated from further analysis.

The Cronbach alpha coefficients per newly defined factors were as follows: *Honesty-Humility** - 0.6447, *Agreeableness** - 0.6538, *Extraversion** - 0.703, *Openness to Experience** - 0.7270, *Emotionality** - 0.6752 and *Conscientiousness** - 0.3881. (The coefficients may be interpreted as follows with respect to the scale [26] – 0.00–0.20: less reliable; >0.20–0.40: rather reliable; >0.40–0.60: quite reliable; >0.60–0.80: reliable; >0.80–1.00: very reliable). The result of Spearman's rho that was performed to compare the rankings of the factors on the components of the TPB is demonstrated in Table 1. The coefficients were interpreted as follows: > = ± 0.4, "strong relationship"; ± 0.2- ± 0.4, "moderate relationship"; < = 0.2, "weak relationship" [27]. For the sake of brevity, we identified the most pertinent results to report here. There was a moderate positive relationship between:

- *Honesty-Humility** and attitude (rs = 0.253, p < 0.01), perceived behavioural control (rs = 0.262, p < 0.01) and social norms (rs = 0.270, p < 0.01);
- *Agreeableness** and perceived behavioural control (rs = 0.215, p < 0.1) and social norms (rs = 0.221, p < 0.1), as well as
- *Conscientiousness** and perceived behavioural control (rs = 0.222, p < 0.1) and social norms (rs = 0.286, p < 0.01).

Table 1. Correlation matrix

VAR	AT		PBC		SN		HH		AG		EX		OP	EM	CO
1. AT	—														
2. PBC	0.453	***	—												
3. SN	0.547	***	0.652	***	—										
4. HH	0.253	***	0.262	***	0.270	***	—								
5.AG	0.192	**	0.215	**	0.221	**	0.229	**	—						
6. EX	0.071		0.056		0.148	*	0.123		0.029		—				
7. OP	0.166	*	0.192	**	0.155	*	0.139		0.035		0.094		—		
8. EM	-0.028		0.038		0.050		-0.212	**	-0.154	*	-0.065		-0.086	—	
9. CO	0.158	*	0.222	**	0.286	***	0.050		0.052		0.095		0.045	0.058	—

*p < .05, **p < .01, ***p < .001 (**Abbreviations**: Attitude (AT), Perceived Behavioural Control (PBC), Social Norms (SN), Honesty-Humility* (HH), Agreeableness* (AG), Extraversion* (EX), Openness to Experience* (OP), Emotionality* (EM), Conscientiousness* (CO))

6 Discussion of Findings

This exploratory factor analysis should support researchers in identifying the personality constructs that should be considered for security-related research. We found that the *Honesty-Humility** trait has a moderate influence on all three constructs related to insider compliance intention. It has been argued that the Dark Triad of traits is negatively correlated with the honesty-humility trait [21] and thus this construct can be used to covertly identify high-risk insiders with dark traits. The *Agreeableness** and *Conscientiousness** traits had a moderate influence on perceived behavioural control and social norms. van Winsen [28] found that individuals with dominant agreeableness and conscientiousness traits are more likely to behave safely online and therefore less likely to be victims of cybercrime. This suggests that these are important traits to minimise reputational damage to organisations.

Shropshire et al. [29] argue that the traits of extraversion, neuroticism and openness have no impact on security-related studies. However Gratian et al. [30] purport that extraversion is a good predictor for good cybersecurity behaviour and the study in hand found that *Extraversion** has a weak effect on social norms. van der Schyff and Flowerday [31] found that the trait of openness is related to information security awareness of privacy within the context of Facebook use, but not with regard to the intention to review

Facebook's privacy settings. They argue that such an individual could be persuaded to secure their personal information. The current study found that *Openness to Experience** has weak correlations with intention constructs.

It is important to note that traits in the HEXACO model do overlap with the OCEAN traits. Whereas the traits of extraversion, openness and conscientiousness are mostly similar, the traits of honesty-humility, agreeableness and emotionality do not correspond directly [21]. Van Gelder and De Vries [20] found that honesty-humility, conscientiousness and agreeableness correlate with criminal choice and there was an indirect negative effect of 'emotionality' on criminal choice. Similarly, the current study found that the revised *Emotionality** factor has no bearing on compliance. Emotionality contains desirable and undesirable traits such as sensitivity and cowardice [32] respectively. It is possible that participants did not want to be associated with undesirable traits. van Winsen [28] found emotionality was unconnected to cybercrime victims' online behaviour, while Smith [33] found that high emotionality might describe the victims, but not the perpetrators of cyberbullying. The applicability of emotionality to an understanding of the perpetrators of cybercrime is inconclusive, and it may not be effective for uncovering high-risk insiders. However, the remaining traits may be more applicable, which has clear implications for theory and practice, as is discussed next.

7   Implications for Theory and Practice

We now present a conceptual model (see Fig. 1) based on the significant correlations that emerged from Table 1. The categories of cybercrime for which this conceptual framework would have implications include insider sabotage, insider theft of intellectual property (IP) and insider fraud [1]. Our conceptualisation will be valuable to cybersecurity practitioners and researchers who attempt to minimise the insider threat problem. For practitioners, it may underscore the importance of applying psychological scales in recruitment, particularly for jobs that involve interaction with highly sensitive information. For researchers, the conceptual model subsumes the refined personality scale with the relevant facets for security-related studies.

Hypothetically, *Emotionality** appears to have no bearing on the components of information security compliance intention, while *Extraversion** has a bearing on social

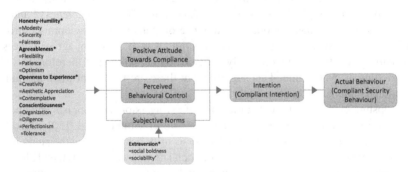

Fig. 1. A personality-ensconced conceptual model for insider compliance

norms only. Appropriating from De Vries et al. [34], we proffer situations that may activate specific personality traits within organisations. The *Honesty-Humility** persona gravitates towards situations that are ethical, due to their inherent facets of modesty, sincerity and fairness. The *Agreeability** persona is less likely to engage in retaliation or to seek revenge due to their inherent facets of flexibility, patience, and optimism. The *Conscientiousness** persona gravitates towards being dutybound, owing to their inherent facets of organisation, diligence, perfectionism, and tolerance. The aforenoted traits are indicative of individuals who would in theory comply with an information security policy.

It is presumed that the empirical results from Johnston et al. [14], who found that individuals with the meta-traits of stability (i.e. 'conscientiousness', 'agreeableness', and 'emotional stability') were more risk-averse and avoided risks and sanctions (i.e. a positive association with compliance), would also apply here. The *Openness to experience** persona is creative, aesthetically appreciative and contemplative, and gravitates towards ingenuity and discovery situations. Perhaps such a persona may be utilised as an early adopter of new information security policies. People with traits of high *Extraversion** – displaying facets such as social boldness and sociability – will seek out social activities and therefore respond to social norms (i.e., subjective norms). Thus, it is important for organisations to ensure that a culture of information security compliance prevails. This is evidenced by the research conducted by Gratian et al. [30] who suggest that extraverted individuals will be more responsive if there is messaging that shows that "good device securement practices" are benefitting others in their social group.

8   Conclusions

This research undertaking had several limitations. First, the respondents were mostly South African and future research will need to consider the involvement of other culture groups (European, Asian, American, etc.). Second, the purposeful sampling method that was used here had inherent biases. Thus, future research would have to consider alternative data collection sources. Forthcoming research should also involve regression analysis to understand the variation of each construct in terms of compliance. It is hoped that the present study will be useful in enriching the general understanding of personality traits with regard to information security compliance and security-related studies.

Appendix A: Rotated Factor Loading

Item	F1	F2	F3	F4	F5	F6	F7	Facet
48."I want people to know that I am an important person of high status" [R]	0.57	0.01	0.11	0.06	-0.16	-0.19	-0.22	HH^{Modesty}
24."I think that I am entitled to more respect than the average person is" [R]	0.54	-0.06	0.04	0.12	-0.04	-0.04	-0.04	HH^{Modesty}
30."If I want something from someone, I will laugh at that person's worst jokes" [R]	0.52	0.10	0.02	0.00	-0.19	0.06	0.01	HH^{Sincerity}
60."I would be tempted to use counterfeit money, if I were sure I could get away with it" [R]	0.47	0.14	0.08	0.03	0.05	0.19	0.07	HH^{Fairness}
54."I would not pretend to like someone just to get that person to do favours for me"	0.46	-0.16	-0.05	0.10	-0.04	0.10	-0.02	HH^{Sincerity}
12."If I knew that I would never get caught, I would be willing to steal a million dollars (or rands)" [R]	0.40	0.09	0.12	0.01	0.01	0.03	0.17	HH^{Fairness}
20."I make decisions based on the feeling of the moment rather than on careful thought" [R]	0.36	0.28	-0.20	-0.00	-0.08	0.33	0.35	CO^{Prudence}
6."I would not use flattery to get a raise or promotion at work, even if I thought it would succeed"	0.34	0.04	0.05	0.01	-0.02	0.10	0.10	HH^{Sincerity}
42."I would get a lot of pleasure from owning expensive luxury goods" [R]	0.31	0.18	0.01	0.01	-0.04	-0.15	0.07	HH$^{Greed-Avoidance}$
27."My attitude toward people who have treated me badly is 'forgive and forget'"	0.30	0.26	0.27	-0.05	0.10	0.05	0.03	AG^{Forgiveness}
33."I tend to be lenient in judging other people"	0.26	0.08	-0.14	-0.11	0.07	-0.15	-0.08	AG^{Gentleness}
3."I rarely hold a grudge, even against people who have horribly wronged me"	0.25	0.09	0.18	0.01	-0.05	-0.01	0.01	AG^{Forgiveness}
18."Having a lot of money is not especially important to me"	0.24	0.09	0.06	-0.00	-0.17	-0.01	-0.01	HH$^{Greed-Avoidance}$
15."People sometimes tell me that I am too stubborn"[R]	-0.03	0.54	-0.11	-0.06	0.09	-0.07	-0.08	AG^{Flexibility}
21."People think of me as someone who has a quick temper" [R]	0.10	0.52	-0.06	0.11	-0.03	-0.02	0.11	AG^{Patience}
57."When people tell me that I am wrong, my first reaction is to argue with them" [R]	0.31	0.45	0.03	0.01	-0.16	0.16	0.01	AG^{Flexibility}
52."I sometimes feel that I am a worthless person"[R]	0.04	0.44	0.08	0.07	-0.21	-0.01	0.11	EX$^{Social\ Self-Esteem}$
9."People sometimes tell me that I am too critical of others" [R]	0.12	0.40	-0.02	-0.11	0.08	-0.27	-0.07	AG^{Gentleness}
22."On most days, I feel cheerful and optimistic"	0.27	0.38	0.31	0.04	-0.12	0.06	-0.03	EX^{Liveliness}

Item	F1	F2	F3	F4	F5	F6	F7	Facet
4. "I feel reasonably satisfied with myself overall"	0.03	0.37	0.16	0.05	-0.11	0.12	-0.07	EX^{Social Self-Esteem}
56. "I prefer to do whatever comes to mind, rather than stick to a plan" [R]	0.04	0.32	-0.07	-0.02	-0.14	0.27	0.32	CO^{Prudence}
39. "I am usually quite flexible in my opinions when people disagree with me"	0.11	0.27	0.18	0.01	0.02	0.13	-0.21	AG^{Flexibility}
45. "Most people tend to get angry more quickly than I do"	-0.02	0.24	-0.03	0.16	-0.05	0.01	-0.00	AG^{Patience}
51. "Even when people make a lot of mistakes, I rarely say anything negative"	0.13	0.20	0.01	-0.05	0.03	0.02	-0.28	AG^{Gentleness}
34. "In social situations, I am usually the one who makes the first move"	0.04	0.01	0.67	0.08	-0.08	0.06	0.04	EX^{Social Boldness}
40. "The first thing that I always do in a new place is to make friends"	0.02	0.01	0.58	-0.02	0.06	0.10	0.08	EX^{Sociability}
58. "When I am in a group of people, I'm often the one who speaks on behalf of the group"	0.08	-0.20	0.54	0.08	-0.11	0.04	0.09	EX^{Social Boldness}
16. "I prefer jobs that involve active social interaction to those that involve working alone"	0.02	0.15	0.52	0.00	0.08	0.08	-0.04	EX^{Sociability}
10. "I rarely express my opinions in group meetings" [R]	0.12	-0.04	0.45	0.08	-0.03	-0.09	0.07	EX^{Social Boldness}
36. "I would never accept a bribe, even if it were exceptionally large"	0.11	-0.00	0.16	0.00	-0.05	0.15	-0.02	HH^{Fairness}
13. "I would enjoy creating a work of art, such as a novel, a song, or a painting"	0.03	0.05	0.01	0.71	0.14	-0.06	0.10	OP^{Creativity}
25. "If I had the opportunity, I would like to attend a classical music concert"	0.02	-0.09	0.02	0.66	-0.05	0.08	0.05	OP^{Aesthetic Appreciation}
1. "I would be quite bored by a visit to an art gallery" [R]	0.00	0.04	0.08	0.57	0.01	0.01	0.00	OP^{Aesthetic Appreciation}
55. "I find it boring to discuss philosophy" [R]	0.04	0.05	0.00	0.50	-0.08	0.05	0.18	OP^{Unconventionality}
49. "I do not think of myself as the artistic or creative type" [R]	0.03	0.13	-0.04	0.48	-0.05	-0.00	-0.08	OP^{Creativity}
31. "I have never really enjoyed looking through an encyclopedia" [R]	0.13	-0.12	0.05	0.40	-0.07	-0.13	0.33	OP^{Inquisitiveness}
43. "I like people who have unconventional views"	0.07	-0.06	0.17	0.34	-0.10	0.32	0.17	OP^{Unconventionality}
37. "People have often told me that I have a good imagination"	0.13	0.05	0.18	0.29	0.06	0.29	-0.09	OP^{Creativity}
47. "I feel strong emotions when someone close to me is going away for a long time"	-0.03	-0.09	0.10	0.02	0.57	0.16	0.16	EM^{Sentimentality}
17. "When suffering from a painful experience, I need someone to make me feel comfortable"	-0.02	0.09	0.14	-0.15	0.56	0.08	-0.22	EM^{Dependence}
59. "I remain unemotional even in situations where most people get very sentimental" [R]	-0.02	-0.08	-0.11	0.05	0.49	-0.20	0.04	EM^{Sentimentality}
35. "I worry a lot less than most people do" [R]	-0.18	-0.14	-0.20	0.07	0.44	0.04	0.04	EM^{Anxiety}

Item	F1	F2	F3	F4	F5	F6	F7	Facet
23."I feel like crying when I see other people crying"	-0.04	-0.04	0.12	0.12	0.44	-0.08	-0.12	EM^{Sentimentality}
41."I can handle demanding situations without needing emotional support from anyone else" [R]	-0.13	-0.06	-0.15	-0.20	0.40	-0.31	-0.04	EM^{Dependence}
29."When it comes to physical danger, I am very fearful"	-0.13	0.18	-0.05	-0.13	0.39	0.11	-0.21	EM^{Fearfulness}
11."I sometimes cannot help worrying about trivial things"	-0.11	-0.26	-0.11	-0.03	0.36	0.06	0.04	EM^{Anxiety}
53."Even in an emergency I would not easily panic"	-0.16	-0.08	-0.11	-0.13	0.27	-0.05	-0.18	EM^{Fearfulness}
5."I would feel afraid if I had to travel in severe weather conditions"	0.06	0.04	-0.02	-0.07	0.26	-0.02	-0.23	EM^{Fearfulness}
2."I plan ahead and organise things, to avoid scrambling at the last minute"	-0.05	0.14	-0.06	-0.11	0.09	0.55	-0.08	CO^{Organisation}
50."People often call me a perfectionist"	0.00	-0.32	0.01	0.06	-0.02	0.40	-0.05	CO^{Perfectionism}
8. "I often push myself extremely hard when trying to achieve a goal"	0.00	0.03	0.20	-0.02	-0.19	0.37	0.07	CO^{Diligence}
14."When working on something, I do not pay much attention to small details" [R]	0.18	0.00	-0.13	0.08	0.20	0.35	0.16	CO^{Perfectionism}
19."I think that paying attention to radical ideas is a waste of time"[R]	-0.06	0.03	0.11	0.15	0.02	0.34	0.02	OP^{Unconventionality}
26."When working, I sometimes have difficulties due to being disorganised" [R]	0.10	0.28	-0.15	-0.14	-0.17	0.31	0.06	CO^{Organisation}
38."I always try to be accurate in my work, even at the expense of time"	0.12	-0.11	0.09	-0.06	0.15	0.25	-0.18	CO^{Perfectionism}
7."I am interested in learning about the history and politics of other countries"	-0.03	0.02	0.19	0.32	0.08	0.07	0.53	OP^{Inquisitiveness}
28."I feel that I am an unpopular person"[R]	0.14	0.13	0.23	0.05	-0.26	-0.21	0.48	EX$^{Social\ Self-Esteem}$
44."I make a lot of mistakes because I do not think before I act" [R]	0.18	0.35	0.00	0.06	0.02	0.15	0.39	CO^{Prudence}
46."Most people are more upbeat and dynamic than I generally am" [R]	0.12	0.01	0.35	0.01	-0.19	-0.10	0.36	EX^{Liveliness}
32."I do only the minimum amount of work needed to get by" [R]	0.28	0.00	0.14	-0.01	0.02	0.23	0.36	CO^{Diligence}

Abbreviation: Factor (F), Honesty-Humility (HH), Agreeableness (AG), Extraversion (EX), Openness to Experience* (OP), Emotionality (EM), Conscientiousness (CO) (Scale adapted from [23])

References

1. Cappelli, D.M., Moore, A.P., Trzeciak, R.F.: The CERT Guide to Insider Threats: How to Prevent, Detect, and Respond to Information Technology Crimes (Theft, Sabotage, Fraud). Addison-Wesley, Upper Saddle River, New Jersey (2012)
2. Hunker, J., Probst, C.W.: Insiders and insider threats-an overview of definitions and mitigation techniques. J. Wirel. Mob. Netw. Ubiquitous Comput. Dependable Appl. 2(1), 4–27 (2011)
3. Legg, P.A., et al.: Towards a conceptual model and reasoning structure for insider threat detection. J. Wirel. Mob. Netw. Ubiquitous Comput. Dependable Appl.cations 4(4), 20–37 (2013)

4. Ponemon Institute: Privileged user abuse & the insider threat. http://www.trustedcs.com/resources/whitepapers/Ponemon-RaytheonPrivilegedUserAbuseResearchReport.pdf (2014). Accessed 06 Jan 2015
5. Jiang, J., et al.: Prediction and detection of malicious insiders' motivation based on sentiment profile on webpages and emails. In: IEEE Military Communications Conference, pp. 1–6. IEEE, Los Angeles, CA, USA (2018)
6. Simola, P., Virtanen, T., Sartonen, M.: Information security is more than just policy; it is in your personality. In: ECCWS 2019 18th European Conference on Cyber Warfare and Security, pp. 459–65. Academic Conferences and publishing limited, Coimbra, Portugal (2019)
7. Shropshire, J., Gowan, A.: Identifying traits and values of top-performing information security personnel. J. Comput. Inf. Syst. **57**(3), 258–268 (2017)
8. Whitty, M.T.: Developing a conceptual model for insider threat. J. Manag. Organ. 1–19 (2018)
9. Maasberg, M., Warren, J., Beebe, N.L.: The dark side of the insider: detecting the insider threat through examination of dark triad personality Traits. In: 48th Hawaii International Conference on System Sciences (HICSS), pp. 3518–26. IEEE, Kauai, Hawaii, USA (2015)
10. Radhakrishnan, M., et al.: Proposed insider threat detection model for malaysian government agencies. Open Int. J. Inform. (OIJI) 54–67 (2018)
11. Ong, L., Chong, C.: Information security awareness: an application of psychological factors– a study in Malaysia. In: Proceedings of the 2014 International Conference on Computer, Communications and Information Technology, pp. 98–101. Atlantis Press, Beijing, China (2014)
12. Alahmadi, B.A., Legg, P.A., Nurse, J.R.: Using internet activity profiling for insider-threat detection. In: International Conference on Enterprise Information Systems, vol. 2, pp. 709–20. SCITEPRESS, Barcelona, Spain (2015)
13. Nurse, J.R., et al.: Understanding insider threat: a framework for characterising attacks. In: IEEE Security and Privacy Workshops, pp. 214–28. IEEE, San Jose, California, USA (2014)
14. Johnston, A.C., Warkentin, M., McBride, M., Carter, L.: Dispositional and situational factors: influences on information security policy violations. Eur. J. Inf. Syst. **25**(3), 231–251 (2016)
15. McBride, M., Carter, L., Warkentin, M.: Exploring the role of individual employee characteristics and personality on employee compliance with cybersecurity policies. RTI International-Institute for Homeland Security Solutions **5**(1), (2012)
16. Ajzen, I.: The theory of planned behavior. Organ. Behav. Hum. Decis. Process. **50**(2), 179–211 (1991)
17. Bulgurcu, B., Cavusoglu, H., Benbasat, I.: Information security policy compliance: an empirical study of rationality-based beliefs and information security awareness. MIS Q. **34**(3), 523–548 (2010)
18. Ifinedo, P.: Understanding information systems security policy compliance: an integration of the theory of planned behavior and the protection motivation theory. Comput. Secur. **31**(1), 83–95 (2012)
19. Ajzen, I.: The theory of planned behaviour: reactions and reflections. Psychol. Health **29**(6), 1113–1127 (2011)
20. Van Gelder, J.-L., De Vries, R.E.: Traits and states: integrating personality and affect into a model of criminal decision making. Criminology **50**(3), 637–671 (2012)
21. Ashton, M.C., Lee, K., De Vries, R.E.: The HEXACO Honesty-humility, agreeableness, and emotionality factors: a review of research and theory. Pers. Soc. Psychol. Rev. **18**(2), 139–152 (2014)
22. Lee, K., Ashton, M.C.: Psychometric properties of the HEXACO personality inventory. Multivar. Behav. Res. **39**(2), 329–358 (2004)
23. Ashton, M.C., Lee, K.: The HEXACO–60: a short measure of the major dimensions of personality. J. Pers. Assess. **91**(4), 340–345 (2009)

24. Safa, N.S., et al.: Deterrence and prevention-based model to mitigate information security insider threats in organisations. Futur. Gener. Comput. Syst. **97**, 587–597 (2019)

25. Singh, A.K., Singh, S., Singh, A.: Does trait predict psychological well-being among students of professional courses? J. Indian Acad. Appl. Psychol. **38**(2), 234–241 (2012)

26. Hair, J.F., Black, W.C., Babin, B.J., Anderson, R.E.: Multivariate Data Analysis, 7th edn. Prentice Hall, Upper Saddle River, New Jersey (2010)

27. Mcleod, S.: Simply Psychology. https://www.simplypsychology.org/correlation.html (2020). Accessed 28 Sep 2021

28. van Winsen, B.: Determining secure digital behavior of individuals using hexaco personality traits. Erasmus School of Economics, MSc Thesis. Erasmus University Rotterdam, Netherlands (2020)

29. Shropshire, J., Warkentin, M., Sharma, S.: Personality, attitudes, and intentions: predicting initial adoption of information security behavior. Comput. Secur. **49**, 177–191 (2015)

30. Gratian, M., Bandi, S., Cukier, M., Dykstra, J., Ginther, A.: Correlating human traits and cyber security behavior intentions. Comput. Secur. **73**, 345–58 (2018)

31. van der Schyff, K., Flowerday, S.: Mediating effects of information security awareness. Comput. Secur. **106**, 1–12 (2021)

32. Ashton, M.C., Lee, K.: Empirical, theoretical, and practical advantages of the HEXACO model of personality structure. Pers. Soc. Psychol. Rev. **11**(2), 150–166 (2007)

33. Smith, R.D.: The Relationship between HEXACO Personality Traits and Cyberbullying Perpetrators and Victims. Doctor of Education. Liberty University, Lynchburg, Virginia (2016)

34. De Vries, R.E., Tybur, J.M., Pollet, T.V., van Vugt, M.: Evolution, situational affordances, and the HEXACO model of personality. Evol. Hum. Behav. **37**(5), 407–421 (2016)

Policy Components - A Conceptual Model for Tailoring Information Security Policies

Elham Rostami[✉], Fredrik Karlsson, and Shang Gao

CERIS, Informatics, Örebro University, Örebro, Sweden
{elham.rostami,fredrik.karlsson,shang.gao}@oru.se

Abstract. Today, many business processes are propelled by critical information that needs safeguarding. Procedures on how to achieve this end are found in information security policies (ISPs) that are rarely tailored to different target groups in organizations. The purpose of this paper is therefore to propose a conceptual model of policy components for software that supports modularizing and tailoring of ISPs. We employed design science research to this end. The conceptual model was developed as a Unified Modeling Language class diagram using existing ISPs from public agencies in Sweden. The conceptual model can act as a foundation for developing software to tailor ISPs.

Keywords: Information security policy · Tailored policy design · Conceptual model

1 Introduction

In contemporary organizations many business processes are highly dependent on information assets. Therefore, information security, where the purpose is to safeguard an organization's information assets, is critical. Organizations can choose to implement controls, i.e., measures that address risks, to enhance information security. These controls are often sorted into three main categories: technical, formal, and informal controls [1]. Among the formal controls, information security policy (ISP), is viewed as one of the most important ones. An ISP includes "established rules that provide guidance in the protection of an organization's assets" [2] and thus directs employees' use of information and information systems. However, employees' non-compliance with ISPs is a perennial problem for many organizations [3, 4].

At the same time, half of all information security breaches caused by employees are accidental [5]. It has therefore been argued that there is also an ISP-design related aspect to employees' non-compliance [6], where ISPs can be cumbersome to follow and sometimes even incompatible with existing business processes [7]. As it has been shown by [8], existing research mostly takes a monolithic view of ISPs, where the same ISP is used for the entire organization, i.e., for all employees. Thus, there is a relevance issue with ISPs. Having said that, research has acknowledged that the needs of employees differ [e.g. 9], which suggests pursuing a tailoring approach to ISPs. Furthermore, designing

© IFIP International Federation for Information Processing 2022
Published by Springer Nature Switzerland AG 2022
N. Clarke and S. Furnell (Eds.): HAISA 2022, IFIP AICT 658, pp. 265–274, 2022.
https://doi.org/10.1007/978-3-031-12172-2_21

is a non-trivial task [10], which means there is a design burden of information security managers. Researchers have therefore suggested software to aid the management of ISPs [e.g. 11, 12], however they have addressed the tailoring aspect of ISPs to a very limited extent. One notable exception is [13], who identified two requirements about tailoring of ISPs among a larger set of requirements for software to aid ISP design. Consequently, combining the ideas of tailoring of ISP and software could address both the relevance issue of ISPs and ease the design burden of information security managers. To facilitate consistent and coherent tailoring with the use of such software, an ISP needs to be possible to represent as modules that can be selected depending on the relevance for the audience. Therefore, this paper *aims to propose a conceptual model of policy components for software that supports modularizing and tailoring ISPs.*

2   Related Research

The use of software to aid the design of ISPs is not new in research, but this topic has received limited attention from researchers [14]. The papers that addressed such software [11, 12, 15, 16] address few aspects of tailoring of ISPs. Furthermore, these papers seem to focus on demonstrating the software's functionality and do not present the conceptual models behind the software designs. [12] introduced a framework, which they implemented as a software, helping managers when "evaluating information security policy performance". Consequently, they did not provide design support for modularizing of ISPs. [16] and [11] elaborated further on the information security management toolbox that has been introduced by [17]. The software builds on the information security governance model [18], which is process-oriented model. The software implements two phases, a direct phase, and a control phase, where the design of ISPs is part of the former phase. The direct phase also supports the selection of information security controls based on the ISP. The software enables a dynamic ISP, where supporting security procedures "are presented for selection based on the security controls selected" [11]. Although the software provides a "personalized and tailormade Word-document" [11] it is still unclear to what extent it is tailored to the employees' work situation. The reason is that the controls are selected from the international information security standard ISO 27002. Furthermore, they do not provide any conceptual model to aid the implementation of such tailoring functionality in other software. Moving beyond the research on software that aid the design of ISPs, existing research provides some model/frameworks that support ISP design [e.g. 19, 20]. However, these models are not conceptual models, i.e., models that are representations of software, and they do not address the tailoring aspects. Finally, [13] identify 14 requirements on software to aid ISP design. Among these requirements 2 of them directly focus on tailoring ISPs (1) support a tailorable design of ISPs, and (2) address clear and uniform target groups. The remaining software requirements to aid ISP design are actionable advice, adopted to the work practice, based on identified risks, clarifying responsibilities, clear communicative objectives, clear structure, clearly defined concepts, informed by laws, regulations, and standards, internally congruent ISP actions, keep up-to-date, goal alignment, and styling. Although these requirements as prerequisite for developing software to support tailoring ISP are valuable, they were not turned into a model or a software.

3   Research Method

This research is part of a larger design science research (DSR) endeavor, where the end goal is to suggest a software for tailoring of ISPs. Our particular research follows the DSR approach suggested by [21], but is here limited to the first four phases of the our first design science cycle: (1) Problem identification and motivation, (2) Define objectives of a solution, (3) Design and development, and (4) Demonstration.

The Problem identification and motivation phase is found in the Introduction, showing that there is an ISP-design-related aspect to employees' non-compliance. Existing research has suggested a tailoring approach to ISP, which we combine with the idea of software to aid information security managers in achieving this goal. The Define objectives of a solution phase focused on setting the objective for the first DSR cycle and was operationalized into two design goals: (1) To develop a conceptual model that supports modularized ISP content to self-contained and free-standing parts, and (2) To develop a conceptual model that supports creating tailored ISPs by reusing modules.

The Design and development phase focused on developing the conceptual model of policy components. As an empirical starting point for our conceptual modeling, we had access to 159 ISPs from public agencies in Sweden. Still, we had to balance resources available for modeling and arriving at a stable conceptual model. We therefore divided our modeling work into two steps: (1) developing an initial conceptual model and (2) validating the model. During the first step we selected the three most extensive ISPs that we had access to and used them as input to develop an initial conceptual model. The conceptual modeling of the ISPs took place during three workshops where all three authors participated. During the second step, we validated the initial conceptual model using the ISPs from the database until we reached saturation [22]. This meant, we stopped modeling when modeling another ISPs would not add anything new to the conceptual model. To reduce researcher bias we developed an algorithm to select 10 ISPs from the available ISPs randomly for each validation iteration. We reached saturation after two iterations, which meant that we validated the conceptual model using 20 ISPs in total. During the second step, we used the classes and associations in the model to sort the content of the ISPs. Things that could not be sorted using the conceptual model were noted and later considered as input for revising the model. The refined conceptual model is presented in Sect. 4. In this section we also provide (a) references to existing ISP design research, pinpointing theoretical grounding of the model in addition to our empirical work and (b) show how the model addresses the requirements in [13].

The Demonstration phase consists of two parts. First, we use the conceptual model to elicit policy components from one of the ISPs from public agencies in Sweden that we had access to. Consequently, it is an empirical demonstration showing how policy components are self-contained and free-standing parts (i.e., meeting our first design goal). Second, we use the elicited policy components to create two tailored ISPs targeting different target groups. This part of the demonstration shows how policy components can be reused across two tailored ISPs (i.e., meeting our second design goal). Executing this demonstration as a proof-of-concept is important before investing in software implementation and demonstrating tailoring as a proof-of-value in actual organizational cases [23].

4 Policy Component – Conceptual Model

The conceptual model of policy components is shown in Fig. 1 as a Unified Modeling Language (UML) class diagram. The conceptual model consists of 13 classes: actor, role, information security policy, policy component, structure, policy statement, actionable advice, educational content, general content, consequence, concept, goal, and supplementary sources. Between these classes, we find several named associations.

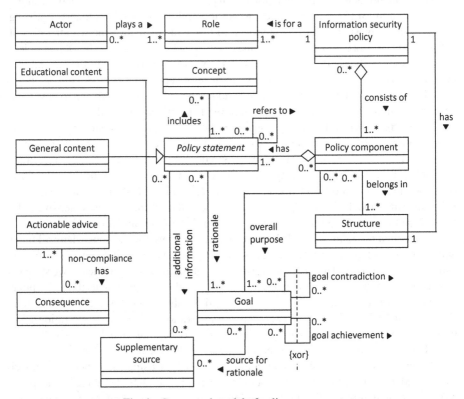

Fig. 1. Conceptual model of policy components

In organizations, many different work tasks are carried out in relation to business processes. Thus, not all parts of an ISP are equally relevant for all roles and existing research recommends that ISPs are divided into several parts that target specific audiences [9]. Organizations define roles in order for employees and other associated actors to know what is expected of them. Thus, starting in the upper-left corner of Fig. 1, an *Actor* is an individual associated with the organization, while a *Role* is a function played by an actor in the organization. Thus, actors playing the same role is a common ground for the addressing the "clear and uniform target groups" requirement [13]. For example, at a hospital, an employee can play the role of a nurse in a ward. The model defines those actors included must have at least one role in an organization, but some roles have no dedicated actors at a specific point in time.

A *Policy component* can both guide and restrict tasks associated with a specific role. Addressing the "tailorable design" requirement in [13], a policy component is a self-contained part of an ISP expressing rules that guide the protection of the organization's assets while executing a defined task. The nurse exemplified above could have several defined tasks, and one of them could be to access a patient's medical record to provide care. A policy component is prescribed in order to achieve one or more goals. A *Goal* is a verifiable state of the world toward which the policy component is directed. Goals can be derived from supplementary sources, such as internal standards, work instructions, laws, and regulations. For example, one goal related to the exemplified task above is to keep patient information confidential. By explicitly stating the goals of the policy components, it is possible to identify any goal conflicts, conflicts that may create future non-compliance situations [24]. Thus, this addresses the "goal alignment" requirement in [13].

The policy components provide a set of *Policy statements* to support an actor playing a role. A policy statement is direction-giving and guides towards the goal of the policy component. Thus, these statements have different communication objectives [6]. As shown in Fig. 1, a policy statement is an abstract class, and there are three different types of policy statements (actionable, educational, general) that serve different purposes. Thus, we address the requirement of having "clear communicative objectives" in [13]. *Actionable advice* provides instructions and rules on how to execute a task [6]. Thus, the actionable advice defines what is allowed and what is not allowed regarding the task [25]. For example, when using medical records to provide care, one part of the actionable advice is to access a patient's medical records that the nurse provides care for only. It means that as a nurse, you are not allowed to access all medical records. One main purpose of an ISP is to limit non-compliant behavior, and actionable advice can be associated with one or more *Consequences.* Drawing on deterrence theory [26], a consequence is a specific sanction for not complying with the instructions and rules found in the actionable advice. For example, the policy components should include the consequences of accessing a patient record without having work-related reasons, clearly stating that the care provider always reports to the police when they suspect unauthorized access to patient records to continue with the running illustration. Consequently, we address the "actionable advice" and "clarifying responsibility" requirements in [13].

Educational content and *General content* serve a different purpose than actionable advice; these types of advice do not have the purpose of regulating. Drawing on [6], separating different communicative functions in an ISP is important to provide clear and efficient communication. Simultaneously, the policy component's design allows referring between these types of advice. Educational content provides information about information security and the task to educate the actor. For example, the care provider can explain that activities in the electronic patient record system are logged and that these logs are audited regularly. By providing this information, the care provider can raise awareness of how the system works. Finally, general content provides information about information security and the task that serves the purpose of generally informing the information security policy user.

It is important that all actors using the ISP have a shared understanding of the terms used and what concepts that they refer to [27]. Information security and business terminology and concepts often come with a certain complexity. The policy component, therefore, includes the possibility to define concepts. A *Concept* is a generic description of how something is conceived in the organization. In the example discussed above, confidentiality is a central concept to understand. Thus, a definition, such as "information is not made available or disclosed to unauthorized individuals, entities, or processes" [28], can be included in a policy component about patient's medical records. The same concept can be associated with more than one piece of advice. This means that we address the "clearly defined concepts" requirement in [13]. Sometimes it is necessary to refer to other documents as a complement to the ISP. Thus, the different types of advice can include references to *Supplementary sources*. A supplementary source is an artifact that contains additional information to specific advice, such as found in laws, regulations, and information security standards [29]. These sources provide background information for the actionable advice that is provided in the policy component. This part of the model addresses the "informed by laws, regulations, and standards" requirement in [13].

A self-contained policy component can act as a building block when constructing tailored ISPs. As is shown in Fig. 1, an ISP tailored for a specific role consists of one or more policy components. We acknowledge the fact that the content of an ISP needs to be presented in a structured way [6, 30] in order to provide an overview for the actor playing a specific role. Thus, each ISP has a *Structure* that organizes related policy components together and addresses the "clear structure" requirement in [13].

5   Policy Component – Demonstration

Below we demonstrate the policy component concept as a proof-of-concept. The demonstration consists of two parts. The first part provides an internal view of a policy component, showing its content. The second part of the demonstration shows an external view of policy components, hiding their content. The purpose is to demonstrate how policy components can be combined to create tailored ISPs targeting different roles.

5.1   Policy Component: Managing E-mails

The presentation is structured using the classes in Fig. 1. Since the existing ISP which is used as starting point was not designed with this structure in mind, we had to move text around and rephrase some parts to create better flow in the text. We strived not to change the meaning of the ISP; however, the text below should not be interpreted as exact quotes from the original ISP.

Policy Component: Managing e-mails.

Goal: To govern the use of the agency's e-mail accounts.

Actionable Advice: The e-mail account is for work purposes only. Received e-mails must be opened and read within one business day. For example, during an absence due to illness, vacation, or other leave, you should grant a colleague the right to read the incoming e-mails. Note that an automatic reply is not considered sufficient. You may forward received e-mails to another e-mail address; however, replies to incoming e-mails shall be sent via the agency's e-mail address. You are not allowed to delete an incoming e-mail without first making sure what the content is. E-mail marked as spam must be inspected before deleting. Confidential information should not be sent via e-mail.

Consequence: In case of violation of these rules, the e-mail account will be terminated.

Educational Content: Spam, also referred to as junk e-mail, is the practice of sending unsolicited messages in bulk by e-mail. There is a central e-mail filter that checks whether incoming e-mails might be spam or not to ease the burden of users. This task is carried out using a predefined set of rules. Spam messages are sent to a specific folder called "Spam". However, there is no definite way to define spam. Therefore, e-mails in this folder must be looked through before deleting. The use of e-mailing lists can be perceived as spam, and it is important to think about the relevance of the e-mail before sending it. The e-mail address represents the agency and thus affects the agency's reputation.

General Content: Every staff receives an e-mail account according to the standard firstname.lastname@[agency].se. If there is more than one employee with the same first and last name, the first letter of the middle name will be used by the firstname.a.lastname@[agency].se.

Concept: Confidential information is information that is made available to authorized individuals only.

Supplementary Source: -

5.2 Two Tailored Information Security Policies

In this part of the demonstration, we have created two tailormade ISPs based on elicited policy components. Since the organization does not have tailormade ISPs today, this demonstration shows what such a design would potentially look like. In Fig. 2, we use an object diagram to illustrate the two ISPs and parts of their content. Due to space limitations, we only show three policy components of each ISP. Still, it is enough to illustrate the basic principle of how the selection of policy components enables tailoring of ISPs and illustrates how the same policy component can be reused across multiple ISPs. As it is shown in Fig. 2, the two ISPs target different roles. The uppermost ISP targets the project coordinator role, and the lowermost ISP targets the finance officer role. We have intentionally chosen two roles where it is reasonable to assume that they do not share many tasks in their day-to-day work.

Starting to the left in both object diagrams, we find the policy component we elicited above, the Managing e-mails-component. In the original ISP, these regulations targeted all employees. Therefore, this policy component is included in both ISPs and shared across both roles. Next, we find policy components that are unique for each role, targeting access to specific information systems. In the uppermost ISP, we find a policy component about accessing the organization's project management system. Project coordinators use this system to carry out day-to-day tasks. However, finance officers do not use this system. Therefore, these regulations are not relevant to include in the ISP targeting financial officers. Instead, we have selected a policy component about accessing the financial management system, which manages the finances of the organization. It is an information system that the financial officers work with daily. This example shows how the difference in tasks is used to tailor the selection of policy components included in the ISPs. Finally, rightmost in each object diagram in Fig. 2, we find a policy component shared across both ISPs. It targets how to access the organization's information assets remotely. The policy component includes instructions on how to use the virtual private network software. This policy component is relevant for both exemplified roles and is necessary when accessing both the project management system and the financial system from a remote location. Thus, this shows that policy components can be included in the ISP to support other policy components.

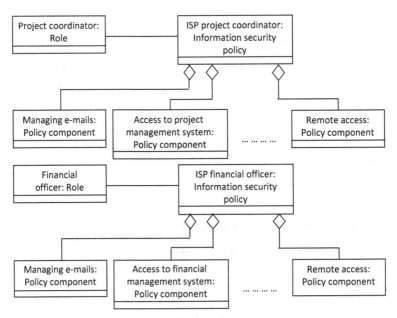

Fig. 2. Object diagram of two tailored information security policies

6   Conclusion and Future Research

The proposed conceptual model can act as a foundation for developing software to design tailorable ISPs, which is also the next step of our larger research endeavor. As it was said in Sect. 2, having software for designing ISPs has received limited attention from researchers [14]. Our model can therefore be considered as one step towards developing a software that aids information security managers in designing modularized and tailorable ISPs. More concretely, the model directly addresses the two software requirements about tailoring of ISPs presented by [13]. In addition, we indirectly address an additional seven software requirements about ISP design in [13] in our design of the policy component concept, requirements that are impacted by a tailorable design.

A limitation of our conceptual model is that we analyzed three ISPs from public agencies and used an additional 20 ISPs from public agencies for validation. Consequently, during our design work we focused on public agencies and did not use any ISPs from companies, and all the ISPs were from Swedish organizations. Consequnetly, we have not addressed any differences in ISP design across industry sectors and countries. It means that the design could be context-bound, making it interesting to further demonstrate and evaluate the model using ISPs from other industry sectors and countries.

References

1. Dhillon, G.: Information Security - Text & Cases Prospect Press, Burlington (2017)
2. Whitman, M.E.: Security policy - from design to maintenance. In: Straub, D.W., Goodman, S., Baskerville, R. (eds.) Information Security - Policy, Processes, and Practices, pp. 123–151. M E Sharpe, New York (2008)
3. PwC: The information security breaches survey - Technical report. Department for Business, Innovation and Skills (BIS) (2014)
4. PwC: The Global State of Information Security Survey 2018. PriceWaterhouseCoopers (2018)
5. ENISA: ENISA Threat Landscape 2014. Overview of current and emerging cyber-threats. European Union Agency for Network and Information Security (2014)
6. Karlsson, F., Hedström, K., Goldkuhl, G.: Practice-based discourse analysis of information security policies. Comput. Secur. **67**(June 2017), 267–279 (2017)
7. Stahl, B.C., Doherty, N.F., Shaw, M.: Information security policies in the UK healthcare sector: a critical evaluation. Inf. Syst. J. **22**, 77–94 (2012)
8. Rostami, E.: Tailoring policies and involving users in constructing security policies: a mapping study. In: Furnell, S., Clarke, N.L. (eds.) Proceedings of Thirteenth International Symposium on Human Aspects of Information Security & Assurance, HAISA 2019, Nicosia, Cyprus, 15–16 July 2019, pp. 1–11. University of Plymouth, Plymouth (2019)
9. Cosic, Z., Boban, M.: Information security management—defining approaches to Information Security policies in ISMS. In: IEEE 8th International Symposium on Intelligent Systems and Informatics, pp. 83–85. IEEE (2010)
10. Kinnunen, H., Siponen, M.T.: Developing organization-specific information security policies. In: PACIS 2018, pp. 1–13 (2018)
11. Coertze, J., von Solms, R.: A software gateway to affordable and effective information security governance in SMMEs. In: 2013 Information Security for South Africa, pp. 1–8. IEEE (2013)
12. Syamsuddin, I., Hwang, J.: The use of AHP in security policy decision making: an Open Office Calc application. J. Softw. **5**(10), 1162–1169 (2010)
13. Rostami, E., Karlsson, F., Shang, G.: Requirements for computerized tools to design information security policies. Comput. Secur. **99**(December 2020), Article number 102063 (2020)
14. Rostami, E., Karlsson, F., Kolkowska, E.: The hunt for computerized support in information security policy management: a literature review. Inf. Comput. Secur. **28**(2), 215–259 (2020)
15. Vermeulen, C., von Solms, R.: The information security management toolbox - taking the pain out of security management. Inf. Manag. Comput. Secur. **10**(3), 119–125 (2002)
16. Coertze, J., van Niekerk, J., von Solms, R.: A web-based information security management toolbox for small-to-medium enterprises in Southern Africa. In: Venter, H.S., Coetzee, M., Loock, M. (eds.) 2011 Information Security for South Africa (ISSA 2011), Johannesburg, South Africa, pp. 1–8. IEEE (2011)

17. Hoppe, O.A., van Niekerk, J., von Solms, R.: The effective implementation of information security in organizations. In: Ghonaimy, M.A., El-Hadidi, M.T., Aslan, H.K. (eds.) Security in the Information Society - Visions and Perspective, pp. 1–18. Springer, Boston (2002). https://doi.org/10.1007/978-0-387-35586-3_1

18. Coertze, J., von Solms, R.: A model for information security governance in developing countries. In: Jonas, K., Rai, I.A., Tchuente, M. (eds.) AFRICOMM 2012. LNICSSITE, vol. 119, pp. 279–288. Springer, Heidelberg (2013). https://doi.org/10.1007/978-3-642-41178-6_29

19. Ismail, W.B.W., Widyarto, S.A.: Formulation and development process of information security policy in higher education. In: 1st International Conference on Engineering Technology and Applied Sciences, Afyonkarahisar, Turkey (2016)

20. Flowerday, S.V., Tuyikeze, T.: Information security policy development and implementation: the what, how and who. Comput. Secur. **61**, 169–183 (2016)

21. Peffers, K., Tuunanen, T., Rothenberger, M.A., Chatterjee, S.: A design science research methodology for information systems research. J. Manag. Inf. Syst. **24**(3), 45–77 (2007)

22. Glaser, B.G., Strauss, A.L.: The Discovery of Grounded Theory: Strategies for Qualitative Research. Aldine, New York (1967)

23. Nunamaker, J.F., Briggs, R.O.: Toward a broader vision for information systems. ACM Trans. Manag. Inf. Syst. **2**(4), Article 20 (2011)

24. Hedström, K., Kolkowska, E., Karlsson, F., Allen, J.P.: Value conflicts for information security management. J. Strat. Inf. Syst. **20**(4), 373–384 (2011)

25. Davis, G.B., Olson, M.H.: Management Information Systems: Conceptual Foundations, Structure, and Development. McGraw-Hill, Inc., New York (1985)

26. D'Arcy, J.D., Devaraj, S.: Employee misuse of information technology resources: testing a contemporary deterrence model. Decis. Sci. J. **43**(6), 1091–1124 (2012)

27. Buthelezi, M.P., Van der Poll, J.A., Ochala, E.O.: Ambiguity as a barrier to information security policy compliance: a content analysis. In: International Conference on Computational Science and Computational Intelligence 2016, Las Vegas, NV, USA, pp. 1361–1367. IEEE (2016)

28. ISO: ISO/IEC 27000:2014, Information technology—Security techniques—Information security management systems—Overview and vocabulary. International Organization for Standardization (ISO) (2014)

29. Tuyikeze, T., Flowerday, S.: Information security policy development and implementation: a content analysis approach. In: HAISA 2014, pp. 11–20 (2014)

30. Höne, K., Eloff, J.H.P.: Information security policy – what do international information security standards say? Comput. Secur. **21**(5), 402–409 (2002)

Security Fatigue: A Case Study of Data Specialists

Anusha Bhana[1] and Jacques Ophoff[1,2(✉)] [ID]

[1] University of Cape Town, Cape Town, South Africa
BHNANU002@myuct.ac.za
[2] Abertay University, Dundee, UK
j.ophoff@abertay.ac.uk

Abstract. Due to the number of data breaches occurring worldwide there is increasing vigilance regarding information security. Organisations employ a variety of technical, formal, and informal security controls but also rely on employees to safeguard information assets. This relies heavily on compliance and constantly challenges employees with security-related tasks. Security compliance behaviour is a finite resource and when employees engage in cost-benefit analyses that extend tolerance thresholds, security fatigue may set in. Security fatigue has been described as a despondency and weariness to experience any further security tasks. This study used a case study approach to investigate employee security fatigue, focusing on data specialists. Primary data was collected through semi-structured interviews with 12 data specialists in a large financial services company. A thematic analysis of the data revealed several interlinked themes that evidence security fatigue. Awareness and understanding of these themes can help organisations to monitor for this and tailor security activities, such as security education, training, and awareness for increased effectiveness.

Keywords: Information security · Security fatigue · Data specialist

1 Introduction

Employees can be seen as barriers but also facilitators of information security. However, creating a security-minded workforce is a persistent challenge. When organisations place policies and procedures at the forefront of their security efforts this can have a negative impact on employees. In such environments employees often face an array of complex security requirements which are difficult to understand and satisfy [7]. Such potentially unrealistic demands may even lead to experienced employees, with good technical skills, struggling to keep up.

Confronted with security-related workload and cognitive demand an employee may experience increased psychological stress, leading to a chronic state of exhaustion [5]. Furthermore, this exhaustion is a core component of

N. Clarke and S. Furnell (Eds.): HAISA 2022, IFIP AICT 658, pp. 275–284, 2022.
https://doi.org/10.1007/978-3-031-12172-2_22

fatigue. Faced with information security stress and fatigue, employees may start to use coping behaviours. These behaviours are often analysed in the context of behavioural frameworks [6,7].

It is also argued that fatigue can lead to employees constantly performing cost-benefit calculations, choosing to accept certain risks to achieve important work goals [15]. If countermeasures are implemented to reduce employees' risky behaviours this can lead to a vicious circle: security policies and procedures → employee fatigue → risky behaviour is displayed → additional policies and procedures, etc. [10]. Wilde [18] suggests employees will weigh the expected benefits of risky behaviour against the costs and determine the level of risk they are willing to accept.

This study explores how security fatigue manifests and affects employees with increased responsibility for sensitive information. In particular the focus is on data specialists, who transform raw data into information. Understanding these factors could assist organisations in creating 'employee-friendly' policies and procedures, choosing appropriate technical security solutions or tailoring security education, training, and awareness activities. This study follows a case study approach, focusing on data specialists in a large financial services company. Primary data is collected through semi-structured interviews with 12 participants and analysed using thematic analysis.

The rest of the paper is structured as follows. First, a literature review provides contextual background on security fatigue and related concepts. This is followed by a description of the research design, including the case organisation and participants. Thereafter the results of the thematic analysis and findings are presented. Finally, the paper concludes by discussing the limitations of this study, along with opportunities for further research.

2   Literature Review

Employees are regularly reminded about security, for example with daily messages to be cautious while performing any online activity. This hyper vigilance can have a potentially detrimental impact on the individual, resulting in a level of despondency. Over time this manifests as weariness and in this context is described as information security fatigue. According to Furnell [8, p. 1], "The term security fatigue recognizes the situation in which users of systems and staff in organizations can tire of dealing with security or encountering messages and warnings in relation to it."

Although fatigue cannot be empirically measured it may be expressed through several factors, such as effort, difficulty, and importance. Effort is described as the energy spent to achieve compliance. Difficulty describes the quantity of energy expended to provide the required effort. Importance is the priority assigned to the compliance task [9]. While fatigue is not a new construct, the appearance of security fatigue has increased in prominence.

Furnell and Thomson [9] describe this as breaching a threshold; becoming weary and desensitised, where compliance becomes too difficult and burdensome. This is the point security fatigue sets in. Stanton et al. [16] describe fatigue as a reluctance to see or experience any more of something. Security fatigue is one cost that users experience when facing constant security messages, advice, and demands for compliance. This cost often results in what security experts might consider less secure online behaviour. Hatashima et al. [10] describe fatigue as a human experience when faced with multiple external actions to mitigate security risk.

2.1 Security Complexity and Fatigue

Security fatigue may manifest in a number of ways. Frequent security decisions, information overload, complexity, and uncertainty may lead to employee stress and consequent information security policy violations [6]. Oto [13] proposes that employees will simply stop making unnecessary decisions. Should they choose to make a decision, it will be the simplest option driven by immediate needs. This irrational behaviour is driven by feeling a lack of control and general apathy, which potentially increases stress.

Internal and external stressors deplete cognitive resources triggering fatigue. Security-related stress includes innocuous and common stressors, such as repetitive security tasks, but also more serious events such as security breaches. Events particularly intensifying fatigue are unclear security tasks and requirements contrary to job expectations. Stress and emotional reactions have been shown as predictors of information security policy compliance [7]. Failure by employees to adhere to such policies can cause security risks to the organisation. It is argued that when employees are overwhelmed by security messages and exhausted with the effort required to keep information safe, they are likely to ignore concerns raised by the organisation [2].

2.2 Managing Security Fatigue

To protect information and systems organisations implement measures such as security policies and procedures, as well as security education, training, and awareness to encourage employees to adhere to security practices [14]. To understand the extent of adherence Beautement et al. [2] introduced the concept of a compliance budget, to be used as one would a financial budget. Here the costs and benefits of security compliance are managed and understood. This constant iterative process takes its toll on the user resulting in the depletion of their compliance budget and security fatigue setting in. However, it is likely that security compliance is a much more complicated phenomenon, stemming from the lived experiences of individuals [12]. Shared viewpoints about security compliance may exist amongst employees, which need to be understood to effectively manage security fatigue.

3   Research Design

The core of this study is to explore the human experience. The study of security fatigue and risk tolerance are human experiences and are therefore well-suited to an interpretivist paradigm. Taylor et al. [17] state that an interpretivist paradigm aims to understand how the world is experienced through an individual's lens. This creates a personal reality, often driven by the desire to understand social phenomena through forming meaningful ideas, feelings, and emotions.

To develop a thorough understanding of the topic a case study approach was adopted. The case in this instance refers to a group of employees within an organisation where the topic was studied. Yin [19] advocates for this strategy when the researcher has no control over the behavioural events and the focus is contemporary.

3.1 Case Organisation and Participants

Alohali et al. [1] notes data management as a key component in information security. With the introduction of data protection legislation covering most countries across the world, there is an increased focus on ensuring information security and legal compliance. To comply with legislation organisations must adhere to strict security protocols and processes. This responsibility may weigh heavily on data specialists and increases the stress placed on those working with sensitive information.

The case organisation is a large financial services company based in South Africa, with a footprint in the rest of Africa. Leveraging information as an asset has increased in strategic importance for the organisation, and there is core team of dedicated specialists supporting the data function. Key positions were created to drive this initiative, such as Head of Data, Head of Data Governance, and Head of Data Acquisition. Another significant appointment was the first Chief Information Security Officer (CISO). Alongside this appointment the information security community in the organisation has grown, focusing efforts on ensuring information security compliance. This is a multi-faceted approach which include security awareness campaigns. With the increased pressure for organisational legislative compliance employees are fully aware of information security requirements. The organisation is thus relevant, both in terms of processing large volumes of sensitive information as well as implementing strict security protocols that could lead to employee security fatigue.

Participants in this study represented both technical and business roles, such as Database Administrator, IT Manager, Senior Analyst Programmer, Senior BI Developer, Data Engineer, (Senior) Business Analyst, and BI Manager. Participants included nine males and three females, and had extensive experience in mid- to senior-specialist roles.

3.2 Data Collection and Analysis

A purposive sampling technique was used to target employees in various data specialist roles with a propensity to experience security fatigue. This approach is often employed when working with a small sample (as in case study research) and allows the researcher to choose cases that are particularly interesting and informative. For this study semi-structured interviews were conducted with 12 participants. Interviews followed a consistent format to ensure repeatability across the study [19].

Thematic analysis was used to analyse the interview data. Prior to analysis the recorded interviews were transcribed and captured in the NVivo computer-assisted qualitative data analysis software. Care was taken to ensure the data was fully anonymised and appropriately stored for analysis. Thematic analysis followed the six-step approach recommended by Braun and Clarke [4], which allowed the discovery of themes and patterns in the data.

4   Analysis and Findings

This section presents four general themes that emerged from the thematic analysis, which include: awareness of risks to sensitive information; the influence of compliance effort with security requirements; the influence of psychological stress; and, the adequacy of knowledge.

4.1   Awareness of Risks

The participants have access to highly confidential information, including customer banking details, income details, medical history, and contact information. When asked about the level of comfort they have with access to such information, the general feeling is one of ease. Participants appeared desensitised to the highly sensitive nature of the information they have access to. They are familiar with the information and do not perceive any risks in having access to it.

A level of unease sets in when participants are called upon to share this information with other parties. Being unfamiliar with the recipient and process increases tension and stress. When asked about sharing information participants do not display a similar confidence as when the information is within their domain of control. Concerning any new situation which is unfamiliar, P4 stated: *"But something new, I don't know how to handle it or the polices and controls around it, then may be I would panic..."*

The severity of any data breach originating in the area where these participants work is extremely high. While participants take on the responsibility to secure information there is a growing concern about data breaches. P12 stated: *"We deal with data, the value of data, we know what happens if a data breach happens. So here it's me who really understands what happens if we have a data breech. It's my responsibility to make sure that the organisation has proper standards and ensure execution to make sure the data is secure."* Most participants had an opinion on how information security should be managed, because while policies are in place, there is no clear guidance on how to execute this, which leads to frustration. P6 explained: *"In terms of actually securing data they haven't specifically given us tools to do so."* Data specialists often created awareness themselves, as P2 explained: *"... we try to enforce and create awareness in our team because we are the ones sitting with most of the data in the organisation."*

Summary of the Awareness of Risks to Sensitive Information. While the task of managing information should be routine to the participants, the increased security consciousness in the organisation has left participants fearful and unsure whether security processes are sufficiently followed. Participants value security and want to do the right thing but perceived a lack of clear guidance, standards, and tools, which increased security fatigue.

4.2 Influence of Compliance Effort

Compliance effort is the energy spent in fulfilling security requirements. This is associated with a cost-benefit analysis, where employees will weigh up the benefits of complying versus the costs of non-compliance. Participants' compliance effort were viewed in the context of: decisions driven by immediate necessity, the use of practical password practices, and choosing the user-friendly option.

Decisions Driven by Necessity. All participants displayed a high commitment to complying with security protocols. As custodians of information, they are fully aware of the need for compliance, but when security related tasks become burdensome and a barrier to their productivity, participants will forego compliance in favour of progressing efforts to achieve goals. For example, P1 admitted to making use of another employee's account to gain access to systems. The security process to get access in the organisation is not efficient, requiring layers of paperwork and approvals. P3 explained that tasks are often abandoned after attempting to log into a system "... *because it is such a mission to go and email them [IT] and wait for it.*"

While access can be circumvented, or in some cases abandoned, the sharing of sensitive information via email is a decision taken regardless of the punitive measures the employee is likely to face if there is a data breach. P2 explained: "*We still had reports with ID numbers ... emailing data is part of the norm, however password protecting it is something that we changed.*" Participants are aware of information security compliance regulation and agreed knowing the POPIA regulation to some degree. However, they often choose to share unsecured sensitive information to ensure business continuity.

Practical Password Practices and Choosing the User-Friendly Option. It was noted that the organization has multiple layers of security. Employees must navigate both physical security measures and systems with multi-factor authentication and other security measures. When questioned about password creation and management participants revealed a few mechanisms employed to reduce cognitive demand. This includes repeating passwords, keeping password creation to the minimum system requirement and keeping a written copy of passwords. For example, P5 used the minimum system requirements to create passwords, with the rationale that the administrators believe this is as stringent as they require the password to be to access the system. P11 provided insight into the rationale as to why keeping simple password algorithms work: "*Having a* *login profile and a password for so many devices and applications is very painful and to remember all of them is a nightmare ...that's why I keep it simple and I do remember."* When questioned about the use of biometrics all participants agreed it would be a welcome and safer alternative, despite representing yet another technology solution.

Summary of the Influence of Compliance Effort with Security Requirements. Compliance is a choice and organisational security goals are secondary when employees primary focus is their delivery of tasks and responsibilities [2]. In the participant group of data specialists, who have the responsibility to manage information assets in the organisation, the effort required to comply with security requirements can become unmanageable. Participants are driven by need and will forego tasks impeding their work. Employees are inadvertently worn down by the energy spent in constant cost-benefit analysis. Compliance is taxing and users become weary, resulting in them choosing less secure behaviour to reduce cognitive overload. Thus there is a strong preference for security solutions which would reduce effort on their part.

4.3   Influence of Psychological Stress

Employees are constantly faced with messages to be safe online and be vigilant about potential cyber attacks. Participants noted how this leads to increased anxiety and a sense of resignation.

Increased Anxiety. Participants expressed feelings of panic, fear of getting into trouble, and fear of being hacked when faced with complex security requirements. The demographic of participants who displayed a high degree of stress are those that are older or experienced security incidents. This led to participants expressing frustration at the organisation. For example, P11 believed the organisation should deal with security related issues and stated: *"So I try my best to keep myself secured but I don't feel like I should be the one to make it secure. I feel that the system or the application should have enough security built in to keep me secure. Why must I do that effort? I feel like the company that created the thing should build in security for my purpose."*

Sense of Resignation. The IT security division in the organisation applies strict user access protocols which can be cumbersome to navigate. Failing a security check sometimes led to the abandonment of tasks, as P3 illustrated: *"I put in my details, well the password, incorrect firstly. Then I tried to reset it and it said to contact the system administrator or something like that. And that was at the first try. It wasn't like we give you a temp password or whatever."* Thus a general sense of resigned frustration could be perceived. While P11 expressed frustration, there is an understanding that the process is in place to mitigate risk: *"I locked myself out of my machine and I couldn't get in ...I will sort* *it out because it will bother me."* Thus employees nevertheless seem to take responsibility for security.

Summary of the Influence of Psychological Stress. The organisation has elevated security to its highest priority and in doing so created a sense of earnestness among the participants. As a result they displayed increased anxiety. As reported in literature, employees are overwhelmed with security requirements and are often not allowed to assimilate these highly complex processes into their frame of reference and work routines [7]. There has not been any clear guidelines from notable authorities on how employees should deal with security-related matters and in the face of the insurmountable effort required on their part, the employee simply gives up. This sense of resignation created a feeling among employees that security is enforced using a dictatorial approach.

4.4   Adequacy of Knowledge

Since the appointment of the CISO the organisation has radically increased security awareness drives. The awareness activities are designed to improve security consciousness across the organisation. Participants highlighted several issues with ineffective security awareness activities, as well as the adoption of new technologies.

Ineffective Security Awareness Activities. Participants claimed to be overwhelmed with the frequency and duration of awareness activities. For example, P9 believed there were too many phishing exercises trying to catch out employees. The time to complete awareness activities could take up to six hours every month, which involved completing online courses and questionnaires. The organisation has been quite unforgiving when it comes to completing these courses, with P7 explaining that access would be removed if employees had not completed security awareness assessments by a stated date. In an environment driven by deadlines this becomes an overload on the employee.

The effectiveness of these activities were questioned by several participants. For example, P11 stated that the activities failed to communicate details on material changes to effectively ease security concerns and *"it doesn't make you want to be more secure ... they [IT] just say you need to do this and the onus is on you only, they just put all the load on the user."* From the perspective of P12 all the activities were grounded in theory but do not offer any substantial guidance to execute on them. The consensus was that awareness activities were often no more than an academic exercise, with P3 summarising: *"Yes we have all the IT security modules but are we just ticking boxes?"*

New Technology Concerns. When questioned about new technologies, and specifically cloud-based technologies, participants perceived security risks. P11 voiced reservations and questioned how secure it would be: *"I would be very* *worried because I don't know how secure that is and how easy that would be for someone to hack."* Participants welcomed and accepted the use of cloud-based technologies, provided the information stored is not sensitive. Regarding sensitive information all participants expressed concerns. Based on their experience participants foresee potential risks they are exposed to in the cloud. P2 worried about placing information in the cloud: *"I worry who is going to be able to access it. What is their intent ... at the end of the day I am not able to control that information."* The perceived risks and lack of control inherent in cloud computing is a concern among the participants. However, P12 believed that conducting adequate risk assessments would be vital for storing information in the cloud.

Summary of the Adequacy of Knowledge. The level of an individual's awareness and knowledge influences behaviour [11]. When organisational security awareness activities do not have the desired effect, employees are not empowered with the necessary skills to perform their tasks. Gaining compliance through awareness activities demand effort and skill, but it left the participants despondent with no desire to comply. In addition, the adoption of new technologies challenge employees to willfully increase their level of knowledge to avert security incidents. This requires considerable effort which can lead to security fatigue.

5 Conclusion

Employees experience higher levels of frustration and fatigue as demands are placed on them to maintain secure environments and to guard against security breaches. Understanding such phenomena provide important insight into the context within which employees operate, providing opportunities to improve human-centred security. This study looked at an emerging construct, namely security fatigue. Security compliant behaviour is a multi-faceted and complex construct, and this research argues that fatigue is an important consideration. This is especially true for roles that deal with sensitive information and a low tolerance for risk. While security fatigue is not readily recognisable, this study identified several themes that contribute to the phenomena. Despite having an awareness of risks to sensitive information, employees can face challenges such as compliance effort with security requirements, increased psychological stress, and doubts of the adequacy of their knowledge. While these are not new concepts, there are behavioural characteristics within these concepts that describe patterns of security fatigue. This study highlights the need to understand the role security fatigue plays in security compliance and in harmonising risk.

This study focused on a very specific population and not all participants showed acute signs of security fatigue. This can be seen as a possible limitation but also an opportunity for further research. This study focuses on the experience of data specialists within a specific organisation, but it is likely that their experiences are mirrored in other roles and organisations.

Acknowledgements. This work is based on the research supported wholly/in part by the National Research Foundation of South Africa (Grant Numbers 114838) [3].

References

1. Alohali, M., Clarke, N., Li, F., Furnell, S.: Identifying and predicting the factors affecting end-users' risk-taking behavior. Inf. Comput. Secur. **26**(3), 306–326 (2018)
2. Beautement, A., Sasse, A., Wonham, M.: The compliance budget: managing security behaviour in organisations. In: Proceedings of the 2008 New Security Paradigms Workshop, pp. 47–58 (2008)
3. Bhana, A.: Security fatigue factors influencing risk tolerance among data specialists [Unpublished manuscript]. Department of Information Systems, University of Cape Town, South Africa (2019)
4. Braun, V., Clarke, V.: Using thematic analysis in psychology. Qual. Res. Psychol. **3**(2), 77–101 (2006)
5. Choi, H., Park, J., Jung, Y.: The role of privacy fatigue in online privacy behavior. Comput. Hum. Behav. **81**, 42–51 (2018)
6. D'Arcy, J., Herath, T., Shoss, M.: Understanding employee responses to stressful information security requirements: a coping perspective. J. Manag. Inf. Syst. **31**(2), 285–318 (2014)
7. D'Arcy, J., Teh, P.L.: Predicting employee information security policy compliance on a daily basis: the interplay of security-related stress, emotions, and neutralization. Inf. Manag. **56**(7), 103–151 (2019)
8. Furnell, S.: Security fatigue. In: Jajodia, S., Samarati, P., Yung, M. (eds.) Encyclopedia of Cryptography, Security and Privacy, pp. 1–5. Springer, Heidelberg (2019). https://doi.org/10.1007/978-3-642-27739-9_1591-1
9. Furnell, S., Thomson, K.L.: Recognising and addressing 'security fatigue'. Comput. Fraud Secur. **2009**(11), 7–11 (2009)
10. Hatashima, T., et al.: Evaluation of the effectiveness of risk assessment and security fatigue visualization model for internal E-crime. In: 2018 IEEE 42nd Annual Computer Software and Applications Conference, vol. 2, pp. 707–712 (2018)
11. Ogutcu, G., Testik, O.M., Chouseinoglou, O.: Analysis of personal information security behavior and awareness. Comput. Secur. **56**, 83–93 (2016)
12. Ophoff, J., Renaud, K.: Revealing the cyber security non-compliance "Attribution Gulf". In: Proceedings of the 54th Hawaii International Conference on System Sciences, pp. 4557–4566 (2021)
13. Oto, B.: When thinking is hard: managing decision fatigue. EMS World **41**(5), 46–50 (2012). https://www.hmpglobalearningnetwork.com/site/emsworld/article/10687160/when-thinking-hard-managing-decision-fatigue
14. Pham, H., Brennan, L., Furnell, S.: Information security burnout: identification of sources and mitigating factors from security demands and resources. J. Inf. Secur. Appl. **46**, 96–107 (2019)
15. Sasse, A.: Scaring and bullying people into security won't work. IEEE Secur. Priv. **13**(3), 80–83 (2015)
16. Stanton, B., Theofanos, M., Prettyman, S., Furman, S.: Security fatigue. IT Prof. **18**(5), 26–32 (2016)
17. Taylor, S., Bogdan, R., DeVault, M.: Introduction to Qualitative Research Methods: A Guidebook and Resource, 4th edn. Wiley, Hoboken (2016)
18. Wilde, G.: Risk homeostasis theory: an overview. Inj. Prev. **4**(2), 89–91 (1998)
19. Yin, R.: Case Study Research and Applications: Design and Methods, 6th edn. SAGE Publications Inc. (2018)

Factors Influencing Cybercrime Reporting Behaviour in South African State-Owned Entities

Karabo Pilane, Zainab Ruhwanya$^{(\boxtimes)}$, and Irwin Brown

University of Cape Town, Cape Town, South Africa
plnlet001@myuct.ac.za, {zainab.ruhwanya,irwin.brown}@uct.ac.za

Abstract. Cybercrime may destabilise organisations and society due to the social, financial, emotional, psychological, and physical impacts. The purpose of this paper was to investigate cybercrime reporting behaviour and the factors that influence it. South African state-owned entities were the focus of attention given their strategic role, which requires that attention be given to improving their cybersecurity practices, such as cybercrime reporting in an increasingly digital society. The conceptual framework was developed using themes from the cybercrime literature, and the Theory of Planned Behaviour (TPB) as a lens. The study used a quantitative method, and data was collected online using a questionnaire survey. One hundred and three complete responses were received from employees working in South African state-owned entities. Factors that were identified as influencing cybercrime reporting behaviour were self-efficacy and facilitating conditions.

Keywords: Cybercrime · Cybercrime reporting · Reporting behaviours · South Africa

1 Introduction

Many terms such as computer crime, digital crime, internet crime, e-crime (electronic crime), hi-tech crime (high technology), online crime, etc., are synonymous with cybercrime. Cybercrime is defined as a crime that utilises computing devices, including smartphones, wearable technology devices, and many others, to defraud, steal, harass, and destroy the property of society [4]. Similarly, cybercrime can be defined as an illegal activity executed through the cyberinfrastructure (computer, mobile device, smartphone, supervisory control, and data acquisition systems, etc.) or the internet to compromise confidentiality, integrity, availability, and privacy of the data in the cyberinfrastructure [20, 37, 44]. Cybercrime may evolve as cybercriminals become more sophisticated using the high speed of technological innovation [5, 19]. Recent technological innovations include bitcoin, drones, blockchain, cloud systems, and augmented reality [20]. The Internet Live Stats [29] indicates that there are more than five billion Internet users, whilst the number of Facebook users has breached the three billion mark. It is, therefore, unsurprising that cybercrime is committed through the Internet infrastructure [16].

© IFIP International Federation for Information Processing 2022
Published by Springer Nature Switzerland AG 2022
N. Clarke and S. Furnell (Eds.): HAISA 2022, IFIP AICT 658, pp. 285–299, 2022.
https://doi.org/10.1007/978-3-031-12172-2_23

Many cases of identity theft, financial theft, phishing, ransomware, cyber-bullying, cyber-stalking, information privacy violations, zero-day attacks, and online surveillance [4, 25, 44] remain underreported [52]. The law enforcement resources are allocated based on reported crimes [12]. Therefore, underreporting of cybercrime makes the work of law enforcement agencies difficult to manage. Reporting cybercrime may help reduce cybercrime to acceptable levels [33] and restore confidence in law enforcement agencies [12]. At the same time, it is worrying that many companies or institutions may not report cybercrime even though required by law to do so [47]. It is possible that internet users will be confronted with cybercrime victimisation linked to cybercrime reporting [18]. Therefore, cybercrime reporting may amplify or diminish cybercrime victimisation [1].

Cybercrime reporting to law enforcement agencies by cybercrime victims is a serious challenge [40, 52]. Cybercrime victims may not share their experiences with family, friends, and colleagues [18], therefore, not receive support from their social environment. Lack of knowledge of cybercrime amongst colleagues, friends, and family does not assist in escalating or reporting cybercrime incidents experienced by a cybercrime victim to a law enforcement agency. In addition, a cybercrime victim's friends, colleagues, and family may influence cybercrime victims not to report cybercrime [33]. Investigation of cybercrime reporting to law enforcement agencies is hence worthy of research attention [33, 52].

The 2021 Internet Crime report [22] notes that South Africa is ranked 6th out of the top 20 international cybercrime victims. There are negative cybercrime trends in South Africa due to poor public knowledge of cyber threats and poor cybercrime legislation [38]. This study will examine South African state-owned entities, given their strategic nature and the recent cyber-attack incidents aimed at these institutions. The research question is thus: *What factors explain employee cybercrime reporting behaviour in South African state-owned entities?*

The research article is structured as follows. Section 2 reviews the academic literature to identify factors of influence and to propose hypotheses. Section 3 discusses the research methodology adopted, while Sect. 4 delves into findings, analysis, discussion, and implications of the study. Section 5 is the research conclusion, inclusive of ideas for future research.

2 Conceptual Background and Hypotheses Development

2.1 Perceptions of Law Enforcement Agencies

Perceptions of Law Enforcement Agencies (LEA) competence may play a role in whether cybercrime is reported or not. These perceptions may arise from LEA's inexperience with cybercrime; the inability of LEA to stay up to date with technologies being used by cybercriminals, the perceived inability of LEA to solve cybercrime, and the lack of collaboration between LEA and industry [14, 34]. Furthermore, where society feels that there will be no consequence after reporting a crime, there will be less likelihood of reporting. Perceptions of cybercrime victims or potential cybercrime victims about LEA competence hence influence cybercrime reporting behaviour [8, 14, 34]. The hypothesis supported is.

H1: Perceptions of law enforcement agencies competence influence employee cybercrime reporting behaviour.

2.2 Emotional Response to Cybercrime

The emotional response is identified as influencing cybercrime reporting behaviour by cybercrime victims and potential cybercrime victims [52]. Emotional responses include a sense of hopelessness that nothing will be done about the cybercrime if the cybercrime is not deemed serious enough [23]. Other emotional responses include guilt, shame, stress, depression, the stigma associated with cybercrime, isolation caused by cybercrime, the fear of disclosure of cybercrime, and fear that they (cybercrime victims) will not be believed [12, 17]. Some emotional responses can be credited as positive influences on cybercrime reporting behaviour, while others may have a negative influence [21, 39]. The hypothesis supported is:

H2: Emotional response influences employee cybercrime reporting behaviour.

2.3 Cybercrime Reporting Awareness

Cybercrime victims may not know or not be aware that cybercrime has occurred in their digital or network environments and that they are compromised [12]. As a result of not knowing or not being aware of what transpired in their digital spaces, cybercrime victims may not report cybercrime to law enforcement agencies (LEA) or relevant authorities and, therefore, not receive support [23]. The cybercrime victims' lack of awareness of cybercrime may influence cybercrime reporting behaviour [48]. In addition, victims of cybercrime may not know or not be aware of whom to report the cybercrime to [17].

The challenge of reporting cybercrime behaviour may be due to cybercrime's transnational nature, which may be unknown to victims [15, 19, 31, 33, 39]. This may leave the cybercrime victim helpless, exacerbating the cybercrime victimisation problem [18] due to no contact between the cybercrime victim and the cybercriminal.

Equally important is that cybercriminals may make use of the dark web using anonymity tools such as the Tor browser, virtual private networks, and secure socket layer encryption to perform illegal and illicit online activities [30]. The illegal activities against potential cybercrime victims in underground markets may include the use of malware, viruses, worms, ransomware, denial of service, and distributed denial of service attacks. Other illegal services may include trading in stolen bank card PINs (Personal Identification Numbers) for debit and credit cards. Online anonymity influences reporting of cybercrime behaviour because victims do not know the identity of their attackers [17, 33, 52]. Bell, Roger and Pierce [10] claim that intention to report cybercrime may be positively influenced by awareness among employees of an organisation's cybercrime reporting mechanisms. The hypothesis supported is:

H3: Cybercrime awareness influences employee cybercrime reporting behaviour.

2.4 The Cost-Benefit of Cybercrime Reporting

Cybercrime reporting behaviour by cybercrime victims or potential cybercrime victims is based on assessing the expected benefit versus the cost of cybercrime reporting

[52]. Benefits may be in the form of financial compensation as an incentive for reporting cybercrime [32], insurance pay-outs, or prosecution and arrest of cybercriminals. Organisations may not report cybercrime incidents to law enforcement agencies if they anticipate reputational damage that may trigger a loss of customers and resultant revenue drops [36, 47]. It may also be cost-effective for cybercrime victims to report online [52]. The hypothesis supported is:

H4: Cost-benefit analysis influences employee cybercrime reporting behaviour.

2.5   Organisational Subjective Norm

Subjective norms refer to social pressures or peer influence on whether to perform a particular behaviour (e.g. cybercrime reporting behaviour) [3, 27]. Subjective norm plays an important role in cybercrime reporting [33]. The organisation may assume that reporting cybercrime will not lead to the arrest of cybercriminals [14]. The organisation and its subjective norms are pivotal in cyber peacekeeping through cybercrime reporting [41]. A lack of positive organisational norms may negatively influence reporting of cybercrime behaviour [33]. Cybercrime reporting is a help-seeking behaviour [23] in the context of organisational norms.

Moreover, cybercrime reporting is a proactive stance that may trigger cybercrime intervention from law enforcement agencies that may improve an organisation's governance. The conduciveness of the organisational culture or control environment to report cybercrime is vital [33]. Where cybercrime victims want to protect their colleagues from cybercrime victimisation, then reporting of cybercrime may improve [33]. Co-workers and other stakeholders of the organisation may either encourage or discourage a cybercrime victim from reporting a cybercrime [17] to law enforcement agencies or any other organisation with a mandate or responsibility of managing cybercrime. Hence the hypothesis:

H5: Organisational subjective norms influence employee cybercrime reporting behaviour.

2.6   Self-Efficacy

Self-efficacy refers to an individual's confidence in performing a behaviour [35, 53]. Therefore, confidence in the ability to report cybercrime has positive effects on cybercrime reporting behaviour [35]. The hypothesis suggested is:

H6: Perceived self-efficacy influences employee cybercrime reporting behaviour.

2.7   Facilitating Conditions

Facilitating conditions refer to facilities needed to ensure that employees report cybercrime as required of them by the organisation [27, 53]. The knowledge, skills, training, and education on reporting cybercrime have a positive effect on cybercrime reporting behaviour [27]. The hypothesis supported is:

H7: Facilitating conditions influence employee cybercrime reporting behaviour.

2.8   Anonymity of Cybercrime Reporting

A factor influencing intentions related to cybercrime reporting is the Anonymity of cybercrime reporting by cybercrime victims or potential cybercrime victims [9, 50]. Cybercrime victims or potential victims may not report cybercrime if they are not assured of their anonymity. The hypothesis suggested is:

H8: Anonymity influences employee cybercrime reporting behaviour.

2.9   Research Model

According to the Theory of Planned Behaviour (TPB) [3], the above factors can be grouped into Attitudinal factors, Subjective Norms, and Perceived Behavioural Control (PBC) factors. Attitudinal factors include perceptions of Law Enforcement Agencies (LEA) competence, Emotional Response (ER) to cybercrime, Cybercrime Awareness (AW), and Cost-Benefit (CB) Analysis of cybercrime reporting. Subjective Norm is represented by Organisational Subjective Norm (SN), and Perceived Behavioural Control comprises of Self-Efficacy (SE), Facilitating Conditions (FC), and Anonymity of cybercrime reporting (AR). These factors are deemed influential on behavioural intentions and actual cybercrime reporting behaviour. Figure 1 below illustrates these relationships.

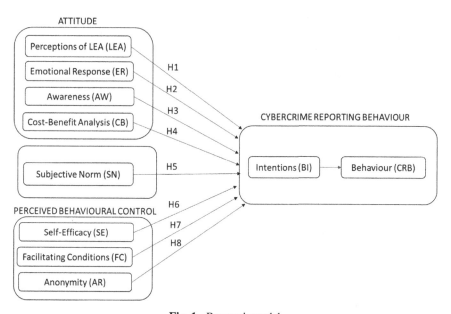

Fig. 1. Research model

3 Research Methodology

Quantitative methods were used through questionnaire surveys that collected data from participants. The study was cross-sectional due to a limited time frame [11]. Measurement items were identified for all constructs in the research model, as shown in Table 1 below. The research instrument items (questionnaire survey) are shown in Appendix A. A seven-point Likert-type scale [11] was used throughout the questionnaire survey where respondents could indicate their extent of agreement or disagreement (1 = Strongly Disagree, 2 = Disagree, 3 = Somewhat disagree, 4 = Neutral, 5 = Somewhat agree, 6 = Agree 7 = Strongly Agree). Participants' demographic data included age, gender, highest education, industry, size of the organisation, their role in the organisation, number of years working in the organisation, and number of years of internet access in the organisation. A web-based questionnaire survey was sent to participants. Qualtrics was used to develop the questionnaire survey. Before distributing the web-based questionnaire survey to participants, institutional ethics in research clearance was received.

Table 1. Items used on the questionnaire survey

Measures	No.	Source
Perceptions of LEA Competence [LEA]	6	[24, 33, 51]
Emotional Response [ER]	9	[24, 51]
Cybercrime Awareness [AW]	4	[24]
Cost-Benefit Analysis [CB]	3	[24, 51]
Organisational Subjective Norm [SN]	4	[6, 7, 51]
Self-efficacy [SE]	3	[13, 24, 35]
Facilitating Conditions [FC]	3	[53]
Anonymity of Reporting [AR]	5	[26]
Behavioural Intentions [BI]	3	[6, 7, 51]
Cybercrime Reporting Behaviour [CRB]	4	[27]

3.1 Sampling Strategy

This study was targeted at participants from South African State-owned Entities. There are more than 200 South African public institutions [42] approximating about a hundred thousand employees. Some entities have five to ten employees, with others in the thousands. Not all elements of the population had access to the internet. A non-probability snowball sampling technique was adopted. Initial respondents identified as working in State-owned Entities were approached and they provided information about subsequent respondents [43]. The sample size in this study was determined, assuming that the minimum sample criteria of the sample size should be ten times the number of variables in multivariate research [2]. There were ten constructs in this study, implying a minimum sample of 100 participants was required [2]. The research instrument was pilot tested by ten participants from South African state-owned entities to ensure that the measures were clear and understandable [11]. No changes were suggested, and data collection proceeded. In the end, 132 responses were received, although some were incomplete, leading to 103 complete responses being used.

3.2 Data Analysis Methods

Factor analysis was performed for construct validity testing [11, 48]. Factor analysis with case wise deletion was performed using the Statistica software package. The factor rotation method adopted was varimax-normalised rotation. For items to be included, they needed to have a factor-loading of greater than 0.5. The extraction method was principal component analysis, using a minimum eigenvalue of 1 as a cut-off value for extraction.

Cronbach's alpha of 0.7 was used as the cut-off to measure the reliability of the research measures [43]. A Cronbach Alpha of 0.7 is considered acceptable for positivist research in Information Systems [45]. Multiple regression was used to test the hypotheses, with the dependent variable being cybercrime reporting behaviour. A p-value of less than 0.05 was considered significant for a hypothesis to be confirmed.

4 Findings

4.1 Demographic Profile

Fifty percent (50%) of the respondents were between the ages of 31 and 40, followed by respondents between 40 and 50 at 31.2%. Respondents were 45.2% male and 52.4% female. 30.4% held Bachelor's degree/B-Tech, 26.4% Certificates/Diplomas, and 24% Honours/Postgraduate-Diplomas. Respondents were from organisations of sizes more than 500 (48%), between 300 and 500 (28%), and between 51 and 300 (16%). In terms of roles, respondents were from Governance, Risk, and Compliance (24%), ICT (19%), and Other (43%). Many of the respondents had worked in their organisations for more than ten years (35%), between 5 and 10 years (29%), and between 2 and 5 years (27%). In terms of the number of years of Internet access, the majority had been accessing the internet for more than five years (70%).

4.2 Construct Validity

When performing factor analysis, items (see Appendix A) LEA1, LEA2, and LEA3 were dropped due to low factor loading. Moreover, EM2 cross-loaded and was therefore dropped, together with EM7, EM8, and EM9 which loaded poorly. Likewise, AWA1, AWA2, AWA3, AWA4, and CB1 were dropped due to the weakness of factor loading. SN1, SN2, SN3, SN4, BI1, BI2, and BI3 were also dropped due to poor loading. Reliability testing (Table 4) was conducted iteratively with factor analysis, which resulted in items pertaining to Cost-Benefit Analysis (CB1, CB2, CB3) also being dropped. Table 2 below presents the factor structure for the remaining items with loading greater than

0.5 and adequate reliability. Items pertaining to Self-Efficacy (SE) and Facilitating Conditions (FC) loaded on the same factor, so the variance inflation factor (VIF) test was used to check for multicollinearity among the independent variables [46]. Low multicollinearity was noted, as shown in Table 3, where VIFs were all less than 5. Hence these factors were still treated as separate [46].

The items that loaded acceptably and were reliable were hence Perceptions of LEA competency—LEA4, LEA5, LEA6; Emotional response (EM)—EM1, EM3, EM4, EM5, EM6; Perceived self-efficacy (SE)—SE1, SE2, SE3; Perceived facilitating conditions (FC)—FC1, FC2, FC3; Anonymity of reporting (AR)—AR1, AR2, AR3, AR4, AR5 and Cybercrime reporting behaviour (CRB)—CRB1, CRB2, CRB3, CRB4, CRB5.

Table 2. Final results of factor loading

Variable	Factor Loadings (Varimax normalised) Extraction: Principal components (Marked loadings are >,500000)				
	SE/FC	AR	EM	LEA	CRB
LEA4	0,020	0,044	0,023	-0,749	0,080
LEA5	0,094	-0,131	0,014	-0,821	-0,252
LEA6	-0,196	-0,059	0,087	-0,744	0,238
EM1	-0,314	-0,043	0,511	0,098	0,315
EM3	-0,017	-0,078	0,653	-0,180	-0,004
EM4	-0,047	0,053	0,628	-0,128	0,103
EM5	0,234	-0,052	0,667	0,103	-0,153
EM6	0,110	-0,021	0,837	0,085	-0,133
SE1	0,709	0,148	-0,028	-0,086	0,058
SE2	0,766	0,147	0,022	-0,184	0,184
SE3	0,704	0,182	0,005	0,008	0,251
FC1	0,738	0,056	0,091	0,223	0,164
FC2	0,730	0,192	0,010	0,104	0,252
FC3	0,790	0,085	0,049	0,103	0,326
AR1	0,201	0,719	0,095	0,172	0,372
AR2	0,204	0,770	0,015	0,157	0,266
AR3	0,086	0,823	0,009	-0,039	-0,080
AR4	0,144	0,868	-0,118	-0,017	-0,023
AR5	0,126	0,890	-0,098	-0,031	0,012
CRB1	0,467	0,047	-0,003	0,048	0,630
CRB2	0,363	0,098	-0,051	0,049	0,612
CRB3	0,307	0,051	-0,067	-0,129	0,784
CRB4	0,449	0,146	0,077	-0,147	0,652

Table 3. Tests for multicollinearity (variance inflation factor)

Construct	VIF
LEA	1,045
EM	1,016
SE	1,870
FC	1,861
AR	1,177

4.3 Reliability

Table 4 presents the composite reliability of each valid construct in Table 2. A Cronbach alpha of 0.70 or higher is considered reliable [45]. All these constructs exhibited adequate reliability.

Table 4. Reliability of research items

Factor	Mean	No.	No. (refined)	Cronbach alpha
LEA	3.3	6	3	0.71
EM	6.4	9	5	0.70
SE	5.3	3	3	0.80
FC	4.8	3	3	0.88
AR	4.3	5	5	0.90
CRB	5.5	4	4	0.83

4.4 Correlation Analysis

Table 5 below shows the Pearson correlations between the refined measures of Law Enforcement Agency competence (LEA), Emotional Response (EM), Self-Efficacy (SE), Facilitating Conditions (FC), Anonymity of Reporting (AR), and Cybercrime Reporting Behaviour (CRB). Factors correlating significantly ($p < 0.05$) with the dependent variable CRB are FC, SE and AR. FC, SE and AR are in turn significantly correlated with each other.

Table 5. Correlation analysis

Variable	CRB	AR	FC	LEA	EM	SE
CRB	1,00					
AR	0,29	1,00				
FC	0,59	0,32	1,00			
LEA	0,03	-0,11	-0,12	1,00		
EM	-0,01	-,083	0,04	0,04	1,00	
SE	0,58	0,35	0,66	0,01	-0,02	1,00

4.5 Hypotheses Testing

Table 6 illustrates the outcomes of multiple linear regression analysis. Hypotheses H3, H4 and H5 were not tested as associated items failed construct validity and/or reliability testing. In addition, hypotheses H1, H2 and H8 were not supported, with only H6 and H7 supported. The adjusted R^2 was 39%, meaning Self-efficacy (SE) and Facilitating Conditions (FC) accounted for 39% of the variance in Cybercrime Reporting Behaviour.

Table 6. Hypotheses testing

		Regression Summary for Dependent Variable:CRB Adjusted R²= 39,15%				
		B	Std.Err.	t(103)	p-value	Supported?
Hypothesis	Intercept	3,05	0,91	3,35	0,001	
H1	LEA	-0,06	0,060	-0,99	0,320	No
H2	EM	-0,02	0,12	-0,15	0,884	No
H3	AWA	-	-	-	-	Not tested
H4	CB	-	-	-	-	Not tested
H5	SN	-	-	-	-	Not tested
H6	SE	0,25	0,08	2,94	0,004	Yes
H7	FC	0,26	0,07	3,68	0,000	Yes
H8	AR	0,06	0,06	0,91	0,365	No

4.6 Discussion and Implications

Self-efficacy (SE) of employees in South African state-owned entities has a significant and positive influence on cybercrime reporting behaviour. This is consistent with research that shows perceived self-efficacy influences information security behaviour [13, 24, 35]. Facilitating conditions (FC) in South African state-owned entities also resulted in a positive and significant influence on cybercrime reporting behaviour. The results are consistent with prior literature that suggests facilitating conditions as an influence on information security behaviour [53]. Perceptions of LEA (law enforcement agencies) competence was found not to have a significant influence on cybercrime reporting behaviour. This is inconsistent with previously discussed literature that suggested that cybercrime victims' negative perceptions of law enforcement agencies may negatively influence cybercrime reporting behaviour [8, 14, 34]. Emotional Response (EM) was found not to have a significant influence on cybercrime reporting behaviour. This is inconsistent with the previous body of work performed by researchers that claimed that emotional factors influence cybercrime victims to report cybercrime [17, 20, 21, 28, 39]. The anonymity of reporting was found not to have a significant influence on cybercrime reporting behaviour. This was inconsistent with previous research [9, 50].

5 Conclusion

The study empirically tested a research model for explaining cybercrime reporting in South African state-owned entities. The research model hypothesised eight factors that were deemed to influence cybercrime reporting behaviour, grouped as (1) Attitudinal factors (Perceptions of LEA, Emotional Response, Awareness and Cost-Benefit Analysis); (2) Subjective Norms and (3) Perceived Behavioural Control (Self-efficacy, Facilitating Conditions and Anonymity of Reporting). This study shows that only the Perceived Behavioural Control Factors—Self-efficacy and Facilitating Conditions influence cybercrime reporting behaviour, suggesting that organisations should focus attention on these two issues to improve cybercrime reporting behaviour amongst employees. To understand how to improve self-efficacy, further research can be conducted to investigate what influences this factor. Facilitating conditions pertain to the various organisational support mechanisms that are put in place to facilitate employee reporting of cybercrime. mechanisms put in place to facilitate employee reporting of cybercrime. Future studies can explore further the most effective support mechanisms.

For the tested hypotheses that are not supported, it may be that as per the Theory of Planned Behaviour, their influence is on behavioural intentions and not behaviour directly. Since the measure for behavioural intention did not exhibit adequate psychometric properties, the effects could not be tested. Future research may hence consider an improvement in the operationalisation of behavioural intentions and those other factors that did not exhibit adequate psychometric properties, i.e. Awareness, Cost-Benefit Analysis and Organisational Subjective Norm.

Appendix A: Research Instrument

Item	Description [Italicised Items dropped]
LEA1	*The Law Enforcement Agencies lack the capacity to deal with cybercrime effectively*
LEA2	*Cybercriminals are more advanced than Law Enforcement Agencies*
LEA3	*Law Enforcement Agencies are too busy to deal with cybercrime*
LEA4	The Law Enforcement Agencies know how to catch cybercriminals (R)
LEA5	The Law Enforcement Agencies do their utmost to help address cybercrime (R)
LEA6	The Law Enforcement Agencies are easy to approach for cybercrime cases (R)
EM1	I fear becoming a victim of cybercrime
EM2	*I am concerned that I can become a victim of cybercrime*
EM3	If I became a victim of cybercrime, it could have serious consequences
EM4	I want cybercriminals to be caught
EM5	I want to prevent cybercriminals from doing harm to the organisation
EM6	I want to prevent cybercrime incidents from happening to me
EM7	*I am afraid cybercriminals can take revenge*
EM8	*I would be ashamed if I fell victim to the cybercrime*
EM9	*I think cybercrime victimisation would be my own fault*
AWA1	*I am aware of my role in keeping the company protected from potential*
AWA2	*cybercriminals*
AWA3	*It is hard to know how I can help protect the organisation from cybercrime*
AWA4	*I understand the risks of cybercrime to individuals in the organisation*
	I do not pay attention to company material about cybercrime threats
CB1	*Cybercrime might damage the reputation of the company affecting revenue*
CB2	*Reporting cybercrime will get the cybercrime damage compensated*
CB3	*Cybercriminals only target a company when there is a financial gain*
SN1	*I will report cybercrime if I see people around me report it*
SN2	*I would never report cybercrime regardless of how many colleagues report it*
SN3	*I feel like I should do according to what my colleagues think about cybercrime*
SN4	*reporting*
	My colleagues would disapprove of me not reporting cybercrime
SE1	I feel confident that I could quickly retrieve accurate contact information of who to
SE2	report cybercrime
SE3	I am confident of my ability to report cybercrime
	I am confident that I would be able to report the signs of cybercrime
FC1	I have the necessary resources to report cybercrime
FC2	I have the necessary knowledge to report cybercrime
FC3	I have enough experience to report cybercrime incidents

(continued)

(continued)

Item	Description [Italicised Items dropped]
AR1 AR2 AR3 AR4 AR5	When I report cybercrime in my organisation, I am confident that others do not know who I am When I report cybercrime in my organisation, I believe that my personal identity remains unknown to others When I report cybercrime in my organisation, I am easily identified as an individual by others (R) When I report cybercrime in my organisation, others are likely to know who I am (R) When I report cybercrime in my organisation, my personal identity is known to others (R)
BI1 BI2 BI3	*I intend to report cybercrime to inform against its illegal activities* *My reporting against cybercrime would positively benefit the victim* *My non-involvement in cybercrime reporting saves lives, prevents trauma, distress, depression, and discomfort to others*
CRB1 CRB2 CRB3 CRB4	I assist my colleagues in reporting cybercrime I always recommend other colleagues to report cybercrime I practise recommended cybercrime reporting behaviour as much as possible I comply with cybercrime reporting policies when performing my daily work

References

1. Abdullah, A.T.M., Jahan, I.: Causes of cybercrime victimization: a systematic literature review. Int. J. Res. Rev. **7**(5), 89–98 (2020)
2. Ahmad, A., Ahmad, R., Hashim, K.F.: Innovation traits for business intelligence successful deployment. J. Theor. Appl. Inf. Technol. **89**(1), 96 (2016)
3. Ajzen, I.: The theory of planned behavior. Organ. Behav. Hum. Decis. Process. **50**(2), 179–211 (1991)
4. Al-Khater, W.A., Al-Maadeed, S., Ahmed, A.A., Sadiq, A.S., Khan, M.K.: Comprehensive review of cybercrime detection techniques. IEEE Access **8**, 137293–137311 (2020)
5. Almazkyzy, K., Esteusizov, Y.N.: The essence and content of cybercrime in modern times. J. Adv. Res. Law Econ. **9**, 834 (2018)
6. Alotaibi, N.B.: Cyberbullying and the expected consequences on the students' academic achievement. IEEE Access **7**, 153417–153431 (2019)
7. Alrwais, O., Alhodaib, E.: What derives people to use reporting functions on social networks? Int. J. Appl. Inf. Syst. **12**(25), 10–16 (2019)
8. Apau, R., Koranteng, F.N.: Impact of cybercrime and trust on the use of ecommerce technologies: an application of the theory of planned behavior. Int. J. Cyber Criminol. **13**(2), 228–254 (2019)
9. Baror, S.O., Ikuesan, R.A., Venter, H.S.: A defined digital forensic criteria for cybercrime reporting. In: International Conference on Cyber Warfare and Security, pp. 617 626. Academic Conferences International Limited (2020). https://doi.org/10.34190/ICCWS.20.056
10. Bell, A.J.C., Rogers, M.B., Pearce, J.M.: The insider threat: Behavioral indicators and factors influencing likelihood of intervention. Int. J. Crit. Infrastruct. Prot. **24**, 166–176 (2019). https://doi.org/10.1016/j.ijcip.2018.12.001
11. Bhattacherjee, A.: Social Science Research: Principles, Methods, and Practices. University of South Florida (2012)

12. Bidgoli, M., Grossklags, J.: End-user cybercrime reporting: what we know and what we can do to improve it. In: 2016 IEEE International Conference on Cybercrime and Computer Forensic (ICCCF), pp. 1–6. IEEE (2016)

13. Burns, S., Roberts, L.: Applying the theory of planned behaviour to predicting online safety behaviour. Crime Prev. Community Saf. 15(1), 48–64 (2013). https://doi.org/10.1057/cpcs.2012.13

14. Cheng, C., Chan, L., Chau, C.L.: Individual differences in susceptibility to cyber-crime victimization and its psychological aftermath. Comput. Hum. Behav. 108, 106311 (2020)

15. Christou, G.: The challenges of cybercrime governance in the European Union. Eur. Polit. Soc. 19(3), 355–375 (2018)

16. Collier, B., Thomas, D.R., Clayton, R., Hutchings, A., Chua, Y.T.: Influence, infrastructure, and recentering cybercrime policing: evaluating emerging approaches to online law enforcement through a market for cybercrime services. Policing Soc. 32(1), 103–124 (2021)

17. Cross, C.: Expectations vs reality: responding to online fraud across the fraud justice network. Int. J. Law Crime Justice 55, 1–12 (2018)

18. DeKimpe, L., Ponnet, K., Walrave, M., Snaphaan, T., Pauwels, L., Hardyns, W.: Help, I need somebody: examining the antecedents of social support seeking among cybercrime victims. Comput. Hum. Behav. 108, 106310 (2020)

19. Dlamini, S., Mbambo, C.: Understanding policing of cybercrime in South Africa: the phenomena, challenges and effective responses. Cogent Soc. Sci. 5(1), 1675404 (2019)

20. Dremliuga, R.I., Korobeev, A.I., Mamychev, A.Y., Miroshnichenko, O.I.: Trends and methods of fighting cybercrime in the Russian Federation in terms of the transition to a digital economy. Laplage em Rev. 7(2), 191–200 (2021)

21. Eboibi, F.E.: Concerns of cybercriminality in South Africa, Ghana, Ethiopia and Nigeria: rethinking cybercrime policy implementation and institutional accountability. Commonw. Law Bull. 46(1), 78–109 (2020)

22. FBI IC3: Internet Crime Report 2021. Technical report I, FBI Internet Crime Complaint Center (IC3) (2021)

23. Fissel, E.R.: The reporting and help-seeking behaviors of cyberstalking victims. J. Interpers. Violence 36(11–12), 5075–5100 (2021)

24. Hadlington, L.: Human factors in cybersecurity; examining the link between Internet addiction, impulsivity, attitudes towards cybersecurity, and risky cybersecurity behaviours. Heliyon 3(7), e00346 (2017)

25. Hall, T., Sanders, B., Bah, M., King, O., Wigley, E.: Economic geographies of the illegal: the multiscalar production of cybercrime. Trends Organized Crime 24(2), 282–307 (2021)

26. Hite, D.M., Voelker, T., Robertson, A.: Measuring perceived anonymity: the development of a context-independent instrument. J. Methods Meas. Soc. Sci. 5(1), 22–39 (2014)

27. Humaidi, N., Balakrishnan, V.: Indirect effect of management support on users' compliance behaviour towards information security policies. Health Inf. Manag. J. 47(1), 17–27 (2018)

28. Ibrahim, S.: Social and contextual taxonomy of cybercrime: socioeconomic theory of Nigerian cybercriminals. Int. J. Law Crime Justice 47, 44–57 (2016)

29. Internet live stats: internet live stats-internet usage social media statistics (2020)

30. Jadoon, A.K., Iqbal, W., Amjad, M.F., Afzal, H., Bangash, Y.A.: Forensic analysis of Tor browser: a case study for privacy and anonymity on the web. Forensic Sci. Int. 299, 59–73 (2019)

31. Jerome, B.: Criminal investigation and criminal intelligence: example of adaptation in the prevention and repression of cybercrime. Risks 8(3), 99 (2020)

32. Jhaveri, M.H., Cetin, O., Gaiian, C., Moore, T., Eeten, M.V.: Abuse reporting and the fight against cybercrime. ACM Comput. Surv. (CSUR) 49(4), 1–27 (2017)

33. Kemp, S.: Fraud reporting in Catalonia in the Internet era: determinants and motives. Eur. J. Criminol. 1477370820941405 (2020)

34. Kshetri, N.: The simple economics of cybercrimes. IEEE Secur. Priv. **4**(1), 33–39 (2006)
35. Kwak, Y., Lee, S., Damiano, A., Vishwanath, A.: Why do users not report spear-phishing emails? Telematics Inform. **48**, 101343 (2020)
36. Lagazio, M., Sherif, N., Cushman, M.: A multi-level approach to understanding the impact of cybercrime on the financial sector. Comput. Secur. **45**, 58–74 (2014)
37. MacDermott, A., Baker, T., Buck, P., Iqbal, F., Shi, Q.: The Internet of Things: challenges and considerations for cybercrime investigations and digital forensics. Int. J. Digital Crime Forensics **12**(1), 1–13 (2020)
38. Mcanyana, W., Brindley, C., Seedat, Y.: Insight into the cyberthreat landscape in South Africa. Technical report (2020). https://www.accenture.com/_acnmedia/PDF-125/Accenture-Insight-Into-The-Threat-Landscape-Of-South-Africa-V5.pdf
39. Monteith, S., Bauer, M., Alda, M., Geddes, J., Whybrow, P.C., Glenn, T.: Increasing cybercrime since the pandemic: concerns for psychiatry. Curr. Psychiatry Rep. **23**(4), 1–9 (2021)
40. Riek, M., Bohme, R.: The costs of consumer-facing cybercrime: an empirical exploration of measurement issues and estimates. J. Cybersecurity **4**(1), tyy004 (2018)
41. Robinson, M., Jones, K., Janicke, H., Maglaras, L.: Developing cyber-peacekeeping: observation, monitoring and reporting. Gov. Inf. Q. **36**(2), 276–293 (2019)
42. RSA National Treasury: Public Institutions Listed in Pfma Schedule 1 , 2 , 3a, 3B , 3C and 3D As At 30 April 2015. Technical report May, RSA National Treasury (2015). http://www.treasury.gov.za/legislation/pfma/publicentities/2015-04-30PublicinstitutionsSch1-3D.pdf
43. Saunders, M.: Research Methods for Business Students. Pearson (2014)
44. Stratton, G., Powell, A., Cameron, R.: Crime and justice in digital society: towards a 'digital criminology'? Int. J. Crime Justice Soc. Democr. **6**(2), 17 (2017)
45. Straub, D., Boudreau, M.C., Gefen, D.: Validation guidelines for IS positivist research. Commun. Assoc. Inf. Syst. **13**(1), 24 (2004)
46. Tan, M.T., Teo, T.S.: Factors influencing the adoption of Internet banking. J. Assoc. Inf. Syst. **1**(1), 5 (2000)
47. Touhill, G.: New study reveals cybercrime may be widely underreported even when laws mandate disclosure (2019)
48. Umlauf, M.G., Mochizuki, Y.: Predatory publishing and cybercrime targeting academics. Int. J. Nurs. Pract. **24**, e12656 (2018)
49. Venkatesh, V., Brown, S.A., Bala, H.: Bridging the qualitative-quantitative divide: Guidelines for conducting mixed methods research in infomation systems. MIS Quart. Manag. Inf. Syst. **37**(1), 21–54 (2013). https://doi.org/10.25300/MISQ/2013/37.1.02
50. Wang, H., He, D., Liu, Z., Guo, R.: Blockchain-based anonymous reporting scheme with anonymous rewarding. IEEE Trans. Eng. Manage. **67**(4), 1514–1524 (2020). https://doi.org/10.1109/TEM.2019.2909529
51. Van de Weijer, S., Leukfeldt, R., Van der Zee, S.: Reporting cybercrime victimization: determinants, motives, and previous experiences. Policing **43**(1), 17–34 (2020). https://doi.org/10.1108/PIJPSM-07-2019-0122/FULL/XML
52. Van de Weijer, S.G., Leukfeldt, R., Bernasco, W.: Determinants of reporting cybercrime: a comparison between identity theft, consumer fraud, and hacking. Eur. J. Criminol. **16**(4), 486–508 (2019). https://doi.org/10.1177/1477370818773610
53. Srirama, S.N., Lin, J.-W., Bhatnagar, R., Agarwal, S., Reddy, P.K. (eds.): BDA 2021. LNCS, vol. 13147. Springer, Cham (2021). https://doi.org/10.1007/978-3-030-93620-4

Online Security Attack Experience and Worries of Young Adults in the United Kingdom

Najla Aldaraani, Helen Petrie[✉], and Siamak F. Shahandashti

University of York, York YO10 5GH, UK
{nga505,helen.petrie,siamak.shahandashti}@york.ac.uk

Abstract. Online security issues continue to grow as a concern, amplified by the coronavirus pandemic. The current cohort of young people (aged 18–30, "Generation Z") are the first to have grown up with digital technologies, but to what extent are they worried about online security attacks and what experience do they have of them? An online survey of 81 young UK participants investigated their experience with 12 scenarios presenting online security attacks, asked about their level of worry with 9 online security attacks and their knowledge of computer and online security, and their confidence in their ability to identity an attack. Experience with the online attacks ranged widely, from over 50% of participants experiencing spear phishing to attempt identity theft, to only 2.5% experiencing a spoofed website. A principal components analysis showed that worries clearly fell into two components: Theft Worry and Phishing Worry. Levels of worry on these two components could be predicted from the number of different online security attacks participants had experienced. These relationships may be useful for developing education and advice to encourage better online security behaviour.

Keywords: Experience of online security attacks · Worries about online security attacks · Young adults · Generation Z

1 Introduction

Issues of online security continue to grow and have been further amplified by the coronavirus pandemic. In 2020 it was estimated that in the area of identity theft alone, the number of stolen online credentials available for sale on the dark web had quadrupled in two years, with 15 billion sets of credentials available as a result of more than 100,000 data breaches [5]. It is well established that human error or risk-taking is often a source of these security issues [4, 20].

Research some 15 years ago by Furnell and colleagues [9–11] showed that users were superficially aware of online security issues, but often lacked detailed knowledge and appropriate strategies to protect themselves online. More recent research suggests the situation has not improved greatly. Furman et al. [8] conducted in-depth interviews with 40 American adults and found that they were aware of and concerned about online security, but lacked skills to deal with the issues. Ion et al. [13] investigated the practices

© IFIP International Federation for Information Processing 2022
Published by Springer Nature Switzerland AG 2022
N. Clarke and S. Furnell (Eds.): HAISA 2022, IFIP AICT 658, pp. 300–309, 2022.
https://doi.org/10.1007/978-3-031-12172-2_24

that novice and expert users considered most important to protect themselves from security attacks. They found that there was little overlap between the groups, with novices relying on antivirus software, changing passwords frequently and visiting only those websites they know, again suggesting that novices lack appropriate strategies. Fagan and Khan [6] found that users were strongly motivated by a convenience/security trade-off when considering online security, quite possibly to their detriment. A similar result was found specifically in relation to password behaviour, although the relationship between perceived risk and benefit varied between different types of password behaviour [17].

Recent research has also explored the individual characteristics which might predict poor online security behaviour. McCormac et al. [14] used the Human Aspects of Information Security Questionnaire (HAIS-Q) to investigate the relationship between knowledge, attitudes and self-reported behaviours in relation to online security and personality traits, age and gender. They found that a number of personality traits predicted online security variables, but age and gender did not. A number of other studies have also found that age is less important that might be expected in relation to online security [2, 15]. However, other studies have found age differences [16, 25], although both these studies were about password-related behaviour in particular, with both showing that younger people were more likely to undertake at least some risky password behaviours.

One factor which may affect online security attitudes and behaviours which does not seem to have been studied is whether people have experience with online security attacks. Given the very robust psychological phenomenon of "optimistic bias" (that people consistently overestimate the likelihood of positive events and underestimate the likelihood of negative events [22]), when people experience online security attacks do they become more worried and more cautious in their behaviour? In this research, we set out to study the first component of that relationship–whether people who have experienced online security attacks are more worried about online security issues.

Given the inconsistent results on age differences in online security attitudes and behaviours, we decided to concentrate on a specific age group of young people, currently aged from 18 to 30 years. This group is also of particular interest, as they are the group often referred to (particularly in the popular media) as "Generation Z", the first generation to grow up with access to the internet and a wide range of personal digital technologies [23]. However, this does not mean that this generation is more expert about digital technologies than older generations. For example, in a large recent survey in the UK, only 28% of 18 to 24 year olds and 34% of 25 to 34 year olds were aware of four main ways in which companies can collect personal data about us on the internet [19].

Compared to previous generations, research is beginning to show that this generation of young people at least perceive themselves as more thoughtful and responsible and less risk-taking than previous generations [21]. Given their familiarity (if not necessarily expertise) with digital technologies, how does this play out in their attitudes to online security? To explore this further, we decided to present participants with a range of different online security attacks, and investigate whether they have experienced them, how worried they are about them and what the relationship between these two sets of variables.

2 Method

2.1 Participants

The inclusion criteria for participation in the study were to be aged 18–30 years old and to be a self-defined British person currently living in the United Kingdom. 84 participants were recruited via the Prolific participant recruitment website (prolific.co). Participants were offered compensation of GBP 2.00 for completing an online survey taking appropriately 15 min. Data from three participants were omitted as they failed an attention check (see Sect. 2.2), leaving 81 participants. Table 1 summarizes the demographics of the participants. Unfortunately, due to a technical error, participants were not asked their gender. However, a gender balanced sample was requested in Prolific, so we can assume the gender balance is good.

Table 1. Demographics of the participants

Age	
Range (Mean)	18–30 years (24.0
Highest educational level	
High school	28 (34.6%)
Bachelors degree	34 (42.0%)
Postgraduate degree	15 (18.5%)
Professional qualification	3 (3.7%)
Prefer not to say	1 (1.2%)
Self-rating of general computer knowledge	
Median (Semi Interquartile range)	5.0 (0.5)
Z score (probability)	6.25 (<0.001)
Self-rating of online security knowledge	
Median (Semi Interquartile range)	5.0 (1.0)
Z score (probability)	4.90 (<0.001)
Self-rating of ability to identify an attack from a cybercriminal	
Median (Semi Interquartile range)	5.00 (1.0)
Z score (probability)	5.57 (p < 0.001)

Participants were asked to rate their general computer knowledge, their online security knowledge and their confidence in their ability to identify an attack from a cybercriminal, on 7-point Likert items (scored as $1 =$ not at all knowledgeable/confident to $7 =$ very knowledgeable/confident). Ratings were not normally distributed, so nonparametric statistics are reported. Participants rated themselves significantly above the midpoint of the rating item on all three items (Wilcoxon one sample ranked sign test with a H_O that the median rating is 4, midpoint of the scale, Z scores are used as sample size is greater than 25 [12]).

2.2 Online Questionnaire

An online questionnaire was deployed through the Qualtrics survey software.

The questionnaire consisted of three parts: a set of 12 short scenarios about online security issues; a set of 9 statements about online security worries; four attention check statements; and a set of demographic questions.

The 12 scenarios were designed to describe in non-technical language the range of online security attacks that young people in the UK may have heard about or experienced (see Table 2). A very simple version of the frameworks from Lockheed Martin (the "intrusion kill chain") [24] and Mitre [18] for describing the lifecycle of security attacks was used to classify the types and stages of attacks. The range of attacks and the concrete examples of these attacks were developed through a reading of the research literature, documents advising people about attacks and how to avoid them, and several brainstorming sessions of the authors. The attacks were then transformed into short scenarios to reflect the experience of users possibly with little technical expertise.

The presentation of the scenarios in the questionnaire all followed the same format. Firstly, presentation of a scenario. Participants were asked "has something like this has ever happened to you?" on a 7-point Likert item (1 = never to 7 = many times). If a participant answered "never", they moved to the next scenario. If this type of scenario had ever happened to them, they were asked a short set of questions, always very similar, but appropriate to the scenario (not analysed for this paper, so not discussed further).

The full set of scenarios is listed in Table 2. For each scenario, we identified the adversarial strategy used for the delivery of the attack and the eventual exploitation phase of the attack following the attack lifecycle frameworks. The order in which the 12 scenarios were presented to participants was randomized to avoid practice and fatigue effects [7].

A set of 9 statements was developed to assess how worried participants were about the various types of security attacks (see Table 4), using a similar method to the development of the scenarios. Participants rated each statement on 7-point Likert items (1 = not worried at all to 7 = very worried).

Demographic questions checked for nationality and location (these were filtered in Prolific), asked for age and highest educational level, and asked participants to rate their general computer and online security knowledge and confidence in their ability to detect an attack from a cybercriminal (all on 7-point Likert items).

Table 2. The 12 scenarios representing online security attacks

Scenario	Attack type and stage
1. I click on a link (e.g. on a website, in social media, in a SMS) and then notice my device acting strangely (e.g. the device freezes, runs slowly or crashes repeatedly). I realise this may have been caused by clicking on the link	Delivery: *Phishing* (website, social media, SMS) Exploitation: *Denial of Service*

(continued)

Table 2. (*continued*)

Scenario	Attack type and stage
2. I download an attachment (e.g. from an email or website) and then notice my device acting strangely (e.g. device freezes, runs slowly or crashes repeatedly). I realise this may have been caused by downloading the attachment	Delivery: *Phishing* (email, website) Exploitation: *Denial of Service*
3. I download a free app or game from an unknown or possibly untrustworthy source. Then I notice my device is running slowly or crashing more frequently than normal	Delivery: *Malicious Code* (in free app or game) Exploitation: *Denial of Service, Trojan Horse*
4. I install some software or a file on my device from a link or attachment I received in an email, then notice the device acting strangely. I can't access some or all of my files and then I am asked to pay a ransom to be able to retrieve these files. I realise this may have been caused by installing that software/file	Delivery: *Phishing* (attachment in email, website) Exploitation: *Ransomware*
5. I realise that someone has made a purchase using my credit card or bank account details. I remember that I have recently entered these details online and they may have been stolen	Delivery: unknown Exploitation: *Data Theft, Identity Theft*
6. I realise that someone has used my personal information or something I have stored online (e.g. your name, a photo). I remember that I have stored that online and they may have been stolen	Delivery: unknown Exploitation: *Data Theft, Identity Theft*
7. I download some anti-virus/malware software to try to protect my device. But it does not seem to be effective and it keeps showing me advertisements on the device	Delivery: *Malicious Code* (free app) Exploitation: *Adware*
8. I click on a link (e.g. on a website, in social media, in an SMS) and then notice strange things happening on my device (e.g. pop-ups appearing frequently, unrecognized apps being installed). I realise this may have been cause by clicking on the link	Delivery: *Phishing* (link on website, social media, SMS) Exploitation: *Malware*
9. My friends report receiving strange messages from me (e.g. requesting money because I'm in trouble, including suspicious links). I realise someone must have illegally used one of my accounts	Delivery: *Spear Phishing* Exploitation: *Identity Theft*
10. I receive a message or call from what seems to be a trustworthy source (e.g. via email, social media, SMS or phone call) asking me for personal information (e.g. account details, password) for a legitimate reason (e.g. updating data). At some point I realise this is a fake message or call	Delivery: *Spear Phishing* (email, social media, SMS or phone call) Exploitation: *Data Theft, Identity Theft*
11. I receive a message or call which seems to be from someone I know (e.g. via email, social media, SMS) asking me to give them urgent assistance (e.g. transfer money). At some point I realise this is a fake message	Delivery: *Identity Theft* (of another person), *Spear Phishing* Exploitation: *Theft*
12. I need to undertake an urgent task on the government website (e.g. renewing my passport or driving licence). I search quickly for the website in Google. The website asks for personal information (e.g. my name, date of birth or credit card details). After entering my personal information and making a payment, I realise it was not the actual government website, but a fraudulent one with a very similar address and information	Delivery: *Spoofed Website* Exploitation: *Data Theft, Identity Theft*

3   Results

The 12 scenarios were analysed for whether participants had ever experienced this kind of online security attack, and if they had how frequently they had experienced it, summarized in Table 3. It shows that the scenarios vary greatly in how many participants reported having encountered them, from over half the participants (55.6%, 45) reporting having encountered a spear phishing attack to obtain personal data (Scenario 10) to only 2 (2.5%) who had encountered a spoofed website (Scenario 12). It is notable that the two scenarios which most participants had encountered involved spear phishing and identity theft.

Table 3. The 12 scenarios by number of participants and frequency of encountering

Scenario No	% (N) participants encountering	Frequency of encountering Median (Semi Interquartile Range)	Type of security threat
10	55.6% (45)	6.0 (2.0)	Spear phishing identity theft
11	38.3%	3.0 (1.5)	Identify theft Spear phishing
1	34.5%	3.0 (1.5)	Phishing, Denial of service
8	29.6%	4.0 (1.5)	Phishing Malware
9	27.2%	3.0 (1.5)	Identity theft
7	24.7%	4.0 (1.0)	Adware
2	23.4%	2.0 (0.5)	Phishing Denial of service
3	21.0%	3.0 (1.5)	Malicious code, Denial of service, Trojan horse
5	17.3%	2.5 (1.5)	Identity theft
6	13.6%	5.0 (1.0)	Identity theft
4	3.7%	5.0 (n/a)*	Phishing ransomware
12	2.5% (2)	2.5 (n/a)*	Spoofed website

* Semi interquartile range could not be calculated, as too few ratings

The 9 statements assessing how worried participants were about different security attacks were initially analysed individually, as shown in Table 4. Levels of worry ranged from on average just below the midpoint of the 7-point scale (median of 3.0 for 4 statements, 2, 3, 8, 9) to quite high (median of 5.0 on two statements, 6 and 7). Ratings on all statements were significantly above the "not at all worried" point on the scale, and one of the two statements with ratings of 5.0 was significantly above the midpoint of the scale (Statement 6: $Z = 2.09$, $p = 0.036$), the other was not (Statement 7).

Table 4. The 9 statements measuring level of worry about security attacks

	Question	Attack types	Median (SIQR)
1	My device will be accessed by an attacker and my data will be destroyed	Data theft/ destruction	4.0 (1.5)
2	I will receive an email with a link leading to a fake website	Phishing Website spoofing	3.0 (1.5)
3	I will receive an email with an attachment that may include malicious code	Phishing Malware	3.0 (1.5)
4	Someone will lock me out of my device(s) and demand money to restore access	Ransomware	4.0 (1.5)
5	Someone will access my device(s) or account(s), look at my information and use it to blackmail me	Ransomware	4.0 (2.0)
6	Someone will steal my online identity and misuse it	Identity theft	5.0 (1.5)
7	Someone will access my device(s) or account(s), steal my data and use it for malicious purposes or to their advantage (e.g. make illegal purchases)	Identity theft	5.0 (1.5)
8	I will receive a phone call from someone asking about my confidential data (e.g. password, bank account details)	Spear phishing Identity theft	3.0 (1.5)
9	I will click on a link in a SMS message or email from a source that I cannot verify its origin, whether it is trustworthy	Phishing	3.0 (1.5)

A principal components analysis[1] was conducted on the ratings of the 9 statements and produced a very clear result with two components accounting for 71.7% of the variance in the ratings. The first component (which accounted for 58.6% of the variance) included Statements 1, 4, 5, 6 and 7 (factor loadings above 0.74 in all cases) and clearly related to data/identity theft and ransomware (for simplicity we will call this the Theft Worry component). The second component (13.1% of the variance) included Statements 2, 3, 8 and 9 (factor loadings above 0.68 in all cases) and related to phishing and spear phishing (for simplicity we will call this the Phishing Worry component).

Median scores on these two components were calculated for each participant in order to investigate the relationships between these two major worries and experience with the security attacks, as measured by the scenarios and the individual characteristics of self-reported computer and security knowledge and confidence in identifying security threats.

---

[1] Principal Components Analysis is a technique to reduce a number of variables to the set which describes the data in the smallest possible number of variables with the least loss of information. It is a non-parametric analysis method. A requirement is that at least 5 observations are needed for each variable in the analysis. With 9 statements (i.e. variables), observations from 81 participants comfortably met this requirement.

There was no significant relationship between either self-reported computer or security knowledge and scores on either Worry component. However, there was a significant relationship between self-reported confidence in ability to identify security attacks, but only with the Phishing Worry component (Phishing Worry: rho $= -0.27$, p $= 0.015$; Theft Worry: rho $= -0.15$, n.s.). This showed that people who were more confident in their ability to identify security threats were less worried about phishing attacks.

There were also interesting relationships between participants' experience of security attacks and their scores on the Worry components. In terms of whether participants had experienced attacks at all, the more of the scenarios they said they had experienced, the higher their scores on both Worry components (Theft Worry: rho $= 0.27$, p $= 0.027$; Phishing Worry: rho $= 0.23$, p $= 0.036$). The effect of how frequently participants had experienced an attack was less clear. Linear regressions were conducted to predict Worry scores from the ratings of the frequency of experiencing the different scenarios. The result for the Theft Worry scores was just above standard significance level ($F_{12, 80}$ $= 1.80$, p $= 0.066$) with Scenarios 1 and 4 being individually significant predictors (Scenario 1: p $= 0.008$; Scenario 4: p $= 0.027$). The result for the Phishing Worry scores was significant ($F_{12, 80} = 2.06$, p $= 0.031$) with Scenarios 1 and 10 being individually significant predictors (Scenario 1: p $= 0.014$, Scenario 10: p $= 0.042$). So Scenario 1 is particularly predictive of being worried about security attacks.

4 Discussion and Conclusions

This study investigated the experience of online security attacks by a sample of young British people ("Generation Z") and their worries about online security, and how these two groups of variables related to each other.

Firstly, we found that this sample of young people rated their knowledge of computers and online security highly and were confident in their ability to identify a security attack, with median ratings on all three aspects significantly above the midpoint of the rating scale. This finding is in agreement with the findings of Cain et al. [2] who testing their American participants' "cyber hygiene knowledge" with a multiple choice quiz. Participants in the 18–24 and 25–29 age groups achieved mean scores of over 80%. However, our results contrast to a very recent survey of over 2750 participants in the UK of 18 to 34 year olds, who were not very aware of how their personal data were collected by companies [19], showing a distinct lack of awareness of security issues.

To investigate the numbers of participants who had any experience of a range of online security attacks, and the frequency of those experiences, we created a set of 12 short scenarios presenting such attacks from the user's perspective in non-technical language. Participants were asked not whether they had experienced exactly the scenario, but "something like" it, to allow for a range of similar experiences. There was a wide range of experience with the security attacks, with over half the participants reporting experience with spear phishing for identity theft purposes (Scenario 10), which was also reported as occurring very frequently, but only a very small number of participants reporting having experienced a spoofed website (Scenario 12).

To investigate what participants are most worried about in relation to online security, a principal components analysis of the 9 statements provided a very clear answer–over

70% of the variance in the ratings was accounted for by two components. The first component was worry about identity and data theft and ransomware, this accounted for over half the variance in the ratings. Identity theft featured in three of the five scenarios reported as experienced by most participants, although ransomware has been experienced by very few participants. However, in the period before and during the coronavirus there was a considerable about of publicity about ransomware attacks, particularly on hospitals in the UK [1, 3]. Of course, these attacks were on large organizations, not individuals, but this publicity may have caused young British people to become more worried about this type of attack. The second component was worry about phishing and spear phishing, this accounted for a smaller proportion of the variance (13%). It may be that participants are more worried about identity/data theft and ransomware as they feel less in control of that aspect of their online security and that the consequences can be very serious. Given their confidence in their knowledge of online security and ability to identity attacks, they may well feel able to identity and deal with phishing and spear phishing attacks. This was borne out by the fact that participants who were more confident in their ability to identify attacks were less worried about phishing (as measured by the Phishing Worry component), but there was no relationship between their rating of their confidence and their worry about identify and data theft (as measured by the Theft Worry component).

There were also interesting results on the relationship between the two Worry components and the reported experience of online security attacks. The measure of the number of different scenarios (therefore the number of different security attacks) participants had experienced was the best predictor of how worried they were, on both Worry components. The frequency of encountering the attacks produced less clear results, with a significant relationship on the Phishing Worry component and a near significant relationship on the Theft Worry component. Thus, the experience of attacks may well mitigate the optimism bias which young people may have about online security. Further analysis of our data may reveal more about these relationships as we also have information on what the consequences of a attack was, which may affect the level of worry. However, at the moment, this suggests that any experience of an online security attack adds to the level of worry about online security.

The challenge for security educators and advisors is how to build on that worry into strong security behaviour. Given that some kinds of online attacks are encountered by many young people, if these could be automatically detected, that may be a very useful opportunity to provide advice and reinforcement of good security practices. On the other hand, even if young people have not experienced an attack personally, creating information in formats that appeal to them might be an effective substitute. For example, TikTok videos about how security attacks occur and the consequences and how to detect them, might help Generation Z become more careful about online security. Further research is needed to test this idea.

References

1. Beaman, C., Barkworth, A., Akande, T.D., Hakak, S., Khan, M.K.: Ransomware: recent advances, analysis, challenges and future research directions. Comput. Secur. **111**, 102490 (2021)

2. Cain, A.A., Edwards, M.E., Still, J.D.: An exploratory study of cyber hygiene behaviours and knowledge. J. Inf. Secur. Appl. **42**, 36–45 (2018)
3. Collier, R.: NHS ransomware attack spreads worldwide. Can. Med. Assoc. J. **189**(22), E786–E787 (2017)
4. Crossler, R.E., Johnston, A.C., Lowry, P.B., Hu, Q., Warkentin, M., Baskerville, R.: Future directions for behavioural information security research. Comput. Secur. **32**, 90–101 (2013)
5. Digital Shadows: from exposure to takeover: the 15 billion stolen credentials allowing account takeovers (2020). https://resources.digitalshadows.com/whitepapers-and-reports/from-exposure-to-takeover
6. Fagan, M., Khan, M.M.H.: Why do they do what they do? In: Symposium on Usable Privacy and Security (SOUPS), USENIX Association (2016)
7. Field, A., Hole, G.: How to Design and Report Experiments. Sage (2003)
8. Furman, S., Theofanos, M.F., Choong, Y., Stanton, B.: Basing cybersecurity training on user perceptions. IEEE Secur. Priv. **10**(2), 40–49 (2012)
9. Furnell, S., Bryant, P., Phippen, A.D.: Assessing the security perceptions of personal Internet users. Comput. Secur. **26**(5), 410–417 (2007)
10. Furnell, S., Jusoh, A., Katsabas, D.: The challenges of understanding and using security: a survey of end-users. Comput. Secur. **25**(1), 27–35 (2006)
11. Furnell, S., Tsaganidi, V., Phippen, A.: Security beliefs and barriers for novice Internet users. Comput. Secur. **27**(7), 235–240 (2008)
12. Howell, D.C.: Fundamental Statistics for the Behavioural Sciences (8th edn). Cengage (2013)
13. Ion, I., Reeder, R., Consolvo, S.: " … no one can hack my mind": comparing expert and non-expert security practices. In: Symposium on Usable Privacy and Security (SOUPS), USENIX Association (2015)
14. McCormac, A., Zwaans, T., Parsons, K., Calic, D., Butavicius, M., Pattinson, M.: Individual differences and information security awareness. Comput. Hum. Behav. **69**, 151–156 (2017)
15. McGill, T., Thompson, N.: Old risks, new challenges: exploring differences in security between home computer and mobile device use. Behav. Inf. Technol. **36**(11), 1111–1124 (2017)
16. Merdenyan, B., Petrie, H.: Generational differences in password management behaviour. In: Proceedings of the 32nd International BCS Human Computer Interaction Conference (HCI 2018). British Computer Society (2018)
17. Merdenyan, B., Petrie, H.: Two studies of the perceptions of risk, benefits and likelihood of undertaking password management behaviours. Behav. Inf. Technol. (2022). https://doi.org/10.1080/0144929X.2021.2019832
18. Mitre Corporation.: MITRE ATT&CK (2022). https://attack.mitre.org/
19. Office of Communication (Ofcom): Adults' media use and attitudes report 2020/21 (2021)
20. Safa, N.S., Maple, C.: Human errors in the information security realm–and how to fix them. Comput. Fraud Secur. **9**, 17–20 (2016)
21. Seemiller, C., Grace, M.: Generation Z goes to college. Jossey-Bass (2016)
22. Sharot, T.: The optimism bias. Curr. Biol. **21**(23), R941–R945 (2011)
23. Turner, A.: Generation Z: technology and social interest. J. Individ. Psychol. **71**(2), 103–113 (2015)
24. United States Senate, Committee on Commerce, Science, and Transportation.: A "Kill Chain" analysis of the 2013 Target data breach (2014)
25. Whitty, M., Doodson, J., Creese, S., Hodges, D.: Individual differences in cyber security behaviours: an examination of who is sharing passwords. Cyberpsychology Behav. Soc. Networks **18**(1), 3–7 (2015)

PowerQoPE: A Personal Quality of Internet Protection and Experience Configurator

Enock Samuel Mbewe[(✉)], Taveesh Sharma, and Josiah Chavula

School of IT, Department of Computer Science, University of Cape Town,
Cape Town, South Africa
{embewe,tsharma,jchavula}@cs.uct.ac.za
http://www.uct.ac.za/

Abstract. Security configuration remains obscure for many Internet users, especially those with limited computing skills. This obscurity exposes such users to various Internet attacks. Recently, there has been an increase in cyberattacks targeted at individuals due to the remote workforce imposed by the COVID 19 pandemic. These attacks have exposed the inefficiencies of the non-human-centric implementation of Internet security mechanisms and protocols. Security research usually positions users as the weakest link in the security ecosystem, making system and protocol developers exclude the users in the development process. This stereotypical approach has negatively affected users' security uptake. Mostly, security systems are not comprehensible for an average user, negatively affecting performance and Quality of Experience. This causes the users to shun using security mechanisms. Building on human-centric cybersecurity research, we present a tool that aids in configuring Internet Quality of protection and Experience (referred to as PowerQoPE in this paper). We describe its architecture and design methodology and finally present evaluation results. Preliminary evaluation results show that user-centric and data-driven approaches in the design of Internet security systems improves users' Quality of Experience. The controlled experiment results show that users are not really stupid; they know what they want and that given proper security configuration platforms with proper framing of components and information, they can make optimal security decisions.

Keywords: Usable security · QoE · QoP · Internet security · Cybersecurity

1 Introduction

Internet usage has become part of our daily life, with its technologies affecting every part of our daily activities. The prevalence of smartphone usage has

Supported by Hasso Platner Institute for Digital Engineering.

© IFIP International Federation for Information Processing 2022
Published by Springer Nature Switzerland AG 2022
N. Clarke and S. Furnell (Eds.): HAISA 2022, IFIP AICT 658, pp. 310–327, 2022.
https://doi.org/10.1007/978-3-031-12172-2_25

transformed the technology landscape, pushing the responsibility for one's digital data to the individuals. Security is one such responsibility that one must master to ensure cyber safety. Until the recent past, security has been considered corporates' responsibility and confined to a perimeter [1]. In this paradigm, most security systems are not designed for average users who form a greater part of the Internet user base. This kind of security implementation is referred to as *stupid user* or *paternalistic* security implementation [2,3]. The exclusion of users in the security systems design robs them of the opportunity to acquaint themselves with necessary security knowledge, further deforming their security mental models and paralysing their online security practice [4]. The rapid penetration of mobile devices and personalised computing platforms has demolished security perimeters calling for a paradigm shift in security implementation. Security authors agree that security systems should be human-centric, considering three fundamental concepts: User, Usage, and Usability [1].

The latest advancements in technology, such as smartphone, the Internet of Things (IoT), and Wireless Sensor Networks (WSNs), however, has completely changed the landscape of cybersecurity. We now witness the increased cyber-attacks targeted at individuals abolishing any perimeters that existed. This means that individuals must be vigilant to protect their digital assets, making security configuration a personal responsibility. Some security researchers have proposed a paradigm shift from the human out-of-security loop to the human-in-the-security loop (human-centred cybersecurity or security orchestration). The argument is that if humans are involved in security decision making, they would have better security mental models, reinforcing their security practice. However, the Internet users' mental models have been reported to be flawed by the stupid user security implementation. Their proposal follows results from a series of usable and security usability research which found that certain user behaviours either positively or negatively impact their practice [5]. Such behaviours usually are maintained throughout one's lifetime [6]. For example, overconfidence ("nothing bad can happen to me") and hyperbolic discounting (trading of security for short term benefits). These result in a privacy paradox, a situation where users' needs for privacy do not match their practice. The unfortunate part is that usually, users often underestimate the risks associated with such behaviours [7].

Internet security mechanisms and applications such as IP Security (IPsec), Virtual Private Networks (VPNs), Domain Name Systems (DNS), and Content filtering, among others, are some of the security systems that are yet to be designed for average users. DNS, for example, a fundamental component of the Internet, is barely understood by many users. Attackers exploit this weakness on one extreme who then successfully manipulate DNS records, monitor user transactions, and inject unsolicited ads and malware. Research shows that much as these can be configured by the user, they are usually hidden from the average user and are not fully comprehensible by this class of users. Demographics determine socio-technical approaches, which are very key in the Human-cyber space interaction. As such, security systems should target diverse classes of users. Usable security mainly focuses on systems and platforms. It seldomly touches on the usability of the underlying components of the Internet. Building on previous research, this paper focuses on the intersection of Quality of Security Services (also known as Quality of Protection (QoP)) and Quality of Experience (QoE). This paper collectively calls these services Quality of Protection and Experience (QoPE).

Previous work shows that most users do not configure Internet security, citing configuration complexity and overhead. Despite the failure to implement security, most Internet users acknowledge the need to stay safe online. Other reasons behind the non-implementation of security mechanisms include the negative effect of security on performance, especially in poorer network conditions. A user study by Mbewe and Chavula [4] showed that "flawed security practice does not only result from users' negligence, but also lack of sufficient Internet security knowledge". They, therefore, suggested that Internet security configuration frameworks should be designed with capabilities to reinforce users' security knowledge and mental models. This study focuses on DNS privacy, VPN, and content filtering. We follow a data-driven approach to ensure that the designed system reflects the network conditions under which the device is operating. We also incorporate nudging in the form of the high-level costs of the security settings. The contributions of this work lie in the quality of protection and experience. We argue that if the users are provided with different security configuration levels with their associated costs, they would be able to comprehend some of the security concepts that have been obscure to them and, in the long run, reinforce their security mental models leading to better security practice.

2   Background and Related Work

Security is generally defined as the collection of all measures to prevent loss of any kind. The security concept is as old as humankind, implying that human assets have been at risk ever since humanity existed. It can be categorised into two main groups: physical security and digital security. Physical security is mainly a personal responsibility, and, over time, humans have developed complex physical security mechanisms. This may be partly attributed to regular interaction and regular experimentation with the systems. Individuals can choose the level of security they need depending on the circumstances and on what they are protecting. Digital security, on the other hand, mostly follows a delegated approach modelled after power. Security researchers have for so long argued that security concepts are too complex to be understood by human beings. Hence, it is better to manage their security centrally where knowledgeable people can understand the concepts. Security was often seen as mathematical and technical. Following this line of argument, the same argument has been repeated by different researchers, with others coining humans as the weakest link in the security ecosystem. Thus, this kind of security implementation made sense in the era when the Internet was for the elite and corporates. In this paradigm, perimeter defence made sense.

2.1 Quality of Protection

The early research about human involvement in deciding the level of digital security was coined Quality of Security Service (QoSS) and later Quality of Protection (QoP) [8–13]. This kind of research is aimed at balancing security and performance (throughput, latency and delay) or at least allowing the resource management systems to tradeoff security and performance. The idea came about because, generally, adding security to service increases the resource consumption and the delay of information exchange, thereby decreasing the Quality of Service(QoS), which, in turn, degrades Quality of Experience (QoE) [14–19]. Due to the multi-attribute nature of security, different researchers have focused on measuring the impact of specific security mechanisms on QoS and Quality of Experience (QoE). In an attempt to understand the impact of different encryption mechanisms on VoIP, studies [14,15,18] have shown that the IPSec protocol reduces jitter but significantly increases latency and end-to-end delay. They, however, recommend increasing bandwidth which might be expensive in low-resource networks. However, implementation of the proposed solutions followed the same paternalistic paradigm suiting the technological advancements of the time. The security applications developed using the recommendations from QoP research suffered a Single Point of Attack (SPoA), leading to a Single Point of Failure (SPoF). For example, Nahrstedt [8] proposed a middleware adaptation scheme to provide End-to-End tunable delay (QoS) and security. The scheme was later proven by Chen et al. [10] to be susceptible to Denial of Service bandwidth attack. To solve the identified weakness, Chen et al. [11] proposed a framework for integrating QoS and security and developing a security advisory system. Again, this solution was later proven to be susceptible to attack broadcasting. Despite the shortfalls, QoP research inspired the emerging human-centred security and Quality of Experience research.

For the majority of the users and applications, increased security cannot be achieved with technology that decreases usability. A study by Cardoso [20] proposes that the system interface be designed for ease of use so that users apply the protection mechanisms correctly. He argues that mistakes will be minimised if the users' mental image of their protection goals matches the security mechanisms. To design this mental model, Irvine [21,22] developed a Quality of Security Service costing framework for quantifying costs related to security service. The study uses a security translation matrix developed by Ivirne [23], which maps the elements of a simple user interface i.e. *high, medium, low* to a detailed security invocation mechanism. The study quantifies the cost from *CPU time, memory, bandwidth, disk space, delay, jitter* and *latency*. The authors conclude by proposing that further research be conducted to determine formulae for calculating resource costs for a range of security services and determining the best units for cost measures. Much as their work focused more on resource management systems, they tried to untangle the misconceptions about security, users and QoS. Such works inspire our work in conjunction mental modelling research. We use the measurements approach to provide device-based security-performance costs.

3   System Design

3.1   Design Goals

The primary goal of our system is to assist Internet users, especially those with limited computing skills, to easily configure internet security settings on users' Internet access devices such as smartphones. These settings should be selected based on the network resources available on the device as well as the user's desired security level. For example, suppose the user experiences sub-optimal network performance at a given security level. In that case, they should be able to switch to a security level that provides better network performance. The system should also cater to the advanced category of users who have better understanding of their security configurations. These users usually desire autonomy in choosing the parameters that govern their smartphones' security and network performance. To achieve this, the system should allow a user to choose from all possible combinations of security parameters. Once a particular configuration is chosen and activated by the user, they should be able to also be able to test and monitor the performance of their connections. In addition, the system should be able to schedule tests periodically on the devices to collect performance data. The system should also be able to learn from this data and provide better informed security choices the next time a user requests for security configuration.

3.2   Choosing Parameters

Studies [24,25] have shown that choice of DNS resolver preferences are pivotal to the level of QoE for users. Mbewe and Chavula [26] further measured the impact of applying DNS filters on QoE. Their results showed that apart from providing the user with an opportunity to choose an extra layer of protection, choice of filters impacts QoE. The authors also conducted a user study investigating Internet users' security mental models, their security configuration experience and general security practice [4]. Their results show inadequate Internet security mental models in self-reported expert and non-expert Internet users. Their mental modelling and task analysis revealed that the flawed security practice does not only result from users' negligence but also lack of sufficient Internet security knowledge. They finally recommended reinforcement of users' Internet security mental models through personalised security configuration frameworks to allow users, especially those with limited technical skills, to configure their desired security level easily. This work, therefore, builds on such works and presents a personal Internet security configuration companion. The following paragraphs outline the architecture, system components, and configuration parameters.

PowerQoPE integrates three privacy-centric protocols: DNS privacy (including DNS-based content filtering), VPNs and Transport Layer Security (TLS). These have been discussed in literature [4,27–30] and they offer a multiplicity of protections based on use case but mostly difficult to many novice Internet users. We use public DNS services as shown in Table 1, which have extensively been used in DNS privacy performance measurement works. All DNS providers except for Google have filter instances such as Security, Adult, Family and Ads filters. DNS filtering is a practice of blocking access to a domain for specific reasons such as content filtering. A site will be blocked if the contents it presents are deemed inappropriate by the configuration, such as gambling, malware, pornography, and unsolicited ads, among others. PowerQoPE uses known blocking databases and filter-enabled DNS services to help the user easily configure content filtering with minimal hustles. It further classifies commonly negotiated ciphers into strength levels using classes 3 to 5 as implemented in openSSL (level 5: high, level 4: medium and level 3: low).

The user interface of our application is designed to provide four main levels of security - *high, medium, low, advanced*. Essentially, the user choice levels are determined by DNS protocol, VPN, web-filtering and cipher strength. For example, in the *high*, we use non-logging DoH (which is more private than DoT), remote VPN, and a stricter web filter. In the *medium* security option, we use DoT, local VPN, cipher strength level 4, and family filter. Finally, we use Do53, local VPN, cipher level 3 and Do53-based family filter in the low-security level. The outcome of a security decision by the server also depends upon the type of network to which the user's device is connected. For a given network type and configuration combination, the system returns the configuration with the least page load time. In the current implementation, only two network types are supported - *mobile (4G, 3G) and WiFi*. Once the user decides to use a particular configuration level, our system makes a security decision by allowing the configurations to be chosen from each of the below sets:

1. $\mathcal{D}$: A set of recursive DNS resolvers. Our current implementation supports the below recursive resolvers and their respective security filters as shown in Table 1. Each recursive resolver provides different options for the type of security filters. Each filter has three variants - DNS over port 53 (Do53), DNS over TLS (DoT), and DNS over HTTPS (DoH). In Table 1, for example, Cloudflare provides three distinct security filters, and each can be implemented with either Do53, DoT or DoH, giving $3 \times 3 = 9$ distinct options for the system to choose from.

Table 1. Different DNS providers and their security filter variants.

DNS provider	Security filters
CloudFlare	No filter, Security, Family
Google	No filter
Quad9	No filter, Security
Cleanbrowsing	Family, Adult, Security
Adguard	No filter, Ad block, Family

2. $\mathcal{C}$: A set of preferred cipher suites: As the name suggests, a cipher suite is a suite or a combination of ciphers responsible for authentication, key exchange, bulk encryption and signing.
3. $\mathcal{V}$: A set of publicly available VPN servers. Whenever the VPN mode is enabled in our system, the user's smartphone connects to a remote VPN server. These servers are chosen from a predefined list that contains servers that are freely available for academic use.

Formally, a security configuration can be denoted as a member of the set $\mathcal{D} \times \mathcal{C} \times \mathcal{V}$. Whenever the user chooses the advanced configuration, they have complete control over which member to choose from $\mathcal{D}$, $\mathcal{C}$ and $\mathcal{V}$. In all other cases, the system decides based on historical data, the user's current network type and the security level chosen. In our current implementation, VPN servers are only used when the user selects the high-security level or chooses to enable VPN at the advanced security level.

3.3   System Overview

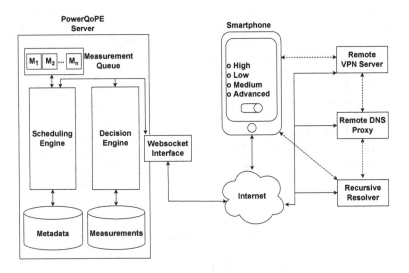

Fig. 1. An architecture of the proposed system, PowerQoPE. In this figure, the dotted arrows represent configuration-specific connections.

The PowerQoPE system (Fig. 1) is equipped to assist Android phone users in taking charge of their device's security. In the current implementation, the system can be used to collect measurement data and store it in the measurements repository for further analysis. All the security decisions made by the system are static and based on what has been observed previously by experimentation.

An orchestration engine forms the heart of the PowerQoPE system. A user can initiate three types of measurements from the Android application. These include speed tests, HTTP tests and video tests. Speed tests measure the latency, upload and download speed of data transfer between the nearest server and the user. HTTP tests provide insights about DNS response time, page load time and other related parameters when a website (either user-defined or system-defined) is visited from within the app. Video tests measure the buffer, load time and bandwidth for a system-defined video file. In the current implementation, these tests can only be initiated by the user.

For users who may be unfamiliar with terms like DNS, filters, VPN, cipher suites, the system provides three main security configurations - low, medium and high. As per previous experiments, if a stricter security level is chosen, the performance of applications that access the Internet is expected to degrade for poorer connections. Thus, users with a very high-quality internet connection can enjoy the benefits of maximum security that could be configured.

The Android application provides an advanced options radio button for a technically capable user. On tapping this button, they can choose the specific DNS provider and the type of filter (family, advertisements, security) depending on whether it is available with the provider or not. Since the list of supported cipher suites is large, the application only provides the category of the cipher (low, medium, high) as an option. If a user selects a specific cipher category, all ciphers belonging to that category are sent to any subsequent HTTP request made from within the app.

3.4   Architectural Components

PowerQoPE Server. This component is responsible for orchestrating the measurements, including HTTP webpage downloads, speed tests and video tests. The design of this measurement server is a modified version of QoSMon, an architecture proposed by Sharma and Chavula [31]. One key modification to this design allows measurements to be scheduled on a specific device instead of any device.

- **Measurements Scheduling Engine:** This component allows measurements to be scheduled periodically on end-user devices by minimising the contention between network and CPU resources used by measurements. This engine can be configured to use four existing measurement scheduling algorithms [32].
- **Decision Engine:** There are two main categories of decisions that the PowerQoPE server is involved in. The first decision is related to selecting the best DNS configuration for a user. The decision engine searches the historical data and finds out all the configurations with the same network type and chosen level of security. Then, it chooses a single configuration that corresponds to the least page load time. The second decision is related to choosing a VPN server when the user has selected a high configuration. The PowerQoPE server maintains a list of freely available VPN servers and updates it every 30 min with their latest configurations. Then, when asked to decide, the server chooses a single VPN server with the lowest latency and the highest throughput.

– **Remote DNS proxy:** This proxy is used in configurations where remote VPN capabilities are enabled. Our application uses OpenVPN [33] for configuring a new VPN server, and it requires the recursive resolver's IP address to be written in a configuration file. This works well for Do53 and DoT, but not in the case of DoH because it requires the complete URL of the recursive resolver instead of the IP address. Therefore, we decided to relay all DoH requests through a proxy that we configured beforehand with a particular DoH-based resolver.

User Application Module. The user application module (See Fig. 2) handles user configurations and user-initiated measurements. It comprises a user interface, measurements module, nudge generator and the QoPE configuration module. The user module handles user preferences and configures them on the operating system. In the current implementation of PowerQoPE, only Android phones are supported. The Android user application is designed so that it persists its connection with the server even when the user switches from one network to another. We now briefly describe each of the user module components:

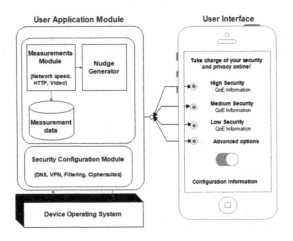

Fig. 2. User application module components and user interface wireframe

– **QoPE configuration Module:** The QoPE configuration module handles user preferences based on the decisions and classifications made by the PowerQoPE server and configures them on the device. The user can as well overwrite server recommendations by performing the advanced configuration. Currently, the module can configure DNS (Do53. DoT and DoH), web filtering, VPN and cipher suites. We provide the user with high-level choices; low, medium, high and advanced. The app connects to a local VPN server in low and medium configurations. It resolves any subsequent HTTP requests via a recursive resolver recommended by the server. In high configuration or any other configuration with VPN enabled, the app connects to a remote VPN server. This remote server can either be chosen by the user or recommended by the system, depending on whether the advanced configuration is selected. All subsequent HTTP requests are sent through the VPN tunnel and resolved via a remote DNS proxy in this type of setting.

4 Evaluation

4.1 Methodology

This section describes the procedure followed to evaluate the components of PowerQoPE. We conducted an evaluative controlled user experiment to test the effectiveness of personal Internet security configuration tool, especially on the configuration options and security-performance cost. The experiment aimed to assess whether providing Internet users with levels of security configuration and accompanying the levels with their associated performance or privacy cost would modify user's security choice.

Participants. To ably evaluate the usefulness and inform further design of the app, an initial usability study was carried out with 14 participants (seven females and seven males). These users were novice frequent Internet users with a basic understanding of computing. Purposive sampling of participants was used to get ideas from a specific cadre of Internet users, i.e. novice Internet users. All the participants completed high school and understood English.

Design. Three interfaces (See Fig. 3) of security configurations were designed to assess whether adding the performance cost of different security configurations would help users make an informed security decision. The first interface had only the security configuration levels (High, Medium, Low and Advanced). The second screen was activated by toggling a button. On toggling, descriptive costs of the underlying security mechanisms were added under each security option, categorised under network quality, video streaming quality and security/privacy. We decided to use a within-subject controlled user experiment [34] approach to fully measure if the protection motivation features of the app would modify users' security and QoE mental models. Within-subjects experimental design demands that each participant tests all the conditions under study. In our case, each participant performed all the three tasks.

In order to test whether security costs and visual cost framing, in addition to the security levels, would improve the security mental models and encourage users to configure better security, we provided different interfaces of the personal security configuration tool, enabled by toggling different combinations of the configurations. First, we have security levels with no cost information (LCn) as control (See Fig. 3a). Then, security levels with textual cost Information (LC, Fig. 3b) and security cost with visual cost framing (LCV, Fig. 3c). We further randomised the order of the security options for each task.

(a) First screen containing security configuration levels only

(b) Second screen containing security configuration levels with their associated textual cost information

(c) Third screen containing security configuration levels with their associated textual and graphical cost information

Fig. 3. Configuration screens for tasks 1 to 3

Materials. The experiment required the following materials:

- A smartphone with android operating system.
- A mobile application which we developed iteratively for this purpose.
- Deliberate configuration of three different interfaces that visibly showed different elements.
- An interview guide used as a follow up between tasks.

Procedure. The Ethical clearance was sought from our University's ethics committee. The experiment was conducted at a telecentre on Likoma Island in Malawi. The location was ideal because there was an ongoing project to sensitise the youth on general cybersecurity. The researcher had no relationship with the participants, and the experiment was not related to the project.

The convener welcomed the participants, and explained the aim of the experiment. Then the participants were given an online informed consent form to read and, if in agreement, sign. It was emphasised that participants were free to withdraw from the study. Then the participants completed a pre-experiment questionnaire that captured demographics and assessed their Internet security knowledge. No identifying information was collected. Finally, the participants were assigned unique IDs.

The participants were asked to install the app on their smartphones. The experiment began when participants indicated that they were ready. Participants were asked to open the PowerQoPE app they had just installed. Then they were asked to choose their desired protection level from a list of radio buttons

(High, medium, low, advanced). Then the participants were asked to run the measurements module (both Internet speed and web QoE) using their security choice. This was specifically done to collect empirical performance cost of the selected security level. The participants were asked to give a rationale for their choice marking the end of the first task. The researcher recorded the responses on a notepad. There was a lapse of 15 min between the tasks.

Then the researcher toggled the cost information for each security option. The order of the security options was shuffled (i.e. medium, low, high) to minimise learning effects. The participants were asked to choose their desired level of protection, this time, based on the cost information visible. Again, they were required to run the measurements module if their choice in Task 1 differed from their choice in Task 2. The researcher asked them to explain their choice, and the responses were recorded.

Finally, the researcher toggled visual cost. This setting only appended simile faces to the cost information. The participants were asked to repeat the tasks. Participants' preferences were recorded for each task and summarised.

5   Results

This section provides two sets of results; analysis of the user experiment and results from the measurements.

5.1   Influence of Security Cost Information on Users' Choice of Security Level

Users' security options for each task were tabulated and compared. Figure 4 shows participants' security preferences against conditions. Recall that Task 1 only provided the security levels from which the participant was required to choose one option based on the PMT's framing of the options and their mental models. Task 2 added textual cost information to the security levels. The cost information was qualitative to avoid suffocating the participant with technical details. The costs were based on network performance, browsing/streaming experience and security/privacy.

The results show that 100% of participants chose the high-security option in Task 1. When textual information was added in Task 2, 50% of the participants changed their preference to medium while 21% chose low security. Finally, when visual cost nudges were added to the cost information, 71% of the participants chose medium security, 21% chose high security, and only 1 (8%) chose low security.

When asked why they configured high security in Task 1, many responded that they "care about security and secure connection". However, when presented with cost information, the same 71% of the participants changed from a high-security configuration. When asked about the sudden change of preference, one participant said,

"Slow internet flustrates, I would rather have a combination of good Internet performance and security, hence my change from high to medium-security.."

Three (3) participants switched from high security to low security. When asked why they chose low security, the participants said they would rather compromise security but not Internet speed.

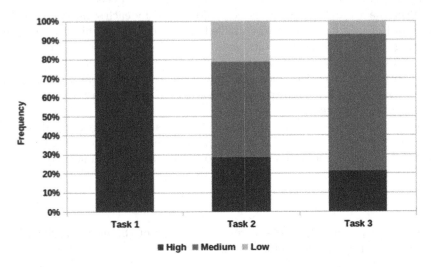

Fig. 4. Participants' security preferences for each condition (Task 1: Security levels only, Task 2: Security levels plus textual performance cost, Task 3: Security levels, textual and visual performance cost)

Task 3 results did not differ much from Task 2's. However, two of the three who chose the low-security option in Task 2 changed to medium-security. When asked why that change, one participant attributed the change to the images that accompanied the cost information saying that the visual nudges made the costs more visible.

We finally run paired t-tests between tasks to determine whether the differences were significant. We first compared Task 1 and Task 2, then Task 1 and Task 3 and finally Task 2 and Task 3. In short, we present the combinations as $T_1 - T_2$, $T_1 - T_3$ and $T_2 - T_3$, where T stands for "Task" as shown in Fig. 5.

Paired Samples Test

		Paired Differences							
					95% Confidence Interval of the Difference				
		Mean	Std. Deviation	Std. Error Mean	Lower	Upper	t	df	Sig. (2-tailed)
Pair 1	$T_1 - T_2$	-1.071	.730	.195	-1.493	-.650	-5.491	13	.000
Pair 2	$T_1 - T_3$	-1.143	.535	.143	-1.451	-.834	-8.000	13	.000
Pair 3	$T_2 - T_3$	-.071	.730	.195	-.493	.350	-.366	13	.720

Fig. 5. Paired samples test

From Fig. 5, we observe a significant difference between Task 1 and Task 2 ($p = .000$), Task 1 and Task 3 ($p = .000$). We observe no significant difference between Task 2 and task 3 ($p = .720$). This tells us that cost information, whether textual or combined with graphical costs, can modify users' security preferences. The results also show that adding a visual nudge to the textual cost information does not significantly affect users' security preferences.

5.2 Empirical Performance Impact of Users' Choice of Security Level

Descriptive statistics were used to analyse the measurements data. Figure 6 show empirical performance impact impact of users' security choice. Metrics of interest were page load time, DNS response time, network speed and SSL time. Due to space limitation, we will consider pageload time and SSl time.

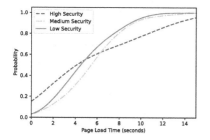
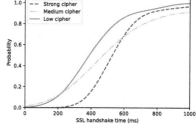

(a) Page load time for each of the security configuration levels

(b) SSL handshake time for each of the security configuration levels

Fig. 6. User initiated measurement results

Figure 6a shows page load time CDF for security levels. Generally, we see that high security is slower than the medium and low-security options. However, we see that high-security options outperform both medium and low levels for faster loading pages. We suspect that such faster loading websites are at the top of the tranco list and have caches within Africa. In general, we observe that high-security configuration results in longer page load time while medium level has moderate PLTs followed by low-security level. Similar patterns are observed in Fig. 6b which shows the impact of cipher suite strength on SSL time which in turn affects page load time. However, higher strength ciphers outperform medium strength ciphers for the not-so-famous websites, i.e. websites at the tail of the tranco list[1]. This is because most preferred stronger ciphers perform 1 round trip while medium ciphers perform 2 round trips. Therefore, higher latency domains will incur longer SSL handshake time.

---

[1] See https://tranco-list.eu/latest_list.

6   Discusion

Thus far, we have presented the design and preliminary evaluation of a security configuration tool called PowerQoPE. Using the concepts of the Protection Motivation Theory (PMT) [35,36], we included some features that would nudge the user into implementing a desired level of security. We then conducted a controlled user experiment to evaluate the feasibility of such features, i.e. QoE impact of different security mechanisms.

From the results, we observe that the participants implemented a high-security option in the absence of cost information. However, when cost information was added, most participants changed their preference. In this case, the users weighed the negative effects of relaxing security in trying to enjoy good Internet speed. The change was also possible because options were within reach of participants. The participants were novice Internet users. The complex underlying security constructs were hidden under advanced security options. This simplified and minimised novice participants' search space. Using this prototype, novices could configure VPN, DNS and content filtering, defeating the stereotype that security is so complex for an ordinary user.

We further note that other users would still choose suboptimal security configuration even in the presence of the options. This fact cannot be ignored for Internet users with a persistent slow connection. To this type of users, it makes sense to restrict the options to ensure that there always exists a minimum possible security level; otherwise, such users may give up security for speed. This cognitive bias is known as hyperbolic discounting [2]. In this situation, one chooses short time benefits disregarding the long time consequences.

Empirically, we found that the cost displayed to the user closely represented the actual impact of the underlying security mechanisms. We also note that the choice architectures implemented in the prototype maps the objective measurement results. This suggests that data-driven security decisions would improve the QoE even if the user configures a high-level security option. We see from the empirical measurements results that participants used slower networks as evidences by longer page load times. These are typical speeds offered by mobile service providers in most parts of Africa. Therefore, adaptive security configuration solutions such as PowerQoPE would assist users under such network conditions to decide the level of security based on their network conditions.

We argue that properly designed security configuration tools would bridge the divide between novice and expert users while still aiding in optimal security decision-making. This calls for more studies and experiments on user-centric security. This may lead to different use cases integrated into the security configuration interfaces of devices from different vendors and operating systems such as smartphones, SOHO routers and others.

The apparent limitation of this study lies in the sample size and diversity of participants. The sample size of 14 participants may not give us generalisable results. Also, we tested this on novice users from one geographical location. However, we argue that the results provide insights into how Internet security configuration protocols can be designed to involve novice users in the security decision making. Such platforms can be used to reinforce users' security mental models thereby improving their online security practice.

7   Conclusion and Future Work

In this paper, we have shown that complex security configurations can be made available to novice users who have generally been regarded as the weakest link in the security ecosystem. Future work will expand the evaluation with more participants of diverse demographics. Future works also include testing Usefulness, Satisfaction and Ease of use.

Acknowledgments. The authors are grateful for the financial support received from the Hasso Plattner Institute for Digital Engineering through the HPI Research School at the University of Cape Town. In addition, the authors would like to thank *Mr Henry Mikanda* for helping with UI design and *Mr Joseph Kumwenda* for the help rendered during data collection. Finally, we thank all the participants for their time and willingness to provide information published in this study

References

1. Grobler, M., Gaire, R., Nepal, S.: User, usage and usability: redefining human centric cyber security. Front. Big Data, **4** (2021). www.ncbi.nlm.nih.gov/pmc/articles/PMC7968726/
2. Acquisti, A., et al.: Nudges for privacy and security: understanding and assisting users' choices online. ACM Comput. Surv. **50**(3), 1–41 (2017)
3. Wash, R., Rader, E.: Influencing mental models of security: a research agenda. In: Proceedings New Security Paradigms Workshop, p. 9 (2011)
4. Mbewe, E.S., Chavula, J.: Security mental models and personal security practices of internet users in Africa. In: Sheikh, Y.H., Rai, I.A., Bakar, A.D. (eds.) e-Infrastructure and e-Services for Developing Countries, pp. 47–68. Springer International Publishing, Cham (2022). https://doi.org/10.1007/978-3-031-06374-9_4
5. Gcaza, N., von Solms, R., Grobler, M.M., van Vuuren, J.J.: A general morphological analysis: delineating a cyber-security culture. Inf. Comput. Secur. (2017)
6. Van Schaik, P., Jeske, D., Onibokun, J., Coventry, L., Jansen, J., Kusev, P.: Risk perceptions of cyber-security and precautionary behaviour. Comput. Hum. Behav. **75**, 547–559 (2017)
7. Tischer, M., Durumeric, Z., Foster, S., Duan, S., Mori, A., Bursztein, E., Bailey, M.: Users really do plug in USB drives they find. In: IEEE Symposium on Security and Privacy (SP). IEEE, vol. 2016, pp. 306–319 (2016)
8. Nahrstedt, K.: An integrated solution to delay and security support in wireless networks. In: IEEE Wireless Communications and Networking Conference 2006. WCNC 2006, vol. 4, pp. 2211–2215 (2006)
9. Chen, J., Hu, C., Zeng, H., Zhang, J.: Impact of Security on QoS in communication network. In: 2009 International Conference on Networks Security, Wireless Communications and Trusted Computing, vol. 2, pp. 40–43 (2009)

10. Taleb, T., Hadjadj Aoul, Y., Benslimane, A.: Integrating security with QoS in next generation networks. In: 2010 IEEE Global Telecommunications Conference GLOBECOM 2010, pp. 1–5 (2010)

11. Taleb, T., Hadjadj-Aoul, Y.: QoS^2: a framework for integrating quality of security with quality of service. Secur. Commun. Netw. **512**, 1462–1470 (2012). https://doi.org/10.1002/sec.523

12. Ksiezopolski, B., Zurek, T., Mokkas, M.: Quality of protection evaluation of security mechanisms. Sci. World J. (2014)

13. Rusinek, D., Ksiezopolski, B., Wierzbicki, A.: AQoPA: automated quality of protection analysis framework for complex systems. In: Saeed, K., Homenda, W. (eds.) CISIM 2015. LNCS, vol. 9339, pp. 475–486. Springer, Cham (2015). https://doi.org/10.1007/978-3-319-24369-6_39

14. Radmand, P., Talevski, A.: Impact of encryption on QoS in VoIP. In: 2010 IEEE Second International Conference on Social Computing, pp. 721–726 (2010)

15. Mohammed, H.A., Ali, A.H.: Effect of some security mechanisms on the QoS VoIP application using OPNET. Int. J. Curr. Eng. Technol. **3**, 1626–1630 (2013)

16. Hani Haidar, A., Houseini, M., Kshour, M.: The analyse of adding security on QoS parameters. Int. J. Innovative Res. Adv. Eng. **2**, 11 (2015)

17. Lindskog, S., Jonsson, E.N.: Adding Security to Quality of Service Architectures (2002)

18. Al-khatib, A.A., Hassan, R.: Impact of IPSec protocol on the performance of network real-time applications: a review. I. J. Netw. Secur. **20**, 811–819 (2018)

19. Hayajneh, T., Mohd, B., Itradat, A.: Performance and information security evaluation with firewalls. Int. J. Secur. Appl. **7**, 335–372 (2013)

20. Cardoso, L.S.: Quality and security usability. In ITU-T Wksp. End-to-End QoE/QoS, Geneva, Switzerland, pp. 721–726 (2006)

21. Irvine, C., Levin, T.: Toward a taxonomy and costing method for security services. In: Proceedings 15th Annual Computer Security Applications Conference (ACSAC 1999), pp. 183–188 (1999)

22. Spyropoulou, E., Levin, T., Irvine, C.: Calculating costs for quality of security service. In: Proceedings 16th Annual Computer Security Applications Conference (ACSAC 2000), pp. 334–343 (2000)

23. Irvine, C.: A note on mapping user-oriented security policies to complex mechanisms and services (1999). https://calhoun.nps.edu/handle/10945/15290

24. Mbewe, E.S., Chavula, J.: On QoE impact of DoH and DoT in Africa: why a user's DNS choice matters. In: Zitouni, R., Phokeer, A., Chavula, J., Elmokashfi, A., Gueye, A., Benamar, N. (eds.) AFRICOMM 2020. LNICST, vol. 361, pp. 289–304. Springer, Cham (2021). https://doi.org/10.1007/978-3-030-70572-5_18

25. Hounsel, A., Borgolte, K., Schmitt, P., Holland, J., Feamster, N.: Analyzing the costs (and benefits) of DNS, DoT, and DoH for the modern Web (2019). arxiv.org/pdf/1907.08089pdf

26. Mbewe, E.S., Chavula, J.: Measuring QoE impact of DoE-based filtering. In: Proceedings of Southern Africa Telecommunication Networks and Applications Conference. Champagne Sports Resort, Central Drakensberg, KwaZulu-Natal, South Africa. SATNAC, pp. 240–245 (2021). https://pubs.cs.uct.ac.za/id/eprint/1508/

27. Ion, I., Reeder, R., Consolvo, S.: No one can hack my mind: comparing expert and non-expert security practices. In: SOUPS 2015 - Proceedings of the 11th Symposium on Usable Privacy and Security, pp. 327–346 (2019)

28. Maceli, M.G.: Encouraging patron adoption of privacy-protection technologies: challenges for public libraries. IFLA J. **44**(3), 195–202 (2018)

29. Reeder, R.W., Ion, I., Consolvo, S.: 152 simple steps to stay safe online: security advice for non-tech-savvy users. IEEE Secur. Priv. **15**(5), 55–64 (2017)
30. Zou, Y., Roundy, K., Tamersoy, A., Shintre, S., Roturier, J., Schaub, F.: Examining the adoption and abandonment of security, privacy, and identity theft protection practices. In: Conference on Human Factors in Computing Systems - Proceedings, pp. 1–15 (2020)
31. Sharma, T., Chavula, J.: Investigating Measurement Scheduling Strategies in Low Resource Networks (Poster), New York, NY, USA. Association for Computing Machinery, p. 453–456 (2021). https://doi.org/10.1145/3460112.3472310
32. Sharma, T., Chavula, J.: Topology-aware measurement scheduling strategies in low resource networks. In: Proceedings of Southern Africa Telecommunication Networks and Applications Conference (SATNAC), Central Drakensberg, South Africa. SATNAC, pp. 308–313 (2021)
33. Feilner, M.: OpenVPN: building and integrating virtual private networks. Packt Publishing Ltd (2006)
34. Anderson, A.J.: Controlled experiments. Interpreting Data, pp. 183–190 (2019)
35. Rogers, R.W.: A protection motivation theory of fear appeals and attitude change. J. Psychol. **91**(1), 93–114 (1975). Taylor & Francis
36. Rogers, R.W.: Cognitive and psychological processes in fear appeals and attitude change: a revised theory of protection motivation. In: Social Psychophysiology: A Sourcebook, pp. 153–176. Guilford Press (1983)

Author Index

Printed in the United States
by Baker & Taylor Publisher Services